From Light into the Abyss

*Swindling, Web-cams, College
Youth Behaving Badly*

Jim Jacobs

authorHOUSE®

AuthorHouse™
1663 Liberty Drive
Bloomington, IN 47403
www.authorhouse.com
Phone: 1 (800) 839-8640

Published by AuthorHouse   02/27/2016

ISBN: 978-1-5049-7447-9 (sc)
ISBN: 978-1-5049-7448-6 (hc)
ISBN: 978-1-5049-7446-2 (e)

Library of Congress Control Number: 2016900994

Contents

Acknowledgement

This book would not have been possible without the essential and loving support of family and friends. Worthy of mention are Christian men of the cloth, Dr. R.C. Sproul, Pastor Burk Parsons, both preachers and teachers at Saint Andrews Chapel in Sanford, Florida, and Dr. Larry Meyer who ministered at Faith Community Church in Trenton, MN. I would also like to thank Mr. Randall Van Meggelen, Director of Music at Saint Andrews Chapel.

Words are never enough, nor would words do justice for the influence and direction these four men of the faith had on shaping and molding my walk with the Lord. Every person listed in this acknowledgement was instrumental in taking a piece of my soul and breathing life and light into what was otherwise a life lived in darkness.

Finally, all praise, honor, and glory is given to our Lord and Savior Christ Jesus for His gift of Salvation, and the Holy Spirits ongoing good works to transform me into Christ's likeness.

Introduction

I stand alone resting on pardonable merits, the blueprint of all things useful for edification. For in creation thy hand hath provided the harvest whether good or evil. Humankind has opted to live in the sinful nature of the flesh in opposition with spiritual harmony and communion with their creator. During the Authors journey, there was no bartering before Angels. Rather, I became the host of a thousand nights. Knowing night begets darkness; I soon realized night paled in comparison to the abyss where images of immorality exist. Therefore, "From Light into the Abyss" took flight on the wings of the cherubim with feet firmly planted to investigate the matter. No stranger to the abyss (before becoming a born again Christian), darkness never escaped the bottomless pit's grasp where absolute darkness claims its abode. Also, it is where the shadow of pain, suffering, and torment screams for liberation from its eternal home.

The purpose of this manuscript is to inform the public and bring awareness to this nation's state of affairs as seen through the eyes' of the author. There is no pleasurable entertainment value in writing on the subject of immoral decay. There is a misunderstanding in society today involving the serious question of immorality undermining our ability to function as a human race in concert with goodness. It is not a grand declaration as I enlighten the reader why we may be headed in the direction of self-destruction, if the current state of humankind's attitude remains callous and indifferent relating to our current behavior.

We have become distant subjects. Known as territorial isolationist; detached. We turn a blind eye to what is happening around our closed and locked doors. In defense of my allegations, a list that reads like a who's who constituting the whole of the total, draws you into this perplexing dilemma. Web-camming, Scamming, (fraud) and college students behaving irresponsibly, are the main topics we will cover. Moreover, we will look at Drug trafficking, drug use, drug peddling, domestic violence, human trafficking as well as other vices. Furthermore, should we not also cover Illegal border crossings, pornography, prostitution, abortion, and same-sex marriage? Let us also then, address gangs, drive-by shootings, divorce, kidnappings, low wages, jobs, poverty, the decay of our infrastructure, corruption, and a do-nothing Congress neatly incorporated into the sum of the total.

I could add to the list of unresolved issues, but the previous paragraph is a foretaste given as identifiers having a bearing on our future destiny. Nature and its attributes cannot sustain immoral behavior without the cause and effect overburdening our society with chaos. However, why should it matter to you? It isn't infringing on your liberties, at least not yet! The particulars of this subject demand ethical reasoning. We should take it seriously, and it should be considered with profound humility, caution, and reverence. If ignored, it brings us into contact with a subject so wicked and overwhelming, it contributes to the misery of man. Can we deny the vestiges of time, that we overlook this exhausted arrangement of evidence by treating it as nonessential? We have assumed a mentality that we are rational creatures, but our baggage of imperfections surfaces while our country remains in denial about whom or what we've become.

There are no capacities or powers I claim ownership as masterpieces of man's present condition. I have had my share of sorrows, memories elations and fulfillment. The pendulum more times than not swayed in the direction of challenging trials. However, I have no regrets for the yoke I had to bear. The author should have had his life extinguished ten times over, yet here I stand. Firmly convinced the Lord preserved my life for this very purpose. It is at this time, during this hour, and for this season that the manuscript began to breathe life. I am a simple person in retrospect but complicated. I have seldom allowed anyone accesses into my inner sanctuary of ideology. However, you shall witness for yourself where passion and infirmities manifest themselves.

Our focus of the manuscript recognizes four main areas of greater truths that I feel grips the heart and soul of anyone whose eyes' will scan these pages containing stained reality. I use Scripture passages in selected chapters to bolster, define, and justify the rationale for this manuscript.

The author devotes the first four or five chapters indoctrinating the reader about the torturous inquisitions relating to trials, struggles and hardship incurred before his eventual transformation from self-destruction to maturing as a born again Christian. A unanimous testimony the author feels makes him qualified to write on the subject of immorality and internet swindling. I am who I am. It is who I am. Accept me as I am. I am the total of my parts.

The remaining three topics of the manuscript will concentrate on models (prostitutes) web-camming, fraud, and young adults behaving badly. (Moreover, the author addresses all other encumbrances mentioned in paragraph three, page one of the introduction.) Just a brief overview if you will, but they all belong to the same family of immorality. Thousands of women are smuggled across our border's from Mexico every year, sold into the sex slave industry. These women have no freedoms, no liberties, and no life. It has reached pandemic levels. This doesn't include women who flaunt their flesh on live webcam internet sites for money. Thirty percent of all human trafficking goes through Houston, Texas. No less sinister are entities propelling fraud inside and outside our borders where IC3 (Internet Crime Complaints) receives 70,000 complaints monthly relating to fraud and other crimes.

Am I naïve to think there isn't going to be critics or cynics in the public sector who will boldly boast with indifference towards mentionable proclamations? A voice that suggests the author is sensationalizing or exaggerating the truth. What separates this book from others is the author's penchant for his acute observations. Rather than becoming a poster child of these swindlers,' and accept it as a learning experience, I pursued these scamming loose cannons. Having the nature of a pit bull mentality, the author eventually became the hunter rather than the hunted.

Taking meticulous notes and accumulating eight binders of chronicled documentation over a span of time, I was able to place names, residence's, and other personal information on this entity. Swindling then led me on an odyssey of immoral degradation by default, to sites of female web-camming. From there we traverse to men and women behaving badly. Is this what we call civilized freedom? "Drunkenness, vulgarity, drugs, etc." Have we fallen into a trend these past two decades morphing into a lawless Nation? The practical effect of belief is the real test of its soundness. The only hope now is a blessed resurrection of our system of governing.

I wasn't about to sit around, and delight in complacency as most of the brethren have chosen with their selfish motives and self-interests. The highest calling for rejoicing is answering the voice of God. It is unconscionable to desert the deliverer of the message. Am I bleeding fatalism? You do not have to agree with me. You don't even have to like me. After all, you didn't like me as it was when I was amongst you. All too frequently this is what the author defines as exercised dichotomous thinking. Remember, I'm under no obligation to explain all the mysteries connected with my actions. In the past, I have had some in my circle who through unmerited worldly thinking stigmatized and vilified my character with indifference and selfish determination. As if I had an ulterior motive and an agenda that gathered grapes of wrath, or gardens of thistles. There is no stronger inclination than doing an injustice to a person's soul.

The conscience tells us that the things which appeal to us more powerfully at the time, are the things that determine our volition. We have politicians who without rhyme or reason behave with contrite spirits. They live lives of half-truths. We use former President Clinton as an example. Instead of standing and deliver; admitting his transgressions, he chose to manipulate words in an attempt to avoid taking responsibility for his actions. (It depends on what the word is, is.) His ill-conceived demeanor was condescending to the American public and shameful. It is pride and arrogance bundled up in a neat little package.

Former Senator Feingold promised he would only serve one term in the Senate. Reneging on his word, Senator Feingold ended up serving two additional six-year terms. What message does this send to our youth? A colony of other prominent persons of interest include Jessie Jackson, Jim Baker, Gary Hart, Jimmy Swaggart, former President Nixon, Etc., who took the great fall. Where are our role models today? Have we encouraged our youth of today that there is no right or wrong behavior? It doesn't take a genius to see we've elapsed into believing, "It just is," … mentality.

Do these people in positions of authority think the American people are naïve? Men of the cloth exposed for molesting young boys, and we wonder why the pews are empty. Our children indoctrinate themselves into the drug culture and inherit an immoral disposition. I made provisions for these two examples to illustrate a point. The list of influential people who have conducted themselves in a disgraceful manner is endless. The unanimous testimony of history suggests immorality displayed by people of influence didn't go unnoticed in past generations of our youth. The message you were transmitting was that it is acceptable behavior to lie, deceive, kill, and steal. We have instilled in our youth that there is, "no right or wrong." It just is!

This Nation is currently experiencing birthing pains. It has for the past two decades, and unless we begin to act responsibly, you can be sure the wrath of God is going to appear on our doorsteps. Should you decide to challenge the authors warning blessed, I highly suggest the politicians and American citizens who are slothful in reading Scripture, open your Bible and begin reading. We've become a Nation of illiterates neglecting to come into conformance with God's laws and precepts. This manuscript just touches the surface of immorality. To confront this beast head-on it will require VISION and immediate action. If we don't address these issues, I'm fearful all my hours of research will have been in vain.

We need to put our "man pants" on and own up to the mistakes of the past and turn this country around with God's help, so we can return to our former grandeur and receive Gods blessings. Perhaps if our Lawmakers were familiar with Scripture, they wouldn't have committed troops to the Mideast. It was and is a no win proposition. The only Nation we need to concern ourselves with as a true friend and ally is the Nation of Israel. History, history, history, it's all right there in Scripture. These are profound truths that are trustworthy and true. There is no wiggle room in our society for wickedness and evil to overwhelm the moral decay of our country.

I've ranted and raved for four pages. It is not until we embrace biblical truths and repent of our sins, and see a need for Christ Jesus, will you and me as individual's have the assurance of eternal life. Who wants to live in the light, and who chooses' to live in darkness? Only you can make that choice. Free will; Your choice.

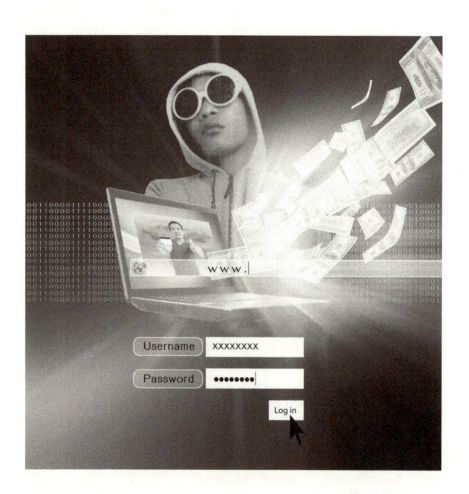

About the Author

The author is what he is. Accept him for who he is. He cannot be who he is not. The author has been on a pilgrimage for nearly seven decades, and during this journey he has experienced trials, brokenness, and has felt the sting of wounds. Certain his life was preserved for this moment, in this hour, and for this time. He has been into the Abyss before (lived in darkness). Yet, by the grace of God; has undergone a transformation as a born again Christian, presently residing in the "light."

Furthermore, it is because of the light he can announce victory over the evil in this world. The author went from alcohol addiction 20-years ago to a crusader for the oppressed and immoral behavior in the arena of an obscene smut laden industry, and out-of-control criminal entities. He gave 18 1/2-years of his life to the military before receiving a medical disability discharge in 1984. His service career didn't end with his discharge. He spent 3-years doing volunteer work in a Nursing Home, and another 6-months volunteering in a battered woman's shelter. The author is not immune from life and death situations, working as an Emergency Medical Technician while station in California on active duty serving my country.

The author witnessed a wrong and paid for a prostitute's freedom when he learned she was enslaved in bondage to a pimp. He remains a champion in the cause in liberating all women who are in the human sex slave trafficking industry controlled by pimps and other entities. Immorality is a priority in his resume of injustices and soiled behavior permeating throughout this Nation. Convinced everything happens for a purpose and not by chance, the author believes this has been his calling in life, touching as many lives of every soul living in darkness and bring them into the light of salvation before it is too late.

A Lie is a Lie is a Lie

From Light into the Abyss, is as compelling as it is engaging. The author guides the reader into the old structures of internet "scams" and "cams" where morality has taken reason into the realm of the twisted single-minded glut of immorality ... A canker sore as troublesome as this Nations firestorm of drug addiction, dealers, pimps, prostitution, human slave trafficking, domestic abuse, and political chicanery. We no longer say this Is an epidemic, but a pandemic gone awry.

The author takes you into the world where the hunted becomes the hunter spending a little over one-year researching, chronicling, and exposing the secret world of fraud, and immorality in the face of pure evil. The struggle isn't outside our borders but has taken residency within our borders.

The tentacles of sin reach much further than "Cams, and scams." Rather, our entire society is in free fall from Government to the Lobbyist, who corrupt and influence our system of governing with their deep pockets of unlimited cash. Why then, would we not deem this as favoritism, and unethical?

To lend authenticity to the manuscripts content, the author used the analogy: "If you want to learn how swine live, eat, and interact with their kind and in their environment, you must live in their habitat." Willing to get in the filth and mire with them to relate to their surroundings.

In this in-depth account, you will witness the deceitful practices employed by swindlers, and how greed permeates in the scamming and female web-camming industry. How the invisible became the visible, and the extremes both entities will go to protect their turf.

Chapter 1

The Serpent's Deception

To one man He grants wealth, power, and knowledge, and breath of freedom.
However, oppression became his master over time and for a season.
To another soul, He allotted the heavyweights of the tempters' manifestations.
Thus, are numbered all the days of his life, suffering trials and hardships.
Jim Jacobs

When giving thought to writing this manuscript two-years ago, I was determined to limit the document to fraud. However, while kicking the can of fraud around the internet, intelligence gathering led to other seedbeds of immoral behavior that the author felt duty-bound to include in the book. I did not expect to be visiting websites that I concluded were college youth behaving badly, and pornography depicting online live webcam prostitutes. (models)

There could be no manuscript without including immoral behavior seen in its darkest hours of demonstrated vile conduct as it is today. The total package was missing essential elements of information to impose maximum effect for the reader. There were just too many variables and observations for this voice to silence this restless soul.

An unknown force was goading the inner conscience of my mind to awaken and broaden the inner circle of swindlers, webcam models, and college youth behaving badly. There was a sense of urgency that propelled this manuscript beyond the pages of dry ink. All the pieces had to fit together sensibly, or the entire structure would collapse and be of little value to the reader.

If the reader does not get a panorama of the author's manuscript, then the message I want to convey will become dismal. My wish is that you read this book with an open mind, lest you render the book mundane. Moreover, I fear the script will become blasé, useless, and lifeless. If that is the outcome, all would be in vain, and I will have squandered your time—and mine.

Entering the confines of this created little world in my study where this project began to sprout wings, I sat down in the black leather swivel chair, scanned the length of a well-organized desk and began the task of writing.

Discipline dictates and demands order in this disorganized mind. Without order, I surmised, chaos would be lurking next door to foil my efforts. Left with a choice, this was going to be the proverbial all-or-nothing crusade. All in. Come or bust. Take it or leave it!

I concluded that the darkness of the abyss had other idiosyncrasies recoiling at the ready. Fraud, college youth behaving badly, and web-camming needed exposure for sure. There are consequences for unacceptable behavior. However, it goes beyond behavior. It is holding people accountable for irresponsible conduct. The author felt it was urgent to scrutinize under the microscope this flotilla of bacterium that knows no boundaries. To put a face on the facts I needed to alert, educate, and inform the public about college youth behaving badly, live online webcams, and swindling. Simply put, they have no place in a civilized society.

There has never existed a beacon of hope on the hill, as former President Reagan so proudly declared to our nation. You would be extremely giddy if American's were fortunate enough to witness a glitter of light coming anywhere close to a rich symbolism on the hill in Washington, DC—or anywhere for that matter. This nation has tethered on the brink of immoral behavior far too long. It has surpassed ninety degrees of separation, spiraling treacherously close to inviting the wrath of God on our nation and the world. These weathered arthritic knuckles of Jim Jacobs would surely turn white with fear and trembling at the thought of God's wrath visiting this country. Not for blessings, but for his uncompromising judgment.

Close your eyes' and imagine this through the history of prophecy. Visualize for yourself with openness, and picture the almighty power, righteous anger, and vengeful judgment God would exact on us for our sinful, stiff-necked ways. It comes from a Holy God. "Would I intentionally put the fear of God in a man? Better believe it!" Let us look in the arena of immorality to mount a frontal attack to justify the reasons for the unchaste decay, and fraudulent bankruptcy we face.

For emphasis, we are discussing college youth behaving badly, internet fraud (scammers), websites that promote live adult sex-camming, and the pimps who operate these flesh-for-money factories on sites devoid of ethics. Exploiting eighteen-year-old girls and older, with the promise of tremendous earnings potential is obscuring the truth. Although a select few prostitutes do earn good wages on cam sites, the majority of women entering this arena of iniquity struggle. It is the most degrading, psychological, and immoral practice this government has allowed to prosper unregulated since antiquity. This so-called entertainment has infiltrated every household in America that owns a computer or television. In the sex industry, there is no shortage of human trafficking in prostitution. Women who are victims of this sex-slave trade by pimps is intolerable and unacceptable.

As an example of the out-of-control human sex trafficking industry, all we have to do is look south of the border to Mexico to see how lucrative this criminal industry has thrived. It is estimated to amass $32-BILLION in revenue annually for the drug cartel and the town of Tenancingo, where the city makes its entire living from sex and kidnappings. Thousands of innocent young victims are kidnaped each year and shipped North to cities like Queens New York, Miami, Phoenix, Los Angeles, Chicago, Dallas, Las Vegas, and foreign countries.

You won't see all these faceless victim's selling their bodies on the streets. These women are hidden and warehoused in dilapidated buildings. Imprisoned in cubicle type rooms with a mattress, lamp, and drape for privacy. These women spend every waking hour in a 10x10 room servicing up to forty clients (perverts) per day. Many have been denied freedom from upwards of ten-years. Our Federal prisoner's receive better humane treatment than women who are involuntarily imprisoned in warehouses.

Writing on immoral conduct must include the pervasiveness of illegal drug smugglers, drug addiction, and those who peddle this poison to our teenage children. We have neighborhood gangs promoting violence on innocent victims. Internet fraud has become the faceless crime that preys on and swallow's victims' assets. Drive-by shootings and the killing of innocent children are on the rise to the degree it has become carnage. Massage parlors promote sex for money. Pimping, domestic abuse, and white collar crime are but a few of this nations ill's that are eroding the fiber of America.

Here is the conclusion of the matter. Governors do not govern, legislators do not legislate, and the President does not lead. It is cronyism, self-interests, and overbearing arrogance by elected officials sitting on their lofty thrones dictating what is in the best interest of self and not we the people. We have become a nation divided. Washington divides and conquers because the citizens of America have become slothful, self-loathing, and uneducated in the ways of right and wrong. There is no middle ground.

Man's callous and constant desire to throw money into the coffers of the sex industry is irreprehensible, deplorable, and unacceptable as evident by their thoughtless inhumane participation in this endless Ferris Wheel of websites that encourages and promotes prostitution. It goes contrary to the moral edicts, proclamations, and God breathed words of Scripture. Was I to turn convicted laurels into blank pages, leaving well enough alone these atrocities; and pretend they didn't exist? I have spent months cultivating these soiled sheets of paper exposing fraud. Therefore, this voice demands this project move forward. Oversight committees have given these issues little creditability. As noted by their failure to legislate known pornographic activity or decaying social issues facing a society that this author has determined is culturally detached.

If a committee exists, then they must be out on an extended leave of absence. The war is right here within our borders. Any resources we may have available to combat this immoral dilemma is nonexistent. Yes, there are conflicts in the Middle East. However, let us reason together and ask the question that begs for an honest answer. "Why isn't Saudi Arabia and its Arab neighbors assuming the lion's share in this Mideast conflict of terrorism and Jihad? Sunni and Shiite's will always be at war with one another. It is a losing proposition for the United States. If you read Scripture, you would know this blessed.

Law enforcement is doing a commendable job attempting to stem the flow of drugs, prostitution, and other criminal activity, but their efforts are feeble. They're taking one step forward and two steps back. We are not making any in-roads in the war on drugs. We are unable to stem the flow of immigrants crossing over into our borders. Our manpower and resources have been diminished to combat the human trafficking of women into prostitution. The atrocities are endless, and as such we are losing the war on all fronts.

The President is commander-in-chief of the armed forces. Regions that we have defended for decades with our tax dollars—Europe, Japan, South Korea, Okinawa, etc.—are capable of supporting themselves as their economy, military readiness, and Armed Forces have become stronger and combat preparedness is at a premium. It is recommended that our men and women in uniform be reassigned back to the homeland where they can assist homeland security as border guards in deterring illegal border crossings and drug smuggling.

Restructuring and retraining in common areas of criminal activity where the military can be active in using their experience and expertise in assisting local and state law-enforcement agencies in their on-going efforts to stem the flow of drugs and drug use in this country. We already have a small contingency on the front lines to stem the flow of drug smuggling; however, it remains insufficient and understaffed. Port cities, airports, and known drug-infested neighborhoods are areas where our military could systematically defuse destructive criminal behavior. If the politicians legislated and left the military, including the National Guard and Reserves; to do the job these men and women have undergone training to combat insurrection, our country would be better for it. As it is, we haven't had leadership in the Executive and Legislative branches of Government for decades.

What puzzles the author is the lack of visibility in Congress. It seems they have all been on furlough for the past twenty-years. Do they have influence in the pornography industry that allows pornography to thrive unabated in every state in the union? It sure influenced Senator

Reid from Nevada as you will discover in a later chapter. Surely, these legislators must know female web-camming is active and prosperous on the internet.

What actions or progress has our commander-in-chief taken to abolish this form of entertainment? I do not hear any voices rising within any branch of our government over this destructive activity. Not even a whimper. Where are the voices of reason from the citizens of this country? I can't even hear a hiccup, let alone a sneeze. Who should we hold accountable for this ever increasing trend? Ownership belongs to us all, Christian and Non-Christian alike. And most assuredly the Executive, Legislative, and Judicial branches of Government. In this fray, we cannot disregard executive, local, state, and county governments either.

Let's be frank. Who is running this government? Are we to assume Congress and the Senate are legislating any of the people's business in the interest of contemptuous criminal activity and immorality? No! Is the President using the bully pulpit to address any of these problems, let alone setting the agenda to submit legislation declaring criminal activity as a priority? The author doesn't think they are managing anything well. It's stalemate, deadlock, impasse!

The recent rulings on abortion and same-sex marriage decided by the United States Supreme Court for these prohibitive social values has become a boiling pot of dissension. Dividing the nation even further. Are we to entrust our Government and the Judicial system with wisdom when it applies to sound judgment and obedience to Gods word? Are the Supreme Court's decisions based on God's Holy law or man's law? There certainly was a lack of forbearance when the court ruled to legalize abortion, allowing women the right to murder babies while planned parenthood and pro-choice advocates defended this carnage as a woman's right. Furthermore, we pushed the envelope when same-sex folks were given the right to marry.

We aren't going to allow a free pass to lobbyist and special-interest posse composed of a galvanized gift-bearing Santa Claus. Lobbyist and special interest are the Holy Grail of a country under siege. They're entrenched deep inside the hidden corridors of Congress. We can conclude lobbyist and special interests have power and influence. Yes! They control the purse strings. Elected officials are there to do their bidding. Lobbyists and the wealthy don't contribute vast sums of money during election campaigns without expecting something in return. Its known as the need for greed manifesto.

Another grave abomination that has gone astray, using the euphemism, "submarines submerge into the deep; out-of-sight; out-of-mind" lending prostitution its legitimacy over airwaves without legislative action curtailing this form of behavior by elected officials. Hollywood and smut peddling producers are testing God's authority by imposing their repugnant unsettling offensive speech, pornography and violence into our lives and homes, distributing tasteless sexual perversion's on videos in unprecedented numbers while television stations glamourizing adult channels on pay-per-view channels is becoming as popular as Mr. Rogers Neighborhood. Society has become indoctrinated, desensitized, and complacent by this low-grade form of entertainment. If this is what Americans want to accept as entertainment viewing, then were getting what we deserve blessed.

Moreover, the cancer is just beginning to spread. Domestic abuse, drugs, escort services, and massage parlors run the whole gambit of illegalities and immorality. Is this really what we want infringing into our lives, accepting it as the social norm? It is already an uncontrolled fire burning dangerously out of control. How much garbage and stench are we going to allow seep into our nostrils like rot before we declare. "Enough is enough!"

Nudity is not an art form, and it is not freedom of expression. It is soiled behavior! Folks like Larry Flint and Hugh Hefner exploit women by devaluing their modesty. It is clear this is unrighteousness in the eyes of God. An abomination in the truest sense of the WORD. Do you think these people searched the word of God first before creating a warehouse of sin that promotes images containing loose pages of nakedness? Are we even living and enforcing God's laws and precepts? Do we leave it to mortal man to discern morally correct behavior?

Where did separation of Church and State get its roots? Washington, Jefferson, Lincoln, Adams; they all governed based on biblical principles. Now the government is attempting to silence the church. What is the problem here? "Why wouldn't your hearts be troubled over this personal attack on the church?" Are we a society or generation that just doesn't care? Are you voting with your pocket book with the notion some politician has promised you a pay raise, jobs, health care benefits, or change?

"Ignore immorality and sin will visit you in the most unlikely places." The infrastructures in many major cities have become eyesores of shame and disgrace. Living wages have reached an all-time low. Poverty is at the doorsteps of the White House knocking at the door, but there isn't anyone at home. National Security is not outside our borders; National Security is within our borders, in the here and now. Open your eyes' that you might see. Medicare and Medicaid is running out of money because of fraud and escalating medical costs. People are having their identities stolen. Illegals are crossing our borders in record numbers.

Who dares approach the podium in the Congressional chambers and announce. "The State of our Union is vibrant and healthy?" Not even, close! Get your pious heads out of the sand. We cannot even agree to disagree any longer. Now is the time we as American citizens take an honest look at the politicians we elect into office. Cronyism by politicians has morphed into a prehistoric animal, quite alive and doing very well for themselves.

The cost savings to this nation would be phenomenal if we recalled our servicemen and women home. Not only would it save billions, but it would also create civil service jobs in America, bolster the construction industry, economy, manufacturing, Etc. We need to take care of America. If we don't, I fear we will stand to lose that which we already have; and that I'm ashamed to say isn't very much right now because there is no leadership. We have become a debtor nation.

Our National debt by the end of the fiscal year 2015 will rise to an estimated 18.628- trillion dollars. Whom do we owe this debt too? Some think we owe the Kings share to China. In reality, we are indebted to China for a mere 1.16-trillion. We owe the Social Security Trust Fund, and Federal Pension Fund 5-trillion, followed by 11-trillion owed to foreign and domestic investors, and private investors, 1-trillion.

The first four chapters are written to inform the reader about the author's character as words are scripted to discuss life's challenges, trials, and struggles with injustice and the unfortunate misfortunes that affected his life. Not all events highlighted in this manuscript will cover every nuance life had to offer, and the challenges throughout his pilgrimage. However, it should clarify why I am qualified to write about immorality. It will serve as a backdrop on how human behavior influences psychic perception.

As ignorance has no equal and knowledge of man derives its existence through physical and emotional bitter herbs, it renders within its members, suffocating elements invisible to the naked eye. The scales of justice fracture with the entanglements of suffering, pain, and grief, while others may prosper with no birthing pains. Nudging man's conquest of fleshly desires, he elevates himself to a loftier position indicative of the purest form of pride. Understandably, insecurity demands a mate, so man reins in ego and arrogance as its cousin. What remains for man who is the partaker of all things unnatural and immoral is the cause and effect syndrome. Dissect it or parcel its meaning and it still equates to one group having superiority and coercion over the oppressed and innocent of the world.

In a quest for rest, there is this desire through the natural course of events for gravity to target the subtle folds of the skin above the eyes to succumb to eternal slumber. The light of day disappearing from life's cadence, ending the minds ability to see worldly corruption and wickedness, as we learn and actively participate in the good and evil that dwells within man's heart. Body, then soul set adrift in a lifeless, motionless, rigid state no longer involved in worldly dysfunctional manifestations. But the remnant shall continue to use their free will to inflict pain and suffering on humankind as history testifies by repeating the actions of years past.

This mortal mind and body have become frail, weak, and sluggish. No longer able to sustain the weightiness and struggles this world has wrought upon itself. I am inconsolable! Years forever measured in trust and not time. It is the time that scales are applied to justify a condition riddled in turmoil. I have surrendered into an agreement with the soul to disassociate self from immorality. The ugliness of it all corralled and captured in the lens of the eye. Waffling, instruments of time has far too long given this quest to lend authenticity through the prism of these eyes into a world so avidly evil, as to wallow in the muck and mire of secular living.

There is an urgency to write this manuscript on such matters taking the author and the reader on a journey, "From Light into the Abyss." Of greater appeal is humanity's folly to hurl degrading insults in the face of innocence. Humankind has a penchant for evil and deceit. The vastness of immorality is overpowering, with an unbiased penchant to inflict extreme pain on fellow man. A topic of great concern making it an unrelenting struggle of heart, mind, and soul. Take a pilgrimage with the author if you wish, and witness the abyss opening its mouth wide to lay claim to the wickedness of humankind. Evil is an equal opportunity employer. Criminals; white and blue collar know this because its rewards outweigh the consequences for their blatant behavior.

Come; come, join the writer as he ventures into the abyss. It is not tidy, certainly not sterile, and for sure not flawless. Making haste, I declare it is soiled with corruption and sinister connections in every contemptible dimension. Dare we streamline these words by discussing them in a forum that invites criticism and hostility? If souls have a free will to choose, are some liberties not a foregone conclusion based on our desire to sin?

Should the author pattern his words so as not to offend a segment of the population or class of people? Did the Supreme Court rule in favor of abortion because they have become Gods in their own eyes'? Have they become scribes of antiquity past? Are we allowing our Executive, Legislative, and Judiciary bodies of Government to slice and dice away at our individual freedoms using an all-out frontal assault on our places of worship? Killing babies and allowing same-sex relationships has man redefining the moral laws as he no longer desires to obey God's edicts while legitimizing sinful behavior too accommodate his sinful desires.

Abolishing public prayer in our schools has now become politically correct. Are we slowly eradicating Gods word by tossing it into a smoldering heap of unwanted waste blessed? Opting instead to chase after worldly desires of the flesh? I have concluded there is a movement in America to censor and silence the Christian faith. We have become a nation of biblical illiterates who much prefer to be entertained in this secular world by sinful desires of the flesh rather than searching for the truth.

The government spends more time, money, and resources catering to immorality than using its legislative authority to act on stemming the tide of the pervasiveness of bacteria that mutates on the internet without remedy. The government is doing nothing! Choosing instead, to ignore immoral behavior and hope it will somehow correct itself through osmosis rather than exacting legislation to terminate the ever increasing colony of pimps, prostitutes, drug dealer's, human traffickers who appear to thrive with impunity like the rat's they've become. What long-term legislation has ever been enacted to stem the influx of renegade misfits turning the world into a lawless society? Whatever life you may have breathed into correcting our wayward ways has proven to be marginal or non-existent at best.

Among the living, there are challenges for mediation with bravado and steadfastness, lest we become afflicted with raindrops of disappointment. What lot of mortal souls amongst the world's billions of people does this population profess to possess ownership of a heart and soul as that of a Puritan? Also, all who have within their nature a zealous predatory taste for the moral code residing in their soul let it shine as a virtue of your character.

If puritan, then be puritan. There is no greater cause than to live and breathe righteousness, and purge the carnage and bondage that is within our midst. It never escapes the presence of God, that is a given. Blessed, to suggest that God is disappointed with us as a people is putting it rather mildly and graciously. It is a stench in His nostrils, a detestable abomination in His eyes'. Do you honestly believe that if it is not God's will, our Armed Forces who are assigned throughout the world, could determine a victorious outcome in a conflict? You can deploy 500,000 combat ready soldiers to engage in the battle, but it is God who determines the outcome.

Our Creator created the cosmos by "His word." Each word has as its component a definition. Words uttered from the tongue have power. They define man's identity, the fingerprint into his soul. Words can be misleading, deceptive, hurtful, crafty, and manipulative. It reminds me of the ferociousness of a Wisconsin Badger. He is unpredictable, aggressive, and mean spirited. While uttered in whispers man is capable of causing irreparable damage. Piercing heart and soul consigned in belligerent sarcastic overtures wounding and capable of breaking man's spirit.

The victim's emotional state and altered self-esteem become a liability. As a result, they create a barrier of a self-made glass house erected as a defense mechanism to defend against future harm. Words uttered in hatred and threats of physical violence set in motion the "fight or flight" ultimatum. It takes on the characteristics of a passive, passive aggressive or aggressive reaction from the person on the receiving end of victimization.

Words written in Scripture set in a motion consistent and reliable truths. Should the reader find the truth too extreme to embrace, then it is likely this manuscript would not compliment your beliefs. Therefore, you will have undoubtedly squandered your time and money on this manuscript. The author through good faith efforts, and a clear conscious with no other obstructions; put his most logical mind to its better reasoning while writing about criminal activity and immorality.

I attempted to piece together for the reader in chronological order all manner of discovery as best this mind could organize this story. The author makes no apologies for any blemish written or spoken through this manuscript. The only way to measure success from this manuscript is by the number of people who read it and accept it as a worthwhile symphony ensemble free from partisan interests while demanding change. For it is the truth as I have come to believe the truth, setting aside pride and prejudices as I disassociate myself from the darkness of the abyss.

If man truly desires truth as millions has come to believe Scripture as the infallible word of God, then using Scripture as our moral compass it is important that we seek, identify, reveal, and unearth the stench, deceit, filth, and evil intent of man's heart. You may discover the book too controversial between the lines and pages of this manuscript. That is understandable. Why, you may inquire? When the human body suffers a cut with a sharp instrument, perforating the skin it draws blood. This sets into motion the "cause and effect" outcome (pierced skin; cause. draws blood; effect). We can apply the same principal when addressing good versus evil. The good is a Christian, who is in obedience to God's moral laws and exemplifies Christ-like behavior. Evil is its polar opposite, a child of Satan, the great deceiver and destroyer of soul's.

There is the evil, sinful behavior of man. One who knowingly and actively participates in opposition to Gods laws and precepts. Research has shown people who engage in pornography eventually take it to another level. They rape, sodomize, there into bondage, pedophilia, and fetishes, just to name some of the inner trappings. Women, unfortunately are more likely than men be the victims of sexual assault. Society views them as sexual objects of gratification. A commodity. Women are the weaker gender in this male dominated society. Men who flaunt money, power, prestige, and importance can become the gladiators of wickedness.

Prostitutes who perform lewd acts on websites as self-imposed cam models via the use of the internet, display their wares on these sites while catering to the perversion of man's unquenchable lust for the female flesh. It is delusional, sick, and perverted. The exploitation of women on cam sites creates an imaginary fantasy featuring room settings and grotesque role-playing, known as the fantasy illusion, directed towards the perversion of thousands of men who appear each night on these sites. One website alone can foster up to ten-thousand male perverts.

Moreover, there are thousands of live cam sites on the internet peddling woman's flesh. We have other men trolling web pages containing X-rated videos of every conceivable sexual perversion. While visitors can hear audio sounds from the prostitute's room, she uses her audio sound in an unrelenting plea to her audience; begging visitors and premium members for tokens (money). If the money isn't flowing into the coffers of the host website, the prostitute often becomes more creative and a little more desperate to solicit members to ante up more tokens so she can meet the topic goal.

Bartering for tokens, she may begin the process by exposing a part of her anatomy in this never-ending prop of sensual seductions. If the model determines that her topic goal will not meet a pre-determine timeline established by her, she will discontinue broadcasting. The prostitute and the industry keep all tips received up to where she discontinues the broadcast. However, the contributing member loses' out on whatever tips she received from them up to that point. The entity uses skillful wording by cautioning members, tokens given to a model are gifts and not an incentive to get the model to perform. I don't know about you, but this is unethical and in my opinion stealing money based on ethical laurels. Moreover, this whole business from the standpoint of God's righteous laws is morally wrong.

None of this would be possible if you did not have the owners of these live cam sites (pimps in suits), and the prostitutes working in this flesh for money industry. This flesh for cash industry has become too promiscuous and widespread to remain legitimate for a nation such as ours to continue receiving the Lord's blessings.

When choosing to take this pilgrimage down the path of porn, fraud, and college youth behaving badly while in their wickedness and pure evil behavior, it is essential for openness and honesty to become part of the curriculum. The soul that resides in every living person is not pure and clean as some might surmise when highlighting sinful behavior as the major theme in this manuscript. During years of foolishness and rebelling in my life, indulgence in pornography became a way of life for me, much to my shame and guilt.

However, after God spoke to my heart, enlightened, and convicted me of this heinous sin I indulged in, He revealed the destructive and sinful nature that lust plays in the flesh. As a result of irresponsible choices and sin, I discovered that anyone can be led like lost sheep into the valley of the abyss. It was at this point in my life of sin that a spiritual awakening occurred. Prior to this, God allowed, and I made the choice to experience all the egregious sexual exploits sin had to offer. That said; we fast-forward to the present.

There came a stirring of the soul. The Holy Spirit was convicting this vile man (Jim Jacobs) over the iniquities of pornography and all the entails, harm and disgrace that accompany this sin. It began with "scams," and from "scams," I was taken down the path of pornography. With organized copious notes and research, I was drawn to discover what was behind the darkness of pornography. I wanted to know what drew men and women into this web of deception, and so begins the journey into the abyss. A distinction required a definition between web-camming, college youth behaving badly, and swindlers. That is if a difference can be determined. Testimonials seem to dictate all three are taking money by sinful and dishonest means.

The objective in the first few chapters is to capture your attention by laying down a foundation. Awaking the reader through means of stoking the soul to where this manuscript will prod your conscience into taking up residency in your minds. Another objective is to nudge the viewer to turn page after page until you have read the manuscript from cover to cover. Engage! Engage! Engage! Weigh the immoral implications this book has on all segments of this nation's population and around the world.

There are also safety precautions that need scrutiny concerning a possible backlash the writer may encounter when or if the manuscript goes public. However, weighing possible repercussions outweighed the benefits. I rationalized that to do nothing, "is to be nothing!" Something I have taken a step further in the next paragraph. Rejecting one's allegiance to Christ, and His teachings would be the same as denying the Savior. "From Light into the Abyss," is not a sacrificial duty overloaded with burdens, but for the sanctity of what is right, just, and honorable. We must always strive to do what is pure and just for the Glory of God.

Before we begin framing these chapters, it is with the wisest counsel for the reader to peer through the lens of this renowned author of literary works. The poetic works suggest to us that on occasion life's challenges suggest that we all can connect when poets have penned for discernment and meditation. C.S Lewis wrote a poem I could connect with through his words and works.

15

The Beloved Works of C. S. Lewis

"There is no safe investment. To love at all is to be vulnerable. Love anything, and your heart will certainly be wrung and possibly broken. If you want to make sure of keeping it intact, you must give your heart to no one, not even an animal. Wrap it carefully round with hobbies and little luxuries; avoid all entanglements; lock it up safe in the casket or coffin of your selfishness. However, in that casket—safe and dark, motionless, airless—it will change. It cannot suffer harm; it will become unbreakable, impenetrable, hopelessness. The alternative to tragedy or, at least, the risk of tragedy is damnation. The only place outside Heaven where you can be perfectly safe from all the dangers and perturbations of love is Hell."

"I believe that the most lawless and inordinate loves are less contrary to God's will than a self-invited and self-protective solitude for loneliness …. We shall draw nearer to God, not by trying to avoid the suffering of all loves, but by accepting them and offering them to Him; throwing away all defensive armor. If our hearts should break, and if He chooses this as a way in which they should break, so be it."

--From the Four Loves--

How could such a finite mortal mind comprehend life's obstacles in the wake of trials? Each soul arrives from the secure confines nestled and surrounded by fluid and attached to the umbilical cord that connects to the navel which is further connected to the fetus with the placenta and through which respiratory gasses, nutrients, and wastes pass. In the Lord's preordained time a child is born from the womb of a woman. This human form has within its framework a complex brain organ comprised of three main parts, cerebrum, cerebellum, and the brainstem. The cerebrum, Frontal Lobe; controls behavior, problem-solving, attention, inhibitions, judgment, physical reaction, libido, and eleven other functions. The cerebellum functions to control balance, posture, cardiac, respiratory, and vasomotor centers. The Brain Stem involves the motor and sensory pathways to the body, face, and the vital centers cardiac respiratory vasomotor. It is the cerebrum that most captures and fascinates the authors curiosity. It is where we discover Gift-love and Need-love.

Gift-love and Need-love have so eluded the author for over six decades of his pilgrimage on earth. It is during these many decades of life, where I learned you cannot live without them. One or the other, or both has eluded man. Having both is rare. Becoming the recipient of chastisement, vilification, and vestiges of trials during a lifetime of undisciplined discipline transfixed by erratic hostility, and cruelty became the norm. If you slowly peel away self-identity, you learn that I suffered long endless days of sadness and grief. Can this then be my lot in life?

Reconciliation of self is but a distant reality. Locked forever in the channels of the cerebrum until the lungs deplete themselves of oxygen supply, and I am no more. For you, oh man, have taught this soul extremely well indeed! The barrier so dense, that I have encased myself in a protective cocoon, disbarring you from entering into a secluded sanctuary gripped by the uncertainties this life had to offer.

To be blessed with vision that I might see. Ears formed to gather auditory sounds into the inner hearing canal so that one can hear. Senses' to give credibility to emotions both physical and psychological. Each living person has a brain to process further all that has been seen, heard, and experienced, and then planted between the pages of the mind. Some will take their secret life of despair to the grave. Others will keep it to themselves, but act out their pain publicly. While still others will eventually abandon the protective armor, and seek reconciliation with the Lord, who is the great physician.

I invite the reader to join the author on this wayward journey. Come down from your lofty preconceived ideas about how the world should package and bundle this earthly existence to accommodate your unreasonable expectations. Therefore, I challenge you to take on the character and personality of the author in this manuscript. "Whoa! Whoa! Whoa!" Your shoulders will bear the weight of the facts. How I should wish it not to be so for you! There is no mystery for that which is known, or familiar to you. No. No. No. Each person mentioned in the manuscript; if authentic so be it. Fiction then a fictional character it is.

I have never been my own! The opportunity has never afforded the author this luxury. The heart became void and empty inside, worse than death itself. This man assumed ownership of this soul after being wounded, and within a short span of time, began the process of repairing, healing, and reconciling a life littered with molestation and abuse. From adolescence it spilled over into the military. Therefore, any foreknowledge of happiness, peace, and joy assumed its polar opposite.

Man has stripped away all identity, innocence, and self-worth. Rather than being created in the likeness of our creator you sought to find and destroy through the course of six decades, life, liberty, and happiness. You denied a child of simplicity by creating a mountain of molten lava sending gaseous vapors skyward laden with debris from the likes of an active volcano. Like volcanic eruptions; anger, wrath, and rage would occupy the members of my body.

The outcome produced a neatly packaged rebellion against authority. A bondservant to anger, I was branded an out-of-control time bomb. Reruns of old classic movies continue to play themselves out between the pages of Jim Jacobs mind. Cursed are these dreams and unpleasant memories that serve as a reminder of years lost opportunities. Counting it as all loss, I now see it as victory through a renewed faith in Christ. However, each day continues to be a work in progress. After all, I'm still in the world, bearing witness to immorality, pain, injustices, and disparity in all corners of the world.

Every word uttered brings an unbearable ache to heart and soul as the author painstakingly leads you down the unpaved road of a defeated human Spirit. I am not a whole person, as one should well like to think. Nor dare we ascertain completeness is inevitable. That is to say, not until the Lord welcomes this tent (physical body) into his Heavenly kingdom in a glorified body.

However, man, being the creature that he is, is predisposed to possess a snippet of boldness along with a cluster of brevity; rendering up images of machismo masculinity. There is no desire on the author's part to cling to notoriety or fortune. I am a man absent the bloodlines and pedigree of nobility. I am a commoner at best. The sum of my parts whether mind, body, or soul. "No more … No less!" I never cared in what light humankind viewed me as a person. I wouldn't allow anyone to make me into the person I am not, nor conform to their standards under peer pressure.

Let us explore the reality of the matter! "These eyes' see and the ears hear, and this body and mind have been under siege, ravaged with the taste of bitterness and painful alms over decades of abuse. Here stand I, standing as tall as the majestic California Redwood's towering towards Heaven, reaching heights of three-hundred feet. They withstood the violence of nature's unpredictable fury, holding fast to the test of time. Should we then, continue the struggle inwardly to capture any small scraps of insanity that dare challenge the endurance likened to the Redwood tree? "Oh but for the Grace of God go I."

Nevertheless, there remains within this whirlwind of turmoil an understanding of life as expressed in the example of the rapacious hawk. Soaring high above its prey, circling the landscape waiting for an opportunity. Evaluating perhaps even more so, predisposed to allow its foe to scatter into a vulnerable area of open space so it can claim its bounty. Through gravity, it saturates the air with lightning speed. Within seconds, the talons of the predator have carried away the prize with unexpected expediency, relying on the element of surprise and skill. The seemingly strong and cunning nature of man exudes this method of assault, just like the hawk.

Humankind is a self-driven creature that preys on the weak, defenseless victims of the world. With sadness of heart and soul, I have just defined man in his primitive element. It is darkness residing in his heart. It is our sin nature. Nobody, I mean nobody, likes being told, reprimanded, or welcomes correctness when man's flaws become visible. God frowns upon this behavior as genuine bona fide pride blessed, A sin. Many choose worldly secular living opting for material possessions rather than focusing on the spiritual world.

Love has always remained a mystery to this author. There are no understandings or feelings about human love. Nor have I known love. I have never been able to give love willingly or accept man's form of love. In retrospect, it is a thorough summary. It has been most difficult for the author to reciprocate true love until I met Darlene. It is Godly love discovered; agape love The author is quite familiar with conditional love.

However, love! What is unconditional love? We know the definition of love as defined in Webster's dictionary. Strong affections for another arising out of kinship, and personal ties. Attraction based sexual desires. Affection and tenderness felt by lovers. Affection based on admiration, benevolence, or common interests, terms of endearment, unselfish loyalty, good for the concern for another, and fatherly concern for God, and humankind. Love has eluded us as a people in recent decades. Just look at the divorce rate and single-family households and you can't help but see the devastation and impact its had on our youth.

The parody is reminiscent of a trail of light such as a comet or asteroid blazing through the eternal universe leaving in its wake a long streaking white trail of particles and ice. As it draws closer to earths gravity it is pulled closer to earth's orbit. The violent collision would strike and hit either land or water. Depending on the size of the comet on impact, it could be extremely deadly, as its explosive force creates a crater hundreds of miles deep, causing massive destruction to man and beast for decades.

If the asteroid were to plunge into any one of the seven oceans, it would cause such a swell of water that the amphibious creatures, sea life, and every living creature within hundreds of miles would vaporize! The destructive power would disrupt and obliterate our food supply, hinder all forms of production, deplete our natural resources, and essential amenities society takes for granted. Therefore, love I reasoned has components inherent in the explosive power of a comet. Love, affection, kindness, humility and forgiveness are a summons for awe, wonder, and beauty.

However, continuing to use the asteroid as an example, if sin enters into loves orbit humankind would collapse, and destruction would soon follow in its wake. It is this writer's conclusion that we have experienced the collapse of the family unit for decades now. We now reap what we have sown with single parenting on the rise, and couples preferring to live together without a commitment in direct disobedience to God's edicts. If the woman gets pregnant, unwed couples will opt to kill God's ordained creation. This is a heinous disregard towards a Holy God.

Before there is any misunderstanding, the seal of admission extends beyond the realm of ordinary. I have never been one to elevate myself as equal to, or boastful of the title Saint even though Christ gives believers this exclusive distinction. Participation in any particulars through means of deceit or as may otherwise implicitly imply misleading social tendencies, may lead the reader to conclude the author has latched himself into the victim's role. It is far from the truth.

"Woe, woe, woe; am I." May it never be! This author assumes full responsibility for his life whether good or bad. Consequences for bad behavior I own. It is all about the business of glorifying God. There are distinctions where scrutiny requires steadfast truths. Sin is sin; harm begets injury, and abominations are iniquities. You cannot dissect these words to make them appear as minor hiccups. Neither can humankind sugarcoat transgressions against a righteous God. Righteousness in the broader context (living righteously in Jesus Christ alone), is a person acting in accord with the moral and Divine Decrees' of God.

When rebelling against God, there is always an overwhelming sense of stirring inside the inner depths of the soul and Spirit. Having an understanding of Scripture, we can know the Holy Spirit is about the business of convicting people for transgressions committed against God's moral laws and Christ's teachings. It is during sin and turmoil brewing like a raging fire out of control where I have had to refer to another literary book kept within arm's reach on my desk. It lives in me since purchasing it from Saint Andrews Chapel. It is entitled, "The Valley of Vision". One particular passage this book inspires and helps keep me grounded in the faith. The chapter is entitled, "purification."

Purification

I sin ... Grant that I may
never cease grieving because of it,
never be content with myself,
never think I can reach a point of perfection.
Kill my envy, command my tongue,
trample down self.
Give me grace to be Holy, kind, gentle, pure,
peaceable,
to live for thee and not for self,
to copy thy words, acts spirit,
to be transformed into thy likeness,
to be consecrated wholly to thee,
to live entirely to thy glory.
Deliver me from attachments to things unclean,
from inverse associations,
from the predominance of evil passions,
from the sugar of sin as well as its gall,
that with self-loathing, deep contrition,
earnest heart searching
I may come to thee, cast myself on thee,
trust in thy cries to thee,
am delivered in Thee.

It is a daunting undertaking that one should and must confess the gravity of their sin's, (mine) in a public forum. You cannot make them disappear in between the pages of this manuscript. It is beneficial for a man to reveal sin where it manifests itself. Allow Christ to declare the person's innocence or guilt. Search, read, and see if there is any justification for immoral behavior. As mentioned earlier under formally hidden agendas of justice, the author knowingly, freely, and willingly searched the internet looking for pornographic sites. It is a vile, shameful act of betrayal as I attempted to conceal sin from a faithful spouse. These motives man uses as a tool to browse the internet may appear inconspicuous at the time, but its subtleties can also draw you into pornographic websites before you realize you have ventured beyond the boundaries' of decency.

Images of female erotica can captivate the user with imaginative fantasies that are limitless. The computer along with the internet was intended for constructive, useful purposes. But man has made the computer and internet into a den of iniquity. It inflicts psychological wounds with lasting consequences to the unsuspecting victim. Remorse for the grief and sufferings brought upon Darlene has created an atmosphere of mistrust, and rightly so. The adoration, esteem, and respect I have towards Darlene has always been highly cherished. If not for the grace of God through Christ Jesus, I'd still be under the law and dead in my sins. However, Jesus, our righteous and sinless Son of God atoned for our sins for those who seek Him as their Savior. Our Lord and Savior was beaten, scourged, humiliated, and killed on the very cross we continue to trample our feet under.

What led this soul into this carnal dungeon of pornography? It was denial pure and simple. The circumstances, actions, and conclusions about the sexual mores and decay of this country had awakened a dormant soul. There is nothing better in writing a manuscript than scripting something unknown that will become known. There wasn't any intention on my part to enter into the abyss. The fantasy and imaginary amounted to nothing more than observing the degradation of the female anatomy.

We were members of Saint Andrews Church in Sanford for nearly ten-years. We were in fellowship with other Christians of the faith. Regular attendees for the Sunday morning worship service. Our involvement in the church included Sunday school lessons, senior group Bible studies, church functions, and lecture presentations by Dr. R. C. Sproul Senior, Minister of Preaching, and Teaching. Doctor Sproul along with Associate Pastor Burk Parsons are very passionate teachers, orators, and lecturers in the doctrine and knowledge of Biblical teachings. If there was anyone who entered into agreement with the spirit; was motivated, inspired, influenced, and spiritually fed by these two highly regarded teachers of Scripture, it was the author. Words spoken, will prove to be inadequate while describing these two faithful men of the cloth. Not only were the New and Old Testament Scripture's preached, but they walked the walk, and talked the talk.

I was briefly engaged in individual singing lessons by a tutor before stepping aside for health reasons. I also participated in the Saint Andrews choir before health issues forced me to leave. The privilege and honor of participating in one of Saint Andrews annual Christmas programs under the guidance and direction of the church's Chief Maestro, Randall Van Meggelen, a godly man of the Christian faith and deserving accolades of praise is warranted. I developed a great deal of respect and admiration for Mr. Van Meggelen. He had a gift that manifested itself in his gentle, persuasive mannerisms, unrelenting persistence, and patience. He was soft spoken and overseer of those men and women under his charge in a fatherly sort of way. He attempted to fine-tune my vocal cords so I could sing bass, but I don't believe I came close to his expectations.

Brilliant, firmly fixed in the faith, and word, Dr. Sproul and Pastor Parsons had delivered a myriad of sermons on the inner trappings of pornography on the internet. The dangers, sinfulness, and immorality it posed to Christians and society. A member can expect excommunication from the church for pushing the envelope while engaging in internet pornography. Sin will always be at war with the flesh, and a continuous thorn humankind must struggle with, but also conquer. Scripture tells us that if we break one Commandment, we have broken them all. Christians have a helper who is the indwelling of the Holy Spirit whose job it is to convict us of our sins. Once you have the spirit, it will tirelessly mold, shape, and perfect the heart and mind while condemning sinners, so they can grow and become more

Christ-like until that great and glorious day when they will be called home to be with the Lord. A day I yearn with anxious anticipation, where sin will not reside, nor evil known any longer.

Everyone has guilt. It is what you chose to do with guilt that matters most. There is no conflict in guilt which takes up residency in the subconscious mind. It cannot deny the Gospels (the good news). Sharing the good news is something all Christians should partake in with the spiritually dead (unsaved souls). I empathize with anyone unfamiliar with Scripture and the New Testament of Acts. I impart the reader to assume the author's great compassion for the exploitation of the oppressed.

I am convinced God had His hand in this crusade by using the author as his instrument to expose pornography and fraud for their degrading and exploitive harm to women, society, and victims. It is the driving force behind the illegal greedy promoters of this smut-laden industry. It ignores the long-term psychological scars, and the independent nature entities in the porn industry want women to do. These faceless victims may have just turned eighteen. At this age they are very impressionable and naïve. Prostitutes who willingly or unwillingly entered this sinful industry with false promises make this morally irreprehensible. Allowing pimps in suits to cower behind closed doors while lining their greedy pockets off the degradation of innocent, naïve women is demeaning.

Chapter 2

Persecutor to Saint

Beginning in the book of Acts, Chapter 9: we read from Scripture about a man named Saul. Later Saul, now called the Apostle Paul, commissioned by Jesus Christ to become the most faithful messenger and writer of the New Testaments in antiquity. Saul started out as Christianity's most zealous enemy of the church and was infamous for breathing threats and murder against the disciples of the Lord. Saul was from Tarsus in Cilicia, now present day Turkey, and was from the tribe of Benjamin. He had a brilliant mind, commanding knowledge of philosophy and religion. Paul could debate with the most educated scholars of his day.

Saul approved of the stoning of Stephen and was a merciless persecutor of the early church. His mentor was a famous rabbi named Gamaliel. Saul was a tent maker by trade and belonged to the party of Pharisee's before his conversion. Saul would go to the high priest and ask him for letters to the synagogues at Damascus so that if he found any belonging to the way that he might bind them (Christians) and bring them back to Jerusalem; there to suffer and die on the cross. NOTE: Saul was his Jewish name and Paul his Roman name probably going back to his life in Tarsus.

Luke uses the occasion of the conversion of a prominent Gentile official Sergius Paulus, to introduce the familiarity of the apostle to the Gentiles (person of a non-Jewish Nation). Paul was the Apostle to the Gentiles, emissary, and representative. (One sent with the authority of the sender.) Disciple means pupil, rejecting the Apostles is rejecting Jesus.

As Saul was walking down the road to Damascus, suddenly a streak of lightning flashed around him. Falling, he heard a voice saying to him, "Saul, Saul, why are you persecuting me?" Moreover, he said. "Who are you, Lord?" Also, he said. "I am Jesus whom you are persecuting. But rise and enter the city, and you will be told what to do" Acts 9: 1-7. It was at this point in antiquity that Saul was commissioned by Christ to be an Apostle to the Gentiles.

Of the twenty-seven books contained in the New Testament, Paul receives credit with authoring thirteen. The Romans martyred Paul for his faith in Christ in 64 or 65 A.D. Although all Scripture has redeeming qualities, faith, and truth, I cannot in good conscience abandon this trail of blazing everyday words penned by the Apostle Paul in the book of Romans. "Should man think of himself in higher regard?" Perhaps man should begin a sojourn of his soul. Law and Sin are written in Romans Chapter 7: 7-25 would be a good starting point.

"What then shall we say? That the law is sin?" By no means. If it had not been for the law, I would not have known sin. For I would not have known what it is to covet" (what belongs to another), if the law said, "You shall not covet. Nevertheless, sin, seizing an opportunity through the Commandment (laws), produced in me all kinds of covetousness" (having a craving for possessions or another's possessions).

"For apart from the law, law lies dead." Just said, if there were no laws there can be no sin, and therefore, no guilt. "I was once alive;" apart from the law, because if there is no law, there isn't any feelings of guilt or wrongdoing, "but, when the Commandment came (God's word), sin came alive, and I died. (Man became aware of his sin nature through the Commandments.)

When man sins; guilt, feelings of culpability, and responsibility begin to trouble his soul, and conscience. It is not a physical death Paul refers to, but Paul's spirit; through the manifestations of Christ's word. (Make certain by showing) And the infallible word (incapable of error), that it has been made known to every soul born, each governed by, and subject to any violation of god's commandments. Breaking the law or sinning, against god's law now makes us accountable for our sin nature. The wages of sin are death, Romans Chapter. 6: 23.

The very commandment that promised life proved to be death to me, Paul writes. (The law can serve to bring happiness and contentment.) "However, where sin is present there is now pain, suffering, and death. For seeing an opportunity through the commandment, it has deceived me and through it killed me". The metaphor used here is the forbidden tree in the "garden of Eden." The Lord allowed Adam and Eve to partake and eat of any fruit in the garden except for the tree of good and evil; that was in the midst of the garden.

However, the Devil deceived (diluted the truth) Eve, who in turn, shared the fruit with Adam. Therefore, they ate from the tree of good and evil. Because of their disobedience, sin entered into the world. God cast Adam and Eve out of the garden. "Therefore, the law is Holy, and the commandment is Holy, righteous, and good." The law shows God's character as Holy. Man having been created in the image of God (This is good). "Did that which is good then, bring death to me, by no means?" Paul continues. "It was a sin, producing death in me through what was good so that sin might be shown to be sin and through the teachings of Christ Jesus might become sinful beyond measure," (Paul describes an unnatural and unhealthy spiritual condition).

"For we know that the law is spiritual (supernatural beings or phenomena), but I am of the flesh, sold under sin." All creation is now in bondage (slaves to sin), because of Adam and Eve's disobedience. "For I do not understand my actions. For I do not do what I want, but I do the very thing I hate. Now if I do what I do not want, I agree with the law that it is good. Therefore, it is no longer I that do it but sin that dwells within me. For I know nothing good dwells in me; that is, in my flesh for I have the desire to do what is right but not the ability to carry it out."

"For I do not do the good I want, but the evil I do not wish is what I keep on doing." As with Paul, I cannot adequately elucidate sin except when disobedience has taken residency within my heart. Therefore, I have a difficult time processing when sin and grace polarize together (mercy or unearned pardons). Paul continues. "Now if I do what I do not want it is no longer I who do it but sin that dwells within me." (Here Paul is not absolving responsibility for sin, free will.) But merely stating that there is this continual struggle or warfare going on between our sinful flesh and the spiritual realm (good versus' evil).

"Therefore, I find it to be a law when I want to do right but evil lies nearby." Paul delights in the law of God in his inner being. Nevertheless, Paul sees in his members, (perhaps referring to the heart and soul) another law waging war against the law of his mind making him captive. (To be under the control of another such as a prison) To the law of sin that dwells in his members, "wretched man that I am!" I am positive beyond everything sacred that the author identifies with the Apostle Paul as he wrote thirteen books of Scripture based on the inspired word of God. Paul states, "Wretched man that I am! Who will deliver me from this body of death? Thanks be to God through Jesus Christ our Lord!" Romans Chapter 7: 24-25.

Many professing Christians have misinterpretations of the word of God because they seldom find time to get into Scripture and read it. Including but not limited to other denominations, religious cults, and sects. Refer to John Chapter 14: 6. God used men under the inspiration of the Holy Spirit, as His chosen instruments to write Scripture. Reflect if you will on the Dove. When they mate, it is for life. Watching a dove perched high above the ground on a telephone line, they chirp in harmony with their own or other species. They sing a melody in concert which sounds like a well-tuned orchestrated musical play.

However, what is unique about the Dove that separates it from most other birds are its nurturing characteristics. When the mate is injured, sick, or dying, the other Dove remains with their lifelong partner protecting and watching over its welfare until it has recovered or dies. Forever pacing back and forth in distress or a defensive posture when necessary, distracts unwanted intruders away from its mate. What is the big ado about Dove's and the written word? Disenchantment comes in many forms. The answer is rather simple really. The Dove has a lifelong relationship with its partner. They are docile creatures man is not. Humankind is aggressive, often mean-spirited, uncaring, uncommitted, and selfish while the dove is the opposite. Learn from the Dove!

Also, Jesus said to Thomas, John Chapter 14: 6. "I am the way, and the truth, and the life." That is life eternal with Jesus. The alternative is eternal Hell. Scripture tells us it is a place of fire and darkness, torment and separated from God forever. "No one comes to the Father except THROUGH me." Though this is a prepositional phrase that when combined with a noun or pronoun, "me." Together they comprise the function word "through me."

What this means is that Jesus Christ came to Earth, and while taking on the form of human flesh through the virgin birth of Mary, and at the age of thirty-three, given over to man though He was without sin, was crucified on the cross as a living sacrifice for our sins. To consider yourself saved you must receive Him and acknowledge a need for Him. Praying for the forgiveness of your sins and showing true repentance (complete turning away from your sins). The alternative is condemnation to eternal pain and torment in Hell. Unrepentant sinners are cast into total darkness in the abyss forever and ever!

It will become evident why there was a willful yearning to write this manuscript. It will reveal what the author learned about "Cam's, scams, and college youth behaving badly." These sculptured, influential, and deceptive practices of a subtle invitation used by site promoters to draw women into their web of exploitation are nothing short of patronizing. And fraud does not take a back seat to other forms of criminal activity.

However, before we go there, I feel it is important for the reader to be given an introduction into the author's character traits, trials, and hardships. More of these traits will enlighten your taste buds in future chapters.

Why did the author carefully lend consideration and place certain passages of Scripture where they appeared? There was no intent to display intellectual superiority concerning Scripture. This entire acquisition relating to the seriousness and rationale divested in human rights, dignity, and immorality needs our attention. Women deceived by pimps in suits, who entice girls into web-camming through skillful and misleading statements drooling from their deceptive tongue, while sweet honeycombs of lies cascade with reckless abandon from their lips, need to be informed that society no longer has the stomach nor spiritual conviction to tolerate this form of entertainment.

These pimps promote and boast of unlimited earnings potential to women applying for these live sex cam jobs. The prostitutes are told they would be working in an open atmosphere. However, these skillful pimps with their tarnished tongues filled with empty promises amount to nothing more than wolves in sheep's clothing. Jackals without shame… Brood of vipers.

These pimps advertise to prospective prostitutes that the only qualifications are to be personable, friendly, and to entertain a massive audience of men, and in some instances women. Eventually, this leads to other areas that can and do leave emotional and psychological scars. The scars I bear from the deceit, lies, betrayal, sexual assaults, and rejection along with other manifestations encountered throughout my life has strengthened my resolve to combat immoral behavior. So why does a Christian grounded in the faith suddenly find himself stumbling?

You would suppose this question imposes a dilemma that one is unable to affirm logically. However, I have given much thought to this rather contentious vulgarity and have come into agreement once again with Scripture. It is the sin in us, which accounts for our hardened hearts to stray. We have hearts that are disobedient causing us to go astray. No less an offense is that humankind takes for granted the grace in Christ Jesus walking contrary to His commands for obedience. This is clear. The only way to the Father and Heaven is through God's Son Jesus Christ our Savior, period!

Another reason we may find ourselves falling out of grace is our free will. When given choices, we can choose to live according to Gods laws and precepts, or we can choose to be disobedient and face his punishment. It isn't any different from the rules our parents imposed on us during adolescence and teenage-years. Bad choices made during adolescent had consequences, as did my addiction to alcohol. Whether Christian or Non-Christian, when anyone in the flesh is in opposition to godly living, sin takes over which is then deserving of Gods judgment. Let there be no illusion, sooner or later the deceiver comes when you least expect it, and when you are at your weakest. This author does not have all the answers. I am Gods vessel, used as He sees fit and for his Glory.

On the following pages are some poems that exact words that are penned denoting humankind's fears in its present state. Maybe you will discover yourself in these poems if you allow yourselves to be open-minded. Several poets composed these poems. However, do I pre-suppose I am among this elite group to be considered an accomplished poet? Never, absolutely not.

Poems to give aid and enrichment of the soul.
What is it that troubles you? Is it Death?
Who lives forever?
Can it be because your foot has stumbled on the earth?
No man has never stumbled.

Unknown

What is it that troubles you?
Is it the fear of mortality?
Could it be fear of manner of death?
Your fears are unfounded; it is worldly; set your sites on the Cross!

Jim Jacobs

Kindness in words creates confidence.
Kindness in thinking creates profoundness.
Kindness in giving creates love.

Lao-Tse

Mind is the master power that molds and makes.
Moreover, man is Mind, and evermore he takes.
The tool of thought, and shaping it what he will,
Brings forth a thousand joys, a thousand ills:
He thinks in secret, and it happens, Environment is but his
* looking-glass.*

James Allen

If we could cast the gift of a lovely thought into the heart
Why would the heart then not cast upon another what we say, its
* dues impart?*
For everything beautiful done from the heart resonates in harmony,
Would it not be giving as Angels nearby give, absent all disharmonies?

Jim Jacobs

Chapter 3

Reflection's

*Speak of your faith with boldness; let your heart be
steadfast. Be gracious and merciful.
Announce your weaknesses', always repent; be humble
and meek towards your adversaries.
Proclaim Scripture to all; read Scripture; embrace
it, obey it. Remember well, words carry.
Your Father, who is in Heaven, acknowledges a faithful
servant, lifting up the cup of salvation.*
Scripturally Based

I have had the good fortune of knowing godly men who were ordained by our Lord. Gifted and ordained to preach and teach the word of God to their sheep. These ministers repeatedly showed divine forbearance, vanguards who orchestrated through biblical teachings and instruction with purpose and determination for a congregation thirsting for the word. Darlene and I jointly shared in this pilgrimage, foremost because of the spiritual food that served to nourish our souls under the tutelage of Dr. R.C. Sproul. A man after Gods' heart. One of the most mesmerizing orators we have ever had the privilege of hearing as a member of Saint Andrews Chapel in Sanford, Florida. R. C. was nothing short of a blessing.

In addition to his preaching and lecturing, Dr. Sproul authored countless books, including books of the Bible explaining in detail and clarity the supreme authority of Scripture. Dr. Sproul is the founder and chair of Ligonier Ministries. Ligonier Ministries holds a national conference every spring in Orlando, Florida with other prominent ministers who give lectures and testimonials throughout this 3-4-day event. Also, Dr. Sproul provides taped messages on the doctrinal truth of Scripture. Doctor Sproul holds a doctorates degree in theology and philosophy. Since 1979, Ligonier Ministries started publishing the daily Bible study magazine, TABLETALK. In 1994, Dr. Sproul began to broadcast Renewing Your Mind with sound in-depth teachings of the word of God. He also founded the Bible College in Sanford, Florida.

Pastor Burk Parsons is the editor of TABLETALK and co-pastor of Saint Andrews Chapel. He is currently completing his Doctor of Ministry degree. Pastor Parsons has also authored books and has written many journals. He is currently authoring a new book. "Why Do We Have Creeds?" Pastor Parsons was instrumental as editor of the books "A Heart for Devotion," and "Assured by God." These, in addition to other notable achievements has earned him creditability. He is currently under the tutelage of Dr. Sproul. Pastor Parsons has an extraordinary mind and exceptional knowledge of Old and New Testament books. However, if I were to take a straw vote, I'd much prefer Dr. Sproul's sermons during Sunday morning worship service, even though they are both esteemed preachers in their own right.

Notwithstanding, Dr. Sproul is perhaps more profound and deliberate when delivering sermons than Pastor Parson. However, regardless of who preached the sermon, Darlene and I never went out of the church doors without receiving spiritual nourishment and refreshment to the full. I once remarked of Dr. Sproul's lectures and sermons. "It is as if I were sitting at the feet of Jesus, never tiring of his words to the promises anyone can receive in Christs' grace. We love these two godly men, and we want you to love them too.

Either preacher could hold your attention with equal clarity; preaching with fluency as they articulated the message in truth and spirit as prompted by the indwelling of the Holy Spirit. The only distinction that separated these two Ministers was their age. Dr. Sproul I would characterize as aged vintage wine while the ever-principled Pastor Parsons was still fermenting in the vats.

Dr. Sproul had tenure and longevity to compliment his other credentials as a teaching professor and preacher. Pastor Parsons was quite young as his boyish features testified. Pastor Parson's knowledge and teaching skills complimented his authoritative posture using his powerful presentations with boldness, and confidence. Pastor Parson; handpicked by Dr. Sproul to replace the outgoing associate pastor proved to be an excellent choice by Dr. Sproul. Assuming the associate pastor position on short notice was a tremendous responsibility. Pastor Parsons deserves high praise for accepting the challenges placed upon his young shoulders. He never forgot a person's name, and when he preached, he had a habit of calling people in the congregation, "folks."

Pastor Parsons was preaching a sermon one Sunday morning, when suddenly in the middle his sermon, he paused briefly in deep thought. After much reflection, he began to go into a soliloquy of a personal nature. He began by telling the congregation that the day had arrived when he would approach his future father-in-law who was lounging quietly in the living room nestled in his favorite chair. Pastor Parsons stood in front of his father-in-law with his soon to be bride by his side. Pastor Parsons thoughtfully and respectfully asked his father-in-law for his daughter's hand in marriage. If ever there was humble reverence for your elders, it was this act of unselfish respect. Now if this is not a true Calvinist or Puritan, then I am reading the wrong books. How many men do you suppose, in this present era, would bestow reverance to this humbling approach to their future father-in-law? Hum! You see folks, this is how Christians are supposed to conduct themselves at all times. Not just in the house of God, but when living in the secular world. (Away from the church)

The last Pastor to have a positive and lasting influence on my soul was Dr. Larry Meyer, who evoked inspirational words, showed meekness, and uplifted the lowly in heart through edification. Dr. Larry Meyer was the Pastor of Faith Community Christian Reformed Church in Trenton until he felt a calling become a church planter. The church had a congregation of approximately 150 members. Before my initial introduction to Dr. Meyer, there needed to be some prompting from Darlene. I have to admit, had it not been for Darlene; I would still be spiritually dead in my sin. I was clearly a Carnal person, a slave to sin in conduct and behavior. Alcohol was the catalyst this body, heart, and mind worshiped and idolized. Another part of my past I would just as soon defer from discussion because it engenders open wounds and destructive behavior.

I met Doctor Meyer one might say, quite by "Providence" while volunteering at the care center where Darlene worked. Darlene widowed for approximately three-years at the time of our brief introduction by the Director of Nursing at Trenton Care Center where I was to eventually meet and marry my future quintessential angel.

Darlene worked the second shift as an ambulatory care nurse. During our initial greeting, Darlene had no knowledge of my past. Especially the court ordered community service adjudicated against me because of an incident that happened at Carla's home.

Carla and I had been living together after our divorce. Alcohol was the monster lurking in the darkness of the abyss for both of us. Dr. Meyer had a gentle, quiet spirit. He did more listening than talking. I bonded with him immediately. Something rarely observed or would be allowed by me in recent memory. Dr. Meyer was the first person to show a genuine understanding of the maligned pain resonating from within the recesses of my soul. Dr. Meyer was yet another true living testimony of a godly man of the cloth.

Living in a squalid one-bedroom hotel room with a bath, small kitchenette, and small living quarters was not one of the better choices for a place to lay my head. Despite the drinking issue, I remained steadfast in my laurels when it involved cleanliness and personal hygiene. This hotel I called home with its well-worn couch that sank in the middle as soon as the backside hit the cushion was a gem. If that wasn't insulting enough; once you thought you were comfortable on the couch, it would draw the buttocks deeper into a bowl-shaped position inflicting pain on the lumbar spine. Moving into this antiquated hotel was about as low as one could fall from an ordinary life, short of homelessness. It was while living in solitary confinement that serious consideration had surrendered to the thought of committing suicide. The evening of July 4, 1993, was the date selected to accomplish mission suicide. Bye people.

I was living at the hotel because Carla insisted on a quick exit from her home. Only one of endless demands Carla burdened me with during our marriage, and after a mutually agreed upon living arrangement following our divorce. Walking on eggshells while married to Carla was a common theme throughout our marriage. Her mood dictated whether you were in her good graces, or needed a send-off to greener pasture. There wasn't a structured democracy in this relationship, it was a dictatorship favoring Carla. Either conform to Carla's unattainable rules or face her wrath.

It became more egregious and tense whenever Carla consumed too much alcohol. Then she behaved like a caged animal. She would go into fits of rage that were frightful and unpredictable. There was no place to run, no gofer hole to crawl into and hide to avoid the onslaught of her violent physical rage. It was becoming an unsustainable crescendo of sickness. The madness of it all was the deciding factor in ending this unhealthy relationship sooner than later. I felt as though if something didn't give; one of us would end up on death's bed. I didn't want it to be me, not on her terms.

Not only did I want to leave, but Carla made my decision easy; too easy, but I wouldn't begrudge her decision. She gave me an ultimatum. Carla demanded I forego fishing, or our relationship would come to a screeching halt. Carla was an avid lover of nature and animals. All creeping, crawling, or aquatic water creatures, and mammals were off limits for hunting or killing. Worms and minnows included. Fishing meant dead fish. Needless painful suffering, she felt. Fishing was out of the question; taboo. My defiance of Carla's warning soon had me evicted from her home. I was out of her life.

It seemed to fit into her agenda rather well. Behind the scenes and unknown to me, Carla had already formed a very close friendship with another man who did not believe in, or worship God, but worshiped the Gods of nature. Bill was a vegetarian and didn't believe in killing all life forms either. So there you go; now she had herself a perfect match. They would make for the ideal couple. Although difficult at first to let go of the past, it turned out to be a pivotal life-changing turning point in my life.

Perhaps by divine Providence and intervention, this soul guided by the steady hand of Almighty God turned out to be the greatest eviction notice I soon relished from Carla. Call it divine intervention with a purpose. Whatever it was that had me go to the care center I can't say. All that matters is that it changed my life dramatically, and no one was better off for it than me. Darlene did not realize it at the time, nor did I, but we were going to become an item.

Furthermore, I didn't even know I would become her beau. However, for this to gain momentum, there were hurdles; big hurdles for this man to explain. With a blighted past, Darlene would need to know the particulars. There was blossoming dreadful discomfort creating heaviness of heart and a tremendous feelings of agitation at the thought of breaking the news to Darlene. Eventually, Darlene would need to hear the details about this misguided person's efforts to end his life.

The first thing that defined the language of admiration about Darlene was the magic in her dark blue eyes'. Only to discover much later Darlene wore contacts. Not that it was a defining moment in the courtship. Another attachment that mesmerized and occupied my attention was this endless array of thunderous billows of luminous gradations. Warm colors were cascading with structured wonders ablaze, as likened to the face of an Angel. Whoa! An enlightened impression of Darlene when first we met and were introduced to each other.

I had to be careful when shaking Darlene's hands because they appeared fragile and dainty. A clumsy lot such as I known as a thousand winds that can blister flesh without realizing one's strength. Immediately, the mind was transmitting integers' of Fermat's last theorem, for I lacked the wisdom to understand these phenomena. Could we reasonably expect that the chemical stimuli pheromones were echoing the sound of heartbeats without hesitation within the members of my being?

As a volunteer, I developed a bond with the residents and employees at the care center. Promoting a mutual atmosphere of respect for the commitment, dedication, and loving care that soon became a labor of love. Realizing compensation for services rendered was not the reward. Rather, assisting and comforting the elderly residents in all facets of care was my recompense. Deriving a real sense of usefulness was the catalyst that generated a sense of purpose that had long since eluded the writer. Helping the patients during lunch and dinner meals was always challenging and gratifying. It nurtured within the heart a sense of humility. A much needed therapeutic healing of the soul. During Darlene's dinner breaks, we would meet downstairs in the lunchroom. If time allowed, we would engage in light-hearted discussions while she ate her noon meal. I was bewildered at times when the talks appeared to gravitate towards religion.

"And where are you in your Christian life Jim?" Darlene inquired with curiosity.

"Well," as I paused briefly to ponder the question. "I have not been to church in years except to marry Carla seven-years ago," I replied nervously.

That was the wrong answer to give Darlene. Now Pandora's Box was starting to peel back the layers of skeletons hidden in the closet as Darlene looked puzzled and perplexed by the frankness of my response.

"Well, why not?" She asked with a determined look on her face. "You know Goo wad (there was merriment when Darlene extended the word God) should be the center of your life. Reading Scripture, prayer, and worship service, it is all inclusive Darlene concluded."

Replying as if I were defending my actions or lack thereof. "I do pray every night. Besides Darlene, there aren't many good churches around here to attend," I said hoping this would end the questions about church service.

Sensing a lecture coming, I braced for the worst-case scenario. Perhaps I would fall out of favor with Darlene, and she'd no longer want any part of me. Was it fear, doubt, or paranoia driving my thoughts?

"That Jim is just an excuse people use to avoid going to church," she replied sternly, with a scolding gesture. "Christians," she said, "encourage, edify, and pray for each other. We lift each other up in the faith," Darlene announced while nibbling away at her meal of meatloaf.

"Well, I do read the Bible now and then Darlene," I boasted, expecting the answer would appease her so she would know I wasn't illiterate in Scripture.

There was a further correction by Darlene as she said. "The Bible tells us that we should not neglect the gathering together of people." Then Darlene cited Hebrews, Chapter 10: 24-25, to justify her response.

"Darlene, I have no ill will towards the church," I said. Not really wanting to belabor the point. "I realize church should be a priority in my life and I should have a passion for God as well, but, I don't know," I said. "Sometimes Darlene these Christians can be such clicks. That rubs me the wrong way," I elaborated. Long winded I continue unabated. "I have seen a lot of professing Christians act as if they are superior to everyone else outside the church," I declared with a smug air of confidence.

Darlene countered with a terse response. "That is just another excuse that has been heard all too often in the circles of Non-Christians who don't know Christ," Darlene said, resolute in her response. "We are fundamentalist grounded in biblical doctrine." Then Darlene added. "Goo wad desires that we are to come under the word, so where else would you find it but in church?" Then, Darlene hit me with a follow-up question. "Are you even saved through the blood of Christ Jim?"

She sure is raking me through the hot coals, thinking to myself as I reply. "You expect me to walk thru the doors of a church I have never stepped foot in by myself Darlene? Besides, I never heard of "Reformed Theology" before this, let alone stroll into a new church setting alone amongst strangers who I do not even know."

"Pastor Meyer is our Minister, and he is very easy to get to know Jim. I would encourage you to visit the church and get to know him," Darlene responded with conviction.

"I don't know Darlene, I'll have to give this some thought," I responded with caution.

Without hesitating, Darlene interrupted my response with a flat-line in-your-face remark. "I don't think I would ever marry a man who was not a Christian;" Darlene hinted with intense deliberation.

She has stated her position with sincere conviction. I thought to myself quietly.

As time would lend itself to its just dimension's in resilient harmony, as words can display unpredictable outcomes. There was a brief pause while I considered Darlene's persuasive appeal to attend worship service at her church. However, commitment might bring with it anxiousness. We were just beginning to share more about our sojourns, becoming comfortable with each other. There was a greater degree of defensiveness on my part. We were candid about our private lives. Still, feelings of discomfort were surfacing.

Should I disclose how it happened that I came to volunteer for the community care center? Darlene knew about my retirement from military service, receiving a medical disabilities discharge. Volunteering an up-to-date account of the nature of my disabilities. I wondered, could this lend credibility as to why Jim had so much free time on his hands while offering volunteer services. However, I took a silent posture, fearful at the very thought of discussing the dreadful events of July 4, 1993, to Darlene. It continued to weigh heavily on my conscience.

There were many evenings within the still of my new apartment, alone with fear and trembling. Struggling while attempting to redress these past inner demons. How shall we muster the strength and courage to explain without despair and anxiety, the events of July 4, as they unfolded during those fateful and dreadful early morning hours? Ultimately, it would have life-changing effects.

From hospital staff, immediate family, doctor's, Law Enforcement Officials, Attorney's, and the County Courthouse were all unwelcomed guests intruding on my lifestyle. It's their fault I surmised, convincing myself. It was easier to shift responsibility for my actions on a third party than accept accountability for my behavior. However, upon further reflection, there was no one else but Jim to blame in the end for his addiction to alcohol. Eventually, confronting these cunning

42

demons would become the chief mission, so a more wholesome quality of life would finally taste fulfillment.

A month before the July 4, 1993, incident, the Boy Scouts of Trenton were informed a future assignment was being prepared by their Scout Master. To earn their Eagle Badge, the Scout Leader handed out to every Boy Scout a set of instructions. They had to choose a project that would earn them their Eagle Badge. Danny, one of the Boy Scouts, gave thoughtful consideration to a headstone engraved in honor of two soldiers killed in Vietnam who grew up and lived in Mobile County. David, my brother, and another homegrown soldier would have their names engraved on the monument. These two young men from Mobile County became casualties during this undeclared war. Danny felt these two young men were worthy of recognition.

After learning of my whereabouts, Danny's parents paid me a visit in the hotel and asked if I would consider the honorary position as keynote speaker when the date of the dedication ceremony arrived. "How could anyone say no?" I humbly, accepted their request to be the keynote speaker. I could never have imagined that Danny's project would open battle wounds of controversy from the local Veteran's organizations in town, not to mention some of its residents. In this city if you do not have status, or you are outside the inner circle of this group of do-gooders known as the "click;" or the "elitist,' you may as well be an insignificant gnat in the town dumpster.

There was so much unmentionable bickering filling the plates with disingenuous spitefulness amongst the Veteran's organizations that it turned my stomach. They were petty complaints about the monuments location. Where it could, or could not find its quiet repose on the cities valuable property. They trumped up issues with easements, costs, and maintenance. Another example of this unpopular war. How sad! Frankly, after having had my fill of hearing these grown men quibble and whine over something as minute as a location, prompted me to draft a letter off to the Editor of our local paper.

All these naysayers needed to hear another point-of-view and I wanted it printed in the journal. It is most unfortunate one has to resort to extreme measures sometimes to get your point across to grown men acting like teenagers.

The relationship I had with my parents had the strained appeal of imploding on contact. They were at the site seated behind the podium in the front row chairs reserved for them when I arrived at the dedication site. There were no cordial greetings or words exchanged between us, just head nods. There would be other dignitaries there to address the crowd gathering at the memorial site as well. I'm sure the relationship with Carla along with my abuse of alcohol was a constant thorn in my parent's side. Mother never did approve of Carla, but then again, mother never quite took a liking to me either. People often commented that if mother liked you, it was the better of two worlds.

However, if you rubbed Mom the wrong way, she could turn on you in a Nanosecond with feisty fury. You ended up on the ten most wanted list; public enemy number one. She would often carry that mean streak to extremes. It took forever to get back into semi-grace with her. I just happened to end up on the, "I do not like you list." It was always pins and needles between the two of us. That said, the ceremony featuring other distinguished speakers delivered their speeches with eloquence and conviction of heart as they paid tribute to two fallen soldiers, twenty-six-years removed from our midst. I loved David, and I want you to love David too!

When I took the podium, the theme of my address came from the mouth of Cain, which is based on Old Testament Scripture. Cain replied to god's question in Genesis Chapter 4: 8-9. Abel was Cain's brother. Cain was jealous of his brother Abel because God favored him. Abel always gave the best of his first fruits of the harvest to God; Cain didn't. When they were in the field alone, Cain rose up against his brother Abel and killed him. Then the Lord said to Cain. "Where is Abel your brother?" He said. "I do not know; am I my brother's keeper?"

"Am I my brother's keeper? Are you your brother's keeper? Do you want to be your brother's keeper? Have you been your brother's keeper?" If you replied "yes," you just succeeded in raising my eyebrows without giving the questions much thought.

I began my opening remarks by declaring. Each and everyone who came before us, those in the present, and those who are yet to come without exception, have a moral responsibility. In fact, we are commanded by Jesus Christ to become our "brother's keeper." Whether the crowd gathered on the grounds of the site or whoever was listening to the commemorative speeches on the radio station; the emphasis was God-centered. He gave us the commandment to love one another with unconditional love.

The draft board had classified David as ineligible because of a severe ankle injury and other disqualifiers that temporarily excluded him from enlisting in the Army. How David eventually pulled this off to meet the Army's eligibility requirements for enlistment remains a mystery. I knew this about David. Determination fueled his goals to succeed. If David set his efforts on success, there wasn't anything that would discourage him from achieving his goal.

The address mentioned the struggles and hardships many in the service encountered throughout their military careers. Too many enlisted soldiers faced mistreatment because of jealousy or just out of pure meanness from senior grade sergeants. I was no exception. I had to endure chastisement. I was vilified, disparaged, defamed, isolated, abused, and labeled worthless. It ran the gambit of trials. Despite all the trials David faced in his young lifetime, he overcame adversity and enlisted in the service. He received orders to deploy to Vietnam shortly after basic and advanced training. David paid the ultimate price.

You see, David ended up as just another statistic, killed by friendly fire a few months into his tour. "Am I my brother's keeper?" I would hope we would all have that inner thirst in our hearts to be our brother's keeper. Apparently, we are falling dramatically short of God's commandments. Read further into future chapters of this manuscript and determine for yourselves if I am making a convincing argument for immorality.

Today, we live in a world where labeling, or classifying society as either elitist, rich, powerful, middle America, poor, smart, dumb, average, below average, successful, failure, and on it goes. We love to classify and group people based on Maslow's hierarchy of needs. The focal point of the entire address centered on an individual's value. God created man for Himself. God did not create man for man. Each person is unique, and all have a special gift they bring into the world. A gift received from God for his good pleasure. We all didn't receive God's blessing's to be Rhodes Scholars, Lawyers, Doctor's, or Kings.

Come head-to-head in consortium with eyes' wide open with this author for tools of thought, and the shaping of it. There is much stench and manure inlaid in temples of logic evolving into illogical. When dissecting addictions, logical processing becomes cloudy. Wrought with intermissions in life at a point in time where it suggests all behavior is lawful and sorrows become craters of the soul. A mind absent sound judgment by the "cause and effect" factor, presumes with conscious awareness in what society now believes to embrace as, "no right or wrong" behavior. To the mind, heart, and soul this is not healthy. "There is a right, and there is a wrong. There just is!" End of debate. Search Scripture! Hold this thought as your directional compass leads you. Let us give serious thought to addictions and bad behavior. Give them a place in history during this our hour. So come! I cordially invite you, the reader to join me on this pilgrimage.

In the following weeks, I struggled with everything Darlene, and I discussed during her dinner breaks at the care center. Home alone at night, some genuine spirit was searching for a new life. A life seeking guidance in the direction this troubled soul should journey. Turning forty-six-years-old, the relationship I had with the Lord was non-existent. Of equal significance, I intentionally withheld information from Darlene over what had occurred during the early morning hours of July 5, 1993. Secluded in private thoughts accelerating at warp speed within the parameters of this spacious apartment I now leased, all thought surrendered to the "what if" questions.

As I sat in the lounge chair pondering my options, waffling became the name of the game. How would Darlene respond, let alone react should revelations about how I ended up at the care center doing volunteer work come to fruition? Every time thoughts arose to explain my reckless behavior to Darlene; it made me cringe inside. The pit of my stomach felt like a suitcase full of skeleton bones. Ugh! Palms filled with sweat, hands tremoring, and tears rolled freely caring this burden of baggage concealed in a time capsule that I knew would someday be exposed. It might prove a good omen from the liberation of alcohol addiction once it was out in the open.

To say I was overwhelmed with fear and trembling would be an understatement. I was not looking forward to explaining in depth the dire consequences, guilt, and shame that would haunt me for many years to come. I finally rationalized that to prolong the truth served no useful purpose. Hiding this from Darlene was not going to last long. Eventually, she would find out. Darlene could hear about these atrocities through any number of friends in her inner circle. Furthermore, she could read it in the local paper once it was printed in the local paper under "In the Courts." With the liberties of limitless formalities, I finally inhaled the moral courage; approached Darlene, exhaled the growing pains of the truth of what occurred during the twilight hours of July 5, 1993.

Chapter 4

Insanely Suicidal

*Under hidden vanities camouflaged with the faceless
vessels of the unknown, lurks fear.
Coffers are overflowing in conquest; man's penchant
for harm draws Nye, it's made very clear.
Death is nothing; subscribed innocence my delight; this never ending game of life,
Know 'Est circumstances ever stamped with contempt; its tear's, its pain, its strife.*
Jim Jacobs

The date, July 4, 1993. Confined within the four walls of this dirty hotel room, I sat on the couch pondering my options about the future. I had begun the methodical process of neutralizing the inner sanctuary of the cerebrum. Reacting without fully understanding the consequences; surrendering to the ever-increasing cessations striking a chord through vessels of the mind while endorsing extreme measures to do the unthinkable; commit suicide. I had rationalized the option of suicide in concert with an unwillingness to coexist with humankind in their environment of hostility and vindictiveness.

It was an allotted portion of painful agony and miffed conflicts drenched in darkness. Wanting to disappear from societies grip on my soul. It is best to see this through now rather than later. Overloaded to the brim with anger, pain, and mistrust, the time had arrived to utter my indignation with this world the only way I knew how. From childhood's hour at the tender age of five to the present, the mission of constructing barriers had already taken place around a privately designed space where the wounded could reside isolated from the intrusion of outside influences.

Rarely could anyone observe signs of euphoria in my demeanor as I courted this wounded heart. Moreover, trials and hardships arose out of the abyss changing ambivalent behavior. I now surrendered to the indignation of a consuming agitated heart; bereaved by grief deserving of an exclamation point. From underground springs, exploding skyward in unpredictable spurts derived from intermittent jets of hot steaming liquefied geysers, is a testimony to man's penchant for conflict. When all of Heaven displays its colors with the richness of blue, these blue eyes' swelled with the stain of wet tears as they cascaded downward onto cheeks of innocence. Mucous trickling in steady streams from my nostrils, finding its resting place on the upper lip. Wiping it away with a swipe of my hand only to have the cycle repeat itself.

Already entombed forever in memories vaults where reminders of three failed marriages coupled with years of physical, emotional, and psychological ruin lying dormant until something or someone triggered it back to life. Adolescence was only one of many painful experiences molding a frivolous dark cloud that lingered around an eventful childhood while festering inside hearts garden for countless years. Years in the military did not help matters. It only served to compound additional berating's adding to an already disingenuous life. Oh, what should a man do with these persistent rivers of wounds? The nightmare did not end there but appeared to impose its will, riding piggyback throughout the duration of this complex life.

There have been many souls who came before me wanting to take a late life without much care. I had purposed to commit suicide on quite a number of occasions while serving in the military. Stationed at a secured military installation on the Nevada-California border was one such incident. While experiencing unmanageable, unrelenting pain and discomfort because of an injury sustained while unloading a freezer from the back of a truck caused an unexpected back injury. Relief from pain medications had little or no lasting value. The doctors were passing the injury off as a muscle strain or inflammation of the skeletal muscles. The military doctors dismissed it as an insignificant hiccup you might say. After a short while, I had had enough misdiagnosis' by military doctors and their continued refusal to refer me to a specialist. So I came up with my own cure-all to end all. I had a sure-fire way of taking care of pain.

In my mental aberrations and backward thinking, this did not pose a problem. Given the distinction as the three amigo's, the other two men would undergo a litmus test before I allowed them into my inner sanctuary of trustworthy friends. Men who I could trust with my life. We hung out together even though these two men had families of their own. You might say there was a joining at the hip. Inseparable… Band of brothers. We drank, bowled on the base bowling league, went camping and fishing together, and socialized as one big contented trustworthy family. Their wives occasionally joined us on these social outings.

I still have fond memories of our times together. However, when I suffered this injury to the back, my irritability, and unpredictable behavior skyrocketed out of control. The pain was unbearable, depression and anger came alive making its presence known for reasons unknown to me. The beers offered some relief, but when the effects of the alcohol left the bloodstream, it was back to feeling miserable again.

One evening I made the decision to venture out on my own to one of the local bars off the post. After gulping down endless glasses of beer, it would be only a matter of time before my mind would slip into one of those self-imposed pity party doldrums. Over indulgence was a force to reckon with on many occasions. It allowed a person to remain in a fog and lesson internal fears. The conscious decision to drink alone off base this night without inviting the other two amigos was intentional. Sometimes it was necessary to declare the exclusionary clause into our friendship because we knew each other's strengths and weaknesses. I did not want to risk the chance of involving these two over my ill-conceived plan to do myself harm. We all knew John. He was the bartender and owner of a tavern off the post. Most notable, closing hours often meant playing cards until the wee hours of the morning. The beers were always on him. I never declined the offer for free alcohol. John was never great at cards. Another bonus for me. John was always a day late and a dollar short when it came to gambling.

After leaving John's place around 4:30 in the morning, my system full of brew, I was confident my blood/alcohol level measured off the charts. No question, I was intoxicated, but that is what alcoholics do, they get stone-cold drunk to erase the pain. Arriving back at the post barracks (sleeping quarters), all enlisted personnel, regardless of rank at this outpost, where assigned private rooms that served as a living/sleeping quarters. At least, it allowed a sense of security and privacy from outside perverts. The barracks accommodated eight such individual private rooms. However, we all had to share one latrine. It was never a comfortable position to solidify an inner sense of security.

The lights were out as I entered the barracks. Once inside, I went directly to my room and undressed. Struggling to put on faded pajamas, I then went over to the dresser where the medications were stored and took out every bottle that was in the drawer. Enjoying the luxury of a small refrigerator, I went and retrieved a can of soda. Grabbing a cup, I poured the soda into the Styrofoam container. I poured a handful of pain medicine from the bottle into the palm of my left hand and flushed them down my throat with the soda. This process continued, until all the bottles of medication were gone.

This cocktail of alcohol and painkillers worked quickly traveling south and coming to a halt at the bottom of the stomach. I would not know from whence my last breath would come as I laid down on the bed thinking silently before the eyes' closed. There would be one less foot print to contend with shortly. I would become a distant memory to some, as this mind processed final thoughts before going silent. Whatever portion is mine; it is to woe or delight. Is this my legacy? Suddenly as quickly as the eyes' had closed and apparently still in a stupor, I heard a loud percussion noise at the door. Someone or something was forcefully kicking in the door to the room. I could barely make out the figure standing at the entrance of the room. The shadowy figure resembled the hospital First Sergeant. He was calling out. "Jim, Jim." However, his voice was barely audible. I could not hear the voice calling out explicitly. With a faint muttering sound piercing the air, I managed to utter the word. "What?" Deciding the response was troublesome, the First Sergeant summoned another enlisted member, and the two of them lifted my nearly limp frame from the bed. Securing me on either side of their shoulders, they immediately whisked my hapless form from the barracks and rushed me to the hospital emergency room.

If frankness took on the characteristics of a dead man walking, everything of differing faculties and interventions had just compromised my best-laid plans for death. Lending itself to a distant memory, I gradually returned to reality. Recovering and returning to duty after a near death experience, I felt dismayed by a guilt-ridden sea of turbulence of my choosing. I had failed miserably, having lamentations seething with contempt for my well-intended rescuers.

"Why so?" That it might render pyramids of injustice this life was subjected to throughout this sojourn, as it continued unabated to bring about more visitations of these tenacious sufferings of past physical and emotional traumas. What is most disturbing about this unfortunate failed attempt is the ugliness of what we do not wish to see or admit too. But it is hidden in the shadows of alcohol, littered with the debris of delusional realities. For in my infirmities, there was not a recollection from the morphed time capsule I laid in, until awakening from a prolonged slumber. Only then did I become aware of the day times days that I was in a state of diminished capacity. Only after awakening from my altered state of comatose, was the infection of despair becoming apparent?

Every enlisted member assigned to the hospital regardless of rank was assigned additional duties as Emergency Medical Technicians. Given the significant task as first responders, we were responsible for reacting to civilian and military injuries, accidents, or casualties within a vast geographical area. We were generally the first to arrive at the scene of an accident, or residential medical emergency. We often stabilized the patient and then transported the patient or patients in rare cases, back to the base hospital, where an attending physician would evaluate the patient's medical needs, stabilize them, and if necessary, have the patient transported to the city of Reno, Nevada some fifty miles from our military base.

Extensive training was a prerequisite to qualify as an EMT responder. There were many emergencies I responded to or witnessed causing flashbacks, nightmares, or unpleasant memories. Life and death situations were often difficult to deal with because of the seriousness of the patient's condition or medical need. However, I tried to separate patient care from my professional duty when rendering aide. Some nuances' during this period in my life affect me to this day. You never get over witnessing a person take their last breath of air and expire on your watch, despite all efforts to render life-saving treatment.

Fast-forward seventeen-years later, July 5, 1993. I have been out of the service since 1984. As an afterthought, the reader should know that addiction to alcohol or for that fact, any substance with addictive mind-altering chemicals is unhealthy and destructive. It creates an environment of isolation from family and separates the individual from what is fantasy and reality. It is a miserable co-existence. Habit's you thought harbored peace. Yet, when all the layers are uncovered exposing the truth, you are able to see your alienation from family and friends in a different realm. In essence, you create your own abyss.

We return to the less-than-stellar hotel I loathed as my crib. Shortly after the commemorative speech honoring the two Vietnam War Veterans; for reasons I am unable to process definitively, a sense of hopelessness came over me. I became tearful…Distressed. The way to cure feelings of gloom was to resort to Satan's brew to arrest this cloud of pessimism. The irony of suicide, and therefore by extension, it seemed to me, a plausible solution. Nothing would deter me from another attempt at dismissing myself from this world. In my altered state of reasoning, this life was still too complicated and painful.

Preoccupied in thought with too many uncertainties in futures path, the kettle was overflowing with irrational behavior and thoughts of despair. I had observed and tasted inexplicable deceit and evil from man's heart. Contentment is not such a comfort when torrents of pains veins pump rivers of melancholy. I found this misfortune much to my disliking. This insurmountable overwhelming distress forever laden with ashen piles of scars was a constant nuisance knocking at miseries door.

There is a growing feeling about how to feel what, or why even to feel at all? A compulsion to change, however, I am insolvent when it rivals change even when I have tried to spread wide my wings. However, when I hear the call of the wild, I am none the better for my efforts to respond. Days when understanding life does not make any sense, and therefore, any understanding of life is in the here and now! Therefore, onward and forward trek I in an attempt to accomplish in the former what I failed to do in latter days. Would the reader exhaust all efforts in his manicured environment to polarize by foreknowledge through engaging the writer in doubtful disputations?

"Naysay I. I say, Nay!" Careful management of words and having observed all that is true, one should then lend credibility to another who has seen many seasons. I am not callous enough that it warrants preconceived ideological notions. First, you need to walk the walk through history before you label the author an out-of-control invalid. I am amazed at the institution of frailty that Jim Jacobs is still around to write this manuscript. Now convinced the Lord kept me here for His purpose, you are now witnesses' to his handiwork.

Although the first attempt at bidding farewell to society had met with unequivocal resistance while under the gaze of embroiled controversies and pain, the mission statement remained intact. A primary means to disassociate self with evil human behavior all but botched on my last attempt, my determination to repeat was holding its own. But the consensus would prove there may have been divine intervention.

Knowing just enough about the body and its ability to absorb alcohol, I understood how it can overwhelm the blood stream, body tissue, and kidneys. Drinking in excess can cause blackouts and alcohol poisoning. Alcohol, combined with liquor is a potent combination. Your system can only absorb, purify, and pass through the kidneys only what the organs were intended to filter through the bloodstream within a given period-of-time. Therefore, it is natural to expect that when a person consumes more toxins than the kidneys can process, it begins to overload your internal organs and starts to back-up in the layers of tissue and organs. Eventually, the body begins to shut down sending the person into toxic shock and possible death.

Rendering immoral and unethical purposes,' I concluded many times that no virtuous conduct raised more contempt than my numerous attempts to overload and abuse the body with alcohol. When consumption of alcoholic beverages had trumped self-pity and the atmosphere was in prime season, I would become engulfed in a deep dark depression. When these feelings surfaced, it was lock and load time. The alcohol had taken control of these misguided faculties within the subconscious mind.

Therefore, thoughts driven by desire suggested that it would be judicious for everyone if I consumed large quantities of alcohol to the point where it would alter rational thinking. An initiation would define this moment of no return driven by a defeated spirit. Thus, when eyelids encapsulate the eyes', there is finally closure. Never any hope of arising from the imaginary orchard fields, or beautiful raised colored petals bringing about the refined expression on the faces of women. However, like anything that displays exterior beauty, the rose bush contains thorns that produce the sought after rose. However, if flesh brushes against the thorns, it pierces or scratches the skin, leaving in its wake an unpleasant irritating wound.

As you digest this package of conflicts relating to self-harm of God's temple; all efforts to keep this hidden from society seemed like a plausible scenario to end one's life without casting suspicion from others. It isn't something I relish talking about in a public forum as a whole. Attached admirations have since concluded through the Lord's intervention biblical truth's. "But for the Grace of God go I!"

The literary approach of the soul grieves at the prospect of having lived in this deep abiding well of the abyss. Life is very brief. Therefore, before it is lost in memory and it gets to the point where one is unable to ad-lib an oral account, I determined the power of the pen would be the weapon of choice. As man becomes feeble with age and memory, I felt compelled to share these hardships and my pilgrimage into Jim's world with the reader now.

Where certain elements of an experience where intentionally shortened in description, and tethered in restraint, it is because it was omitted for personal reasons. Future chapters will reveal further, this broken world in more depth and detail. Factors guiding the author towards hidden nuances' in this journey catapulted into reality through months of research on cams, scams, and college youth behaving badly. A time for reflection is about the business of looking into your own soul. For lurking in darkness is evil prepared to invade the members of your flesh. You cannot dismiss undesirable pride and the like. We need to illuminate the distinctive qualities of goodness and love. This said, let us move on to chapter five.

Chapter 5

Lethal Intentions

Under vessels vanities, hidden faces, camouflaged
with fanciful faceless veneers of fear.
Driven by individual conquests, man's desire to inflict
pain and suffering so abundantly clear.
Death is nothing, our destiny once to die; this to
claim as my own; that which is known.
Know 'Est well; arises from pools of melancholy,
kindling tears with fire; pains Torrid Zone.
Jim Jacobs

As we begin to describe the facts as common sense surrenders to the orderly dissemination of information without grandstanding within the boundaries of trust, I write what needs to be said. The manuscript grazes over appearance and form and is written solely for its literary content involving swindlers, cam models, prostitutes, and the like. It also bids that I draw your attention back to my final attempt at suicide. To do this, we must retreat to the hotel setting. After registering at the front desk, the clerk assigned me a room on the third floor at the end of a long corridor where my new living quarters for the next six months greeted me. I christened the apartment the crib. Tall vertical windows conjoined with one another in a one-bedroom setting. All windows faced the west side, giving the resident a partial view of our beloved city of Trenton. The hotel was five stories tall and constructed on the corner of Jupiter and Clemens Street long before I was born.

Blinds were the source of shade from the summer's sun. There were no drapes and no curtains. I loathed the thought of taking up residency there. However, the monthly rental fee was reasonable. This hotel was on the short list of apartments because it accommodated my meager budget at the time. However, it did allow for extra disposable income to support my alcohol addiction. I was a binge drinker, yet I also knew based on knowledge of the disease, "alcoholic" fit my profile to a tee. Once alcohol touched the taste buds of the tongue, it was a given that I would be in for a long date with the Devil's brew. After inhaling the taste of an alcoholic beverage, its grip took ownership of me like an Andromeda strain.

Downtown Trenton in the early fifties and sixties was bustling with merchant stores peppered with bars. However, the eighties and nineties saw more and more merchants closing their doors and moving to the mall north of the city. Downtown Trenton had become a mere shell of its former grandeur, leaving behind nothing but bars, and a few diehard retail stores. Even the hotel, where I once worked as a part-time kitchen helper/ waiter on weekends was losing regular customers. The hotel drew crowds on the weekends for their infamous fish fry on Friday evenings, and the deep fried chicken dinner special featured on the menu for Saturday and Sundays.

While sitting in the hotel room late one afternoon on July 4, 1993, I was recessing on the couch contemplating how I would go about the task of taking my life without calling attention to myself. It consumed me on every front. It had weighed heavily on my mind for months now. Flashbacks were overloading a steady stream of unrelenting thoughts that could surely justify liberation from the desolation of it all. There was a simple beginning at one time but seemingly became prey to a bottomless pit of this never ending turmoil.

With all these contentious uncompromising entreaties of betrayal and deceit, the least of which were these intimidations that continually preoccupied minds thoughts at every level, building to a crescendo of hostility. It muddled muddy waters of my life indefinitely. You cannot arrange to greet happiness for just a few hours a day, and then pardon anguish for the remainder of your waking hours. It shall happen then, where all proper terms life has to offer with free will and freedom to choose becomes yours. Misery exhausts all energy, and, therefore, I concluded the taking of one's life was justified.

Beginning to stew on this miserable excuse for a couch, I took a panoramic view of my life. Perhaps to reinforce the desolate shores of wilderness as whispering sounds skim caverns floor to awaken this soul into action or inaction as the situation deems appropriate. Mind unbound with thousands of vexed agitations, grounded in images chasing haste before blue eyes'. Rehashing Carla's decision to evict me from her home and from her presence was just another unpleasant reminder. Another one of her skewed knee jerk tiffs.

Carla had gotten into one of her enraged out-of-control tantrums over something that offended her. Sometimes I got the feeling she relished conflict. It was always over trivial matters unworthy of time or attention. Carla could be cunning and very crafty, especially when engaged in one-on-one dialogue. She had a knack for aggressive behavior if the discussion did not conform to her illogical thinking. She could make you feel as small as a gnat without much provocation or as desirable as royalty.

When Carla persistently went into the stratosphere with these tantrums of hers, I knew the droplets of wrath were about to infringe upon my liberties. The more you tried to ignore Carla's antics the more out-of-control her aggressive and learned behavior became. It was never comforting to be on the receiving end of her tirades.

Like a skilled tactician, Carla's antagonistic demeanor engendered trigger points that kept the argument going until it would spiral out of control. When I realized where the discussions were headed, I would try to remove myself from her presence, usually by telling her I was headed to bed. However, Carla always had her own agenda. You did not go to sleep until she allowed you to retire to the bedroom. As swift as a gazelle, Carla would be on your heels faster than flies' attracted to fly-paper.

Following me down the steps to our room, while I begin to undress, Carla kept the barbs coming fast and furious. Once undressed, I slid into bed. No sooner had I nestled into bed than Carla did a full body slam on top of my stomach with unexpected force. Screaming at the top of her lungs, Carla declared. "You're not getting any sleep tonight buddy! Do you really believe you can come into my home and do as you please?" She yelled. "Buster, you better think again." Her face contorting as she spoke. The more rambling in her arsenal of choice words, the more diminished became my chances to recant her verbal assaults.

"I don't feel like talking right now Carla, leave me alone," I objected loud and clear. "Were not accomplishing anything by you screaming, pushing, and lashing out at me … Now, enough is enough Carla," I demanded.

Yeah right. As if a truce were going to impede her agenda.

Carla switched gears without warning. In a condescending tone, she said. "Come on, I'm feeling frisky, come on, I want to make love!" As she is disrobing while lying on top of my stomach, clawing at her clothes as if she were a prairie dog burrowing itself a tunnel, her clothes flying in every direction.

"No, Carla," I objected. "I don't want to, and I don't feel like it," I insisted, objecting to her demands.

"Who do you think you are mister?" Carla hissed while rolling off my stomach and applying pressure to the midsection with her elbows digging into my ribcage with her fingernails. "You think you're too good for me now? I'm not sexy enough for you all the sudden?" Carla declared sarcastically with a twist of indignation in her words.

There was a brief pause before I boldly screamed. "Knock it off and leave me alone. I want to get some sleep." I shouted again. This time with more authority.

"Oh yeah, see what you've done to me now Jim," as she gets herself into my face. Placing her mouth near my nostrils while grabbing both arms and holding them down on my chest Carla declares. "Smells good doesn't it, huh…huh?" I notice the smirk on her face, as her lips curl upwards. "I'll show you," she said screaming uncontrollably, arms flailing about. I detested this part of her personality. She takes on the behavior of a rabid animal.

Up and out of the bed she leaps landing feet first on the carpet. She disappears into the utility room located around the corner of the bedroom. Thank the Lord now maybe I can get some peace," thinking to myself silently while she's gone doing whatever. I can't imagine, and I don't really care.

The thought no sooner escaped my mind when I realized Carla was now standing alongside the bed. In her right hand, she held a twenty-two caliber pistol two feet away, pointing the barrel of the gun in the direction of my head.

"I'll kill you," Carla uttered, saliva drooling out the right corner of her mouth. She had more than enough to spit in my face, which she did with precision.

"You'll regret ever knowing me, I hate you," she screamed uncontrollably like a wild opossum who felt cornered and threatened.

Lying there for a few seconds in disbelief, flashbacks now resurfacing to other expressed intentions to inflict evil, injury, or damage by infringing on my liberties. With Carla hovering over me at arm's length, the hammer cocked, Carla was poised to do some damage; perhaps putting an end to my life within seconds.

"Oh no not again," I said to myself lying there thinking of the worst-case scenario. Then I cried out saying. "Carla, this circle of violence needs to cease right now!"

This indignation from her seems misdirected at the wrong person. At times life just gets too uncomfortable; so demanding. My mind was adrift with unpleasant memories, and now Carla was prepared to tip the scales out of balance again.

"Look, Carla," I remarked in a raspy tone. "If you want to kill me just pull the trigger, I really don't care anymore. Just don't stand there with a gun pointed at my head with idle threats," I insisted. Becoming rather annoyed by now.

"Think I won't?" She threatened without showing any signs of emotion. "I could do it without blinking an eye, and I will tell the police I was defending myself against you…Hah," Carla said grinning while her face goes into a fogged expression again. "They've been called out here before, or have you forgotten," she declares sarcastically.

"Yeah, that's because you are predisposed to deceive. They don't know you as I do. You can be very convincing in planting the seed of lies while masquerading as this harmless innocent person in distress," I countered, attempting to make my point understood. "You know very well that the only thing I've ever done to you was to keep you at arm's length to prevent your fists from lashing out at me. Not only that, you use your fingernails as a weapon, clawing and scratching away until you draw blood. So don't try to make me out to be the bad guy here!" I declared in defense of her distorted view.

"So what you big cry baby," she said. "They believed me, didn't they?"

"Whatever you say Carla," I complained. "Carla you compromise ethics to achieve your goal. Apparently, the end justifies the means. It's your way or the highway Carla. Just shoot me and get on with it!"

By now, I am tiring of her antics and threats. "Go ahead and put this disgusting crybaby out of his ungrateful mind and be done with it then," pleading. "I have just about had it with you, Carla," I said dejectedly, pointing my finger at her in displeasure while she continued with her babbling tirades.

After what seemed like hours of bickering back and forth over nothing, other than Carla's mean spirited "free will" to make something out of nothing in a seemingly never-ending melodrama, she quit. If for no other reason than pure exhaustion. However, before she retired just before sunrise, she walked away to put the pistol back in its hidden space in the utility room. Apparently, she was exhausted, which I welcomed with relief. The light now switched off, Carla's head hit the pillow like dead weight, and in no time, lights out Carla.

Meanwhile, my mind was preoccupied with how I would go about the business of vacating her premises without another outburst or confrontation. Tired of dealing with Carla's unpredictable behavior, I needed a plan implemented to seek refuge outside this volatile relationship. It would require timely action. Whatever I finally decided, it would leave her no other option than to remove me from her home permanently.

She would never allow the object of her affection to leave voluntarily, not without another confrontation; this was a given. I could do this! Call it blindsiding, grandstanding, or bucking her…Whatever works. Within a matter of days, I had accomplished the mission and was out the door. However, it would come with a huge price tag later on.

Burdened by life's troubles negotiating with the mind into death's arms was I. After reflection, in the sadness of life's evasiveness … A secret that the bitterness of heart has already spoken. The past lies in the dark corners where Hell and nightmares foresee no end. Yes, indeed, what lame corner of the world has humankind created for me to rest my head? I lamented because nobody believes in the cause…Believes in the purpose … Believes in me! I have been chastised, vilified, betrayed, despised patronized, the victim of sexual molestation, times-four. It is endless…Used, abused, teased, hated, traumatized, victimized by mean spirited souls, even when looking at deaths doorstep through the barrel of a gun times-three, threatened with knives, held in contempt, harassed, and four-times married.

"But now, I consider that the sufferings of this present time are not worth comparing with the glory that is to be revealed to us." (Romans chapter 8:18.) This was my conclusion of the matter. With memories comes loves unknown. Through this lost love, I know not. Therefore, mistrust encircled with suspicion for all humanity became my companion. For thinking it best to let the moon dim as blinded kindred have diseased this soul of mine for all time.

Deep wounds incurred during military service had yet to heal when Woe, straight into the firewall of resistance and controversy, what should await my arrival? The incompetent, do-nothing bureaucracy of the Veterans Administration. Should not grievances with a bloated, inefficient bureaucracy insist there be a plea of "nolo contendere" for collateral malfeasance? These wolves in sheep's clothing do not understand that I refuse to retreat, yet there is a desire to conceal the wounds that continually fester and never heal. A meandering stream of gloom loomed heavily embedded and buried in the recesses of this mind. It binds man and government equally towards the wanderings of the walking wounded. Do you see the empty stare in their eyes'? Taste the lingering injustices of arrogance and pride that fill this cup of struggles. All is vain.

These eyes' have seen far too much, and these ears have heard the art of deception while man masquerades in shades of gray. Accountability it seems exists only when people agree to work in concert with reality. However, if it does not conform to their agenda, then accountability leaps from the window. Then it is no longer reality but glossed over mechanical manipulation for personal gain. Having been afflicted in every way, yet never defeated, perplexed but resilient, driven to despair but a survivor. Persecuted but still alive. Struck down but not destroyed. Through it all by some divine purpose, I was always carried in the body of Jesus so that the life of Jesus may also be visible in our bodies. II Corinthians chapter 4: 7-10.

What may appear as conventional wisdom rendering allegories of doom and gloom leaving the reader with the impression of self-loathing; I would suggest the viewer not get carried away by perceptions. This is shallow thinking. It lacks substance. The truth lies within the parameters of survival of the will and a strong faith. If this has tainted man's view, then I recommend you embark on a neutral position until all the facts and information in the manuscript has been composed and written.

"Just the facts ma'am," Sergeant Joe Friday of Dragnet frequently found himself saying to a witness. For those too young to know, Dragnet was a sixties television series aired in black and white featuring the Los Angeles police department robbery, homicide division thirty-minute mini-series.

Before the attempted suicide, there were routine consultations with a local psychiatrist in Trenton because of my depression and anxiety.

However, we should have been treating the author for PTSD, (Post Traumatic Stress Disorder). These psychological disorders can dramatically affect daily life. It had gone untreated and never diagnosed before and after discharge from military service for decades before the symptoms were finally diagnosed in concert at the Veterans Hospital. The psychiatrist I visited in town knew something was wrong but could not quite put her finger on the problem. I saw Dr. Chapman about five or six times before the July 4, 1993, holiday.

"Would you like any medications?" She would ask during our therapy sessions.

"No, I would prefer not to have any thank you," I replied. "I want to be able to function without living like a zombie." The question of prescription medication was always front and center during every consultation session with Dr. Chapman. Each time the answer was the same. "No thanks."

"Do you have any intentions of harming yourself or others," she would inquire. Another frequent question she would continue nagging me about.

Again, the reply was the same. "No, of course not. Why would I do such a thing?" I answered. My eyes' and head drooped down staring at the carpet of her neatly manicured office; unwilling to engage my eyes' with hers.

I kept everything inside. Determined to keep feelings of hopelessness and despair in the corridors of the mind. Since adolescence to the present, I would remain steadfast in my mistrust of authority. The constructed barrier of protection did not discriminate with those in positions of power, and who lord it over others. Some in the inner circle of "clicks" have a tendency to abuse their position by influencing the outcome of other people's liberties. As such, it causes me to remain entrenched.

Let it be said, as it is written. I will continue to be defiant to those who see fit within the interest of superiority, to bridge this safety net. Not all the details need discovery when it pertains to the author's inner sanctuary, including but not limited to traumatic life changing events in his life.

Our attention once again brings us back to the hotel room where it is time to leave the hotel for a brief late afternoon grocery run to purchase beer and liquor. Walking down the corridor of the hotel towards the elevator and down to the main lobby, I head out the door to my car for the drive a few blocks down the street. I had been down this route numerous times before in the direction of the local store in Trenton to purchase a case of beer and some vodka.

It was a beautiful day. Blue skies, feeling the warmth of suns' rays on tan skin made a person feel jovial. A stiff, warm breeze offered a refreshing sensation one delights in inhaling as footsteps impact the concrete sidewalk underfoot. As the body moves, it parts the thin air and just as suddenly, the air returns to where the body has been. Time and space were something that occupied my thoughts. Shopping complete, I swagger back to the car for the short drive back to the hotel.

It was not long before I was back in the room at the hotel. I bought beer, snacks, pint of vodka, and orange juice to make screwdrivers. The orange juice was to dilute the vodka to take some of the bitterness out of the alcohol. It was still daylight outside. Plenty of time left before sunset to liquefy the body into a stupor before going out to the bars. Reclining on the sunken cushions of the couch drinking in solitude within the confines of four enclosed walls, I sat silently in private thought. The cigarettes and snacks close by on the end table.

The more alcohol that I consumed, the more cigarettes I inhaled, and the greater became the mushroom cloud of smoke emanating throughout the apartment. Soon I would not have to light up at all; just inhale the smoke floating like cumulus clouds throughout the rooms. Just another addiction added to my tarnished profile. I was well into the process of hitting a pre-determined goal of self-destruction. I could not begin to tell anyone how many times I have been down this path before. The goal was always the same routine. Drink with reckless abandon, and sink into oblivion only to awaken the next day with a hangover, headache, and diarrhea. Sometimes, never remembering how I had arrived back in the hotel room. It was insane…Destructive…Foolish.

There was no one to blame but the person lifting the drinks to his lips; Jim Jacobs is his name.

"Do you folks understand now why I am the commander-and-chief of sinner's?" This was no badge of honor…Nothing glamorous about this chosen lifestyle. Sitting sluggishly on the couch with a beer in hand, I start the process of busy think, as I torque another few pages in history locked in memories journals. Subject to recall at a moment's notice, especially when you are in a foul mood to begin with. A complicated question for me is the earthly existence we speak as the quality of life.

Whoever I say that I am, you have already dismissed me in your heart. You snicker about the truth of whom I am in this world where we often meet. Unless you seek the truth in your heart, you will go on rejecting me. As it is, you have made it problematic, and the world continues to smother me with imputed rejection thru selfish actions and motives… Words past and present. I am thought of as an attitude of indifference. Just accept the person for who I am. Because when you do, you may be touched by a slight breeze of the wind.

Yet with so much withheld, and much still unspoken, the revelations will eventually breed its furrowed salts throughout this manuscript. This is not about Jim Jacobs at all, even though you may have that perception. No, the desire, even the wish, is for you to clutch each word as if were a delicate orchid … A collector's trophy.

It is now 9 P.M., I had emptied the pint of vodka and downed nearly twelve cans of miller lite beer. It is at this point, the face begins to feel flush and warm to the touch. The effects have already signaled the brain with its numbing … Dull … Heavy feeling. Looking in the mirror, the eyes' revealed showered veins of red tentacles covering the sclera of both eyes'. They're glazed over, glassy in appearance, quite intimidating.

Before leaving the hotel, I grabbed the seven-inch fillet knife that I use for fishing. Fishing was the only liberation I received from my daily struggle with depression. The knife was a useful tool to remove the thin layer of scales and skin from fish. However, tonight it was going to be the weapon of choice to end life as I had come to define and live it. With the knife secured in my waistband of a pair of faded jeans, I was ready to greet the drab world of bars. Making sure I had plenty of cigarettes to smoke and enough cash for purchasing drinks; I was out the door to execute the plan.

Once out the hotel doors, I walked around the corner of the hotel and crossed the street about six-hundred feet to where the closest tavern was without using the car. Meandering through the door of the bar there was a stool next to the entrance, so I plunked my backside down on it. The more I drank, the more I was convinced this was the way to go. Yes, there was a degree of confidence this would be the last night these feet would tread on mother Earth. In fact, the more alcohol consumed, the more emboldened I had become to see this through to its absolute end.

The one disadvantage of time is that it allowed too much time to probe the inner sanctuary of the brain for negative thinking. Sitting there without any interaction with other customers, I would occasionally glance up at the time. It was midnight, a quick decision to drive closer to Carla's home out in the country, ten miles east of Trenton, and to the small community of Givens. This town was dotted with plenty of taverns in which a person could choose for a sit-down.

Feeling numb, speech slurred, staggering …Understandably so, I was one inebriated, lost soul, staggering with every stride it took to maintain my balance, I had become an unsteady chap treading the nine-hundred yards or so to the car before flopping into the driver's seat. I thought I had better remove the knife from my waistband in the event I was stopped by law enforcement, so I removed it and placed it under the right passenger seat.

Moving on, I drive slowly and cautiously so as not to draw attention from law enforcement. I am getting ever so close to the objective. The private oath I made would occasionally buttress and butcher the ignorance swirling around in my mind to that which I was about to do in short order. While driving East, I went into deep thought. "These are mere collectors, collaborators of man's destiny. Should I continue to remain in the valley of the damned?" I needed to remind myself of the reasons to see this violent, self-destructive violation of the body through to the end. I was demoralized, distressed, and I engendered feelings of hopelessness. End of story.

About two miles from Carla's home there was a small bar sitting off from the highway. "Good as any I thought, have a few more." I will swallow down more of the Devil's brew for an hour or so before driving to my final destination...This seemed right. I had never been in this bar before, so when I stepped inside the door, I noticed the crowd was sparse, and the place was dirty. The patrons looked like a bunch of roughnecks modeled after a motorcycle gang. Most were unclean, filthy clothes, long greasy hair, and foul language. However, that did not deter me from staggering towards a stool near the door again.

About an hour later, feeling as though I had more than enough, I stood up from my seat and left, leaving a gratuity for the bartender. After all, I had no need for money anymore. I was already blistering drunk. There might be a problem driving; we'll see. Once inside the vehicle, I grouped around searching for the knife. Finally finding it, I secured it inside my waistband again. Turning on the ignition, I headed towards Carla's home. It didn't take long before the car pulled into her driveway. Shutting off the engine, I sat in silence giving thought on how best to proceed. I was about to embark on a series of calamities that drove the will to see this to its end. Present conditions notwithstanding, Carla was going to witness firsthand how badly she had wounded, betrayed, and made a mockery of our eight-year relationship.

Plans do not always go according to the manifesto, as I had hoped they would in this diary of misadventures. Now isolated, with darkness all around, the voice of the soul silent as well, there was an eerie quiet outside the car. From inside the house, there were no signs of activity coming from within ... Nothing. It was not a complete surprise; after all, it was passed 2:00 AM. Even the crickets and frogs were silent this night. Did these creatures know something and were keeping it from me? It was dismal and gloomy. It was giving me the creeps.

"What to do?" Sitting in the car thinking aloud, I had to remind myself that I did not come all this way only to turn around like a coward, and hightail it back to the hotel without seeing this through. It was a now or never proposition. Should I strike the horn, maybe take the knife, and go knock on the door? Perhaps that will alert Carla or her new beau that a visitor was on their doorstep. Dismissing the idea of going to the front entrance, would just spook them so that was out of the question. I wouldn't want them forming any crazy idea that I was there to cause physical harm to them. No, I would use the horn to get their attention.

Beeeeep ... Beeeeep ... Beeeeep ... No response! The bedroom is down in the basement. Maybe they didn't hear the horn; remaining in the car in deep thought. In my drunken stupor it occurred to me, there was another option I had not considered. This second choice seemed doable. If I just place my right foot gingerly on the accelerator and ease the vehicle forward, it would strike the garage door with the front bumper ... Wham! Carla was sure to hear the percussion. This was defined stupidity in its primitive form. However, an alcoholic with a blood alcohol level of 0.32; rational thinking becomes irrational.

Well Jim, sitting in the driver's seat mumbling words that made no sense. What about this pending assault on the body. It is an either-or proposition. Do it or go back to the hotel. Chalk it up to mission impossible. I have nothing left of lesser known instruments of unfinished affairs. This all-consuming depression was not helping matters. It was just another instrument of discontentment in which to justify an assault on the body, lending it legitimacy.

"Such as it was, it is." I cannot change history. Sitting here having a panoramic flashback is not what I came here to do. "It is time to get with it pal. Get it over with Jim boy." The decision made, turning on the ignition, I put the foot on the accelerator, and with my headlights glowing brightly against the garage door, the car jettisoned forward a little faster than I had intended. Thump ... Boom, as the front bumper struck the garage door. "Oooops," I gasped putting the car in reverse. I slowly backed the car fifteen feet from the door and waited to see if I had aroused anyone from their restful sleep. I had already taken the knife out of its sheath before arriving at Carla's house. I sat until I noticed the lights come on. I saw Carla part the curtain slightly to look out. Wasting precious little time, I brought the knife up to my abdomen and thrust it into my stomach.

"Ugh!" Came a curdling cry from my mouth. However, it did not penetrate deep enough to do any damage other than to draw some blood that had begun trickling through the white short-sleeve shirt I was wearing. Carla and her new earth worshipper boyfriend did not open the front door, which was no surprise. "Why are they ruining my plans? Come out! What's going on in there, I thought."

The first thrust apparently did not accomplish its intended purpose. Either valor or stupidity, it must go one way or the other. This meant another thrust into the midsection. Without any forethought, I lifted the knife forward and with a firm grip on the handle, gravity took over as the knife headed in the direction of the abdomen one more time, only with a little more force. The knife penetrated deeper, the pain much sharper as it reeled my frame backward against the backrest of the car seat.

"Ugh. Ugh," I gasped, as the knife was withdrawn from the abdomen. The amount of blood seeping out of the stomach was flowing steadily now. However, a muffled voice was declaring another missed opportunity gone awry. Carla and her eccentric, conformist vegetarian boyfriend still had not shown any sign of coming outside. Perhaps they were looking out through one of the dark upstairs bedroom windows where curtains could hide them from view. I remained in the car, applying pressure to the stomach wounds. I started to question whether this was a success or failure. The pain from the abdomen was by now increasing in intensity. I was barely holding my own. She could have called 911 alerting the county sheriff's office. If this is the case, then it will not allow me much time to get this right.

Again, I brought the knife upward without fear or trembling; extended the arm and hand at a greater distance from the abdomen than the first two attempts. Drawing the knife in a downward motion, while directing the arm towards a different area of the abdomen, the knife penetrates the air striking the midsection of the stomach once again with quickening speed. Penetrating even deeper, inflicting a wound into the bowels of the stomach, I grimace in pain. Extracting the knife out quickly, I grunted through pierced lips, "Oooooooh, that is painful. Ahhhhh, man, this hurts." The last blow caused me to bleed steadily from the self-inflicted wound. "Dang, does this ever bother me now.

"Why haven't I succumbed to a comatose state yet?" I mumbled. "Why am I still here?" I begin to ponder my motives and apparent failures.

I think it is time to get out of here before the Sheriff's Department gets here. I'm sure she called them. I can't risk it. Putting the car in reverse, I made haste backing out of Carla's driveway and speeding in the direction of some back roads. I hoped the sheriff's office wouldn't think of cruising there. The blood was flowing onto my trousers by now, and onto the car seat forming a small pool of wet blood.

I thought if I could only make it back to the hotel and park the car in an inconspicuous spot, there might be a success in this after all. I could stagger into the hotel and up to that dirty room, get into bed and bleed out unnoticed; I could accomplish the mission. Sometimes we hope for the best well-laid plans but it never comes to fruition. This means God wasn't finished with me yet. For only he knows the days I will live during my sojourn on earth. Therefore, no matter what I do, my plans appear futile.

I had evaded any sheriff's vehicles up to this point, beginning to think I was free and clear. Maybe Carla did not call. Yet, no sooner had I dismissed this thought when, driving slowly but steadily down Highway 12, five miles from Trenton, I glanced into the rearview mirror. Behind my vehicle was the county sheriff cruiser approaching from behind. As the sheriff's car approached, my worst fears were confirmed…I am toast.

The county sheriff cruiser is a mere two feet behind my rear bumper. The gig is up! I gradually merged to the right shoulder of the road applying my foot to the brakes. Bringing the vehicle to an abrupt halt, I sat there and waited for the officers to approach the car. It didn't take them long before they noticed blood coming from my abdomen. They immediately called for an ambulance. The bleeding alerted the officers of a possible weapon. When asked, I told them about the knife.

"Look somewhere in the front passenger side on the floor board," I groaned. "You should find the knife there," I said, barely able to speak.

"Did you harm anyone, or did someone do this to you?" The officer asked. "What's your name sir?" He inquired.

"Jim, Jim Jacobs," I responded, grimacing in pain. The officer asked. "Jim, did you do this to yourself? I need to know," the officer asked.

"Of course, I did," replying to the officers' question. "I wanted to kill myself," I replied incoherently.

"Just hold tight, we have an ambulance coming for you, it's on its way," the officer assured me.

Arriving at the Trenton hospital, I was wheeled into the emergency room on a gurney where an attending physician was standing at the ready. Grabbing forceps, the doctor used them to probe the wounds for any internal damage to vital organs or tissue. I was none too happy with how the doctor went about probing into the wounds looking for possible harm. Apparently, he knew what to look for even though there were times I wanted to jump off the gurney and give him a roundhouse to the jaw. If I had not been handcuffed to the gurney, the physician would have seen the full force of my pent-up anger. It would not have mattered if the deputies were there. I was already upset because I was aware I remained this living breathing creature who now found himself in a lot of trouble.

The emergency room physician determined immediate surgery would be necessary. A specialist would need to be summoned to do the emergency surgery. The deputies were not without their demands. They insisted on a blood draw to determine the blood/alcohol levels in my bloodstream. Voicing opposition for the blood draw just made them more determined to move forward, whether I cooperated or resisted. There were many occasions when consumption of too much alcohol, created a combative disposition. I would morph into an uncontrollable belligerent, obnoxious, and rude beast of burden. After sobriety I realized how nasty my behavior had affected others. It made me feel like an ostrich wanting to bury its head in the sand for the shamefulness of it all.

After surgery, I had a four-day hospitalization stay to recover from the self-inflicted wounds. While I was an inpatient Mom and Dad came to visit once. mother let Dad do all the talking while she stood in the background with her familiar stern expression and penetrating eyes'. I felt if were feasible she would have me sent into orbit using a booster rocket. Nothing new about Mom's indifference towards her third oldest son. She never had to verbalize her outrage because the message could be seen written in her eyes. Nothing surprising. But Mom would eventually undergo a transformation as seasons turned into years and she finally mellowed. Sister Sally came to see me, which was refreshing. I knew she cared about my health and welfare. She uplifted this wretched soul on many occasions when I was down on myself.

When the doctor finally signed the release papers discharging me from the hospital I thought the worst was behind me, and I was about to go back to the dingy hotel room to finish the healing process. However, without my knowledge the County Courthouse had their own agenda, taking the next step for my benefit. Best kept secret in the hospital. Even the nurses maintained their composure without letting on to me about my next destination until my discharge day. Timberline Mental Health Institution fifty-five miles from Trenton would be my port call. The Court wanted an evaluation completed to determine my mental state. I should have known something was amiss when the nurse gave me permission to get dressed, but insisted that I remain in the room.

"Yes, get yourself ready," the nurse instructed me. "You are leaving today, however, once you are finished dressing, please stay in the room until "we come to get you," the nurse instructed stone-faced.

So there I sat for what seemed like hours waiting for the discharge papers. Eventually, the head nurse looked into the room to greet me. Accompanying her was a deputy from the county jail to transport me to Timberline Mental Health.

"Surprise! Oh my what a surprise," I thought to myself.

"Stay in your room until WE come to get you." That was the key word. "We!"

Now I knew for certain the final boarding destination was planned well in advance and it was done without consulting me, as if this were a requirement Jim Jacobs expected. I was none too happy to be going to Timberline.

Chapter 6

Loathsome Journey

*Wounded words, grasp them securely to the beating of
the heart, weary soul gone to Timberline.
Realities dire condition awakens demonic creatures
of underlying motives, off to be refined.
Inhale this demise as whispering winds awaken;
history's forgotten claim; wayward spoils;
In men are devised schemes; to which is no end;
absent sensibility, his thoughts, soiled.*
Jim Jacobs

Observing the emotionless face in the mirror consigned to eternal whispers of a thousand past and present defeats. It is where we unearth the great divide. The sense's draw Nye the turmoil within. When despair for the world grows smaller, I summon the polarized strength to carry me to the end. This is humiliation in its purest form. There is no comfort when a man finds himself treated like some disposable outcast of society. Yet, while lying here languishing over many thoughts passing before downcast eyes', prospects seem to grow dim and bleak for a peaceful co-existence with humankind.

Sitting transfixed in futures destiny that secures only pain and turmoil. These thoughts that appear to surface most frequently. "What do I do now," as I contemplate this question in seclusion and silence. A future surrendering with uncertainties, I begin to sulk. What a terrible mess to have gotten myself into. I needed to hope that once I was admitted into Timberline Mental Health Institution, I would not be held there indefinitely. If they do, Trenton Hospital might just as well have left this soul there to die on the hospital gurney. Liberty is a precious commodity. The only intangible thing man has to cling too. Now, I must surrender to its outcome.

Impressionable contours characteristic of a prison environment greeted every person who walked through the doors of Timberline. I immediately observed a containment area comprised of thick impenetrable glass at the nurse's station as the deputy escorted his prized patient to the admissions window. Here, they had a three-hundred-sixty-degree view in which to observe the movement of every patient, visitor, and staff member in the institution. Security cameras dotted the walls like a checkerboard. I was told by the deputy to stand in front of the admissions counter while he went a distance of fifteen feet to hand over the medical reports from Trenton Hospital.

The nurse, who took possession of the records, cordially thanked him and informed the deputy. "We were expecting Mr. Jacobs." They would begin the preliminary registration process for inpatient admissions. "Wonderful," thinking sarcastically to myself. "I can't wait for the show to begin." This new environment wasn't to my liking. I would rather endure the pain of a self-inflicted stab wound than be here right now. This wasn't my cup of tea, as they say.

After the deputy had left, and the staff was finished with the registration process, the nurse pointed her finger in the direction of a small room next to the nurse's station. As I passed by the nurse's station to have a seat on the hard plastic chair, the nurse instructed me to remain in the chair until permission was given to move about. If I needed to use the restroom, I was told to raise my arm.

Someone was going to shadow my every move today according to Ms. Jennings. When to expect what … And what to do when. Just how long was my stay going to be? I had to remind myself to slow down the gears churning in my head. This was beginning to resemble the movie "One Flew over the Cuckoo's Nest" featuring Nurse Ratchet. The longer I remained here, the more became my resolve to get out. Sitting in isolation reminded me of my childhood. I spent as much time on the chair as I did with outside privileges. The only difference is the belt that was measured out first, and then the hardwood chairs awaited your flat backside. While you sat in the chair, there was to be no interaction with your siblings. "Mum was the orders for the duration of your punishment.

Occasionally, a team of doctors would arrive for a consult. Even the meals were eaten in this small containment area with its bland walls, no TV … No magazines … No radio … Nothing!" Zip, zilch! Occasionally, one of the patients would walk by, stick their head through the threshold and gawk at the newbie. The meals were bad, tasting like torn pieces of cardboard. Military c-rations tasted better than the bland slop we were served.

Separation from others just served to validate my utter resolve about the beast in man. This was my assessment of Timberline. Descend your eyes' upon this physical specimen until your heart is content. Peer over in this direction until your neck hurts Nurse Jennings. I'm not about to add fuel to the fire. I refuse to give you any ammunition to use against me. Not even a snippet of information that will negate this man's chances of getting outta here. This forsaken Mental Health Facility will not receive anything of value that will warrant keeping me here one minute longer than necessary. While I'm here, for whatever dark mystery this mind may secure as protection, you will only document what I force-feed into your heads. "No more, no less."

The staff charted appearance, mannerisms, interaction with other patients. Their written conclusion noted a forty-six-year-old male patient whose appearance was rather paunchy, wearing a bloodstained white short-sleeved shirt. Dah, where did they think the patient was going to get a change of clothing. If that wasn't a no brain conclusion warranting documentation, then what they noted next was void of any balanced thought process.

What was written in the medical charts next, alerts my mind to throw caution into the wind as it left me questioning the medical staff's ability to practice ethical medicine. A staff employee entered the room where I was seated, leaned forward, his head moving towards my body and begins sniffing my torso for any offensive body odor. "Who is in need of mental health counseling here?" Was this really a "need-to-know" medical issue; this personal hygiene thing? Especially since I just arrived at their facility.

A useful tool in establishing man's state-of-mind I presume. Pick, pick, pick! Then, the medical staff found it noteworthy to mention in the chart. "Jim sat in the chair with his arms crossed." I was finding myself questioning whether or not these folks were interns, out to lunch, out of touch, or had been working here too long. Who really had the problem here, the staff, or Jim Jacobs?

I went into Timberline Mental Health Institute on July 8, 1993, and was discharged July 12, 1993. If I was paunchy going in, then I left there fifteen-pounds lighter. If you're searching for a reputable weight reduction program, I highly recommend Timberline for instant results. The strangest situation to happen that involved interaction between all the patients occurred when an actual tornado threat and alert notice was announced. All patients were to get in line and marched through the corridors to the safe zone. This was in the semi-secluded section of the building away from the windows.

When we arrived at the designated location, Nurse Jennings gave the order for the patients to take a seat on the floor while Ms. Berry counted heads. Everything was uneventful until one patient started crying out five-minutes into the alert.

"I want to go to my room now!"

Ms. Jennings replied. "Not now Jeremy!"

Nurse Jennings no sooner finished her sentence and Jeremy pipes in again. This time, he was a little more vocal. "I wanna go to my room now! Why can't I go to my room now?" Jeremy demanded loudly.

This contentious exchange went on for ten minutes without the stillness of the air being silenced. Jeremy continues to exercise his vocal cords.

"I wanna go to my room now, why can't I go to my room now?" Jeremy kept repeating.

It hit a crescendo when the patients, finally tiring of Jeremy's outbursts and his whining yelled in unison their displeasure towards Jeremy. "Shut up Jeremy! Shut up Jeremy! Shut up Jeremy," they shouted, making a game of it now.

This exchange between the other patients and Jeremy went on for an additional three-minutes, and then it escalated, elevating to a fevered frenzy. Now nurse Jennings had to call backup. It was becoming rowdy and unmanageable.

"We need Crowd control here," I thought to myself.

After almost five days at Timberline, the assessment was completed and a report sent to the County Courthouse. Judge Marcus was the official who signed off on this emergency detention, after all. Even after Timberline discharged me, there was no guarantee I was going back to the hotel. Nah, it wasn't that simple. I was escorted from Timberline in handcuffs mind you, by the deputy sheriff, and taken straight to the courthouse and a date with Judge Marcus.

How could I have known that my problems were just beginning? While waiting for our scheduled appearance, I had an opportunity to review the discharge summary from Timberline. The Judge signed the emergency order because he had previous reports handed to him by the Sheriff's Department stating I had stabbed myself three times in the stomach with a fillet knife while intoxicated. Additionally, it was reported I told the deputies of my intentions to kill myself. I certainly cannot defend driving drunk, or the attempted suicide. There will be a hefty fine for driving under the influence for sure. Oh well, "take the bitter herbs and learn from it, Jim."

I held fast at Timberline. I volunteered only that information which I felt was pertinent to my current predicament. I informed the medical evaluation team I had a volatile off-and-on relationship with a woman I married and eventually divorced. Further telling the staff there was always a pattern of mixed messages coming from Carla. "My ex-wife would implant false hope hurling in my direction, leading me to believe we were going to re-marry, and a minute later she would say our relationship had bottomed out." "Mind games, Carla loved to play on a person's emotions," I informed the staff.

The week before my admission to the Trenton hospital, Carla would call frequently singling out one particular song sung by Dolly Parton. "I will always love you." Then after the song was finished, Carla would say repeatedly. "I don't want to get back together with you." As usual, Carla always enjoyed playing the "victim" even to the extremes of threatening to put a restraining order out on me because, as she put it. "I fear Jim will harm me."

Yeah right Carla! In hindsight the measure of one's perception for an event after it has happened, should have alerted me to Carla's unpredictable disposition. This was a woman in need of psychological counseling based on personal observation of Carla's mood swings which dictated her thoughts, words, mood, and deeds.

The problem escalated when I made a call to Carla's residence and a male answered the phone. I was accused of becoming upset that she might be seeing someone else. The truth of the matter, I was getting angry because of all the wrangling back and forth between Carla and me was because she kept trying to play these silly head games.

I admitted to the staff how I would occasionally apply reverse psychology on Carla just to confuse her train of thought before she could land a blow in my direction. Therefore, I made plans to go over to Carla's house and stab myself after getting drunk. I wanted Carla upset, and in a strange way show her the pain she had inflicted on me all these years. Looking the doctor in the eyes', I intentionally lied to him when denying I wanted to kill myself. No way was I staying at Timberline any longer than necessary, so I told the evaluators it was pre-meditated planning and I wanted Carla to witness the act of self-harm on her property; strange as this might appear to the novice ears that wanted to hear.

Yet, she wasn't the only candidate. There was a litany of prospects on my list of agitators who had provoked and challenged my mental state of reasoning to the breaking point. I described myself when drinking as inheriting a split personality. Worthy of mention, they were told how violent, irritable, belligerent, and hostile I could become when confronted by aggressive agitators when I was drinking. When asked by the doctors about my mood, I stated matter-of-fact. "I am not happy." The doctors wrote in their report. "Patient had no mental thought process." Boy; my role playing is paying dividends.

"Impulse control appears to be impaired when under the influence of alcohol." This determination was within the boundaries of an acceptable conclusion. "Judgment seems impaired." (Also true) Four failed marriages confirms this observation. "Insight is adequate." If they only knew how far out in left field they are on this one. "Patient was cognitively intact." (Right-on my man) I didn't need anyone to document what got me into this mess. How does wrong choices sound? I would take full responsibility for all the irresponsible choices I made, with great shame I might add.

Cognitive functioning as to time, place, and person indicated that patient was oriented in all three spheres. However, they minimized intellectual functioning as average. Grading me average was fine, as it seemed good to me. Memory was within normal limits. I accepted this assessment as well.

The three-member panel focused on current effect. Mood was somber, serious, and he expressed remorse about stabbing self. Jim appears most sad. After a few more questions and answers, they derived at a preliminary diagnostic impression using Axis I. Their opinions indicated an adjustment disorder, alcohol abuse, alcohol dependence, and intermittent explosive disorder. Again, these were conclusions I could live with for now.

On the Axis II scale, it was determined that this patient had an antisocial personality disorder. Antisocial? Of course I'm antisocial, and then some. I can accept that characterization with eyes' wide shut. However, I wasn't going to show and tell everything with this group and exchange dialogue they could use to profile me further. Lest they find more reasons to extend the evaluation process further and keep me detained any longer than is absolutely necessary.

Timberline also performed what is referred to as an (MPI-2), Minnesota Multiphasic Personality Inventory-2, and the, (MAST) Michigan Alcohol Screening Test. During the MMPI-2 testing, results indicated.

Even though the test was conducted in a somewhat defensive posture (evasiveness) by the patient, the test suggested difficulty with repressed hostility and was, therefore, a valid diagnosis. The report went on to say the patient displayed signs characteristic of a person who is sullen, argumentative, and suspicious of others and their motives.

Their assessment was spot-on when they reached this conclusion. I resented people of authority who were opinionated, proud, and greedy. The MAST score was 32, (cutoff is 5). Observing the test results realistically, you could indeed find a substance abuse problem. I could have saved them the time. I knew I was an alcoholic. If the casual observer evaluates the visible, yet neglects the invisible, turmoil will affect the external in a profound way.

This anger, has it not already taken up residency in the chambers of a darkened mind? Indulging in the excesses of alcohol has been indicative of associating the substance abuse with underlying traumatic experiences. There were patients at Timberline with every conceivable mental, emotional, and psychological manifestation making it tough for them to function without the aid of mind-altering medications. Even on the drug, you never knew when a patient would lash out on an unsuspecting patient setting off a near riot.

Spending hours in my room lying on a thin mat Timberline calls a bed, I immersed myself in deep meditation, taking a journey into the recesses' of my mind. I found myself analyzing what was haunting inner fears and insecurity. The hurt and pain I had caused so many people in my life, as well as my encounter with the enemy. I resolved to abstain from alcohol in spite of the painful and hurtful experiences from present and past traumatic events that were securely embedded like tumors in this heart, and mind.

I needed to ferret out my inner demons and alcohol addiction. There had to be a sterilization of the old by reigning in the new. After a twenty-eight-year courtship with alcohol, I knew it would be difficult separating myself from the fermented beverages, but it would not be impossible. Cold Turkey was the only alternative. Once committed there is no turning back, its full throttle moving forward. Surrendering to a commitment requires discipline of the mind. I could conquer and defeat the demon inside me. Apologizing to those closest to me would be easy, they were few in number. Dealing with trauma was another animal. The question. "How do you confront this beast head-on?" I cannot count the number of times I would get into fits of rage. I thought someone else was occupying space and time inside me. I have come within a breath's width of accidently killing predators infringing their will in my space on numerous occasions.

So it bears repeating. "But for the grace of God, go I."

What still remains an impasse and impedes all progress is the Post Traumatic Stress Disorder. It accounts for these feelings of hopelessness, despair, depression, anxiety, mistrust, anger, objectionable indifference towards persons of authority. These symptoms suggest a remnant containing hundreds of knives piercing the heart all at once. These psychoneurotic or psychotic disorders are marked by and linked to Post Traumatic Stress Disorder, which is more apt to be attributed to the military, and adolescent trauma.

When the addiction to alcohol was conquered and sobriety achieved, other feelings began to surface more frequently to the degree that PTSD had become a somber reality. I was not consciously aware of the reasons behind my unpredictable behavior. The answer is complicated. My conduct was masked far too long by substance abuse to grasp its manifestations to the norms of a peaceful co-existence with humankind. However, since liberated from alcohol, I am now forced to deal with past traumatic events. Whether counseling will be useful in addressing PTSD issues remains the subject of debate. Something one cannot assess at this point.

The assessment was a mouthful of cotton. Was I uncooperative? Yes! Did I appear evasive and defensive with the Psychologist and his meddling team of associates? Of course I was! Were they accurate in their assessment of the patient's mental state? By far, they reported the information exactly as it was spoon fed to them. I refer to it as, "garbage in … garbage out." They knew I wasn't truthful with them during certain stages of the evaluation. And I knew they knew. We all knew it! Anyone who thinks I am going to give them a life history on traumatic events that have injured and wounded this soul has their priorities backward.

Especially, if the person or persons are attempting to glean information from me for the first time. So, Timberline can write in their assessment report, and document whatever they wish, it would not have any bearing on how I viewed man. Yes, anger and drinking were a major problem, and that is where the energy and focus were placed.

Admitted to Timberline Mental Health for four days was no picnic. However, standing before the County Judge was unpleasant indeed. Dad had come to the Courthouse to support me. Mom was absent… To be expected. We had a brief opportunity to talk thanks to Attorney Allen. I could see the tears well up in Dad's eyes'. His compassion and concern were genuine. He was always there for his children in the best of times and during periods of affliction. How Dad knew when I was being discharged from Timberline; and then have insight to know the date and time of my court appearance surprised and astounded me. This in itself told me volumes about how much he loved his children.

Attorney Allen had a few choice words to say in our closed-door conference before our appearance before Judge Marcus.

"Consider yourself a very lucky man," he stated in all candor. "I had to jump through hoops with the Assistant District Attorney to keep you out of the County Mental Health Facility," Attorney Allen said sternly.

This was not good. Yet, in some respects it was good. I think I can taste freedom for the first time in eight days. As Attorney Allen and I went into Judge Marcus, the Judge first questioned Attorney Allen and the ADA about their pre-arranged agreement. After getting the preliminaries off the docket, Judge Marcus looked over in my direction where I was sitting alongside Attorney Allen and ordered me to stand. Judge Marcus paused for a brief moment; lifted his head slowly, and in a stern, authoritative voice proceeded to give me a history lesson in anger. With open rebuke over my conduct, behavior, and actions. Judge Marcus put it into perspective.

"Mr. Jacobs you're forty-six years' old. Retired from military service for our country, for which we are grateful for your service," Judge Marcus declared. "However, it is now time for you to get your problems under control and take responsibility." When the Judge finished his elongated speech, I felt as if it was me against the Judge, caught between dueling banjos.

Judge Marcus ended his marathon discourse with these final words. "The only thing that separates you from a home at the Holiday Inn, (County Mental Health) is your military service record," Judge Marcus remarked. "But I caution you Mr. Jacobs, this bench will incarcerate you if I see you in my courtroom again. I will bring the full force of the law on your head. Do you understand me, sir?" Judge Marcus looked at me with a piercing stare directed into my line of sight as he concluded his scolding with me.

"Yes your honor, completely," was my response. "You will never see me again Judge Marcus, I promise you." In closing, I stated. "I give you my word Judge Marcus." I have kept my word ever since my appearance before the Judge since that dreadful day.

Out of mountains of adversity enters a keen silence that only the mind can build upon. Springs of living hope brings forth tranquility to heart and soul. I should never remain silent with words until my life is touched by delivered care and the manifestations of sweet innocence are delivered. As I sat in my hotel room, giving thought to lingering questions not easily defined. I gave pause to reflect on where I should now leave my footprints on society.

"Love stand with me while your silence debates something into nothing and nothing into never and never into forever." If you should open my skull and view the prism of turmoil that remains unsettling and littered with disappointment, you might become horrified. Open your eyes' and you will discover an Angel whose name only God and I know. The task had begun renewing and reshaping what otherwise should have been continued embodiment in the grip of the abyss. I would gradually make slow strides in my recovery efforts.

There comes a time in man's education when he finally arrives at the crossroads and acknowledges that indifference is ignorance, that sometimes trusting is suicidal, and that he must accept himself for better or worse as his portion in life. No vestige of nourishment can come to him but through his toil, bestowed and given to man to work the soil. That which resides in man is not new to life's journey and none but he who partakes in life knows what that is of which he can do with their portion in life, nor will they know until they try.

It is something or nothing. One face, one character, one act can define the person. It appears the rule of wisdom should remain. Never rely on others alone, even in acts of pure innocence and sincerity. To bring the past into perspective, with a thousand eyes' ready to endorse what wisdom is unwilling to entrust to you, you will have to be content with what you have or cultivate the bad soil until wisdoms court is once more your recompense.

Dad drove me to the hotel. No words needed exchanging except when we arrived at the hotel; Dad informed me he would see me the next day. There was lurking in the back of my mind, a hint of apprehension and anxiety wondering what Dad was, or wasn't going to discuss with me in the morning. Would he have me give a full account of all the painful hindrances that drove my heart to end my life? I had considered too, how disappointed he must have been by bringing disgrace upon the entire family with my behavior and conduct. I finally rationalized there was no point working myself up over the could have, should have, and would have possibilities.

I decided for the sake of peace and tranquility I would just take this valley of despair one day at a time. Talk about one happy camper, grateful to be free. Even the hotel started to look like the majestic MGM Grand in Las Vegas. At least, that is what I wanted to believe, but it is all wishful thinking. It was and always will remain a depressing place to lay one's head. It would take getting used to going to bed at night sober. This was a given.

The following day Dad arrived. I am expecting another reprimand as I open the door to greet him. However, no reprove was forthcoming from his lips. Instead, it was casual, an atmosphere of serious dialogue that had goals as its central theme. Dad wanted to know my intended goals for the future. "Had I given it any thought?"

"Morning Jim, how was your night, feeling any better?" Dad asked, concern still showed on his well-weathered face.

"It was a pretty uneventful night as evenings go, but I did give serious thought to issues that may trigger my reaction to unacceptable behavior…What the cause of my drinking problems might engender," I informed Dad.

"I don't think we need to go over the reasons right now; save it for later," Dad implied. "What needs to happen; your number one priority as I see it Jim, is to get yourself out of this hotel and find yourself a decent rental apartment." Exclaimed Dad. "This environment is not conducive to your mental stability," Dad said with conviction. "I see this hotel as one of your major problems Jim." Dad expressed with a tone of panic.

Then Dad confided to me something that was totally unexpected, blindsiding me… Catching me off guard for a split second. In the end, I was not disillusioned by his revelation.

"Jim, I do not understand why your mother dislikes you and Sally so much," he remarked bluntly. Then added. "You know I can't force your mother to love you. I have to live with your mother too, and you know how unreasonable and stubborn she can get." Dad expressed with much sadness.

Dad wasn't finished, as he continued. "I really hate that I have to choose sides. I hope you understand this Jim," came his confession, as I sensed the utter pain in his tone while he turned his to look over at me.

After a long pause, I commented. "No Dad, I perfectly understand. I don't know why she dislikes me either, but then, only mother has the hidden mystery to that question," as I affirm Dad's comments. "Mom has had forty-six years to take this wrong and make it right, but I doubt she will." shaking my head from side to side while taking a deep breath.

"If it is any comfort to you, Jim," added Dad. "I have loved your kid's equally," he reassures me.

"I've always known you loved us Dad. There has never been any doubt about your love," I responded. "However, mother's indifference towards me has been known since I was a child," I informed Dad in all frankness.

"I am just sorry the outcome couldn't have been different Jim," Dad tells me.

While Dad continued to express his disappointment as he referred to it as; "this whole mess," as he calls it, while I sat and listened.

"Jim," Dad iterated. "Finding you suitable living accommodations for an apartment that offers breathing space, scenery, and easier access to retail stores is what I feel would best accommodate your emotional welfare. It really isn't healthy for anyone to live confined in this hotel that has seen better days," he concluded.

Dad continued. "You have too many bad memories and experience's living here that contribute to other issues facing you at this time, and I am fearful if you stay here this place will pull you down again," he emphasized. "Carla has been the source for many of your problems right now. She is no good for you, Jim," remarked Dad. "Look at how many times she has caused division in this family while you were both married to each other." Continuing, Dad added. "You have to forget about her and get on with your life before she destroys you," Dad said with his insightful advice.

"I know it has been a very volatile relationship. She is manipulative, unpredictable, and very crafty. She has her own psychological issues," telling Dad something he already knew. "Yet, she refuses to recognize she has a problem. The only thing we had in common was the intimacy. It is what kept us trolling for the others physical affection," I responded in an attempt to defend our courtship.

"You know what has to be done Jim. This is your time and the place to prove you can be the person I have known before all this happened," Dad quipped. "You really aren't at peace with yourself unless you escape the clutches of your problems," Dad exclaimed with no-holds-barred advice.

"I know you're right," I replied. "I am going to need some time to find an affordable apartment that will fit into my budget so I can arrange the move," adding. "I have these hospital debts hanging over my head and they're going to want their money," I concluded with a sigh, overwhelmed by the mounting bills to come from my hospital stay.

"Jim, I just think relocating is your best option. You'll see a difference on how much a simple change in environment can play in the healing process," he pleaded with me. "Put an end to this roller coaster ride you have been on since meeting Carla," Dad insisted. He then suggested with fatherly advice. "Pay what you can on these bills until you get straightened around; it will be just fine, you will see," Dad tried to reassure me.

"Okay," I remarked. Surrendering to what I knew to be the practical approach. This is what I had languished over earlier in Chapter two. The notion that a price would be paid after leaving Carla's home. How would Darlene react to all the fines levied against me by the Court? The Court ordered community service, required me to report to a parole officer each week for two months. Restitution for the damaged garage door to Carla's residence. A fine for the DWI.

This was heavy stuff for a Christian like Darlene to digest let alone accept. The worst-case scenario I feared would occur when confessing my transgressions to Darlene. This may result in another reprimand. Could a blatant response be forthcoming from Darlene? Would she say, "Sorry, but I am no longer interested in your friendship Jim? I don't think we should be seen together anymore. Your choices and questionable decisions make me feel uncomfortable around you right now."

I'm sweating bullets about now, believing my future with Darlene may soon come to a screeching halt. When we finally had our face-to-face sit down, Darlene's reaction was most unexpected. She was understanding, kind, and accepting of my past indiscretions. Perhaps, a touch of empathy was indicated for good measure. Darlene recognized my flaws, but also acknowledged and observed that I had a profound sense of compassion for other people. This caught me completely off guard. No one has ever showered me so much genuine understanding and patience.

I had asked Darlene if she would join me for some coffee after finishing her evening shift. Initially, Darlene had politely declined when first approached. She informed me that she was dating another man. Because of this revelation, I decided to leave well enough alone and approach this as a wait and see proposition. What else did I have but time. A few months later, just like water off a ducks back, Darlene accepted an offer to join me for some coffee. It was conditional, however. I had to attend one of the Sunday morning worship services at Faith Community. This was not debatable. So, we entered into an agreement, church for coffee.

It was an informal, casual, relaxed atmosphere at the local restaurant. We started our conversation listening and learning about the other person's profile, qualities, strengths, and weaknesses'. Throughout the discussion, I would comment on how remarkable her dark blue eyes' captured my attention. A signature profile of sorts. Flattering comments solicited a crimson blush on her face whenever I mentioned her eyes'. After two hours of casual conversation, and enjoying one another's company, we agreed to meet again. Finally, I thought. Just maybe I have found someone with character. She was delightful, soft-spoken, sincere, honest, and dignified.

While attending Faith Community Church, I listened very intently to the sermon and teachings of Dr. Meyer. I made an abrupt decision to become a member of the church. I was enamored with Dr. Meyer's and the intriguing approach he took ministering his sermons. He carried himself as a man of the cloth in a very professional and humble manner. Also, Dr. Meyer was a person's person…Hands on. He not only walked the walk he talked the talk. He has a remarkable gift for making people feel important and valued. He instilled confidence and a sense of self-worth in everyone. His family exemplified his example. I loved them all very much and wished they had not left the church.

It was during a "Promise Keepers" rally at Soldiers Field in Chicago Illinois that I became a born again Christian. The year was 1994. The year I experienced a rebirth (Born again). I felt an awareness of the Holy Spirit entering every part of my body, heart, and soul. What happened was beyond the established norm and difficult to explain adequately in human words. I can only impart; it was an overwhelming experience, sending goose bumps throughout my entire body causing emotions that led to weeping uncontrollably for hours. I recall going down underneath the atrium and sitting on the concrete floor while I sobbed. It felt like a purification process was cleansing the inside of my body that contained a soiled soul littered with sin.

I have kept my reader's in a state of limbo and long-suffering far too long as I rambled on about a small element of my trials, character, and personality. There is much to say yet, too few pages in which to include all the information. Perhaps a biography or memoir's may be in the works after this is completed. The thrust of the manuscript has to do with (cams), Internet Pornography, (scams), internet fraud, and college youth behaving badly. You cannot cover one without uniting the others…Conceived as triplets, born to work evil. It is the immorality of it all. Through Providence, Divine intervention and purpose; I cannot say with complete assurance, knowledge, or understanding what part any of it played in constructing this story. All I know is I am here, becoming the instrument of a higher power to bring these abominations to the forefront.

Let us examine for ourselves then, starting with chapter seven and beyond, this joint cancer that in all likelihood needs immediate legislative attention and action. Accountability must start with our lawmakers. Society cannot allow immoral corruption and decay to permeate the airwaves unchecked. That said, onward and forward we shall proceed, struggling to make visible the invisibility of immoral, sick, and intrusive conduct by persons engaged in illegal, and unethical behavior.

Chapter 7

Internet's Foreplay Playground

Restless spirit, overwhelmed in deep sorrow, laden with shattered uninvited blight.
Life's past is present, footsteps blistered in carnage,
cumbersome; dreadful, painful to my sight.
Ears of thunder, embrace the teacher's truth during
this, humankind's suffering hour.
Man's bondage to deceive curries favor; abuse alive
in bitterness embraces much power.
Jim Jacobs

There is one such as I, who, being appointed by the Lord to proclaim with odious pain, that which permeates every nook and cranny in this nation threatening to de-rail our very survival with our stiff-necked attitudes and behavior. Should we not then testify concerning affirmations which reside in darkness? Let us lead them into His marvelous light. Given thought to this matter, we must surrender this plight into God's power and might. The internet is a tool of misgivings. Its images of fantasy all but saturate the computer screen by parties intending to spoil the minds of the innocent.

Through the accomplishments of pimps in suits, we've now exposed an ungodly trend that not only defines humanities seductive end, while acting indifferent towards the blood-stained cross for which Christ died, so that man may live, we've far exceeded our blessings from the Lord. As it were, we have denied Jesus Christ in place of the one we identify as the tempter ... the Devil ... Satan. You and I are going to take a journey into the very depths of the abyss, (Hell) where Satan and the unrepentant will reside forever and ever. There will be complete darkness, void of any light, separated from God for all eternity. There will be no end to the wailing, weeping, gnashing of teeth, and torment. The lost pass this off with their prideful hearts as if it were a fanciful fairy tale. "I am a kind person you say." This you claim, is enough to be granted passage through the gates of Heaven." That is simply dichotomous (contradictory qualities) thinking Satan would have you believe.

Humankind is a diverse people with different views, religions, and beliefs about whether God exists as three. Father, Son, and Holy Ghost. Does He exist? If so, what god is it that you worship? Are you Muslim, Buddhist, Mormon, Islam, Judaism, Christian? What do you believe? Other groups might include Agnostics, Atheist, Holistic, or Heretic. Let us ruminate in our finite minds the implications these belief systems face. Whoever places their seal of approval on any number of views other than Christ's teachings will be disappointed come judgment day. Some in the world have said Scripture is the biggest fabricated lie in human history; written by man.

Too much evidence unearthed since antiquity in the Mideast supports and proves Christ was born God/Man in the flesh and was crucified for our sins. Scripture is the infallible word of God, and it is God breathed that humankind may know God. Everyone has their individual beliefs, but if your theory goes against Scripture, then I would argue that you are to be most pitied. Regardless of your religious beliefs, one fact that can never escape your subconscious…Guilt.

If you admit to your guilt, then the question begs for an answer. What do you do with your guilt? We have guilt because we are under the law. Therefore, when we commit an act that we know is wrong, guilt seeps into your soul and mind. You feel remorse and guilt. You did not mutate yourself into existence. You cannot create something out of nothing. Only a higher power, a Divine God can do this. God is Glory. Glory is the Light. Moreover, light is God.

People who are not of the faith can procrastinate from now until they take their last breath. If humankind wants to gamble with their lives by refusing to see a need for Jesus as their Savior for the sins they commit, then it is their choice. I will never know if you come to a saving grace in Christ because you may be separated from God and Heaven forever on the day of judgment.

Where do we go from here? The remainder of the manuscript will touch on webcams, frauds, and college youth behaving badly. This is not the first book of its kind alerting the public on the wares of internet pornography, scams (fraud), and college youth in the same venue. Countless citizens who are, were, and will be victimized by swindlers, or who participate in live sex cams, and college youth behaving badly on the internet know this behavior is wrong, but they keep on doing what they know they should not do. Immoral behavior demands serious dialogue. It is in need of constant scrutiny by this nation's lawmakers. All three are equally sinister, wicked, evil, and destructive. These are not peccadillo offenses we merely write and discuss in the news media, or air in the format of a documentary on some television network.

Apparently, law enforcement agencies did not take the fraud complaints I submitted seriously. To my knowledge, none of these elite government agencies have yet to respond to complaints I sent to the Criminal Complaint Center alleging this author had been swindled out of merchandise and money. You might classify this phenomenon (scams) as an epiphany that occurs by hit and miss swindlers. Some webcam prostitutes (I address cam models as prostitutes) are involved in this sordid occupation of fraud as well. It is getting as prevalent as dating scams and other fraud activity found on the internet.

Examine for a brief moment a trend breeding another form of internet rave scorching these pages. When I first encountered this so-called entertainment on the internet, my jaw dropped to the carpet. An egregious vista into what I was witnessing convinced me that American citizens needed to be informed on what, in this author's view is immorality without boundaries in an uncontrolled frenzied environment.

When my eyes' first observed this behavior, I wondered how many parents are funding some, or all their college kid's tuition and aware of what is going on in campus dormitories. Moreover, it doesn't end with on-campus shenanigans, but off-campus as well in fraternity houses.

I would highly recommend parents Google, "search engines" for sites with titles that advertise: "College Rules, Dare Dorm, Krazycollege. com, In the VIP, and College Dorm," just to name a few. You might discover your child is engaged in group sex and drunken party orgies. In most cases, such as (expletive), and (expletive), camera crews offer college kids cash to do immoral sexual acts, and then peddle it on the internet. Another scenario may have students taping themselves and selling the tapes to scrupulous sex peddlers. The same applies to students who rent apartments off-campus where the melancholy goes into free-fall.

Initiation into a sorority or fraternity by some who have been videotaped going through a right-of-passage ritual that requires girls to submit to the demands of the fraternities' president, or their representative; encouraging undergraduates of the female gender, to perform acts of immorality. This entails lewd and lascivious acts on other (expletive) It is (expletive) immoral acts done against Gods moral laws. These are videos of a sexual nature where student participants can receive upwards of ten-thousand dollars per video. The video is then marketed on the internet or smut-laden retail stores.

Is this role-playing by professional models? No! I don't believe it for a second. This is unrehearsed spontaneous acts of self-gratification by both genders. Do you really believe parents who see their child involved in pornography would approve of their child having other students or strangers film them in compromising situations while housed in dormitories? Do you know your child is guzzling down beer and liquor drinking themselves into oblivion, and then allowing men to impose their will on your daughter?" If you're not offended, then you live your lives in a glass house. More than likely you are in denial; an enabler.

I have observed these orgies and hazing parties broadcast on the internet in every major university and other learning institutions in the United States. Yes, I've witnessed it all! These students swarm to the dormitories or frat houses like a colony of busy worker bees from Florida, New York, Indiana, Texas, California, and Ohio, to mention a few. Can you imagine if it is happening in dorms and apartments what mischief spring-breakers must be getting into when you have thousands of kids gathered together in one place! Add drugs to the mix and you have one out-of-control orgy leading to the bottomless pit of the abyss.

Is this the standard, or lack thereof, we've set for our children? Do we passively sit by and allow this immoral behavior displayed on the internet, in dormitories, fraternity houses,' and beaches without parent's objecting to this sordid conduct?

Through the eyes of this author who has made this his crusade involving immorality for the past few years, has concluded that we have become a society who have taken the low ground as reactionaries rather than the proactive stance. Collectively, we are part of the problem and not the solution. We do not want anyone intruding in our comfort zone. We apparently have programmed our brain to think that if it does not directly interfere with our lifestyle, then it is someone else's problem. Are we divided into mutually exclusive, or polarized groups and families unwilling to divide and conquer the airwaves with this endless stream of pornography? Have we become so desensitized to pornography and "scams" that shock and awe used by then-Secretary of State Colin Powell during the Iraq war of March 19, 2003, doesn't apply to immorality as well?" We need to torque our moral compass if this is our position.

If I knew my son or daughter was violating God's moral law, I would have shock and awe. Not to mention the anger and outrage I would feel. Where are our youth's morals and priorities today? Of equal concern is the risk of sexually transmitted diseases' and unwanted or unplanned pregnancies. Some of these girls come straight out of college and into the pornography business. "How do you suppose they ended up there?"

Pimping is big business in the human trafficking arena. These are bloodsuckers in suits calling themselves agents or commodity service providers. Even more troubling are the webcam sites flooding our airwaves with impressionable young girls. The majority claim to be between the ages of eighteen and twenty-six-years-old. I have numerous reasons why these sites need to be shut down. At the center of this controversy is all that was, is, and is yet to come…Our Lord and God. He sees this lewd and reckless behavior as an abomination, while perverts and prostitutes see this as a form of entertainment.

Furthermore, written in Psalms Chapter 53: 1-4. The fool says in his heart. "There is no God." They are corrupted by evil iniquities. There is none who does good, no not one. God looks down from Heaven on the children of man to see if any understand, who seek after God. They have all fallen away; together they have become corrupt. Have those who work evil no knowledge, who eat up my people as they eat bread, and do not call upon God? Has this nation left God? Are we losing our sense of decency?

In I Corinthians, Chapter 6: 9-10, we read. Do you not know that the unrighteous will not inherit the kingdom of God? Do not be deceived. Neither the sexually immoral, nor idolaters, nor adulterers, nor men who practice homosexuality, nor thieves, nor the greedy, nor drunkards, nor revilers, nor swindlers," will inherit the kingdom of God.

"What do you believe God is uttering in a loud voice now?" WOE! WOE! WOE! (Calamity, affliction, sorrow, and ruinous trouble) From I Corinthians these sins become a condemnation of judgment. "Woe to you idolaters." "Woe to you adulterers." "Woe to you who practice homosexuality." Scripture reveals how serious God takes immorality and the consequences of facing his wrath from people who do not turn from their wickedness and detestable practices. John Wayne (The Duke), was the first person to coin the phrase "lock and load," in the 1949 film classic, "Sands of Iwo Jima."

This nation must, and should come to terms with our passive mindset towards internet pornography, and initiate a frontal assault on this disgusting industry that thrives with impunity, mutating like an infested home full of bed bugs … "Lock and load!" If you think your children, especially young teens, are exempt from exposure to these websites outside of your roving eyes', I would strongly urge you to rethink your position. What may appear as an open pop-up on someone's computer screen mimicking an advertisement may steer the unsuspecting user to pornography sites. These are master manipulator's who want nothing more than to get you into their web of immorality.

We have established through Scripture how seriously God regards sin. However, I have heard from skeptics relating to their cynical denial of Scripture. They defend their position by arguing that Scripture was written by the hand of man. Christians, Pastors, and Ministers of the Faith will not deny this fact. However, the evidence is overwhelming. All of the Scripture is God-breathed, using immortal man to put God's word on man's heart.

These same naysayers, who deny Scripture as the authentic word of God will rigorously defend the Constitution of the United States, and the Bill of Rights, written by man. The staunch gun lobbyist uses the Bill of Rights as their right to bear arms, freedom of assembly and freedom of speech. We have been guaranteed life, liberty, the pursuit of happiness, and of expression. The man writes laws for humankind to obey, and most of society complies with these manmade laws. If human hands wrote Scripture, and human hands wrote our manmade laws, then how can you make the case against Scripture written by man through a Holy God that He doesn't exist?

What happens when administrators attempt to impose restrictions on rules and policies on dorm etiquette? At the Barnard College of Columbus University, Cosmopolitan, written by Anna Breslaw, reported that a controversial (already met with resistance), new dorm rule has been enacted at the college. The all-girls sister school of Columbus University restricts overnight guests to no more than three consecutive nights, and no more than six nights total in any thirty-day period. Dorm desk attendants were issued logbooks to keep a record of guests. The women are required to come down with their guest to sign them out in the morning.

Who are they signing out? Some undergraduates at the college interpret this new set of rules as the administration's patronizing way of "slut shaming," and policing the student's sex lives. Dah! This is exactly what is needed. You go to college for an education, not to drink yourselves silly and have orgies thrown in for entertainment.

These students say that the new rules harken back to the bygone days of all-girls' colleges back in the sixties. Monitors would walk the halls after dark and make sure that there was no male guest tomfoolery going on. It is not what they signed up for when they chose to attend the liberal, progressive Bernard College. What did they sign up for if not to be educated?

However, Avis Hinkson, Dean of College, responded via email that the new rules required implementation because certain students were angry with their roommates' frequent hosting of guests. The following paragraph contains responses, pro, and con to Ms. Breslaws article.

A woman commented. "Hey Dean Hinkson, I wholeheartedly agree with the restrictions. If you have a single room, feel free to have your guest sleep over as you like, but in a double room. It is just disrespectful for you to expect your roommate to be happy with a persistent extra roomie! It's hard enough to adjust to a roommate much less the roommate's significant other. You both paid the same housing fee, the significant other didn't. So why should his behind take up residence in your room? This rule lessens the friction that will arise when you have to ask your roomie to cease and desist with the rude behavior", she concluded.

Another woman's view echoed these sentiments. "This is not a return to the sixties. Such rules were in play when I was a Resident Advisor at Barnard in early 2000. The reason behind the rules, as explained to us, was to provide the highest quality residential life to students. Desk attendants had the responsibility of assuring the security of residents and visitors. A logbook is standard at any large reputable institution; from luxury apartment buildings to the Fortune 500 corporations. When a resident assumes the visit is over, this is when the guest should exit the building. More often than you might think, it does not work like that. Bernard women are incredibly charming, and guests try to linger on for innocuous or questionable reasons." She stated.

Just a senior in High School, this student, asked college students how prevalent and public sex is in the dormitories. If this isn't a dead giveaway on where our moral compass is heading, then I guess I'm odd man out. With shameless arrogance and bragging rights, college students advocating bad behavior wrote their version of dorm life.

Jerry. "It is very, very, very common to have sex in the dorm."

Dave. "Where else would we engage in sex?"

Dixie says. "Exactly!" She bragged. "I don't live on campus, but my boyfriend does. Where else would we go that is so freaking convenient! As long as some roomie is not around, it is pretty much a free for all." She concluded her common defense of this behavior with a smiley face icon.

Mitchel, in unabashed candor, contributes favorite locations. "Two high sex places he boasts, are prime breeding areas. On his short list were college dormitories and nursing homes."

Jeff another boastful protégée chimed in. "I used to, (expletive) my girlfriend in her room even with her roomie in there all the time."

Donald concurred with Jeff. "I as well, her roommate didn't mind as long as it wasn't often," He admitted. "Most of the time you know your roommate's schedule so you hope they have a social life as well." Donald finished saying

Timmy explains his experience. "Yup, but the schedule doesn't always prevent walk-ins. I came back from a canceled class once to see my roomie's girlfriend (expletive) him. I got a great look at her (expletive), and then went to get something to eat so I didn't (expletive) block him." Timmy then added. "She looked shocked at the time, but winked at me the next time I saw her."

Let us just say Timmy's language was not very sanitary. Joash, role-playing and an advocate of bad behavior unashamedly discuss' his experience. "Yeah, that is the way you gotta do it, it is nothing to be ashamed of so you might as well make the best of the situation and have a good laugh." Joash goes on to say. "My best story was my sophomore year when my roommate had his girlfriend staying in our dorm with us because she was from out of town." Continuing Joash said. "I woke up at 3:00 A.M. to the sounds of heaving, breathing, and moaning but I did not dare get up and interrupt them." (Expletive) "Nope, I rolled over, put a pillow over my head and went back to sleep. The next morning, I met him coming out of the bathroom and high-fived him."

"He was confused until I told him what happened." This was Joash scathing account of free choice.

Clayton writes with bravado. "There are certain general rules of etiquette. Do not be the loudest couple in the hall if people are trying to sleep." Adding additional advice, Clayton said. "Work out a schedule with roommates, etc. However, beyond that, it is pretty much a sexual chaotic situation. There is no need for your own apartment. Why would you when it is all right here in the dorms?" Clayton said, adding to his valuable insight.

"Is this cause and effect? Is it part of the solution or part of the problem with society?" No wonder rapes occur on student campuses.

One more commentary and we will move on. There are however, pages upon pages of this sort of loose talk that could make for another book. The author just wanted to give make a case for the reader's benefit so they might grasp the mindset of this generation, and how they disavow moral behavior. Apparently, there are no internal feelings; shame is nonexistent, little if any feelings of impropriety…Makes me cringe with fear and trembling. This no-holds-barred anything goes mentality coming from the younger generation is troubling. I call it, "fright night fads."

Thorton writes with regrets. "I lived with my parents at home during college," They said. "You will still get the full experience of going to college," the parents added. "Join some clubs that should help," They said. Trevor said in disappointment. "If you want to get laid in college do NOT live at home. I regret not being able to live in a dorm or a fraternity house," said Thorton. "Who cares if you do not have any debt? You miss a (expletive) ton of fun, and just being in clubs does not help your chances either it seems," Trevor mentioned in disgust. "Maybe I need to join more fun clubs I guess," Thorton concluded.

I wonder if this kid has a face full of ache, wears glasses,' and is fitted with braces? After editing Thornton's comments, I believe his focus and energy ought to be on improving his grammar, rather than his obsession to conquer the female gender. As a young adult returning to the sixties, I never had the inclination to divide and conquer women even when the opportunity to do so presented itself. Abstinence was honorable, instilling character in a person. I valued women as the Lords prized possession.

Even when I was silly drunk, I reframed from taking advantage of women. We were not raised this way in our household. Furthermore, we did not view women as play toys or a commodity. The prevailing attitude today seems to be how many women a man can add to his trophy case. This lack of indifference towards immoral behavior has consequences. Not because I said it. No … No … No. God imposes judgment!

Man will also endure trials. The righteous will suffer alongside the unrighteous. Socially transmitted diseases', (STD) Aids, unwanted pregnancies, reputation, modesty, embarrassment, shame, and guilt are just a few of the conclusions we can draw from immoral behavior. Within the deepest recesses of the soul, my mind's eye has already shown me a panoramic view of these young combatants who are snickering and sneering with an air of condescending haughtiness about them. It's okay, I have the lord on my side.

You may ask. "How do you know they will try to embarrass you Jim?" Simple, it is based on personal experience while attempting to disciple men and women on www.LegofLambCams.com, and other sites found in the principal cities of the United States. I can announce to you that I was not welcomed with open arms. If anything, I was greeted with indignation, condemnation, and in many instances, banned from the prostitute's room and twitter accounts. Even if you dole out unlimited tokens into the prostitute's account, she can still ban you without cause. It's goodbye hose'.

Whom among us has not heard about rapes, gang rapes, date rapes, forced abductions, and trafficking women into the sex industry?" These vicious acts of barbarism have been written about in countless articles, journals, books, and newspapers in the United States and overseas. It is pandemic, touching every social class in the world. Yet, what progress have we made to coral this headless monster and put it to bed? Our legislators can enact laws from now until Harry Reid leaves the Senate, but if you don't have the workforce or resources to enforce these laws; it is counterproductive.

As a result, assaults continue to rise. Countless numbers of victim's lives are shattered and ruined forever. Date rape drugs used to incapacitate victims such as Rohypnol, also called roofies, or GBH. Gamma hydroxybutyric acid, (this was a mouthful) ketamine, zolpidem, or z-drug, known as club drugs. In some areas, these drugs are associated with gangs. Moreover, the medicines in some circles are known as a predator drug. Drug-facilitated sexual assault (DFSA). Also identified as a predator rape, which is a sexual assault (rape or otherwise) carried out on a person after the person has become incapacitated due to having consumed alcohol or was intentionally administered another date rape drug. One study of the general population of American women who believed they were victims of DFSA's found 81% knew the perpetrator before the rape. Another study focused on college students and found 83% knew the perpetrator before the crime.

Before Bible study class one afternoon, the group was sitting around the table sharing weekly adventures before the start of our study session. A wheelchair-bound elderly woman who attended the class regularly began to relate to the group about an incident that happened to her granddaughter the week after our last study session. As she was explaining the incident, I visioned in my mind the image of a sweet, innocent, young lady with a mountain for a soul that would be forever changed. The darkness of the abyss had taken away, all that her profile defined as morally responsible and transformed it into an empty voice of silence. The wheelchair-bound woman was sharing something very personal and tragic.

Her Granddaughter was attending college in the mid-west and was invited to a party at an off-campus fraternity house. Sometime during the festivities, she was lured to a room upstairs where, unknown to her, a group of men were waiting. No sooner had she entered the room when this mob of animals grabbed her and began to viciously gang rape her. Furthermore, they were not satisfied with the act of rape; she was then beaten into submission. The more our friend went into detail about this horrific violation of her Granddaughter, the more I would seethe with anger.

What qualifies me to address women who have been raped, beaten, and battered? I spent nearly six months doing volunteer work at a shelter for beaten and abused women. This service allowed the author direct insight into the plight of women who became recipients of verbal and physical abuse. My concern for the oppressed has always been associated with people who are in the minority. Faceless victims of homelessness, and innocence. I have seen the after effects first hand, leaving its victims hopeless and defeated.

You see, when I became a born again Christian, my entire view of this world changed as well. How could these eyes' not see the error of my ways if I continued drinking, and making stupid decisions in life? That part of my past is behind me now. I submit unto Gods care. This is the charge. The hour is the way of my thoughts. Love stands with me. This does not mean I become slothful in the cause of the oppressed. Until there is a radical change in the attitude of our government and citizens, shouts of discontent shall remain the voice of reform. I want this manuscript to be a catalyst for significant change in this country.

When you hear reports about the measures rapist use to control their victims, the question arises as to how any rational, sane man can remain neutral and satisfied with the status quo? In 1990, Canadian serial killers Paul Bernardo and Karla Homolka drugged Karla's younger sister Tammy with valium after which Paul raped her. A year later they drugged her with the animal tranquilizer halothane and raped her again, after which she choked on her own vomit and died. This date rape drug can have the same adverse reaction as the tranquilizer halothane.

Furthermore, we cannot escape the undeniable truth when we address rape, date rape, or consensual sex in dormitories. It bears repeating, it is an abomination. Trauma occurs to any girl who shares a dorm room with another girl. It can have its own implications. One girl is sexually active while the other is not. A lawsuit by one of the girls speaks to the core of this issue. I can summarize this in a few short words. Each individuals disregard, and selfish desire to fulfill their needs above others has become the social norm not only in America but worldwide. We have become too worldly, so full of self, idol worshipers of things. Moreover, we have become a stiff-necked perverted generation.

Cedric Colter, the editor for a Business Journal, wrote a piece about a Stonebridge College graduate who sued the school in Federal Court alleging her pre-existing psychological problems worsened after administrators refused to let her move to a single dormitory room to escape her roommates frequent sexual trysts with guests in their shared room. In suing the Aston private college, Carol King cites Federal and State antidiscrimination laws. She argues her mental illness entitled her to accommodations including separation from her roommate's alleged behavior. The roommate was having online internet trysts and sex right in front of her, the suit states. A resident hall director did nothing to alleviate the problem, the complaint adds.

After Summit administrators had refused King's request for a single room the Suit states, she fell into a dark and suicidal depression requiring her to take a leave of absence from the school and undergo extensive psychiatric and medical treatment. King, who eventually graduated while studying at home in Texas, is seeking $150,000 in damages.

Whether Ms. King wins or loses' her lawsuit is irrelevant. The greater good is not served by her roommate's insensitivity to Ms. King's expressed wish not to become exposed to her roommate's immoral behavior. Out of darkness rages the smoldering ashes buried in the heart and soul of humankind. Kindness is not in his soul. Nor is love discovered in his heart. Obedience is a dead language. What should not linger in the dwelling places of man's brain are sins, the likes of which we can identify as arrogance, pride, covetousness, greed, selfishness, and deceit. Find a bright and sweet soul who will take up the cause. For it is the unseen that is seen.

Dr. Meyer frequently ended his sermons with an eloquent metaphor. "So what does this mean for you and for me?" He then went on to explain how it tied into the sermon. I challenge you, the reader to meditate on the question. "So what does this mean for you and for me?" Are we a society vulnerable to playing into the hands of Satan using secular thinking as I hear indifference reverberating from the four corners of the wind?

"There is no right or wrong! It just is!" This is present human thinking. I love poems and poetry. It is rich in content and emotion. It speaks volumes about the character and thoughts of the poet that can include pain, suffering, and life's traumatic events as seen through their experienced eye.

Where do these college kids go after graduation, or in some cases while still in college? Some will join the ever-increasing number of prostitutes on live webcam sex sites…Pay for play. Even married couples and couples involved in relationships are entering into this arena of ill-repute. "Why?" Some girls told the author it was to pay back student loans. Some girls admitted to attending college while camming part-time to earn extra money. While other girls work and webcam on the side. Still others do it just for the money.

At this point, I want to inform the reader that a lot of the information I share with you came at a cost monetarily, and as the result of another divorce. I regret Darlene and I had to go through the divorce proceedings. However, if the manuscript results in a change for the greater good, these efforts will not have been in vain.

On many sites, in order to solicit information from a model, you must establish trust. Trust gives you access to information and information underscores the depth of the abyss people are willing to choose as their final destiny. I often spent many hours in one room. A pull over secondary obstruction hid my identity so I could eavesdrop on conversations between prostitute and pervert. Other times I entered their room to ask personal questions, paying out tokens to construct their story.

Furthermore, there were times when all I did was listen without sacrificing tokens. I could learn a lot of substantial information on a Prostitutes profile just by listening. Occasionally, they would have a slip of the tongue that spoke volumes about the prostitute's character. There are girls (I resented associating them with models) on sites who are controlled by their pimps, boyfriends, or other entities. Pimps are usually outside the range of the camera so you cannot see them, but their shadows are seen none-the-less in some cases. It is a very strict, controlled environment for these girls.

Your minds must be churning before the ink is even dry on the paper. "If you can't see a Pimp, how do you know they are there, you may inquire?" After spending over a year researching webcams and frauds, there are telltale signs that something is amiss when you start seeing shadows in the foreground. The other giveaway is when the model continually looks over in one direction with her eyes' raised, transfixed on an object for brief periods. More than likely she is getting a queue from a pimp, husband, or boyfriend whether or not to remove an item of clothing or to discontinue broadcasting. Women who keep their clothing on for extended periods of time are usually under the spell of pimp.

Sometimes the pimp is absent from the room, but his watchful eyes are never far from his self-proclaimed property. It is likely he is viewing her from another computer. Furthermore, communication between model and pimp comes from smart phone's so the pimp can keep a tight leash on his women. This especially holds water for girls in foreign countries. The Ukraine, Romania, Hungry, United Kingdom, Poland, Russia, or Canada. These folks use our airwaves to do their business. The most critical piece of evidence is the prostitute's body language and facial expressions. Eyes' filled with sadness screams out in desperation. "Help me, please help me!"

"Are these observations I mentioned reliable and verifiable?" No! However, after a while your instincts and intuition take over and you become aware pimps are part of the equation. I can identify with women who are trafficked; lending much-needed empathy. They are victims in a male dominated society. I cannot imagine what these women are subjected to every waking hour of the day. A piece of property…A commodity…Slaves, forever compliant to the demands and evil motives of their pimp.

Do we need government intrusion to monitor misuse of the internet? I for one advocate intrusion in this nasty stain tainted industry. We need to put an end to this ever-increasing demand for immoral behavior. There needs to be accountability, and it begins with supply and demand. Former President Regan coined the phrase, "supply-side economics." Alternatively, Reaganomics, and the "trickle-down" effect with large tax cuts going to big corporations.

I met a young woman on the internet who graduated from college. She made the choice to solicit her body on live sex cam networks. She claimed her student loan was so high she had no reasonable means to make the monthly payments to the government. "It would take her forever to repay the loan," she confided in me. If this is true, what does this suggest about our government? A government whose repayments and interests are so high, that women have to resort to internet sex camming. Minimum wage does not afford them a living wage. I want to go on record as opposing this 21-year-old girl's decision, even if the facts support her. We all have free will when making choices in life. Degrading yourself in front of two-thousand viewers who visit your room is not the moral and ethical approach to embark on, when lending credibility to a person's character and moral convictions.

The following paragraphs sum up a brief history of the prostitute who I have elected to call Jan. Jan claims she attended a prestigious college. This is why her student loan costs so much according to her statement. When Jan mentioned a prestigious school, what came to mind immediately was an Ivy League College such as Brown, Harvard, or Cornell. "Nad-da!" Allow people to express themselves long enough, and eventually, they stumble. The prestigious college she boasted about was Illinois where she majored in music. Jan said she explored teaching, but told the group assembled in her room that starting wages only offered twenty-five thousand dollars or less per year. This would not cover her expenses.

Asked by other curious guests in her room what brought her to camming on the internet, Jan replied. "One of my male friends (here you are, man involved), suggested I look into webcamming on the internet. My friend also told me to get a reputable agent." I declare, friends do not refer friends to go into pornography so they become damaged goods in this industry of ill-repute.

"What agent in this industry is reputable?" These folks are pimps in suits selling a commodity … Human female flesh! Sold into bondage; a slave. After signing a contract (can you imagine this industry requires a signed contract), she spends four to five months in training with a website called (LOLC), www.legoflambcams.com. Jan was then trained under the tutelage of other prostitutes in the industry. They have instructions on how to get men (perverts), to pony up tokens into the coffers for their pimps while the prostitute attempts to increase her commission for the evening's work. This was the goal of every prostitute. Rules, etiquette, how to get men excited, and on and on it goes during the prostitutes probationary training. In-depth details on how these websites operate are covered in future chapters.

Now that Jan has established herself on the website, she is more-or-less an independent operator of her own site (?). Free to perform and talk within the guidelines of the operators (pimps), rules. Prostitutes were not permitted to give out their real names. Thus, they create fictitious names they assign themselves. (Username) Nor are they allowed to reveal their true location for security reasons (I get it).

However, as I said previously, all you have to do is be a good listener, and before long you can almost pinpoint their location. Jan, a loquacious parrot probably reveals more about herself than she realizes'. It did not take more than a couple months, and I knew Jan's city, eating establishments, where her parents lived within a 2-hour radius. In fact, I could pinpoint the town if I wanted just by using a protractor. I knew the population. She mentioned times she preferred eating. Pimps in human trafficking would find this information very beneficial if they wanted to kidnap a moneymaker for their stable. I have reason to believe this has already occurred to one prostitute featured on LOLC.

We have established that Jan graduated from college and became employed by the live webcam sex industry. "Where do we go from here?" It appears Jan wants to graduate again. Her agent calls Jan and wants her to get on a plane to Los Angeles. He has booked her for some photo shoots with Matrix Modeling Agency. However, Matrix modeling is a misnomer and is not what it implies. They are photographs of her doing soft-core pornography photographs.

Again, these pimp shops chase after these impressionable young girl's promising them the glitter, glamor, fame, and fortune by peddling their flesh in front of a camera. Her first appearance going out on location had someone, if not herself taking a selfie (taking your own picture) while sitting in the back seat of a fancy limousine. She was grinning from ear to ear as she is being chaperoned to the photo site. It does not take some of the photographers long before they begin to solicit and impose their will through implied sexual escapades with the new rookie in town. Some pimps (photographer's), are known to be married.

Among some of Jan's other agencies that she has signed contracts with are, digital desire.com, zishy.com, and manyvids.com.

I am not here to promote or approve of Jan's choices. I find it rather shameful, vile, and disgusting that Jan has chosen to support herself in this venue. I also found it disturbing that Jan has no control over her photographs once the photographer is finished. They either become the sole property of the industry or her agent. Her agent felt it was in her best interest to have some of her pictures featured in Carnal magazine, owned by an infamous peddler of pornography. Naturally, Carnal found her photogenic enough to make her a feature in their 2015 centerfold. The carnal magazine also named Jan, Carnal Darling in one of their earlier issues in 2015.

So now, we have Jan flying back and forth from Illinois to Los Angeles, while still committed to LOLC. It did not take the shifty shysters from LA long to approach Jan with a request to do hardcore videos. While still in the editing stages of this manuscript, I believe to the best of my knowledge Jan has declined to do hardcore. However, given time and the smooth talking scoundrels in Los Angeles, I personally feel Jan will succumb to the pressure and go all-in. Jan has already traveled to Arizona, Las Vegas, and Australia for stills and porn conventions There are other prostitutes who are part of this contingent on LOLC who go to LA for photographs and who knows what else. The ink isn't even dry on the paper yet, and it came to my attention that Jan is in the process of relocating to Los Angeles.

I could have written about any number of prostitutes as a facsimile to telling a story as the example. Towards the end, when I had gathered sufficient information on Jan for this book, I began to disciple Jan and some of the other prostitutes in this business. However, any disciplining and interaction I had with these prostitutes and myself soon went south. The perverts and the girls flat-out rejected the gospel. The prostitutes were there to make money and the pervert entrenched to be entertained.

These perverts did not take kindly to me after I called them into account. These men (animals or perverts) make great strides in humiliating and degrading the prostitutes as if this were a rite of passage. Using such offensive ... dirty ... nasty language about a woman's anatomy, while attacking the prostitute's character reviled me to no end. After all, it was felt they were paying the prostitutes for the privilege to say whatever suited their ego at the time. Whether I planted the seed of Salvation remains an open question. I would hope there is a consensus in the nation that we are facing a pandemic of immorality in the darkest caverns of the abyss that requires intervention at the Federal level.

What is equally troubling is the manner in which webcam prostitutes receive their money, including countries beyond our borders who are compensated by the owners of live webcam sex sites that air and are operated within our borders. Prostitutes receive payments on average every two weeks. Using the example of a site called Navigate, the President of the company or his delegated representative issues the checks. It is the authors understanding that when the girls receive their paychecks, there is no State, Federal, or Social Security taxes deducted from the earned income. If this is true, and many prostitutes have confirmed this. "Does our government have a Federal Registry of prostitutes working in this forsaken industry where these sites mutate on the internet?" My guess is they do not!

"Is the Federal or State government requiring sites to provide them with correct names and addresses of ALL webcam prostitutes, foreign and domestic?" My guess is they do not! "Are foreign prostitutes who work on webcam sites using our airwaves, operating with impunity? Do we have any statutes on the books about foreigner's receiving earned income from American owned and operated webcam porn sites?" "Are they reporting their income to our government? Are they required to pay State, Federal, and or Social Security taxes?" My guess is they are not! If the government answered "no" to three of the four questions then, "Houston we gotta problem!" We have a moral dilemma on our hands as it is. To continue allowing this disease of internet pornography to fester and mutate without so much as a whimper within the walls of Congress; not even an echo is shameful and irresponsible.

Moreover, recently I heard Majority Leader, and Speaker of the House John Boehner, a Republican from Louisiana, announce emphatically. "We do not need to monitor the internet."

"Are you kidding me? Get your head out of the sand Mr. Speaker!" The biggest offenders of websites where nasty pimps pull the strings and control the prostitutes every twitch, I consider cowards hiding behind computer screens in foreign countries such as Ukraine, Russia, Romania, and Poland. This is not to suggest there are not pimps controlling prostitutes online in the United States. I suspect there are just as many. They need to disappear.

No less sinister are pimps in suits. Owners and operators of cam sites who get rich off the flesh of women. Earlier, I mentioned supply and demand. If you separate the body at the midsection, you have created two distinct parts. One cannot function without the other. The torso cannot move without signals from the brain and the upper body cannot go anywhere without the lower limbs. They have both become non-functional ... stagnating ... serving no useful purpose. As they remain separated from each other, they will expire and degrade to where the body can no longer function.

The application of supply and demand operates on the same principal. They complement each other. If you have an influx of one or the other, supply and demand are not in harmony with one another and you end up with too much or too little. These overriding factors affect the economy. Either it will reveal a good outcome, or the economy will collapse because supplies is short. Apply this same principal to live sex video cam sites promoting bad behavior. The fundamentals of supply (the infamous prostitute) and demand (pervert) primarily work under the same example. Eliminate the demand and supply goes away. Take away the supply (prostitute) there is nothing to supply (pervert) and you extinguish the fire of immorality.

You cannot construct a house with one nail. Neither can you eradicate this nation's daunting problems without a purpose, cause, and commitment. If the government tells its citizens it does not have the money or workforce, then we need to bring our military back to our own soil. "What can they do?" For one, patrol our borders, work with law enforcement agencies to eradicate pimps, prostitution, and drugs. Shut down filmmakers involved with and who encourage women to partake in hardcore films for money.

It is a sin and has been on the books for over two-thousand years. Soldiers are flexible and can be trained to assist in combating lawlessness. All you need is for the President to give the order. This camming business is not freedom of expression. Nor can you morally define it as an art form. However, we can, and will call it for what it is. That my blessed are what the Bible warns as immoral abomination, leaving a stench in the nostrils of our Lord. The longer this sore persists, and is ignored, the closer we are to the wrath of God poured out on the masses. Sometimes I wonder whether Congress hears any of the words spoken in prayer by the Chaplin at the start of each session. "Now, who amongst us doesn't get it?"

In future chapter's, we will gather in the harvest of live webcamming further. For there remains much to be said about webcamming to allow this information to be blown away by the winds of time. Now, it is incumbent for the author to open up the gates of swindling for the reader, so they can have an inside vista into internet "scams," (swindle…fraud) conducted by scrupulous, heartless and evil operators.

These scavengers will employ any and all deceptive, underhanded, and ingenious ways to deceive or cheat innocent victims out of their income or material possessions. Again, this is not a revelation you cannot identify with, other than its personal intrusion into a victim's privacy. I'm quite sure the majority of the population has heard about or been affected by scam artist operating around the globe before this writing.

Time to move onto chapter eight where we begin to get a foretaste of pure evil.

Chapter 8

Innocence Interrupted

Knit man to self, taking away a load of iniquities,
for absent goodness all sorrows he bears.
Discover victory in life, who finds sacred rest? Take
heed your natural state, despite man's snare.
Avoid darkness breathe in light, lest you drown thyself
in the filth. Vanities honor even this hour.
The man owns his deceit, lofty tongues blister bitter
sorrows, and it worships much-wanted power.
Jim Jacobs

When attending Technical College in 1987 for Accounting, we were required to take a couple semesters of computer technology. Back then, we used floppy disks as the learning tool for the fundamentals in computer technology. I thought it was a big deal then. However, the advancement of the computer technology age made knowledge of computer software appear as if I had studied something out of the "stone age." Now, Cams, Scams, and College youth behaving badly became a topic of interest on the internet when I was victimized by a criminal scam organization.

Not only was I finding myself dealing with a bunch of renegade swindlers. But for me to have even the slimmest chance of catching these misguided soul's, I would need to have remedial training in the use and application of computer technology. Most would come from on-the-job training; trial and error.

Even when I found myself in the middle of this firestorm of contentious seductions of internet predators, I had to step back and take a deep breath. After all, I considered myself computer illiterate. I had just begun the process of learning how to use windows seven programs on the computer. Although finding myself in the unenviable position of victim in this growing industry, this duped individual was determined to do an immediate three-hundred-sixty-degree turn and inhale as much knowledge as time would lend itself to sparring with these adversarial criminals.

Suggesting that I was marked by powerful simplicity relating to the wares of computer technology would be an accurate assessment. The industry of computer technology flourished and the advancement of technology made computers more computer friendly, more powerful, smaller, lighter, and cheaper. With the continued improvement in microcomputer chips, consumption and demand grew remarkably. Their ability to amass volumes of information and process more data on the hard drives was significantly improved.

Adding to this mix, it reigned in more computer programmers, designers, and engineers who by their very nature and talents created more applications to incorporate into this hardware while designing devices that were more compact. An explosion in computer technology had begun. As I started to take notice, the younger generation forged ahead with a purpose and a sense of urgency, learning with rapid intoxicating fervor. They adapted quickly to this new phenomenon. It so made an impression on me, reinforcing a determination to learn and quell the feelings of inferiority and inadequacy towards this younger generation.

Before elaborating further on this pilgrimage long traveled, there is an overwhelming sense to make a statement, if only in defense of my character against cynical folks who are in opposition, when fellowship and the word are in consortium with the Lord. The Lords word in Mathew, Chapter 6: 1-4. "Beware of practicing your righteousness before other people to be seen by them, for you will have no reward from your Father, who is in Heaven. Therefore, when giving to the poor sound no trumpet before you, as the hypocrites do in the synagogues and in the streets, that others may praise them. Truly, I say to you, they have received their reward. Furthermore, when you give to the needy, do not let your left hand know what your right hand is doing so that your giving may be in secret. And your Father who sees in secret will reward you."

The problem I have you see; is that my heart has the propensity to surrender to compassions calling where empathy responds to the hearts bidding, and I become vulnerable often without apparent provocation to humankind facing hardships. Before I am able to realize that I have been blind-sided, I enter into the inner sanctuary of reaching out, only to face the entrails of injury and hurt. Manifestations have pierced this heart and soul, draining any minute trust that may have begun to solidify. I share this flaw with you because I cannot detach myself from this heart in this my only life. Love's evasiveness I have known well. Neither can I reciprocate same admirations. What is perceived as love and spoken about in Scripture, I conceded that as, "common is the opposite of uncommon, then evil is the opposite of good. How then, does one define love if hate is its rival? To what end do the master manipulators of the world deny themselves from hate and begin the love process?"

On a rare day when I was free from guilt, unacquainted with the evils of the internet, liberated from guile or cunning deceit, I powered on the computer and downloaded an application called Skype used as a social media to communicate amongst other Skype users. A medium for exchanging dialogue and information with family, friends, and acquaintance's.

If you recall, computer illiteracy was a weakness compared to my younger counterparts, so I was struggling to navigate and familiarize myself with the functions of Skype. It was purely by chance while browsing this new application, when out of the twilight zone appeared someone, somewhere, attempting to get my attention. Baffled at first, yet amused at the prospect that there was a mystery person on the other end willing to talk in real time drew my curiosity. I was euphoric but guarded.

The person on Skype introduced herself as Henan Asante. According to Henan, she was a Swedish National enrolled in a Nursing College in Ghana. "Hum! This was different; a woman visitor from Ghana?" After collecting my thoughts over the initial shock, the first question I posed to Henan was in the format of an inquiry.

"How did you locate me?" I asked. "Why and how did you happen to discover me?"

She was silent, saying absolutely nothing for about three minutes. This gave pause to wonder why it should take three minutes to answer a simple question. She never did tell me, not yet anyway. During our initial contact, everything was subtle and innocent. Perhaps this was just a chance encounter that will eventually see its days cut short. After all, she was in Ghana. What harm could possibly come from this. However, as time would lend itself through the footsteps of deceit, lies, fraud, and a world draped in pornography, the turnstiles would prove challenging to penetrate, as time drew me into a web of another world.

I wasn't quite prepared to deal with this on an immoral level. This took on a ripple effect, subjecting the author ever closer to disappointment, and in some circle's outrage. After a while, my mind could not phantom and process what I was witnessing. Henan would prove most challenging. An undertaking never fully realized in this my own charge and commitment. I needed something to occupy my time. However, this, this was an obscure melodrama dished up on a platter for the recipient to consume until the bottom of the entrée was finished.

When purchasing a laptop computer for the first time, it was with the intent of writing letters and keeping in touch with family members and friends using the e-mail application. Microsoft installed its own software and applications to operate windows seven. The e-mail began its rise in popularity in 1979 when a server called CompuServe launched an electronic mail service. At the time, it was the most efficient means in which to nurture relationships and keep in touch with family and acquaintances.

E-mail is an appropriate application that allows the user to share private notes, letters, or for businesses' use. However, it can have daunting implications as we gravitate further and deeper into the manuscript. While attempting to become familiar with the computer and windows seven programming concepts I learned everything was programed onto the hard drive. On the hard disk are programmed tiles or applications that are only visible after you turn on the power. To open and use one of the program applications you use a cursor. Your mouse controls the cursor by guiding it to the tiles on the computer screen. When you left-click your mouse, it will open the application you have chosen.

By now, anyone who is anybody living in a home that owns a TV, radio, or cell phone have heard through the medium of communication, or perhaps by word of mouth how vulnerable computers are to falling prey to hackers. The sophisticated computer tech-nerd is well informed and experienced. Some can and do take the road less traveled and make a choice to become malicious hackers or scammers. They have the expertise to gain access to almost any computer despite all the antivirus safety measures taken to secure the computer. They are able do it at will, it's their religion. They ply their trade as if it were a business.

This group will go to any lengths to steal personal information, identity, or relieve you of your possessions. Opening an email from a person, you don't know is the path of least resistance for hackers, spammers, people who phish, and scammers. If they want to gain access to your computer files with harmful intent, they will find a way. These folks are aggressive and persistent malicious pursuers of your possessions.

It would be irresponsible of me if I did not break down some of the computer language and typical applications. As stated earlier, window's has most applications already programmed onto the hard drive of the computer. If an application is not on the hard drive, then most applications can be downloaded free from the store which is included on the computer's hard drive. What this means is selecting applications that you can "add-on" to existing applications on your desktop screen compatible with your operating system. Some programming software you may want to use has a monthly service charge. Additional software is available at most retail stores.

Once Skype is downloaded onto the computer's hard drive as a file, it remains there until you decide to uninstall it. Now that it is downloaded, all you need to do is use the mouse and guide the cursor over the tile or icon, and left click the mouse icon. An icon is no more than a pictogram shown on the computer screen to aid in opening other applications so you can use them. With Skype, you can make video and audio calls, exchange chat messages and more. It is also available for use on most cell phones, I-Pad's, and smartphones. Texting is free. Now they have voice and video on mobile phones making it convenient to share whatever you want with family and friends. They can also be used as a business tool. Although Skype is one of these applications where the user pays for airtime, I eventually concluded it really wasn't practical for my use.

While Darlene and I were in Florida, Skype was downloaded as a source of communicating with family and friends using the voice and video chat features. I thought using Skype was the best choice, as it allowed a person to view the other party in real time in their natural setting. It was an application available to users of computers that might not otherwise be available for contacting family members and friends. However, having the application and using it correctly posed enormous problems. I wanted to give Skype my level best. Eventual my lack of understanding to navigate within the perimeters of this system proved futile at best. Therefore, what is a man to do when he is flustered? Stop using this application for a time, times, time, and a half?

Skype had become a mindset of contention after a while, as I faced one struggle after another. It was literally giving me fits as I laboriously tried to figure out how this Rubik's Cube of an application fused together. Question remained. How to do what, and when to do it?" The application tried to guide me through each step of the process but to no avail. I told you I was computer illiterate! Each trial run showed I was losing ground and losing fast. One-step forward, two-steps back. Setbacks were becoming the signature of failure. Patience was not always a virtue of mine.

Frustrated and irritated were my constant companions for a while. There were times everything was going rather well, or so I thought when something else would unravel on the screen, instructing me of this, that, or the other. I would get so frustrated, I would begin talking and shouting aloud at the computer (Like yeah computer, you can actually hear and understand). Still Other times I had reached the boiling point and projectiles would be flung here, there, and everywhere out of frustration. I cursed it, nursed it, and conversed with it. However, all was vain and I ended up putting the application to bed.

When Henan, through Skype, initiated contact with me, it still wasn't working well. Henan mentioned Yahoo Messenger, another application I wasn't familiar with. However, Henan would talk me through setting up the application. She said it was easier to use and we would not have any problems getting it up and running. Henan said we would have unlimited chat sessions and could video chat as well. After a couple glitches, I was able to get it up and running. However, contact with Henan did not rear its ugly head until we moved back to Trenton permanently.

There is another application called Facebook. Facebook is perhaps the most popular social networking website on the internet. It allows registered users to create profiles of themselves, upload photos, videos, send messages, and keep in touch with friends, family, and acquaintances. It also gives you the option to communicate with just about anyone anywhere throughout the world, provided the person on the other end of the internet accepts your friend request to follow their page.

Most everyone should be familiar with the original founder of Facebook, Mark Zuckerberg, and his partners. However, Mark is Facebook's Chief Executive Officer, headquartered in Menlo Park, California. The decision to include your profile in a network means that anyone on the network can view your profile. Completing a profile of yourself may make you susceptible to vulnerabilities because you can surrender too much personal information about yourself. This hinges on privacy issue concerns. Keep your profile information sparse.

Facebook is worthy of mention because it will re-surface in future chapters in the manuscript along with Skype. Since Facebook was gaining in popularity, it pin-pricked my curiosity. I wanted to see what the big fuss was all about as a means of social networking. I was not trying to be a busybody. It was something new, another application to stretch my brain. Once all the kinks were fine-tuned, my initial impression was that this seemed to be user-friendly.

I downloaded the application and painstakingly went through the process of registering a username, email address, and password that would allow me to sign-in to use its features. Once registered, you can then begin the laborious task of adding friends you may already know. The next step is a judgment decision only the user can make when choosing to follow someone on Facebook. It could be a radio commentator, lawyer, national newspaper, or a random person. You will never know when there might be something you have in common with other Facebook users. More often than not, social network users on Facebook will allow you to follow them, even if it is only to show other Facebook users how popular they are on the web site.

If you randomly choose to follow other users on Facebook, who you may not know personally and add them to your list of Facebook friends, you might be setting yourself up for a potential scam. One way for uninvited strangers to get onto your Facebook page is through popups or advertisements. Popup blocker needs activation on your browser to keep unwanted solicitations to a minimum. However, selecting "follow" to an unfamiliar user is threading the needle unless you have researched their profile and history on the Facebook page and other related searches.

Popup blocker is located in the upper right-hand corner. It looks like a gear. Left click and you see the internet options under privacy settings. If a user declines to use the popup blocker, they become vulnerable to advertisements, and if someone decides to push the envelope, they may begin to receive solicitations directing them to pornography, dating and romance sites, or other unwanted websites.

Phishing is another method scammer's use for their personal gain. The user receives an email from Facebook, or other applications promoting offers that are too good to be true. We do not want to welcome hackers, but they are always in the background lurking to create mischief and infect your computer with viruses,' or worse, steal your information. On your hard drive are some browsers. Browsers are nothing more than search engines such as Google, Google Chrome, Mozilla Firefox, Yahoo, Internet Explorer, etc. It is up to the user which search engine is the most unique for their start page.

I thought it would be a good idea to breathe life back into Skype again. Let it be known that it required time and patience (patient used loosely) to become marginally proficient in the basics of how this application functioned. As with the biblical patriarch Job who experiences a strong taste of adversity, who is written about in the book of the Old Testament. It chronicle's Jobs exploits while going through trials and hardships, but on a much larger scale than I could ever endure. Eventually, God restored Job to his former status, inheriting more than he lost from the Lord.

Job had lost his entire family, wealth, and status. The man Job, was afflicted with sores, boils, and lost many friends during his afflictions. Yet, Job endured his sufferings without ever cursing God. Therefore, Job was declared righteous in the sight of God. Job deserved an honorable mention because of his deep seeded faith in God despite experiencing adversity. Although trials and hardships befell me, I did not handle it as well as Job. Instead, I chose to wear a millstone around my neck. All it did was weigh me down by creating, even more, problems. I have not mastered patience yet, but the old rugged cross remains at work in my life. Working overtime if you please.

Facebook can be a pleasant experience exchanging ideas, points of view, and chatting with friends on the internet. Bonding, sharing, and trusting relationships were my reward. However, user beware. Like Skype, it can become a landmine-laden with swindlers and other evil criminals.

The most impressionable experience that left a lasting imprint in my life involved a single mother raising two boys. The youngest son, Noah, was born physically challenged. Noah diagnosed with a rare form of schizencephalic. (It is derived from the Greek Word Schizoid, meaning to split, and Enkephalins, having to do with disease of the brain.) It is a rare birth defect characterized by abnormal continuity of gray matter extending from the ependymal of the cerebral ventricles to the par matter. Schizencephaly patients may have an abnormally small head, mental retardation, partial or complete paralysis, and poor muscle tone.

Noah had no father. Apparently, the father took flight when it was determined Noah was diagnosed with severe disabilities requiring around-the-clock care for life. This is A-typical of some men when commitment and responsibility interfere with their lifestyle. Flight appears more desirable than a long standing commitment to patient care. Tommy, Noah's older sibling, showered his younger brother with unbridled love and devotion. In addition to sacrificing his own childhood for the welfare and care of his younger brother, he was always seen as a hands-on caregiver.

I esteemed Tommy for his courage, and unselfish sacrifice. Ashley, their mother, doted over Noah and Tommy as if she were a black bear in the wild protecting her young cubs from outside predators. I was afforded the privilege of meeting this family when Ashley accepted my request to follow her on Facebook. I had read beforehand on Facebook regarding the plight of this family. We developed a bond that remained intact even as Darlene and I continued to travel between seasons (snowbirds) from Minnesota and Florida.

These were very unique people with courage and steadfast resolve. Ashley had a passion and an insurmountable reserve of energy as she spent hours educating the public about this rare disease. She became actively involved in coordinating fund raising events within the community to bring attention to this debilitating birth defect. Sometimes it was tough for Ashley to get state or local assistance for transportation needs. How this is able to happen is beyond my understanding. Ashley had an older model vehicle that was unreliable. Noah's disease was becoming more debilitating through the passage of time. Noah needed a custom-made wheelchair and Ashley had a wish list for this lift van. Additionally, an accessible ramp was needed to get Noah in and out of the house, so it was put on the urgently needed list.

"So you think you have a terrible life do you?" Young women like Jan would rather present herself on the auction block, rather than endure struggles for a short time. The mentality of many people in the last few decades is, "I want it, and I want it now. They do not wish to earn it. They feel it is an entitlement and want it given to them." Perhaps it would be useful if we brought back the draft. Like Israel, every young man and woman must serve two-years. Liberty comes at a price.

Salted and seasoned on this platter of uncertainties are written timeless memories to digest. Within perimeters and boundaries, determined am I to put history to rest during this, love's aspirations. There became a dimension of struggle and anxiety obtaining state funding for special needs children like Noah. Because of this, Ashley had few options other than to organize her own fundraising events in hopes of collecting enough money to procure the basics to make life a little more comfortable for Noah.

Ashley was promoting another fundraising event and asked if I would be willing to participate in their crusade near one of Orlando's parks to generate pledges for Noah's much-needed ramp. "Why not?" I asked myself privately. "How could I decline the offer?" Besides, it would allow me the opportunity to meet Noah and his family for the first time.

Before the event, I only saw pictures of Noah that Ashley sent over the internet. We chatted but did not use the video chat on Facebook. A kinship developed with Noah and Ashley immediately. So when Ashley mentioned the fundraising event I was determined to do something special for Noah besides pledging money for his needs. It took nearly a week to think of an appropriate gift that would have lasting value, yet it had to be creative; thoughtful. Then I had an epiphany. I associated Noah's name with the biblical patriarch Noah. Noah's Ark had its place in antiquity with the great flood.

"Perfect, this is doable," I thought. Wasting no time, I searched the internet for anyone who specialized in artisan work. Through yet another blessing, I located a man who had an inventory of carved figurines, and samples of his work advertised on the internet web page. I was ecstatic. What I was searching for he had on display to sell. The artisanship looked flawless, and the price seemed reasonable. If Noah was going to receive a gift, the price wasn't going to be an issue. Purchasing the Ark and figurines that came with it for Noah had now become my personal project.

The Ark; handcrafted as close to the likeness of Noah's Ark as man's eyes' can picture what Noah's Ark may have looked like, complete with animal statuettes was bringing the idea to reality. Ashley had her close friend Mike print hundreds of T-shirts with "Schizencephaly Awareness" embossed on them along with an image of an Angel with a halo, and one broken wing with hands clasped together. It symbolized an Angel praying over one of the Lord's broken creation. The T-shirt's were given to each person who volunteered their time and pledges for the event. When first informed about the angel with the broken wing, it moved me into action. Getting in contact with the artisan again, I asked the artisan if he would have time to carve an angel with a broken wing.

"Could this be done in time before the walk," I asked. "He could do it," He said.

To keep the donor anonymous, I had the completed Ark and its pieces sent to Mike's residence with instruction's that he tell Ashley the Ark was given by an anonymous donor. I contacted Mike by phone and told him to put the Angel on the bow of the Ark where it would symbolize overseer of the Arks voyage during turbulent times. Furthermore, if I didn't acknowledge Ashley for her unselfish dedication to her children, the project would seem incomplete. Words of praise, courage, patience, love, and sacrifice for her unconditional commitment and loyalty would articulate the message that she was not alone during times of struggle as a single parent.

Mike gave me a list of all participants who pledged their support in the fundraiser. In turn, all their names were included in the recognition letter highlighting Ashley's unselfish commitment to her children. Framed; it was sent to Mike, who in turn presented the letter to Ashley after I left the event. Anonymity was crucial in keeping the donor anonymous. I did not want my name attached to anything I contributed, lest I become boastful and proud.

Ashley would later confide to Mike that the gestures of kindness she received that day made her weep for days. She became relentless in her quest to identify the donor. As we continued our chats on Facebook after the event, Ashley would drop subtle hints. She felt the donations came from me. However, I would deny, deny, deny!

"Now why do you suppose I went to great lengths in sharing this sentimental journey of my life with you? Is it boastfulness, arrogance, pompous bragging rights? May it never be!" When speaking of rewards Jesus said in Matthew Chapter 10: 42. "And whoever gives one of these little ones even a cup of cold water in the name of a disciple, assuredly, I say to you, he will by no means lose his reward." The focus is not the reward you receive for good works, as some may define Jesus teaching in verse 42. No, no, beloved. Jesus' remark underscores the importance of accepting and assisting believers and non-believers alike who may require compassion in times of hardship.

The thrust of describing the above experience is twofold. First, I discovered that the computer and most of its applications is an excellent tool for research and developing friendships and keeping in touch with family and acquaintances. Had I not used Facebook for its social mingling; using it to keep informed of newsworthy events in the community, I would not have learned about Noah and a single parent's daily struggles as a caregiver and parent to a physically challenged child.

Noah had numerous seizures. Sometimes they would become so severe it required hospitalization. This opened my eyes' to the needs of so many faceless children and adults like Noah. They desperately need, yet often do not receive the intervention, support, and assistance from the community, state and federal agencies. There is no way of knowing Noah's status since we left Florida. Ashley's username was lost, so I am unable to communicate with them on Facebook.

Noah never frowned; sulked, displayed anger, or showed hostility. What he did have was a never-ending smile. "Priceless!" I love this little man named Noah. I want you to love him too. "Am I my brother's keeper?"

There is a restless spirit within this soul, overwhelmed in deep sorrows. Heavy laden with tears is this broken man and wounded heart. Life past and present are footsteps of carnage. Man becomes a master of his own bondage. Eyes' of thunder duly embrace each truth during uncertain trials, in this my suffering hour. Humanity bound by deceit, it curries favor with hardened heart's while bitterness contends with ever increasing abuse. Entrusted child coveting too much sadness and despair. Withdrawn from society; beguiled in the midst of an impending storm. Wretchedly sanctioned by the perversion of man.

I now surrender all manner of decency, as I ease you into another dimension. There, encamped immeasurably deep we descend into the depths of the abyss where neither light nor goodness resides; only darkness, for evil's eternal soul.

Still, one such as I must clarify, that for me to feed you with the evil intent of man's heart; with what assurance would you be able to grasp this reprehensible conduct unless you received into communion the realization that I ventured into the abyss. That I must reveal sinful man operating with impunity under the cover of darkness. A contrast can be made using Noah as an example which represents goodness and innocence versus evil; wickedness and deceit written with open candor in this manuscript. There can never be enough discussion about assisting the physically and mentally challenged of this world. We should all take a deep breath and learn from their serene environment.

As indicated previously, I am not seeking absolution or forgiveness from man. That comes from God alone, my Lord and Savior, in whom I trust completely. Only God knows this heart, not man. Man is forever judgmental and spiteful. To get an idea on how the military functions as one, you join the military. If you want to experience combat, you deploy to a combat zone. Conversely, to observe how prostitutes and swindlers operate you must take on the persona non grata of the offender. There is no honor given in this research of debauchery.

Moreover, surrendering to decency by wallowing in the muck and mire of a criminal environment left me with few options. When innocent people become victims of this group of wayward, misguided class of evildoers, I became just another statistic, a victim of fraud. I could have viewed it as another hard lesson learned. However, my conscience bearing witness, I could not allow this story to simply be an event, hidden underneath brush in some jungle and hope it would go away. The American public deserves to know the truth about every word printed in this manuscript, including web-camming and misbehavior. This merits government intervention and the voices of our citizens. This is my calling and I challenge the government to lead us through the storm of the night and into the light.

Once a decision was made to write about immoral behavior, the more convinced I became that the Lord's Devine intervention was involved in directing my path. This then is my lot in life, and if it means criticism and condemnation from friends, family, or the ungodly in the pornography industry, then bring your condemnation to the forefront. I am more fearful of God than I am of man. I choose to stand firm in the Lord's favor as my anchor. Placing my faith and trust in Him to see me through this quagmire of sin and shame. I am quite adept at being chastised. Paths towards the light became dim and exceedingly void. I encountered less than outstanding support from various law enforcement agencies as I sought their assistance and intervention in unmasking these malcontents. But it wasn't to be.

The Braxton police department thought I was viewing this odyssey by creating an overzealous fantasy world of my own choosing. "No manpower resources they would tell me." This callous posturing was not a shining seal of approval and I said as much. We definitely have some priority issues. As a result, we have become by-products of chaos and immorality. "If trust is to become binding, is it not fair to argue it has to have irrevocable trust across the board." If not, you become a bondservant to mistrust. Sitting in a position of neutrality, I see nothing but utter ignorance from our three branches of government.

After Darlene and I had arrived in Trenton, it took several moves from one apartment to another until we settled on a place that accommodated our needs. Between moves, I continued experimenting on the computer, browsing websites and trying to acclimate myself to the myriad of applications and programs available on windows seven. Occasionally, a popup would surface on the screen that enticed me to left click my mouse and directed to its website. With pop-up blocker turned on, I never could understand how these annoying advertising ads were appearing on the screen. Some pop-ups wanted me to visit their dating site. Other ads wanted me to migrate to their single's site. While even others, employed subtle means by encouraging me to gravitate into the forbidden zone of immorality.

Eventually, after learning what pop-ups were, there was an immediate delete. I didn't know how to correct this phenomenon looking me in the face. No one can say Jim Jacobs is not persistent, assertive, and a bit stubborn, with a twist of aggressive mystical tendencies. I detest failing. It incapacitates me to the point where I feel dysfunctional. Jim has a type-A personality you see! (It is defined as impatient, aggressive, and competitive.) There is this compulsion to see a problem through until the source is clarified, understood, and resolved. Then and only then, do I feel whole and complete again. I am way, way, too hard on myself. I have known this for decades, but I cannot shake this irritating menace from my personality.

Obviously, for the novice user of the computer with its numerous choices of applications available for use on the internet, it can have a tendency to overwhelm a journeymen user. It was obvious that Skype was intimidating and frustrating for me. Here is one user who can relate to the irritation awaiting a consumer who gives his level best to navigate through an application in pursuit of excellence, but soon gathers a cloudless song of sorrows.

For this platform, I am pulling up my "man pants" and, like a seasoned warrior, preparing myself to meet the enemy… Skype, I'm prepared to engage. With all the dangerous potholes associated with this application, at least in my judgment, I am either this, that or the other. You knew my first attempt at downloading Skype while living in Florida failed miserably. So let the man pants droop, and we will give this nasty little bug-a-boo another try and see what comes of this contentious monster. Somehow, I have to calm these winds of doubt and proceed full throttle.

Therefore, the process of downloading the application begins, and once again, I am met with resistance. More than likely, I continue to miss a step somewhere in the download and install process. Try, try, and try again! This would become the battle cry until I succeeded in getting it right, even if it meant burning the midnight oil. Seemed as though I was burning the midnight oil without remedy. Downloading and installing the application wasn't the problem. It was registering and set-up that was the source of grief.

Success had finally adorned the footsteps of a sweet triumphal fellowship with Skype. After savoring conquest into green pastures of water's cool flow, I was refreshed. "How stupid is a man, that he can be such a spud?" Given step by step instructions, I wondered how anyone could be so impaled to the point they burden themselves downloading one application that proved an orchestrated embarrassment. Regardless, these feet seem firmly established now, and it is time to experiment.

Using confidence to my advantage, I felt comfortable enough to crank up Skype and give it its maiden voyage. I immediately coordinated arrangements with my sister and one of Darlene's daughters. First we had to get their phone numbers (a requirement for live video feeds), and their username. Along with live video feed came audio, a welcomed addition. However, this first run had some rough edges, as I clicked the mouse indiscriminately, using icons on the screen to fine tune contrast in hopes of getting a clearer image. Frustrated is an understatement. It was not going according to the winds experienced in a mighty storm.

Talking aloud, I said, "here today, gone tomorrow!" If I synchronized audio and video, would this solve the problem? Nope! After several failed attempts and getting nowhere, I surrendered to the song of defeat. I had emotions of elation and disappointment within a span of ten minutes, "Poof!" When I finally achieved a successful installation; whose name do you think appeared? None other than Henan Asante.

"Hello," she said. Then she paused briefly and then continued. "Am I talking with; ah, am I talking with you Jim, Jim Jacobs?"

"Yes you are. I see this is Henan I'm chatting with; right?" Adding. "How have you been and what have you been doing?"

Henan replies. "I am still busy with school and such," she concluded.

"I'm not very good at using this application," I explained. "I'm still in the learning stages so I have to try and refine my skills," I said with embarrassment.

"That is ok, we can chat," Henan replied. "We don't have to use the video chat feature. It isn't a problem for me," Henan answered candidly.

"Henan," I began. "I don't know you very well, not even sure if we should be chatting. I need to know a lot about someone before I carrying on a conversation." Hinting to Henan this might not be such a good idea. "I need your age, identity, what folks do for a living. I do not need to be talking to underage teenagers," I informed Henan, adding. "I am not on Skype looking for a platonic tryst with anyone, so if you are here for that, forget it, I am a happily married man."

"Ok, good, I am just looking for a friend so when I have free time, I can chat with someone. I do not have many friends in Ghana," Henan told me.

"That may be Henan," I responded. "However, I will say it again, I do not know your age or what your agenda is by contacting me. I am going strictly on what you are telling me, and at this point, it is not much."

"Well," Henan said. "I am thirty-one-years-old. I graduate from nursing school November 2013. I have been in Ghana for three years. I'm almost finished with school and I am eager to leave this country. It has not been easy living here with so many different people and languages," Henan concluded.

"I am old enough to be your father Henan. In fact, I am twice your age. Why would you want to hang around with someone old enough to be your father?"

There were a few seconds of silence then Henan responded. "Aha, that is not a problem for me. I am okay with this age thing if it doesn't bother you. I just want a friend."

"That would be about it Henan," then added. "What did you do for friends these past three years while you were in Ghana? Who did you have for friends then Henan?" It had taken a while before Henan responded.

"Most students are female and live here in Ghana. You know they are mostly black people. Only a couple different males attend this school, and they don't speak English well. I do not have much in common with hardly any student's; except maybe a couple of the girl's here, that's it," Henan stated.

"I see. That doesn't seem normal to me. Looks like slim pick-ins when you choose a country like Ghana for an education and for developing friendships. I guess that makes you a minority. What made you decide on Ghana anyway? Are you from Ghana?" Asking out of curiosity.

"Yes, very few people here I can find a close relationship and where we have things in common. That is why I am trying to find good people who I can talk with on the internet," Henan remarked.

"Do you live in a dorm, on campus, off campus?"

"No, I live in an apartment in Santasi, Kumasi."

"Henan, aren't you afraid of living by yourself, especially at night?" Inquiring minds wanted to know.

"No!" She replied. "They have the best security where I live, I made sure before I chose to live here."

"What nationality are your parents?" I asked Henan.

"My father, who passed away was from Ghana, and my mother is from Sweden."

"How then, did you receive the name Henan Asante?" I inquired.

Henan responded saying. "My mother and father lived here for a while, so when I was born, they decided to give me the name of Ghana people. It's kinda crazy … Huh!"

I wondered why her mother wasn't residing with her. It didn't seem natural for Henan to be attending a school on another continent without someone in the family living with them; especially in a country like Ghana.

"So where is your mother now?" I inquired.

"She lives in Sweden."

"Why not attend a nursing school in Sweden then? I think you would want to be with classmates who are the same nationality as yourself and who can speak your language and participate in the customs of your country," I declared.

Henan explained it from her perspective. "Ghana has great nursing schools here. They are the best in the world if you are studying to become a licensed nurse," Henan said. "I will not have to take any examination's, no matter where I decide to practice medicine." She bolding stated, then continued. "You ask an awful lot of questions," Henan finally chimed in unexpectedly. "Nobody has ever asked me so many questions as you have on Skype," said Henan.

Getting Henan's attention, I said. "Remember, you were the one who contacted me, I didn't contact you." Adding. "I need to know as much about you as I can. I need to make sure you are who you claim to be Henan."

Henan in a defensive posture stated. "I am Henan that is who I am, don't worry Jim!"

"The only way I will have any peace is if I see you on video so I know I am not talking to an underage girl," I informed Henan.

"Okay," she replied. "Next time we are online, I will show you proof if that is what you want," she added.

"Yes, that would make me feel much more comfortable Henan."

"Where do you live in the States?" Henan asked.

"I live in Minnesota," I informed her.

"Oh, I see!" Then Henan continued. "Do you know there is a time zone difference of six hours? You are aware of this aren't you Jim?" Then she went on to say. "It is getting pretty late here, and I really hate leaving. However, I still have studies to do before tomorrow and will have to get up early for school. I will keep in touch, though. I will surf the internet sometimes and see if you are logged in anywhere so we can talk again, Ok?"

"Sure Henan, that would be okay as long as we know the ground rules," I said.

"Alright then, we will chat some more another time. It was nice talking to you Jim. Goodbye," Henan concluded.

"Goodbye Henan," I replied.

As quickly as Henan appeared, she disappeared from the radar ... Poof! That was eerie; giving it a passing thought afterward. Never encountered anything close to this before, giving pause to reflect on this surprised meeting from a Swedish girl attending some nursing school in Africa. I felt exposed. I could not place a face to the invisible person chatting on the other end of the screen. At least with Facebook, I could compare a photo image with the individuals profile picture even though it was not sure proof. But at least, if they were local, it was easier to verify they were legitimate.

However, without meaning to be labeled an ogre, this appeared awkward and in some respects indifferent because no other foreigner had ever contacted me before Henan. Foreigners were seldom if ever on Facebook, Yahoo, or Google, that I knew. Now every ethnicity in the world is on here. At least, I could check to determine if the college was accredited using Google search. Then I could check out to see if Santasi in Kumasi was a residential living community. This would lend some credibility to Henan's authenticity.

Now I am faced with a dilemma of sorts. Do you tell Darlene about this chance meeting or do you wait and see if she contacts you again? After struggling and meditating on it, I made a decision, right or wrong to pull back on the reigns and see where this is headed. I believed it was just an accidental fluke, and I would not hear from her again. Why must I worry Darlene over a chance encounter that may amount to nothing? Every heart vibrates according to its deeds so I trust myself to a simple purpose. For it seems the rule of wisdom. I shall walk softly and with caution. If there is another chance encounter, I will deal with it then.

However, I did not foresee this happening anytime soon… if at all. For one thing, I seldom used Skype because I was still having issues with video chat. Secondly, I wasn't on the computer every day. Darlene and I were always busy doing something together. If Henan did get in touch with me through Skype, it would be by trial and error.

"There is a time for everything and everything in its time." Patience coupled with virtue! "Oh, you can believe me!" This has been a challenging apprenticeship this word, patience. Eventually, as I probed and prodded this woman for information, it started turning into a crusade of Good versus Evil. I was taken out of the light in short order and led into the depths of darkness. "From Light into the Abyss!" took on a destiny and character of its own. A personal reconnaissance mission to seek and find the unscrupulous secret world of swindlers would begin.

It would be the tortoise versus the hare in-step to see who could outwit and outmaneuver their opponent. Humpty Dumpty took many a fall as the hunted; before Jim Jacobs became the hunter. This would prove to be the greatest challenge of a lifetime, making previous exploits appear as child's play. This research resulted in volumes of binders filled with information that took over a year to accumulate. Some research proved very useful while still others only served to lead me astray and off the beaten path. This was the prima facie of peaks and valleys.

At first, I was not spending excessive amounts of time on the computer. However, when time allowed, I would power on the computer and begin the tedious task of learning about the inner workings of computer software and how it ties into the internet. Moreover, there were unlimited choices of applications and programs available for add-ons or extensions that were available to download and install on the hard drive. I was in a race to bring myself into alignment with the younger computer savvy generation. They were my yardstick to stretch my brain. After all, knowledge and hands-on experience dominate success or failure in a world that is obsessed and driven by information technology.

The man has this inherent propensity to mold and shape kindred after the likeness of themselves. You must attain a predetermined social status. Act a certain way. Be a conformist, subservient, agreeable, amenable and so forth. If you are indifferent ideologically with the establishment, you find yourself on the outside looking in. You are treated as an inferior creation taking up space…Their space.

So what are you telling us, Jim? This self-importance, over bloated, overstated, exaggerated establishment. Too many overpaid self-proclaimed desk jockey supervisors lording it over average America. We have become a nation of the wealthy pitted against the low-income wage earner. The middle class has left the building. You have college educated cost accountants swarming into business's and manufacturing industries looking in every nook and cranny, fine-tuning ridiculous ways to save the company money to enrich the pockets of the bean counters and stockholders while the employee's income stagnates.

Dare we witness the sinful side life has to offer you in your comfortable surroundings. Get outside the four walls of the church, mega churches, and cathedrals. For evil; the battle lurks outside the walls of the church. You profess to love God's creation, desiring that not one soul be lost, but that all should come to the saving knowledge and grace of our Lord and Savior Jesus Christ. Look around you, they live amongst us, you read about them, you hear of their wicked ways on the news. "Who have you mentored? Who has begun good works as a discipline for God's kingdom?"

Chapter 9

Henan Asante Unveiled

While man lies sleeping in peaceful serenity, body
weary; craving much needful rest this night.
Surrender I, to appraise time and space; must soul
sojourn sorrowful lamentations of this plight.
As with humanity's journey; each stride was taken ... do
not his footsteps undoubtedly part invisible air?
While just as quickly the air returns to where his bodies been for lack of care.
Jim Jacobs

In the weaver's skillful hand there is a new day, new ways, new adventures that are unforeseen and may reveal peace or chaos. I had not talked to Henan for quite some time but then again I hadn't been on Skype for weeks either. I was waffling whether this was the morally acceptable thing to do since I was married. Here I was talking to someone I had encountered quite by accident while familiarizing myself with Skype which continued to be a source of contention. Darlene knew I frequently chatted with folks on Facebook with strangers.

She had never objected then. Apparently, Darlene trusted me to that end completely. She also knew I was faithful to her. Joined at the hip. Soul mates. I'm sure you have heard that it has been said. "All married couples have spats, disagreements arise. We were no different. Compromise, give and take, this was usually the path of least resistance. Therefore, I felt justified as long as I remained neutral and approached Henan as a lonely soul looking for someone to have an occasional chit-chat. Nothing more I reasoned. No harm as long as I, in my forbearance clutch onto my moral compass.

There was no guarantee Henan would be on Skype even if I did log onto the site. It would be one of those hit or miss proposition. It was not a defining moment in life even if she never contacted me again. She did not ask for any money during our initial contact so that was encouraging.

It was a slow day. Nothing demanded my immediate attention. Darlene didn't have anything for me, no chores, errands, or plans, so I went to the laptop and powered on the computer and logged onto Skype. I wasn't on Skype more than five-minutes when wonder of wonders, there was Henan again. The icon was lit bright green to show she was online.

"Hello," She said. "And how have you been?"

"I am doing just fine," I replied. "It is 3:00 P.M. here so it must be about 9:00 P.M. in Ghana," I hinted. This comment was made to verify it was Henan. "Yes, it is as you say. I just finished my homework and thought I would go online and see if you were there," Henan stated. Continuing, Henan announced. "We had a test today, and I think I did pretty well, but I will not know until tomorrow."

"It sounds as if you did very well, I'm sure you did," came my response; offering her encouragement. As an afterthought, I inquired. "Am I keeping you from anything important?"

"No… No, that's fine. I need a little break anyway. Besides, I have not talked to you for such a long time, so I thought we should get to know one another better," she said.

Henan occasionally spoke in broken English. However, she was still quite adept at carrying on a conversation. She had a good command of the English language, but when she typed chat message's it often appeared as fractured speech. However, I never had difficulty understanding what she was communicating. I was still puzzled why and how Henan happened to discover me on Skype. Remember, my knowledge on the use of Skype paled in comparison to users who were computer savvy like Henan. I remained skeptical in the early stages of our friendship. Occasionally putting Henan through an interrogation process.

"What test did you take today? Chemistry, biology, psychology? I am interested in the courses you're enrolled in to become an LPN," prodding at her day's activity.

"Oh," Henan sighed. "We had a test on pharmaceuticals," she answered confidently. Perhaps hoping I would be receptive to her response.

"Sounds to me like a hard test Henan," I remarked. Then I blindsided her with a request I longed to have fulfilled the last time we talked. "Say Henan, while I have you on-line do you think you could provide me with a picture of yourself? Although I would much rather see you on video." I hinted. "You know Henan, we talked about this the last time you were online, remember?"

Henan responded saying. "My computer screen is acting strange right now, so we can't do the video," She claimed. "However, I will send you a picture of me, that will not be a problem," Henan replied. "Can I get a picture of you also?" Came her request.

I had to pause and collect myself for a minute. She doesn't realize what she was asking me. If she only knew how computer illiterate, I am. "Should I keep it from her or tell her?" I thought. Since I did not know her that well, I kept scholarly ineptness to myself. Instead, I thought that this would be an excellent teaching tool. Taking a photo image using the computers camera, attaching it to an email, and sending it to Henan would be another learning task among many that required my attention. She does not realize how dysfunctional I am with computers. As an afterthought, this meant exchanging emails, always a risky enterprise when meeting strangers online.

"Alright Henan, that is fair enough," came my response. "However, I said, there must come a time soon, where I'll need to insist on seeing you on live video," okay?"

"Okay!" Henan acknowledged. "What is your email address, Jim?"

I typed the email *jimjones70@gmail.com,* for Henan to copy.

"Here you go Henan," I said. "And what about your email address?" I inquired.

"I'm typing it right now. This is my email address," *henan101001@ yahoo.com*. "I am uploading a picture of myself to send now," Henan informed me. "The picture should be in your email right now, so all you have to do is open email and click on the image icon, alright?" Henan informed me.

"That sounds great! I can't wait to see who I'm talking with."

"Same here Jim," Henan said.

"You will need to wait for my picture until I have a chance to take some, okay?"

"Sure that's fine. I can wait since I'm not going anywhere anytime soon." Henan replied.

Then, changing the discussion in mid-stream, I tailored some of my other questions that were more personal in nature, asking Henan. "Do you have any siblings; brothers or sisters?"

"No, just me, I am the only child in the family."

"Henan," I continued. "I'm a bit curious about something, if you don't mind me asking? Why did you wait so late in life before deciding to attend Nursing School?" Adding. "You said you were thirty-one-years-old, or somewhere in that age group, yes?"

"Yes," Henan said in response. "I spent some time in England with my boyfriend until he cheated on me with my best friend." She asserted. "I got mad, but I still stayed a long time in England. When that happened, I wanted to go to school," came Henan's reply, without giving any further details about her prolonged stay in England after the breakup.

"Yeah, that has to be very painful and hurtful. Realizing your boyfriend and best friend were cheating on you behind your back," verbalizing empathy with her. "I can relate to betrayals," I told Henan.

"Yes!" Henan replied in agreement. "It hurts very much, a lot of hurts," she tells me. Jim, I have to retire to bed now, it has been a long day, but we will talk soon, okay?" Henan said, before logging off.

There would be additional surprises on the horizon for Henan's description of events and how they would unfold during this journey in more detail when we get to Chapter eleven.

"Sure, fine Henan. I didn't intend to keep you long, but I wasn't really sure when I was going to log back onto Skype again."

"Okay, bye Jim, have a good night," Henan concluded as she logged off Skype.

When we finished our conversation, I immediately went to my email to retrieve the picture Henan had sent. Staring at the portrait of Henan on the computer; my first reaction that stirred my curiosity was that of a woman, mysterious in nature, who had this uncanny ability to mesmerize and hold you spellbound as you locked your eyes' on the photograph for minutes. What endeavors the innocence we see in another? As you peel back the layers of the unknown, it soon reveals the known in its own time over many seasons. The portrait would prove useful further into our friendship. She was modestly clothed. No alarm bells suggested anything other than what was natural for a photograph, other than her natural beauty.

Still, there was something about this picture that did not bode well with Henan's birth name. I am looking at a woman with blonde hair and blue eyes'. She said her father was a native-born citizen of Ghana. I was expecting something resembling a shade of pigmentation in her skin color. I noticed too, Henan seldom volunteered much if any information. As I begin to take notice, Henan would wait for me to initiate the discussion. Maybe she was exploring vulnerabilities in my character. Also, Henan never mentions her mother much during our conversations. Moreover, I now have this business about her prolonged stay in England. There are more questions than answers at this point. There is going to be more probing questions into her background the next time we talk.

Have my instincts unearthed something sinister, or am I allowing her character to come to life more out of drama than mere simplicity? Am I introducing something into my mind with my eyes' reflecting a light veiled in oblique illusions? Too many unanswered questions beckoning the soul to dig deeper. I have decided the intelligent choice at this time, is to leave well enough alone. Forget about this chance meeting with Henan, and stay away from Skype until you have a better understanding of programs and some of those demanding applications. Between late November 2012, and April 2013, Henan and I had no contact.

Although, I felt further research was needed into her background whenever time permitted. Inside, I felt two plus two wasn't adding up to four. It kept coming up to three. My eyes' left their imprint on many search engine pages using Goggle search. Eventually, I would begin to understand the importance of the Google search engine. The more I attempted to escape this foolishness, the more I was being goaded to move forward with the search.

I had briefly heard of fraud occurring on the internet and thought maybe Henan could somehow be involved with one of these organized groups. However, the few times we talked, she never once asked for money. Unless I have been misinformed, swindlers on the internet will slowly and methodically spend precious moments with an intended victim before they spring the trap and have you caught up in their web of deceit. Once they identify a soft spot in your armor, you become a soft target and they go for the jugular vein. They usually continue their aggressive pursuit of the victim until they have depleted their intended target of all their possessions and move onto the next. Therefore, I wondered why I seemed to be prompted by an unknown supernatural force to move forward with Henan. "I just did not get it!"

There comes a time when it is prudent to set aside foreign intrusions in your life for a while until you can think things through. After all, Thanksgiving was fast approaching, and if past holidays is any indicator of upcoming holidays, it was going to get hectic within a baby's breath of busy around here. Moreover, the tension in our home was showing birthing pains. The move from Florida to Trenton then from Trenton to Liberty and Liberty back to Trenton within a span of six months had challenged our patience. I was feeling anxious and depressed. Darlene and I were exhausted, emotionally and physically. Thanksgiving was now just a few weeks away. We, like millions of other faithful, were preparing for the onslaught of the holiday festivities with joyous anticipation.

However, the stress could not be hidden. Telltale signs became evident in my actions or lack thereof. I was certain the three moves we made during the past six months was a contributing factor for these mood swings. Reflecting back during those challenging months took its toll in many ways. You sensed an atmosphere of jubilation, and just a few days before Thanksgiving, or Christmas, smiles become interspersed with sounds of indifference. Panic, anxiety, and depression were depleting my body of energy. This would become the most defining challenge in our seventeen-year marriage.

We have lost the real meaning of Christmas. Instead, we have replaced the observance and celebration of Christ's birth with commercialism. It is all about money, sales, and Black Friday deals. Societies moral compass is pointing towards the South in the wrong direction. The things of the world have skewed our priorities. It may seem right at the time, however, if we were to give pause and ask ourselves what Christmas truly represented, we might realize we need to correct our direction and have it pointing North and not South where vertical thinking is focused.

I was unaware when first introduced to Darlene in the summer of 1993, at the Trenton Care Center by the Administrator of Nursing that we would eventually marry. Three- years later Darlene and I walked down the aisle to become husband and wife. Before the nuptials, Darlene and I sat down and drafted what we adopted as the "Constitution of

Marriage." It would represent a bond and seal of our wedding vows. It contained five articles.

- Article I The Seeds of Priority

- Article II The Spirit of Forgiveness and Humility

- Article III The Heart of a Servant

- Article IV Message of Communication

- Article V Exclusive Commitment

It's a seal of our commitment to one another, and it is, has, and will always remain under seal even though we are presently divorced. It is a pact we made. It is more precious than gold. Nothing can keep us from the vows we made to each other seventeen-years ago. The Constitution of Marriage is hung on my wall as a reminder of our commitment. I had waited for thirty years for tranquility to arrive at my doorsteps. Accept me for me, not what you would like me to become. God meant for this labor of love to burst forth with abundant fullness, as he gently bound our lives together and so it shall always remain.

Fast-forward one week before Christmas. I had an appointment that the Veterans Administration made on my behalf to visit a local doctor in Trenton that specialized in Neurologic disorders. Seven years' prior, a Neurologist from the Veterans Hospital in Gainesville, Florida had diagnosed me with "Parkinson's disease." For seven-years, I was on an aggressive regime of medication for this disease that a VA Neurologist prescribed to arrest its progression. When I arrived at the Neurologist office in Trenton; spending no more than perhaps fifteen-minutes in his office, the good doctor had me walk ten feet, observed my hands for tremors, rigidity, posture, weakened facial structure, etc. He asked a few questions, looked up at me, and pronounced me healthy. "Bye Jim, have a long life," he remarked as I was leaving his office.

"You don't have Parkinson's, come off the Carbidopa-Levodopa, and other Meds, and keep on keeping on." That in itself was fantastic news. What the Neurologist failed to mention which in hindsight was one of many medical blunders doctors misdiagnosed in my lifetime. Despite what I saw in the doctors notes, he neglected to instruct me that I should wean myself off the medication before he waved me out the door. Going cold turkey caused my body to shut down, spending 24/7 in the bed in a never-ending sleep marathon for five days. The Neurologist lacked good bedside manners, and had a chip on his shoulders. A poem I wrote about a year-ago may bode well with how I view humankind and their open display of arrogance.

"In Search of Wisdom"

"Invite honor, give honor, embrace honor, earn the honor, this is an honor; our lot in life.

In search of Wisdom, an Intransigent, Evasive, Elusive, Mystical thought; but for humankind its strife.

"What about ... About?" About this entrusted gift, That God, should grant man deserving wisdom court.

Wisdom's voice in denial cursing economics, ideology, God, intellectuals, and evil manipulators who exhort."

"Exist as one, as one to self, all creation has its beginning, and yet; each will meet their own season.

Wisdom, while granted through Grace. Though Grace is therefore given, God remains overseer of wisdom."

Humankind, have they not rejected knowledge? Wisdom's mercies, wisdom's insight we shall depend on.

Doubts and fears, past and present; broken lives, batteries of tears; in Wisdom shall be I defended,"

Power corrupts, corrupts absolutely, as humankind's heart yearns and demands even more ..."

"Bound by history, history reproves. Words spoken in jest and ignorance lends itself to conflict.

Unquenchable thirst for greed; in opposition to need; curries favor with moral decay.

As oversight begets control, senses grow numb, estranged. Then if it were fodder, let come what may.

Where is Wisdom? What becomes of oversight, right and wrong, moral, and immoral, good and evil?"

Dictators, Kings, Presidents, have governed in the shadow of Wisdom, but their efforts but disheveled."

Bias and bigotry, pride and arrogance, elevates humankind to fertile heights.

Cries decry Human Rights, Bill of Rights, Civil Rights. Its end result became history's slight.

In the interest of self-interest, a man shouts power, power! Blind guides positioning for acclaim. As the disenchanted are labeled classifications; blue and white collar, the majority, minority, rich, poor, intelligent, average, beautiful, so-so. Oh, what shame!

Poverty, hunger, homelessness, outcasts; Social Pyramid abused throughout the ages.

Despair, rejection, hopelessness, powerless; all found hidden in the zone of memories pages."

"Equality is of an anemic dysfunctional origin lurking about to a marginal degree.

Lean not on thine own understanding, for trials and tribulations are as decreed!

Bouquets filled with joy; alas, peace, and tranquility. How much more; shall man teary and wait?

Oppression, though, the realistic norm, brokenness and shattered spirit dreadfully understated."

"During the age of antiquity; millennium, and decades since passed. Wisdom eludes us; given a pass.

Weeping, fear and trembling come in all shapes and sizes, hidden under a veil, evil's own mask.

Should wisdom elude you, it is for the best. You live the here and now; yielding no harvest with your plow.

Soon eyes' will close for a time. Wisdom draws nigh, and to the divine, will I bow!"

"Wisdom isn't given to the foolish, nor of a man whose hearts fill with pride; corrupts mind and soul!

Neither is it granted to the simple, for evil intent. Free to execute their crafty, deceitful ways.

As questions unravel, the mystery reaches a crescendo and thus do I postulate, resolved to ask.

Whom amongst the billions of souls; dare God to entrust with Wisdoms tasks?"

Jim Jacobs

Now you may presuppose that I am getting off message with Henan Asante by introducing poetry, medical issues, and additional biographical insight into the personal life of Darlene and myself. What I am doing is setting the stage to unveil Henan in the fullness of her intriguing schemes. The poem serves a twofold purpose. From the perspective of the author, I wanted to express what I consider the present condition of humankind's heart, for it lacks wisdom. Moreover, there is a three-month lull with Henan since our previous contact until we would start communicating again in April.

In the meantime, trouble was becoming a manifest destiny on the home front. Bundling all these revelations into the mix, it stirred my spirit. It prompted a need to write a poem expressing insight, into the state of affairs relating to a person's spirit. Therefore, in poetic form I want the reader to see how words can pierce the heart and wound the human spirit. Once uttered from the tongue, words cannot be taken back. "But then, you knew this didn't you!"

"Restless Spirit"

"Salted and seasoned on a platter overflowing with turmoil, written are timeless memories to digest.

Set in Parameters plumed boundaries; determined am I to engage history, putting it to the test."

"Chastised, reviled, despised, cursed, and rejected; a foregone conclusion … Yes, even forsaken.

As the past does not reveal the present, nor I curry favor with evil intent, heart soon taken."

"Humankind; displays cruelty to man this troubled spirit and soul now confess. No peace announces I, absent needful rest.

Weeping spirit flooding this heart, all emotions forever put into memory I soon confess.

"Eyes' have seen, now cast downward, tears cascading droplets of rain, and unending pain.

Emptiness partners with disdain, a man, leaves behind wounded stains."

"Innocence violated, pierced by words, deceitful hands, all this and more compounded this pain.

"Restless Spirit, decades pass in reclusive isolation, who asked? Who inquired? Oh, what disgrace!

"Burdens too high to comprehend, years plus years have I endured.

Fight or flight was the battle cry, choose your weapon, into the Abyss; show perpetual fear.

"Saturated in distress, include sorrows; safeguard and defend this fractured soul.

Ruthless and vile, humankind's cruelty to man; swallows you whole, taking its toll."

"Mouths wide open, thirsts never satisfied. A man lies in wait looking for its next prey.

Smugness is proud!" Oh, man, we are beyond reproach. Add to it! Add to it! I'm in decay."

"This spirit testifies, justifies, signifies, that which is heavy laden, excuses all but lame.

Heart and soul did our Creator implant in man, but man's character is flawed, as was Cain's."

"Ears of thunder, embrace each truth during this my suffering hour.

Deceit and craftiness scorched and branded on man's heart, affording evil too much power."

"As you lay sleeping; in peaceful serenity; immersed in solitude, and comforting rest.

The struggle this night am I in deep solace, troubled by misty rivers, in restless civil unrest."

"Embers of the Soul set ablaze, rekindles spirit awakening the playlist glued in strife.

Unable to detach self from this restless spirit; all considerations depleted in this my life."

"As man journeys into the known and unknown, his footsteps leave imprints of carnage.

His mind makes ready to satisfy the desires of heart; respect and honor all but silage."

"Dwelling in man's heart too, resides contempt ... jealousy ... hatred, all manner of sin.

The sum of man's parts is his quest for power and greed, he purposes' to win."

"This restless spirit surrenders to the wonders and beauty of love's aspirations.

This love, where can I find it? Is it in you? Where does' thou art hides? Does it not render same devotion?"

"As fingers stretch the horizon seemingly tormented by suffering ... surmountable distress.

Life of drudgery, heartache, concealed depression. Can there be more? Time favors lesser- known tests, embrace this light while it's still within sight.

Yet, should I, in the still of this night, be at the ready?

Surrender I, mind, and spirit to all matter of harm, and yield all to the Lord's power and might."

"For I know the Lord will maintain the cause of the afflicted.

Reside and abide in this spirit of convictions. Scripture reveals exactly as it has been ordained.

Jim Jacobs

Now that you have had a foretaste of some poetry and the stories it transcends into whatever language you wish to define it, we reverse course as I lead you back to where going cold turkey from Parkinson's medication was having a dramatic effect on my system. Although the body was experiencing an adverse reaction to the withdrawal symptoms, I had also been struggling with PTSD (Post-Traumatic Stress Disorder) but was never aware of its crippling effects.

Symptoms fit into three categories. Re-experiencing symptoms like flashbacks. Reliving the trauma repeatedly, including physical symptoms like racing heart or sweating, bad dreams, frightening thoughts, Re-experiencing symptoms may cause problems in a person's everyday routine. They can start with the person's own thoughts and feelings. Words, objects, or situations that are reminders of the event can also trigger PTSD. Avoidance symptoms would be a classic example. There are places, events, and objects that are reminders of an experience that keeps a person with PTSD away.

There is also emotional numbness, feeling strong guilt, depression, or worry. Included is lost interest and difficulty remembering critical events. Things that remind a person of the traumatic event can trigger avoidance symptoms. Also, PTSD patients have what specialist refer to as hyper-arousal symptoms. This causes the PTSD victim to become easily startled feeling tense or on edge. Patients with PTSD have difficulty with sleep and have angry outbursts. Hyperactive arousal symptoms are usually constant rather than triggered by things that remind them of the event. These can make the person feel stressed and angry. Some people with PTSD do not show any symptoms for weeks, months, or years.

I struggled with PTSD daily. PTSD, coupled with the week-long withdrawal from medication for Parkinson's was difficult for Darlene and me to grasp since neither of us completely understood what was causing my erratic behavior. This may, and I emphasize "may," have been the catalyst for bringing down the house on Christmas Eve.

Christmas Eve arrived and I begin to feel some energy rejuvenating my depleted body strength. Still, fatigue in my body sometimes made me feel like a wet noodle. However, I was regaining alertness and my strength was gradually returning. Darlene had asked earlier if I was going with her to Candice house for the annual gathering of Christmas Eve festivities with her family. I declined, as I said.

"I don't feel well enough to go Darlene; I'm staying in bed." Darlene had nagged me for most of the day to go with her. However, I was just as adamant in my refusal to accompany Darlene to her daughter's house, as I voiced my objection once again.

"Darlene, how many times do I have to tell you, I do not feel well enough to go with you?" Eventually, Darlene, knowing she was not getting anywhere, finally left me home alone, and she left for their family Christmas Eve gathering by herself.

I do not know to this day what, or why I suddenly had a strong compulsion come over me to leave the home once Darlene had left. I had never had this anomaly happen in our seventeen-years before this uneventful canker sore erupted. However, here I was packing some casual clothes, hygiene supplies, and survival equipment and placing it in a makeshift backpack. I refuse to use withdrawal symptoms from medication, or PTSD to justify my actions.

There was a sense of urgency that came over me to take flight and go. It is that simple. Go, my mind kept nudging me. Not only did I leave in the dead cold night of winter on foot, but I left the vehicle behind, keys, money and wallet. I was going to get a taste of homelessness. I also didn't leave a note with Darlene telling her I had left. Those two decisions would turn out to be problematic to say the least. However, I was not thinking rationally. I was reacting. I could have, I should have, left Darlene a note, but I didn't. As such, stupid is what stupid does.

Chapter 10

In Thy Future, In Thyself, In Whatever

Equality is of an anemic dysfunctional origin,
submerged in controversy, we cannot agree.
Trials and tribulations, its sown seeds now established, as was so decreed.
Absent bouquets of love, peace, harmony, and tranquility,
this has humankind long awaited.
Oppression, equality, shouts its exact status; brokenness in Spirit understated.
Jim Jacobs

After putting two sets of clothing on while making sure I brought along the critical medications, in addition to my trusty staff used to maintain balance, I stepped out into winter's eve absent any money except pocket change. Heading South in the direction of Arizona, where I would stop along the way to visit my son, daughter, and granddaughter on the first leg of my sojourn. After that, it would be anybody's guess where these legs would carry me. Perhaps, I would continue further south of the State and visit my brother.

In the meantime, we just move forward as I meander up the elevated exit ramp to the major highway going south towards our capital city of Braxton. Once I reached the major artery of Highway 101, I immediately had mixed emotions about my decision to leave home. It wasn't pleasant to dismiss seventeen-years filled with fond memories. Not to mention the mutual respect and love we had for each other. My mind continually migrated towards the positives in the marriage.

I knew the traffic this night would be light if not non-existent because of Christmas Eve. None-the-less, there were not too many options available. When a vehicle did appear traveling south, the thumb came out. I had to depend on the mercy of the driver. As the first car passed by, I considered myself a full-fledged hitchhiker. I was now a seasoned homeless vessel relying on the outside elements to provide for my needs. A badge of honor for this old man treading the ice-capped road that awaited me wherever these footsteps made an imprint.

Approximately three miles out of Trenton the feet and fingertips were beginning to feel the extreme cold temperatures each step I took. The makeshift backpack wasn't holding up very well either. Occasionally, it would slip off my shoulders. I packed more than I realized. An overpass a half-mile further up the highway looked promising. If there were no rides by the time I reached the bridge, the decision to take refuge underneath its structure was a viable and imminent necessity. After all, the traffic was light at best and it did not appear as though anyone was going to stop.

By the time I arrived at the overpass, the cars and trucks that did come my way whizzed past me so fast you would have thought they were racing at the Daytona Speedway. I climbed the steep slippery slope leading up to the ledge under the overpass. It offered some relief from the harsh cold … Not really what I was hoping for. At least the feeling was starting to return to my fingers and feet. While I was taking a reprieve underneath the overpass from the cold, I tried to fix the makeshift backpack so it would not be so cumbersome to handle. After a thirty-minute rest, I slowly negotiated down the slope, until I was back on the shoulder of the highway.

I was constantly thinking about Darlene and the repercussions that might arise and how it would play itself out. Walking three additional miles, the prospects for a free ride looked pretty dismal. Braxton was another thirty-nine miles down the freeway. The frigid cold was starting to affect my body, especially the lower back and left hip where I had undergone surgery two-years earlier. Maryville was still six miles away. If there were no rides by then, I would seek shelter somewhere in that town for the night.

Another mile further down the highway, I noticed a small compact car pass. By this time, I had given up all hope of hitching a ride, so I did not even bother extending my arm outward. As the vehicle passed by, I notice his brake lights being applied five-hundred feet down the highway. The car crossed the median and began to travel northbound. "They must have been confused about directions, as I pondered this latest turn of events." In less than a minute, the vehicle returned pulling just ahead of me on the right shoulder of the road. He waited with the engine running. Arriving on the passenger side of the car with the window partially opened, I crouched down slightly to get a visual on the driver, as he said.

"Where are you headed?"

"Braxton," I replied. "I'm going to Braxton."

"Would you like a ride to Braxton?" he asked. They were a young couple very polite and well mannered. "If you don't mind the cramped space in the back seat, you are welcome to ride with us," the young man said. "We are going to Braxton to visit my wife's family," He informed me, a soft tone emanating from the outskirts of his lips.

"Thanks, thank you very much," I remarked.

Cramped was an understatement. Struggling to get the staff and backpack into the back seat while wedging the legs and body in between the front passenger car seat and the back seat took some time. You almost needed to be a contortionist. I nestled in for the ride to Braxton. Paul and Angela were their names. I introduced myself as Jim Jones.

"Are you from Braxton?" Paul inquired.

"Not exactly Paul, I'm from Trenton, on my way to Arizona," I told him. "However, Braxton is as far as I intend to go this evening." Pausing for a brief moment, I went on to say. "This body of mine is a little worn down yet after coming off some medications prescribed in error." "Look," I said. "I have some candles in my backpack that I think are rather unique, and I want to give these you folks as a token of my appreciation."

"No, no, Jim, that's not necessary. Angela and I are just glad we were able to help by getting you out of the cold," Paul tells me.

"I would really be pleased if you accepted these candles Paul, and Angela. Accept them as a Christmas gift… Please." I kept insisting.

Paul then replied. "That's nice of you Jim. We will accept, but I want to say again, it's necessary. We will make sure they are kept in a special place as a reminder of this night."

We exchanged small talk all the way into the Braxton city limits when Paul turns around to ask.

"Where would you like to be dropped off Jim?"

"Oh, Ventura Street is good. There are plenty of homeless folks wandering around that area of the city," I replied with amusement.

"I suggest we try to locate a shelter for the night. That would be my idea. It is freezing out here tonight Jim. What do you think?" Paul asked.

Hesitating briefly, I told Paul. "If you think this is in my best interest Paul, you're the driver, but I do not want to take up your time either," I remarked with a sigh.

"Don't worry about us Jim, we will get there when we get there." Paul countered. Then Angela said. "Your welfare and safety are more important right now and we would feel terrible if you ended up freezing out here tonight."

"Okay!" I replied. "You convinced me, let's see what's open then."

Paul was beyond patient as he drove around looking for shelters. After three failed attempts, we resorted to plan B. Paul suggested an all-night restaurant he knew that would be open. Paul was polite enough to ask me first if that would be okay before hauling me over to Benjamins restaurant. All in agreement, we headed for Benjamins across town. Just as we arrived within view of the restaurant, Paul takes a left turn into an ATM machine to withdraw some cash. We then drove the short distance down the block to the restaurant.

As he pulled into the parking lot and came to a stop at the front door, I open the car door to exit. Halfway out, Paul turns around to face me sitting in the back seat.

"Jim here, take this. It isn't much, but Angela and I want you to have this." In Paul's hand was a folded twenty-dollar bill that he placed in the palm of my hand.

"Paul," I insisted. "You have done plenty for me already, so please hold onto your money … Please." Try as I might, Paul kept insisting I take it. Expressing my gratitude for their kindred hearts I kept attempting to give it back. But Paul and Angela pleaded with me to accept the twenty dollars.

Finally consenting, I took the money, but with conditions. I wanted their name, phone number, and address. "Jim Jacobs pays his own way through life. I will be refunding this money back to you when I decide where my final destination will be," I insisted adamantly.

With the agreement secured, we shook hands, exchanged a few pleasantries, and they went on their way to his in-law's home. Strolling into Benjamin's, I immediately took a stool away from the few customers who were dining out. I removed my backpack and set it down next to the stool. A sigh of relief came over me while I sat there and silently thanked the Lord for all his blessings. After a few minutes at the counter, a waiter greeted me and asked.

"Is there anything I can get you sir?"

"Sure," I replied. "Coffee with cream and Splenda would be nice."

"You got it, service with a smile and one cup of coffee coming up. Will that be all sir?" the server asked.

"Pretty much I guess, thanks." replying with a grin on my face.

I was grateful the crowd was small. Most of my life has been spent loathing large groups. I especially did not care much for one on one encounters. Never felt comfortable and secure around people. I learned from childhood on, to avoid contact with strangers. I have made it my life's passion to observe body language, pitched sound, mannerisms, eye contact, and how people in groups interact with each other.

Occasionally, I would leave my stool, and retreat outside for some fresh air, take a smoke break, and just stretch my legs taking the carved staff with me. On one such outing, while I was meandering around the front of Benjamin's, my eyes' drifted towards the Northern Hemisphere. To these startled eyes' I beheld the brightest star in the galaxy. I had never witnessed the North Star that bright in my entire life.

Immediately, I could feel goosebumps traveling up and down my back and neck. Was this a physical sign, I wondered? I stood there awestruck the better part of ten minutes, just gazing and looking up in awesome wonder as the erection of the papillae came in successive waves. Many times while sitting on the stool, my mind would drift into the memory bank of my brain, where it would transmit data back to my inner thoughts of Darlene, and the peaceful, happy, moments we shared together.

I was brought back to reality when I noticed what appeared to be a young Middle Eastern man walking through the doors of the restaurant. He took a seat at the counter; two stools down from my location. It was about two in the morning now. He had a newspaper stuck under his armpit. He appeared to be a regular customer because the server came running up to where he had taken a seat.

"Will it be the same breakfast order Mr. Hakim? Would you like some coffee now, or wait for the order, sir?" She asked politely. "Oh, by the way, Merry Christmas folks," she vented out loud.

"Coffee would be fine," Mr. Hakim replied.

While Hakim is eating breakfast, I retreat outdoors and into the cold once again lest I give in to temptation and purchase breakfast as well. Considering my options, I really didn't want to spend any more money than necessary. Preferring to hold onto what I had in the event of an unexpected emergency.

As soon as Mr. Hakim had finished eating the huge platter of food placed before him, I re-entered the restaurant and took my place at the counter. No sooner was I planted back on the stool, when Mr. Hakim swiveled around and extended his right arm, hand opened, and introduced himself to me as Assad Hakim.

"Jim, Jim Jacobs," extending my right arm out to connect with his.

"I couldn't help but notice that backpack on the floor Jim, are you from Braxton?" Assad asked curiously.

I hesitated a moment before giving Mr. Hakim an answer. Be cautious Jim, think before you speak. "Actually, I'm from Trenton. I arrived here yesterday evening," I replied. Responding to his inquiry with guarded optimism.

"Oh," Mr. Hakim said. Giving a surprised look that resonated from his eyes'. "You mean you spent Christmas Eve at this restaurant?" He asked politely.

"Yes, late last evening until now," I told Assad. "However, I will be leaving at daylight, heading South."

"Do you have a vehicle Jim?" Hakim asked for no apparent reason.

Without seeming sarcastic, I responded. "The vehicle is these two legs Mr. Assad."

Assad then asked the big money question. "Are you married Jim?"

"Yes Assad, I'm married. However, after pulling this stunt yesterday evening I don't know what will be in my future."

Assad by now is flabbergasted and beside himself as he begins to counsel me. "Jim, you have to go back home and do what is right," he insisted. "Just tell your wife you made a mistake," Assad pleaded. A seriousness and concern resonating from his heart revealing just how troubled he had become. Probably thinks the elevator doesn't go all the way to the top floor with me.

"It is too late for that Assad," I replied. "I just can't up and go home now. Besides, I have not seen my children for years, and I want to experience homeless life so I can identify with the plight of these faceless souls."

"Very well," Mr. Hakim remarked. "I can't force you to return home, but I won't allow you to walk three-miles to the interstate through this neighborhood." Assad cautioned. "This is a rough part of Braxton, and isn't safe for anyone who walks these streets alone, albeit someone who is white," Hakim elaborated. "And even if you did get through the neighborhood unscathed, I'm not too keen on the idea of you hitchhiking all the way to Arizona," Assad profoundly stated.

I took in everything Assad said, and then I replied with an off-the-cuff remark. "You have a lot of moxie there Assad. You're a determined individual. It's almost as if you were giving me the Grand Torino sales pitch," I remarked, then added. "I want to thank you for your concern for my welfare and safety Assad."

Mr. Hakim continued jabbering away, telling me how financially successful their company was this year as it generated huge profits and that he had received his lion's share of bonuses and other benefit's. Furthermore, Hakim was investing heavily in the stock market and had made a substantial return on his investments. He was willing to use some of this good fortune to help. He said his wife was spending Christmas with her family so he volunteered to purchase a bus fare for me and drive me to the bus terminal in the morning if I would be amicable to this goodwill offer.

I considered Assad's proposal. Dwelling on the feasibility of accepting his offer. However, he was a stranger after all. Although Assad was pleasant company and very persuasive, I wasn't sure. Did he have an end game? Perhaps he was trying to probe my weaknesses by taking advantage of any vulnerabilities he thinks I may have. Assad kept repeating how insignificant money meant to him. Yet, I also wondered what kind of reception would be awaiting him once his wife arrived back home only to discover her husband spent over two-hundred dollars on a stranger he didn't know, for a bus fare.

After mulling it over for some time, I approached Assad with a counter offer, saying. "Assad, I will accept your generous offer with one condition. You have to give me your address and phone number because I want to repay the debt even though you insist on doing this as a humanitarian gesture."

Assad responded by nodding his head in the affirmative, and then he extended his hand out once again to shake hands to seal a done deal. Assad then excused himself by saying. "I'm going down on the other end of the counter to make some calls to local bus companies, get their departure schedules, and costs for bus fare, while you wait here, okay?" Assad told me. "I don't want you leaving."

"Yes Assad, I'll be right here," I promised him, adding. "Where do you think I'm going?"

"Good Jim, this shouldn't take me long, and then I will return with the information we need to get you on your way."

While Assad was at the end of the counter, an elderly man entered the restaurant and sat on the same stool Assad had occupied. I noticed when he walked into the restaurant the old man had a gait as he lumbered up to the stool. Bent over from years of toil, he showed signs of arthritis and skeletal issues. His pace was deliberate; perhaps some balance issues as well. He was unkempt; clothed in old worn out attire that may have suggested a homeless person's lifestyle. Personal hygiene didn't appear to be a priority. He ordered coffee and toast. He deliberately nursed every morsel of the toast, smothering it with the Jams and Jellies sitting before him at arm's length on the counter.

Occasionally, out of the corner of my eye, I could see the man turn his head over in my direction. At first, this made me nervous and uncomfortable. I didn't welcome stares from men. That signal instinctively placed me in a defensive posture. After a while, I realized the man was admiring the staff next to my side. He appeared drawn to the staff like a magnet. The interest in the staff allowed me to let my guard down ever so slightly. After the gentleman had finished his coffee and toast, he got up from his stool, and slowly made his way in my direction.

As he walks towards me, I'm thinking. "Oh brother, now what's he going to do?"

"Hello, young man, my name is Tim." Solidifying his first name to me. "I couldn't help but admire that staff you have next to you," he remarked. "Mind if I take a look at it?"

"No, no! Not at all." "The name is Jim," extending my right hand forward to meet his. Then I offered to let him give the staff a maiden voyage.

"I notice it has this carved turtle on the top of the base," Tim observed. "Yah know Jim, I been looking for one of these for years, where did you get it?" Tim asked out of curiosity.

"I purchased it at Channel's. It was the last one they had in stock," answering Tim's inquiry. "Give it a try if you like," I insisted.

Tim stood briefly admiring the artisans work, placed his fingers around the staff to get a firm grip and started walking from one end of the counter to the next. I noticed right away how balanced and steady his strides were becoming. Returning to where I was sitting Tim was grinning from ear to ear. He seemed quite pleased with the staff. Without hesitation, Tim told me he had been employed on a turtle farm for most of his life and was now retired. This was either a con or Tim was truly reminiscing about his fondness for turtles. Regardless, it was not for me to judge. After all, Paul and Angela had shown me compassion last night? Tim interrupted my thoughts briefly, and with sparkles in his eye's said he was able to walk easier with the aid of a staff.

"Is that a fact Tim?" I said excitedly. "If this will help assist you in walking, the staff is yours ... Merry Christmas," I announced, bringing a smile to my face since who knows when.

Tim opened his mouth in surprise. "No, tell me you're kidding, this is not happening to me," he remarked with shock illuminating from his weathered face.

"Tim, no jokes or pranks." This is not a trick or treat offer, but a gracious gesture of kindness." Looking Tim in the eyes', I repeated his good fortune and what he was about to take home with him. Quickly seizing the opportunity, I commented. "Tim, everything is good here and you need it more than I do. I've had many blessings, so you might say were both in the right place at the right time." "Besides," I continued. "Nothing happens without the Lord's hand involved in his handiwork."

Wiping away tears of joy Tim said. "Thank you very much Jim, I will surely take care of this walking staff for you."

Tim was out the door like "Jumping Jack Flash." Life made easier for Tim than when he came into Benjamin's restaurant. At least, I made a difference in someone's life, as I considered all that has happened since leaving home.

Meanwhile, Assad is still working the phone. He briefly looked up and glanced over in my direction; lifted his right arm in the air, and gave me a thumbs-up. What exactly did that gesture mean?

Finished with his calls, Assad came over to where I was sitting and announced. "I have good news Jim, there is a bus scheduled to leave later this morning at 10 A.M."

I found myself questioning the same generosity I had shown Tim. "Are you sure this is what you want to do Assad?"

"Yes, Assad assured me. You are a very kind man. I saw what you did for that man," Assad said beaming. Assad excused himself shortly thereafter, informing me he was going home for a few hours' sleep. Assad assured me I would see him around nine in the morning and drive me to the bus terminal. Assad hinted about taking me home with him but didn't think his wife would like the idea when she came back home and discovered a stranger was in their home while she was away. I'm glad he didn't push the issue. I would not have gone anyway.

While sitting on the stool, head resting securely in the palm of my right hand, my attention was suddenly drawn in the direction of a group of servers who had gathered in a semi-circle near the entrance leading into the kitchen. One server had her hands covering her face; sobbing uncontrollably. She was making every effort to tell the other servers gathered around her that she had been stiffed (not tipped) by a table of ten people who had just departed the restaurant.

The server said. "I went out of my way to give this table good service, even catering to the four children who were rowdy and demanding." Continuing she said. "I have to rely on tips to support my family yah know."

The servers were trying to be sympathetic, offering encouragement, but it was useless. She threatened to quit as she headed to the restroom for some privacy. Her emotional display of disappointment tugged at my heart. I knew first-hand how difficult and demanding a server's job could be. It had peaks and valleys. Customers demand so much from a server. It was intense work …A thankless job in many respects. Knowing this, I summoned the kitchen helper over to the counter.

I reached into my pocket and pulled out ten dollars. I instructed the kitchen helper to give it to the server who was upset, instructing him on what to say.

"Tell her the man returned and apologized. He had forgotten to include the gratuity before leaving." The young lad nodded in agreement and assured me he would give her the money.

Aha! What a joy it is to give! However, acts of kindness cannot justify the heartache and pain Darlene must be going through when she returned home to an empty house. Guilt, how do I handle this guilt? I have more than enough guilt to last a lifetime for choice's I've made in life. I had taken this too far to reverse the scourge that may await me back home. Why? Why? Why?

Assad arrived at nine in the morning as promised. Walking through the door of Benjamin's, we met each other halfway. The first words uttered from Assad's mouth jettisoned through the thin air like a bolt of lightning in the form of a limited demand. To my utter amazement, Assad said. "Before I take you to the bus terminal Jim, you have to call your wife and tell her where you are; that you are doing well." Putting the final period at the end, Assad added. "This you must do, no ifs, and's, or buts."

Assad handed me the cell phone. With trepidation and uncertainty, I began dialing our home phone number. It rang two times at most before Darlene answered.

"Hi," I said. "This is Jim Darlene, and I'm calling to let you know I'm all right." Emotions began to surface in sadness when I mentioned her name.

Darlene interrupted to ask. "Where are you? We have been looking for you all evening and morning." Then Darlene repeated her first question. "Where are you?"

Giving Darlene the answer to her question wasn't exactly what she wanted to hear. "Darlene, I can't tell you where I am other than I'm fine and doing well, this is all I can say right now," I informed her.

"But the police are here and they want to know where you are," Darlene said.

I didn't realize at the time I called Darlene that the Trenton police were at our apartment listening in the background. They were instructing Darlene to keep me talking on the phone so they could "ping" my location. Suddenly the Trenton police were on the phone.

"Hello, Mr. Jacob's? This is the Trenton police department," the officer said. "Your wife is worried sick," he told me. "You need to let us know where you are. We just want to make sure you are safe. No one will force you to return home," the officer assured me. "We are just concerned about your welfare," he concluded.

"Are you absolutely sure about this?" Asking for reassurance. "Mr. Jacobs, you have my word, we want to make sure you are safe that is all." The officer reiterated.

"I hope so," I answered sternly, adding. "I'm at Benjamin's restaurant in Braxton, but will be leaving for the bus terminal shortly," I informed the officer.

Then the officer interrupted saying. "We want you to remain there. We are going to dispatch the Braxton police department to verify your identity; so please wait there." The officer calmly asked.

Then the Trenton police officer instructed me to give the phone to Mr. Hakim. Whatever they discussed, it wasn't shared after they were finished. It couldn't have been too important. Otherwise, Assad would have told me.

Five minutes later, the Braxton police arrived at the restaurant. After checking my identification, they were satisfied everything was copasetic. Before departing, the officer informed us we were free to go. Gathering my backpack, we left Benjamin's and headed for the bus terminal twenty minutes away. Arriving at the bus terminal, Assad pulled out his wallet and gave me the money for the bus fare saying.

"When you arrive in Calvin, buy your ticket there. I'm giving you an extra twenty dollars my friend."

"Assad, you are one special man to have done this for me when you really didn't have to." Adding. "I will never forget your generosity and hospitality you've shown me today." Tears began welling up in my eyes' and cascaded down my cheeks as I left the vehicle. This has been an emotional roller coaster these past fourteen hours as I wiped away the tears from my eyes'.

"You are very welcome Jim," Assad replied. "I hope you and the Mrs. can work everything out."

"We will see Assad, we will see." As I walked towards the bus to board, debating whether I should turn around and wave a final farewell to Assad. Best I just keep going, fearful it would just generate more tears.

The bus ride to Calvin was uneventful, taking a little over an hour to get there. I'm in a larger city now. Tread more cautiously. Be on guard for anything and everything. Do not look down. Look everyone in the eyes'. Show no fear. Be vigilant with your backpack. You have entered the arena of the unknown, so be careful whom you talk to, and what is happening around you. You want to experience homelessness? Okay, good luck Jim! After purchasing a ticket, I sat in the terminal holding area until they announced boarding for Trinity. Our next destination before another bus change.

Once out of the city limits, my thoughts began to wander. Whatever brought me to this point in my life remains unknown. Thoughts so in depth they dwell within. Private …Strange wonderings, and yet known only to man's soul. It was personal … Suffocating …Overpowering … Lifelong. We muddle and struggle for words past spoken to each other. Is it Rapture or deliverance? Passion, or is it exaltation? Could it be what most the moment needs? Our faint heart lives in it. However, we chase after natural fullness for happiness and peace. Alone now, I have only photographs in memories bank to touch me. Only one who has not shared our love would condemn these thoughts. However, you, my darling Darlene never left these thoughts, even in times where time passes us by as it is now. These eyes' have passed through the chambers with unspoken words as they rain droplets from the eyes'.

You have stretched forth your hand. You have given of your time. No less, you have given of your love. Yet, most of all, you willingly surrendered your trust … And if that wasn't enough, you freely and voluntarily placed your life into the hands of this soul. You have given me the very best that you had to give. Then, of no trivial matter, I received a total eclipse of a fallen angel whose words are revered. To whom then shall I give an account of my selfish actions. This, a personally embroidered message in pure thought, put together as only the mind may be capable of formulating. I have always been elusive in pattern and personality.

Words can be harmful. Words may communicate love and compassion. Words have eyes' that penetrate into the lie, and can see the truth. Yet, more than this, words have hands that make a story come alive. However, nowhere can you find words; when summoned and cultivated more explicitly placed, than in a person's soul. Why, oh why, do I allow these thoughts to infiltrate the crevices in my mind? I wondered why I continue to have these private, personal, thoughts of us; Darlene.

There is not much one can do on a bus but take refuge into the mind and take inventory of traumatic events that mold and shape the foreshadowing history of one's life. Confronting our emotions and feelings can be painful... Facing them head-on. The mind begins to trick your psychic depositing guilt at the doorstep. Everything that happens, and everything that hinders our progression has meaning or reason attached to it. Sometimes it is invisible until you feel it begin to suffocate your memory.

In the book of life. Past, present, and future, you have to remember every page has two sides. In secular living, we fill one side with our plans, goals, dreams, hopes, desires, and financial aspirations. However, on the flip side of the page, Providence writes. Whatever God ordains may conflict with our objectives. For you see, we are always in conflict with the flesh and the things of this world. The foolish and proud do not have access to wisdom and neither is it meant for men with evil intent.

So deep in thought was I, that it had escaped my attention that we were pulling into the next terminal in Trinity, a much larger city than Calvin. Bigger cities meant higher prices, more congestion ...Unorganized chaos. This meant becoming more vigilant, more alert. The more diverse the population, the more apt people are to get agitated. Their real character comes alive. They are more unpredictable. Yah, gotta have moxie in your stride. I will not be buying any food here. Soon we were boarding the bus again. This time, I decided to take a seat in the rear of the bus. Privacy, I needed privacy. I am tired and fatigued, uncertain yet if I have recovered from going cold turkey from the Medication.

We were now soon on the road to Dallas, when my mind, which cannot seem to take a respite was once again languishing over an internal mind driven by thoughts. Can I be loved without fearing love? How about trust? Would I ever be able to trust without mistrust? Love without restrictions, desire without demand, accepting me just as I am? If I say goodbye, promise, me you will not berate me all over again. Give this soul its peace. As quickly as I entered the mind, I reappeared back into the insanity of the real world.

I need to convince myself that I cannot continue to dwell on the would have, could have, or should have probabilities. Master the brain, do not allow the brain to master you, came whisperings from my mind. I managed to get a few hours' sleep before I heard noise coming from the intercom up front. The driver was announcing that we were driving straight into a blizzard fifty miles down the highway. He informed the passengers we were going to stop at the first convenience store and wait it out, perhaps four hours.

I bought a hamburger to eat while we waited out the storm. Then we waited and waited, and waited some more. After three hours, we were back on the highway. We moved slowly at first, but we were moving. We were driving straight through to Dallas, which adjoined Fort Worth. Once in Dallas, I discovered extra money was needed to continue the final leg of the journey, destination Arizona; money I didn't have.

Dallas was another one of those busy terminals. Within sight of all incoming and outgoing passengers were two huge strapping police officers who showed little if any kindness on their expressionless faces. Homelessness meant helpless vagabond. I would have to panhandle for the money. I scrounged around for an empty cup. After finding one, I began to panhandle in the terminal for loose change. Holding out the cup in front of folks who passed in front of me. There were plenty of passengers to approach. I am having some success. However, I wasn't panhandling more than five- minutes when I turned around and noticed one of the officer's watching me. When he caught my eye, he made a quick beeline in my direction. He was an in-your-face officer. Very straight forward; spoke with authority. He looked me straight in the eyes', and with an intimidating stare said.

"It is illegal for you to panhandle inside this terminal, so if you want to continue testing me, we will gladly give you free transportation downtown to the precinct, do I make myself clear?"

"Yes sir, but what am I supposed to do officer? I have come up short on money to continue onto Arizona, and I do not have enough cash."

I was pleading wanting compassion and understanding. The officer's disposition changed slightly, as he said. "You may ask people if they have any loose change. However, there is a legal way to do it without breaking the law."

He began to instruct me in a fatherly sort of way now. "Let's say you have a dollar. You can ask bystanders if they have change for the dollar. If they give you more than the amount you are displaying, that is not breaking any laws and we cannot interfere in that exchange." He said.

I took the officers advice and had the needed amount in no time. Finally, with a boarding pass in hand, which I did not have to pay for after all. And it remains a mystery to this day. When it was given to me by the ticket administrator, he remarked. "Free of charge, go on your way; Merry Christmas."

I could now continue to my final destination. An arduous journey to see my children was within striking distance. I could see the light at the end of the tunnel. Little did I realize there would be trouble as I was about to enter the eye of the hurricane. You see, not only do my children live in Arizona, but so does Pamela, my ex-wife, mother of our children.

Since our divorce, Pamela continues to carry hatred, resentment, contempt, and anger on a scale beyond the crux of human understanding and comprehension. Pamela is a woman scorned. Before we met she was raped, molested, and a victim of spousal abuse. She has gone through more marriages than Ava Gabor and still counting. She blames me for all of her trials and hardships in life. Also, Pamela for reasons unclear, she wants to exact revenge on me for her dysfunctional failures in life. I have never met a person with so much hatred and an unforgiving spirit of the heart that it causes me to be concerned about her salvation. She needs Christ and Christian counseling for sure.

I stopped by to see my daughter Ginny and granddaughter Stella first. Ginny told my ex-wife; Ginny's Mom, I was staying at her home visiting. Why Ginny called her mother, I will never know because I don't want to ruffle any feathers. I was not aware that Pamela, my ex, was scheming while I was visiting. I sure received an ear full when I arrived back in Trenton. It appears Pamela went behind my back, and like a viper poised to strike its victim, she calls the Trenton Police demanding they come to Arizona and take me back to Trenton. When they refused, she said to the officer.

"What good are you? It's your responsibility to come here and take Jim away! After all, he does live in Trenton; it's your jurisdiction, she snapped sarcastically to the officer. "Jim is your responsibility, now come get him she demanded repeatedly." However, her ranting and raving were futile. When Pamela finally realized she wasn't getting anywhere with them, she then contacted the Phoenix police department demanding the same quick response from them. When they also refused Pamela's demands, she hung up in disgust. They must have thought she was brain dead or had a few screws loose.

Unbeknownst to me, later that day, Pamela calls my bank and demands the officer of the bank grant her authority to withdraw money out of my account. How extreme and foolish that must have seemed to the bank. Pamela wanted me out of Arizona immediately based on her own agenda. Was she envious of Ginny and me because we have a stable relationship? It is either that or there are some old skeletons in Pamela's closet she is withholding from me.

Eventually, I departed for Trenton, but only after getting a taste of life as a homeless person, so when everyone retired for the night, I slipped out of the house at night to roam around until all hours of the night and day. I had no regrets. In the short time, I was there, I learned the art of street shrewdness and developed a greater understanding and empathy for the homeless souls. Homelessness is a lost but forgotten segment of our society requiring more resources and attention to the plight of the faceless. No one deserves to live this kind of existence. This also insists upon leadership and action. It is a blemish to human decency that cannot go unattended. It should also be said, this wasn't my first experience being homeless, but I elected not to get into those times.

Just before leaving Arizona, Pamela came over with her husband; they are divorced now; of course. This makes, at least, eight-times now for Pamela. I approached Pamela and gave her a bear hug while her husband stood by, and while so doing, I asked for her forgiveness. As expected, Pamela said, (expletive) no! The irony here, Pamela should have been asking me for forgiveness. But knowing Pamela as I do, it will never happen. This then is Pamela. She is cold, stubborn, hardheaded, spiteful, hateful, and unforgiving. She hates with a passion, and would just as soon have me disappear from the face of the earth.

Chapter 11

Into the Abyss

Part I

Man of darkness displays no shame; mean, contemptible,
bringing with him chaos, and strife.
Cunning; for this, is their craft, crafty indeed. Man
labors and toils, evil, brings deceit in life.
Woe, Woe, woe, to man who resides in darkness, how
clever your schemes, executed in Satan's midst
Love in its truest form embraces the light, treasure
it lest you get entangled and go adrift.
Jim Jacobs

The spring aroma of April is becoming more noticeable as you begin to see families doing yard work and planting gardens; barbecues stoked with the smell of steak cooking on charcoal grills. There is a beautiful sign of life beginning to appear as nature brings forth its wonders. While all this is occurring, I find myself all but left alone in my own inner sanctuary. With nothing else on my agenda but time, I may as well begin uncovering this mystery woman who introduced herself as Henan. I accepted Henan's plea for friendship at its face value. I had nothing more to lose since Darlene and I were separated now.

I wanted to give Skype one more trial run to see if Henan was still hanging around after all these months of silence. It had taken a week before there was any sign of activity. Did she abandon all hope from my long absence? Nope! She was still around to assume our friendship.

However, I informed Henan I still was not comfortable using Skype. I had asked her if she might have any suggestions about some other application that could be used for chatting that might be available. It didn't take long for her to come up with the solution. Henan told me about an application called "Yahoo Messenger." She would talk me through the downloading process.

One advantage to using Yahoo Messenger is its feature to keep meticulous records of chat sessions. This would prove invaluable for me. Although contact with Henan wasn't initiated until the first week of April 2013, any chat sessions we had from the second week of April to May 29, 2013, disappeared when I made the move to Braxton. Therefore, I had to rely on memory for these chat sessions.

A (ding), on the screen alerts the user the person is online waiting for the other party to come online. It was 11:00 A.M. when contact was made with Henan; 5:00 P.M. Ghana time. Her first typed chat message read.

"Hi, I missed you."

Henan repeated the differences in time between the two continents. It was six hours. As it is, time wouldn't really become a factor when arrangements were made for us to chat on messenger because Henan rarely kept the agreed upon time.

Before April 30, 2012, Henan and I had several chat sessions on Yahoo Messenger. I had finally convinced her to have us video chat so I could see whom it was I was developing this friendship with. I needed to know that I wasn't talking to an underage child. She had sent me pictures, but that wasn't really proof of her age. After all, anyone can use another person's image and deceive you into thinking this is them in the photograph; only to discover later it was pirated from someone's web page or an entirely different source. It didn't take long before "red flags" started raising eyebrows northward. Henan had sent me another still photo of her posing in a flimsy negligee …Not good. The next "red flag" came when she agreed to video chat. As we were exchanging chat on video, the live video feed would go black, or as Henan referred to it as "the screen freezing." Every time this happened, Henan claimed it was necessary to reboot her computer so we could continue the video chat.

These hiccups would frequently occur, creating a nuisance and raise my level of suspicion even more about her agenda. Henan told me she was using an older model computer and that it was affecting her academic studies. Furthermore, she said her mother was recovering from surgery and could not afford to send any money for Henan to purchase a new computer. Against my better judgment, if indeed I had any sound judgment to begin with, I piped in and offered to help.

After all, I did have an extra computer in storage, so what better calling than to help someone who is facing financial hardships. At this point, it was a questionable goodwill gesture but I decided to move forward anyway. Offering to send a slightly used laptop to Henan was met with gratefulness. Moreover, Henan wanted to know if speakers came with the computer. I told Henan no, but that I just happened to have an extra set. "How about a camcorder?" She asked. "If you have a camcorder, I can take movies of the countryside and stuff…Like me, and send you the video." Sent!

Everything Henan requested was shipped Express Mail to Ghana on April 22, 2013. Feeling comfortable with my decision? "No!" Yet, I convinced myself it was only stuff. This was a 50/50 knee jerk response. I was hoping against all hope; Henan was not one of these growing number of preying swindlers. Otherwise, if I discovered later she had played me for a fool, Henan would experience the full wrath of my aggressive nature. I can show compassion, empathy, and kindness. However, to the other extreme, I can become very aggressive when I am betrayed and lied too. Stuff is one thing. A person's word to me is quite another.

Since Henan was not logged onto Yahoo Messenger when I went online, I left her a brief message. "Hello, Henan. P.S. This is the landline number Henan. I changed it from 555-555-5555 to read, 555-5566-5565. This is my landline number used for connecting to the internet as well. Hope to hear from you soon." Jim.

Eventually, Henan logged onto messenger; coming online just before noon my time. I initiate the conversation.

"Hello Henan," I said.

"Hello," Henan replies. "I was just writing your new number down on my notepad." Something needed my immediate attention so I told Henan. "Please hold on a few minutes Henan."

Henan must have received my last transmission too late because she immediately said. "How are you?" When I came back and read her message, I typed another message.

"Okay, I need to cancel my TV service right now. I have customer service on the phone."

"Okay dear," Henan acknowledged.

When I returned, I said. "Alright Henan, I can chat for a while and then I have to go downtown. So did you get my instant message from messenger?" I asked.

Henan responded eagerly. "Yes I did love, that is how I got your new phone number."

"Yes, splendid, thanks," grateful she had received my last transmission. My gratefulness will be known very shortly. But I wanted to know if Henan clearly understood the message.

"It is my pleasure, honey." She is apparently grateful that I thought enough of her to give out my personal landline number. I do not know where this "honey business" is coming from suddenly, but since she is addressing me as honey, I may as well play the game.

"So you know my situation, Honey?" Making sure Henan understood me completely.

Henan then replied. "You mean about going into town and coming back later?"

"Yes," I replied, playing coy.

"I do love," Henan stated.

As soon as Henan finished acknowledging my plans, I then asked Henan the question that I have been waiting to ask since our previous conversation. This would become a common theme; "cross-examination".

"Where were you last night?" I asked.

Henan responded without hesitating. "I had a serious headache, but it is good now."

As the friendship developed in the weeks that followed, it would become standard practice for Henan to invent excuses' about missing our agreed upon chat and log-in times. Henan continued to be unreliable when logging online with Yahoo Messenger, or in some cases, she didn't bother logging on at all. Towards the end of April, Henan's actions were becoming more questionable. By this time, I felt I had been scammed. Her behavior was the catalyst that resulted in a chess game and I was going to play the game with her; only Henan didn't know it immediately. Since our friendship was in its early stages the first move in this game of chess was the "sweet-talk," language to keep her engaged so as not to jeopardize what has now become a crusade of getting at the truth.

I had a worthy cause to tell Henan, based on a previous question that I asked concerning her whereabouts the evening before, so I told Henan. "I guess we're going to have a serious talk later."

Henan acting as if everything was normal said. "Okay sweetheart, I will be waiting for you then," she replied.

However, I had a different agenda as I answered. "That is unless you have another commitment again tonight," I said sarcastically without her realizing the remark was meant to be confrontational.

Finally, it dawned on Henan what I had said as she replied with a question of her own. "What do you mean honey?"

Keeping Henan in the dark, I responded by replying. "So you will give me a little of your time tonight sweetheart?"

"Yes, honey, what time will you want me to be on for you?" Henan said, conceding perhaps that our discussion would be on my terms.

"Thanks, I do not wish to keep you from anything important." Dropping another subtle hint. "You know plenty of stuff." However, Henan did not pick up on this either, as she returned her reply.

"Oh no, I don't have anything important to do other than to be with you."

"We will talk about that tonight, I should be back about 4:00 P.M. my time, Okay?"

Henan acknowledges again answering, "Okay honey."

"What are you going to do about the computer Henan?" I inquired.

According to Henan, the computer arrived in the capital city of Accra along with the speakers, etc., but it was retained by customs authorities. Henan alleges customs officials told her there were custom charges due on the packages before she could claim the merchandise.

Henan communicated to me she had insufficient funds available, explaining. "Right now I do not have enough money. Otherwise, I would go there and claim them."

Curiosity, the path of least resistance, in this case, I wanted to know what the charges were. "So how much do they want?" (Customs in Ghana)

"The customs fees totaled $175.00," Henan said. How she derived at this figure is only presumptuous. The amount was excessive based on what I paid to have the packages shipped to her. Pooh, I was irate.

"You must be kidding! I might just as well have sent you the money to buy a new computer," I said in disgust. However, I thought it best not to belabor the point. It was in my best interest to allow the dust to settle until I get over the shock.

When we finally agreed in consortium to appear on live video feed for the first time, I could not help but be awestruck by Henan's beauty and free spirit. She could turn heads this was a given. She was graceful, proper, and appeared content, despite what Henan described as squalid living conditions. She was giddy and all smiles. Putting on quite the theatrical performance on my behalf.

She made the comment on how handsome I looked. I knew better. Age and thinning hair only amounted to flattery, so I dismissed it as "putts." However, I told Henan I felt she could be a model if she ever decided to pursue that career choice. Never-the-less, I informed Henan that in my opinion, the most important aspect of a person's character resided inside of them, in the heart.

"The heart and soul were the most important," I told Henan. Every time the video feed froze, I informed Henan (like she needed to be told) who would then take five- minutes to reboot, only to have the process repeat itself one or two-minutes later.

"Can you see me now? I'm moving now…Aren't I?" Henan would say, looking for validation.

"Yes Henan, I see you moving in your chair," I said. However, I was getting anxious as to when it would freeze again because after you see it happen over and over, you begin to see a pattern develop where you could predict within seconds when it would freeze again. And wouldn't you know, a few minutes later almost to the second, the screen froze. The computer she was using was in black and white … no color … just a plain Jane computer like the one's we used to learn with in college. At least this is the impression she wanted the victims to believe.

"Henan, you froze on me again," she would be told. I was beginning to sound like a parrot.

181

"Darn this computer, it is such an old computer. It hardly ever works the way it should, and I need it for my homework." Henan would say in frustration. I knew what she was hinting. She was suggesting another hand-out so she could travel to Acura and retrieve the packages from customs.

Finally tiring of her charade, I asked. "Henan, do you have an address where the money can be sent so you can claim the packages from customs?"

"Yes," Henan answered quickly. She wasted little time typing her address down for me to copy. Henan Asante, P.O. Box 14781. Adum Kumasi, Ghana. Phone, +2332267820517.

The money was wired to Henan, based on the information she provided. I included some extra money to defray additional costs for the alleged customs fee charges and travel expenses. I knew with a degree of certainty that I was caught between a rock and a hard place." Now it became a battle of wits. If I ever had hopes of determining her true identity, I would have to dole out funds on occasion to keep her on the field of play.

I had begun to hear the sound of alarm bells going off in my head when Henan sent a picture via email showing her posing in a luxurious hotel swimming pool in Kumasi. Henan had said her best friend's father had absorbed the cost of the wedding for everyone who allegedly attended his daughter's wedding. I might have believed her about the wedding except that if it happened as Henan said, you would have seen guests hanging around the pool, especially on a sunny day. However, there wasn't a soul around except Henan and whoever was taking the photograph.

"I have to leave and go downtown now Henan, so I can wire you the money from Western Union."

"Okay love, hope to be with you when you get back," Henan said.

I replied without much fanfare. "See you later then darling."

By now, Henan is on cloud nine. She accomplished what she set out to do, steal money from another victim's wallet. In a lighthearted gesture that came on the wings of empty words, Henan declares. "Good, you are my one and only, take good care."

Although my wallet took a hit, I now became the hunter rather than the hunted. It would not be long now, and I would be taken from my comfortable surroundings and catapulted into the face of the darkest chasm of the abyss, and into another dimension of a world cluttered with immorality and pure evil.

When I finished my business, I went home and logged online. It was four in the afternoon, the agreed time we were to meet and chat.

"Ding."

"I'm here now hon," I said.

"I was sitting at the computer staring at a blank screen for about an hour, and still no Henan. True to her nature, after waiting over an hour I thought best we caulk this appointment up as another no show! This didn't sit well with me. Henan had me reeling on my heels, casting doubt as to whether or not I had done the right thing. Did she take the money and run? If she did, then I had been duped before I ever got started. Therefore, I was limited to one single option, so I typed on messenger, "I'm gone!" These antics by Henan only confirmed my suspicion that she wasn't playing by any rules except her own.

The money for the alleged customs fees was wire transferred from Western Union in Braxton, on May 3, 2013. Henan supposedly picked up the money at the address given to me. I'm now suspecting it was a mule who actually claimed the money for her or them as the case may be.

Before she left for Acura to retrieve the packages from customs, Henan told me she would be spending the night in Accra with a friend. She justified the overnight stay because of the distance from Kumasi to Accra by bus and bad road conditions. This meant she would be missing two days of school. There were just too many small details I could not quite wrap my arms around. So, without much drama, the eyes became attentive to her words. There was a story here, and it needed a voice to carry the message to whoever had ears to hear.

I was now entering the deep dark underworld of live cams and fraud. Was I the only layperson to uncover and unravel these swindler's identities, location, and addresses? Probably not. Eventually, the research would reveal this journey as a two-party operation that involved other siblings, maiden names, national origin, and other vital information. It would prove to be a formidable undertaking, involving over a year's worth of intelligence gathering and data research. It had all the underpinnings of suspense, twists, turns, disgust, disappointments, and intrigue.

Henan was kept in the dark until the very end involving my secret research and intelligence gathering objectives. I was role-playing. It was effortless to play the "dumb fool" role because I carried that label with me most of my life anyway. It didn't require remedial training because I was intellectually inferior. And, I must admit, I was computer illiterate. I had to become my own teacher. Henan was 31-years-old. At least, this is what I was told by Henan. You may think that the author was passionate about this newfound friendship and where it would eventually lead the author. However, nothing could be further from the truth.

I am here to say categorically that I refute this insinuation. It is where heart and soul reside in man. If you see evil for what it is, and a mindset that upon seeing nakedness can resist being tempted by nudity, then one can be very effective in executing the objective. While Henan insisted on feeding me tidbits of fool's brew, I continued looking for evidence that would call into question her truthfulness. Finally, convinced Henan was not the person she claimed to be, I would confront her after she allegedly returned from Accra. I went to applications such as Facebook, Linked-In, YouTube, Myspace, dating sites, adult industry sites, and others, to see if I could connect her aliases' with any of these social network sites.

I was not going to be deterred by this recent setback. We are only in the early stages of determining this mystery woman's identity. That is if Henan did not take the money and run. Another red flag that seemed out of place was a photograph of Henan that she sent through email showing her casually sitting in a high-end nightclub with a large drink in hand dressed in the same negligee she had sent for the month of April, holding a rose up to her nostrils.

However, what distinguished this photo from the first one she sent, was the fur coat she wore covering her negligee. The first thing that struck me as being out of sorts was the fact Henan was wearing this fur coat in Ghana dressed in a nightgown with no other patrons around, sipping a refreshment. Who, I wondered, sits in a public establishment in a negligee? This photo and the poolside photo would ordinarily have a substantial volume of vacationer's milling around, but other patrons were absent in the photographs.

Cognition and insight already produced the answer, and I was about to put Henan under the microscope. Again, this is what I meant when I told Henan we needed to have a serious talk. There were far too many indicators that I felt pointed in the direction of the adult entertainment industry, scamming or both. So it is not just the swindling we are dealing with, but now the adult entertainment industry as well.

This was a hornet's nest filled with busy worker bees'. African bees at that. How brazen can you get? What dexterous craftiness. If this reveals what I believe it will, I have to tip my hat and acknowledge their imagination. To conceive, such an operation is in some respects ingenious. Although I do not take fraud lightly, I thought to myself. What better way to keep law enforcement at arm's length than by establishing your own website featuring adult entertainment! This wouldn't draw attention to their major bread-winning activity marked by fraud. Pornography would likely keep covert and undercover surveillance on illegal activity from the watchful eye of law enforcement agencies. And then take it a step further by locating away from the primary hub of a large city like New York into an isolated piece of property surrounded by a body of water. Very crafty, I should think.

On May 5, 2013, Henan logged onto Yahoo Messenger after allegedly returning from Accra with the two packages containing the computer, speakers, and miscellaneous hardware. Henan kept her line open waiting until I had logged online. Henan was still unaware I was doing behind-the-scenes research on my own using some of our previous conversations that were gathered to run Goggle search in which to prove or disprove the validity of her statements. I had to maintain this cool persona if I expected to continue with "forward thinking … Planning, and anticipating her next move.

Henan. "Ding, ding."

"Hello? Darling, are you there?" Henan inquired.

"Hello sweetheart, I just logged on."

"How are you doing, what did you do today?" Henan inquired as if it truly mattered how I would answer this question.

I was itching to get to relevant and significant issues I unearthed while profiling Henan. However, I waited patiently. So I began the conversation by saying. "I'm doing great. I was out by the pool soaking up some sun."

Henan kept it simple, as she replied. "Okay, that is good."

Unable to contain myself any longer, I decided to go directly into the heart of the discussion. I begin with a precise question that appeared harmless at the onset. Furthermore, Henan had no clue that I was about to open the envelope of a deceiver. Depending on her response, I will either let it rest or continue the line of questioning and begin to interrogate her creditability.

"How about you Henan, what did you do today; school?" Phrasing the question to give the appearance, it was just a routine inquiry.

"Yes, a very long day today. We had another examination. I will be making me some dinner soon, but first I want to talk to you." Henan said.

Ignoring her response, I decided to pose the big question, knowing all along what her response would be. "You think we can video chat for a while? I want to see that prominent; signature smile." Henan didn't realize this was a lead question that would determine how future questions would be framed.

"Not tonight honey, the electricity is out again," Henan replied without hesitation.

There were more times than memory can recollect, where Henan used power as an excuse to avoid showing herself on video chat. When we were not dealing with power outages, then torrential rains were the culprit.

"Interference, she would say." Power outages were the "big bad bogey man." One never knew the unpredictability of outages because control of video chat belonged to Henan. She had absolute control. This was her baby, embracing it to the end as if her very life depended on her decision.

"Isn't power outages unsafe for you when that happens at night?" I inquired as if I was actually concerned.

Henan gave reassurance by saying. "No, it is safe. I am in a safe protected place here."

"What do you do for light when the electricity goes out sweetheart?" As if I didn't know what her answer was going to be again before she even responded to the question.

"I have candles and kerosene lanterns in the house," Henan tells me.

"That's a good thing to have. I feel better now." I told her even though I believed she was lying.

"Thank you, darling," she said attempting to flatter my ego.

"Say Henan, I have to ask you a question," I commented to her. "Remember those two photos' you sent me? The one where you are in a red negligee holding a rose to your nose, and in the other photo, you are sitting on a stool at a nightclub with a refreshment. You were wearing a fur coat draped over your shoulders, and underneath the coat was that same negligee …The third photograph you sent by email, remember?"

Henan would voice her displeasure with the question. Henan could be combative and indifferent especially when she had to give an account of her actions and truthfulness.

"Yeah, right! So? What, you didn't like those pictures of me?" She responded in a defensive posture.

Playing possum, I stated. "No honey it isn't that so much; they are very lovely photos, a bit revealing though, I should think." I informed her.

"Thanks, darling." Henan was delighted I had complimented her, but I had another agenda. So far, Henan is completely in the dark about where I'm going with these questions.

Giving a polite acknowledgment I continue moving forward with my line of questioning. "Henan, I need to ask a few questions about those photos if you don't mind," hinting. "They are out of character based on what you told me earlier about your purpose for being in Ghana, wasn't it to attend nursing school?"

Henan fires back. "What is it you want to know? They are just photos, honey." Henan firmly stated as she begins to show signs of impatience with me.

"This is the point dear. First, whom is the person taking the pictures? Second, what are you doing out in a fancy nightclub wearing the same negligee with a fur coat draped over your shoulders drinking who knows what?" Then I pondered how a young woman going to nursing school can afford a fur coat, but cannot afford to buy a computer?" This was fair game to ask whether she was intimidated or receptive to the questioning.

"Oh, that!" Henan said. "I do some modeling part-time, but it does not pay much money though," Henan concluded, as she attempted to justify and pacify me with her response.

Surprise, surprise I thought. "When did you begin modeling darling?" I asked innocently.

Henan does not realize it, but she is about to go into free fall. The slippery slope is getting slicker by the minute, as she attempts to downplay the photos.

"Henan, it was early in the morning, around 2:00 A.M. would you agree?" Continuing as I remark. "So you telling me you are roaming the streets of Kumasi at 2:00 A.M. During the heat of the summer wearing a fur coat, and underneath that coat is a flimsy negligee. Isn't that asking for trouble?" I insisted on knowing.

Henan, as expected, returned a curt response to my inquiries, as she replied. "No! I took a taxicab."

I was not about to allow Henan off so easily, saying. "Still, Henan, this is really not acceptable. This is not something respectable women do; wearing a negligee underneath a fur coat in a country like Ghana in the early hours of the morning. It doesn't make sense. At best, it shows poor judgment."

"I was with my friend Jenny; she also does modeling," Henan informs me. Not realizing she is digging a deeper grave for herself.

"I really do not know how a person can do modeling. Complete their studies for graduation, and socialize with friends at all hours of the day. When I add two plus two Henan, it doesn't add up to four," applying some pressure on Henan. "Where did you buy that expensive fur coat?" My objective, to put her on the spot and come clean.

Henan had a ready response to my question, as she replies. "My Mom bought the coat for me before I came to Ghana."

"Well Henan, if your Mom has been sending you less money because she is recovering from her recent surgery, is homebound, and currently unemployed, and now you are telling me you work part-time as a model that does not pay well, it gives the impression something is out of sync."

Continuing I add. "Then I see you wearing this fur coat in the middle of summer …Do you see where I'm going with this darling?"

"No. I don't understand what you are talking about Jim." Henan replies. I assume she's beginning to sense where I'm going with these questions.

"Henan, never mind, you understand. You just refuse to acknowledge and respond truthfully to my questions." Venting my frustration and disappointment with her.

Henan decides she is tired of my questions and hints it is time to go. "Jim sweetheart, I must log off now. I have homework that needs to be done before I go to bed."

"Okay, I will catch you later sweetheart," I replied.

More questions were in the pipeline that needed answers, but I did not want to anger her to the point where she would sever ties just yet. I decided I would remand further questioning at another date. Always another day!

"Yes dear, I love you, and will talk to you again," Henan said.

I closed the conversation pleased with what I had learned during this exchange even though it amounted to table scraps of questionable truths.

"All right darling, have a great day tomorrow. Goodnight."

"Goodnight sweetheart," Henan said in closing.

There was no doubt Henan was spewing lies. I gave her one end of the rope, and she took hold. All she has to do now is gather in enough rope where she will have just enough to get entangled in it. The longer you keep someone engaged in conversation, the more likely they are to trip themselves up in the process. Especially when suppressing the truth while living in darkness, rather than the light. I didn't particularly fancy living a life in the abyss for as long as I did, yet if I had counted it as all loss, running from it, then truth and light would be foreshadowed by darkness and the truth forever hidden from scrutiny in the public's eye.

Humankind creates their own abyss whether they want to acknowledge it or not. Adultery, pride, greed, and idol worshiping are the four primary obstacles humankind faces today in this author's opinion. However, it does not matter whether it is one or ten sins committed in violation of the commandments. "If you transgress against one law, you have sinned against them all," Jesus said.

I am almost convinced Henan has partners in this crime of fraud. I begin to strategize. I need to string Henan along until I have reliable evidence; proof positive the research will implicate other folks who swindle victims. But this isn't just me, but perhaps hundreds if not thousands of victims like me over a span alleged to be thirteen years. I have never embarked on anything quite like this. No matter the count. One victim is one victim too many.

I have no regrets, as it has shown the true nature and condition of humankind's heart. My prey would involve live webcams, scams, and college youth behaving badly. All residing in the abyss. Henan Asante would become the hunted …Hounded … Targeted. This would prove to be a challenge worth pursuing. My personal crusade with the Lord's guidance in a quest to bring this evil to the forefront through callous abuse of the internet by pimps in suits. Pushing their sick perversion on society. Scammer's who steal from victims without remorse or conscience while thumbing their noses' at law enforcement officials. And on the tail end of the spectrum, we write about college youth behaving badly. Another of society's blemishes of immorality, arrogance, pride, and abominations.

I would now be forced to engage Henan on her terms. She decided when it was appropriate to chat and when to disappear when the conversation did not go the way she hoped it would play itself out. I was hoping that until I could navigate around the internet and learn the technical features of the computer through intelligence gathering, then I should consider this crusade more than blessed.

To be successful, I need Henan to be cooperative and willing to hang around. I desperately need names that up until now have been behind the scenes; faceless unknowns at the present. Therefore, faces and names needed ferreting out on these unknowns. I wanted to play Henan's own clever "scams." I was convinced Henan was not the only crook. Therefore, I plunged feet-first into the abyss. Remaining in darkness for over a year. This undertaking to reveal their deceptive practices was more complex and more sophisticated than I had once imagined.

"Fool me once, it is on me! Fool me twice, shame on me! Fool me three time's, now you're dealing with me!" Sometimes I get an overwhelming feeling in my members that I have been given the gift of a sixth sense; as I feel the Lord's hand guiding me in this sojourn. I courted these feelings when they overtook me as blessings. There were just too many opportunities and circumstances that opened doors for me that I could not rationally explain other than someone interceding on my behalf.

I was convinced at this point, based on the sketchy information Henan had already voluntarily leaked to me, that a day would come when I would be able to say. "Gotcha!" Henan would prove to be a most formidable and evasive opponent. Yet, not to worry, she would have plenty of missteps along the way. I'm not one who should be talking about missteps. Not when I had more than my share of conniption fits navigating the computer applications.

When searching the adult entertainment sites (entertainment used in this context is a misnomer. There is no intrinsic value in porn.), searching for Henan was proving challenging in itself. Success seemed to elude the author for a time because of the endless porn sites that appeared on the internet. This would be similar to looking for the proverbial needle in a haystack. Henan would have to volunteer some help. Patience was needed waiting for Henan's tongue to babble something pertinent that would reveal some clues. Perhaps even wait for a weak moment during one of our chat sessions. We will revisit the discussion about her mother and father that Henan and I had briefly covered in a previous chapter. The questions had a distinctive flavor about family history. After all, this is where the first red flag reared its ugly head. Especially when Henan claimed her mother was Swedish-born, and her father a Ghana Citizen.

When Henan joined me on Yahoo Messenger, there were inquiries about her ethnicity, family history, and school. I needed personal information and prayed she would not skirt the issue. The following day we were on Yahoo Messenger again. As events are measured in time and spaces of time, the questions became more direct when Henan appeared on messenger so I could decipher truth from the lie.

"Henan," I began. "What is the name of the University you attend again?" I asked soon after she came online after logging onto messenger.

"Nursing Training College in Kumasi," Henan replied.

"How far do you have to travel to get to school?"

"Maybe five or seven miles, I guess," Henan responded.

Since Henan admitted she had no means of transportation, Henan was asked. "How do you get to school?"

"Sometimes friends pick me up, and sometimes I take the bus," She stated.

"How many courses are you taking this semester?" There was a need to know. If for any other reason than to see if the courses she had registered for squared with her nursing degree.

"Biology, Anatomy, general subjects like writing, English, those type of course's," Henan answered with confidence.

The next question asked of Henan was necessary so that I could check Google search after we got off chat to validate the information. "Could you give me the name of one of your professors at the University?"

"Just a minute please," Henan said politely. Sitting and waiting five minutes before Henan returned had become an ordeal in itself. There I sat wondering why she needed to excuse herself so quickly without giving me a reason. This would be another red flag. "Hum, I believe Henan went to Google search during that five-minute delay to search for a professor's name."

"Professor Kofi Anyidodoe is one," Henan informed me immediately after returning.

"Where was that picture of you in the hotel swimming pool taken?" I asked. This would also need verification once we went offline. Henan new immediately where the location of the photograph was taken.

"That's the "Golden Tulip Hotel" in Ghana, and it's a very expensive place," Henan claimed.

"What is the reason you didn't go to school in Sweden where your mother lives," I asked. There was skepticism and I was searching for an honest answer.

Henan informs me there is another relative in Ghana as we were speaking. "I have an Aunt in Ghana that works as a Missionary, so I came with her," Henan remarks.

"How come you didn't take a leave of absence when your mother had her surgery?"

"My mother wanted me to stay in school and finish." Henan said without providing further details.

"Why? Why? Why?" Henan was not too fond of being at the receiving end of my probing questions. Whatever intelligence Henan provided was assessed, and when found to be relevant this information was researched using Goggle search, with the expectations of offering something of value that would validate Henan's answers to my questions. The only issue left open related to her mother and the Golden Tulip Hotel.

Could it be that Henan had indeed spent time with her husband; if married, and they spent their honeymoon in Ghana? And while there, they hired mules to retrieve wire transfers of money and other merchandise sent to that country. After all, everything Henan requested, she insisted that it all go to Ghana. It is plausible, based on information discovered later during further questioning. Passport verification would be a good starting point. Many times Henan was caught wavering on her truthfulness involving times, places, and events.

The first breakthrough came when I asked Henan on April 28 if her mother had an email address. Henan said she indeed had her mother's email address. I informed Henan that I wanted to correspond with her mother to lend encouragement, and support during her recovery from surgery. This would be an opportune time for me to introduce myself to her. Henan, perhaps thinking this was a simple request, went ahead and passed on her mother's email address. Henan provided her mother's address as *jahniquesvennson301@yahoo.com*.

It wouldn't take long to realize this was another fabrication. Time was well spent familiarizing myself with the culture and landscape of Sweden, and then it took an hour to draft and type the email to a fictitious mother. After writing two emails to her Mom, I intentionally made a decision to blindside Henan; putting her on the defense the next time we were on messenger chatting.

When Henan came online, I said. "Henan, did you know I had written two emails and forwarded them to your mother?" She wrote back once … as you know. I was able to trace that email, and it originated right here in the United States, not Sweden." It came from Yahoo out in Sunnyvale, CA. Even the IP was registered in the U.S.,not Sweden Henan," I said.

This was brought to Henan's attention to see if it would prompt a reaction or comment from her. But she remained mute, unwilling to commit one way or the other. After waiting a minute for a reply from my inquiry, I was convinced Henan was not going to volunteer any information about the email controversy, so I moved onto the next question.

"Henan, why is your last name Asante rather than Svennson?"

Time was wasted waiting for an answer to this question as well. However, Henan remained quiet … Speechless. No response was forthcoming from her lips. Henan was also asked again about the bathing suit photograph she sent me, where she was seen posing at the end of the pool. The attire itself spoke volumes about the inappropriateness of Henan's swimwear. The backdrop Henan said then, was the Golden Tulip Hotel where she was allegedly invited to attend her girl friend's wedding ceremony. This had all the earmarks of a pool loaded with the stench of rotting fish.

Again, I challenged Henan with the same question. "Where was that picture of you posing in that skimpy two-piece bathing suit taken darling?"

Finally, Henan responds. "Oh, that picture," she said. "That was taken at a hotel in Ghana. You remember me telling you, Golden Tulip, right?" Henan finally decided this question was non-threatening so she broke her silence, at least for now.

"Why would you stay at the hotel when you live in Kumasi? Besides darling, if the wedding were held there I could not help but notice that there was no one else poolside, it was entirely void of hotel guests."

Henan was stumped again. "I can't answer that. I'm not sure. What is the big deal? Why are you asking so many questions? Don't you believe me when I tell you?" Henan said with indifference.

"Here's the thing Henan, I countered. "Two plus two is not adding up to four. For some reason, I only get three when I use addition, two plus two."

Henan, puzzled by the use of my math formula, inquired. "I do not understand what you mean sweetheart."

Back to the chalkboard to unravel the math problem for Henan, as I attempt to explain to her why one number was always missing to authenticate the solution to the problem.

"Henan, when two-plus-two does not equal the number four it tells me the wrong number is missing when addition and subtraction are used in a math problem. So, every time I try to add two and two it always reads less than four. Some of the information you give me are either wrong or missing. Therefore, the math is in error," I declared.

"But I told you Jim darling," Henan insisted.

"No Henan, some of the questions you completely avoided answering. When you did give the answer, the details were sketchy, incomplete, or staggered. This is not the first time this has happened." Continuing, I said. "There were other times when you told me something which you thought would appease me; stories Henan, which had no merit. This I know Henan because I always verify the information you tickle my ears with to the beat of another drum."

Fearful the explanation may have been too direct in communicating my observations to Henan; the dread of severing this friendship made me concerned that I may have to deploy damage control. I did not want to be on the outside looking in. However, sometimes we must leave our comfort zone to accomplish what needs to be done.

Trying to justify herself Henan said. "Why would I not tell you the truth honey?"

"That is for you to say, honey. I have been more than kind and generous to you. I have always been a straight shooter in this friendship. Therefore, I think you need to come spot-on clean with me, or we can end this friendship right now." (A bluff was in the offering. It was a calculated risk I had to take.)

"You know Henan, sometimes when someone asks a question, they already have a pretty good idea of what the person's answer is going to be before that person even responds to the question. The questions are sequenced and framed in such a way as to get at the truth. So it is with you Henan darling."

"Why are you doing this to me then?" She asked.

Repeating for the third time, I again went into a full blown litany to justify my questions. "Because Henan honey, two-plus-two has never equaled four like it should in the math problem, that's why. You have been misrepresenting yourself with the answers you have been giving me. You have been evasive for the most part, and untruthful. Your motives have become very suspicious Henan. There has not been anything you have said about your life that is truthful." Adding… "If you want us to remain friend's honey, you are going to have to be forthcoming and honest."

As though Henan was about to succumb to a panic or anxiety attack she asked. "What do you want me to do?"

"Tell the truth. Just tell me the truth darling. It is known as redeeming yourself from all the deceit and misinformation you have been feeding me to the full during these chat sessions."

The objective was to frustrate and hopefully secure usable information from Henan by continuing a relentless assault; delivering one question after another and trust, she would bend but not break. Leaving me before I am able to complete my mission was always uppermost on my mind. If she did, all efforts would be in vain. I believe one of the most necessary signatures I applied to keep Henan around was flattery. Henan loved to hear praise's like "princess" and "sweetheart" showered upon her.

There was a high probability Henan was also involved in the adult entertainment industry, (secondary) and fraud (primary). However, at this time, there wasn't any concrete evidence to connect Henan to either organization. It was pure speculation… Suspicion…No hard evidence. Therefore, efforts had to be employed and unleashed in the arsenal of discovery to uncover that which is hidden in darkness and bring it into the light. Patience would prove to be long-suffering.

The floodgates of the abyss would unleash a whirlwind of wickedness beyond the scope of decency and immorality that society should not be exposed to in this lifetime. This phenomenon I compared to as in the days of antiquity involving the cities of Sodom and Gomorrah; history revisited. There is all manner of wickedness, depravity, corruption, and lewdness.

While forsaking my character instead of obtaining information under the assumed role as a theatrical performer expressing affection towards an adversary, then, so it shall be. Whatever it took within the purview of the law to see this through, then time is justified to accomplish this end. Henan had fooled the author twice. Now it would be showtime for the little woman. While we were chatting one day, a matter of a technical nature was asked of Henan about my computer skills.

"Henan," I asked. "Do you think I am knowledgeable enough in computers to discover your true identity?" Henan was adamant in her assessment of the author's technical abilities, which I welcomed gladly for I was seeking a challenge.

"No," Henan explicitly stated. "It would take you too long to find me, she said. You have a pretty good understanding of how computers and the internet work, but you have much to learn yet."

"Princess, that view was very helpful because if it does anything, it will make me more determined," I agreed joyfully. "I have nothing but time sweetheart. Sooner or later I will find you, so you might just as well tell me now," I said speaking realistically. In presenting this ultimatum, Henan was made aware of my intentions.

"With the relentless energy of a pit bull, once I have you in my site, I will never let go of my grip on you until I know I have divided and conquered. As such, so it shall be with you Henan. Therefore, I'm asking you politely to give me some cooperation now and make it easier on everyone." Thus came the battle cry from a determined warrior, to a computer savvy scammer.

"Okay, okay," Henan conceded after I kept badgering her about her model name she uses on the internet. "I am a webcam model that is all. I'm not a scammer as you think."

"Alright then, what is the name you use?" Everything hinged on this one question Henan needed to answer truthfully. Extending a carrot stick to obtain an honest answer, Henan was reassured I would not come to her room. I even used "sweetheart" to nudge her into revealing her identity. Then to sweeten the offer; "Honey" was mentioned as a goodwill gesture. "You know Henan honey, you are like a daughter to me, and I would never betray your trust sweetheart."

"If I tell you, will you still chat with me?" Henan asked candidly.

Using words of affection must be paying dividends as I replied. "Of course, we will continue to chat darling." Two can play this game I thought, but caution must not be readily cast into the wind.

"Okay," Henan replied. My model name is Carnal Carrie," came her helpful answer.

Carnal. Carnal! Now if this isn't appropriate, but very distasteful. Did Henan even understand what this word engenders? If she does, I wonder why she would continue using it. Associating Carnal with pornography was on target.

Henan was panicky as she types. "Honey, honey," she said. "Are you still there?"

Answering Henan's distress call, I answered. "Yes, sweetheart I am still here. I had to take a little break away from the computer for a minute."

Although Henan freely volunteered her model name, and conceded she was a porn model; for reasons that remain unclear, I felt Henan was still residing in Ghana. I didn't have anything to the contrary and Henan didn't volunteer any additional information at this time. Therefore, the chess match continued with more questions.

"Henan Sweetheart, exactly how did you get yourself into the adult entertainment business," I inquired.

Henan hesitated for some time before explaining in detail how she allegedly arrived in Ghana. Henan came from Poland, her homeland. Shortly after graduating from high school, Henan was introduced to a photographer who was from Romania by one of her closest and trusted friends. When he laid eyes on Henan, he could not stop showering her with esteemed admiration. He told Henan she had a face that was very photogenic. When her friend left, leaving Henan alone, the man politely asked Henan if he could schedule a session with her later.

At first, Henan hesitated, but when the man offered her a large sum of money and flashed it before her eyes', Henan could not resist. A date and time had been set for the next meeting. Henan thought that if her friend knew him, he would not pose any danger or harm to her. Otherwise, why would her friend introduce her to him?

This is Henan's version and an account of their alleged photo session. The photo session went without incident. However, the Romanian wanted another session with Henan, and Henan accepted the offer since the first meeting went well and the money was good. During their follow-up session, the photographer had arranged for them to meet at a hotel as before. Once Henan arrived at the hotel with her friend in tow, the man led them up to a room with a bed and chair for furniture. It was innocent enough at the start of the photo session, but then the man began to insist Henan pose with fewer clothes.

Using additional money as an incentive, Henan first confided in her friend, not realizing her friend was an accomplice in this rogue scheme to entrap and enslave women in the human sex slave industry. Henan went along with the friends prodding to disrobe in a manner that looked enticing but tasteful and modest. The session went well. Another meeting was scheduled; only this time, Henan would meet the man without her friend. Perhaps she felt secure since he didn't make any advances.

The following session was identical to the last in accommodations and setting. Except this time, instead of Henan and the photographer, there appeared another man in the room with them. The stranger had a video camera and the photographer still had his camera. The photographer politely asked Henan to sit on the bed. The photographer told Henan they wished to interview her and wanted it videotaped. After all, he assured Henan, she had the potential of becoming a super model.

Now, with the video camera rolling, the photographer asked Henan innocuous questions at first. However, when he felt Henan was comfortable enough, he methodically went about the business of employing his insidious plot to disrobe her. The photographer was a horrible man at that. Grimy, unshaven, unkempt; wearing oversized baggy pants, and carry a load of lard around his mid-section.

"Do you have a boyfriend?" He inquired as the other man stood in the background videotaping.

"Yes, I do. He is a kind gentleman. We are going to marry someday;" Henan would declare in her Polish dialect.

"You are wearing a very cute outfit today. It looks good on you. You wear brassiere underneath your blouse?" He asked.

Henan stunned for a brief moment replied. "Ahhhhh, no. No bra today."

The Romanian continued. "How about panties, you wear any panties today, or keep off as well?"

Henan snapped back after hearing enough. "Your questions are getting too personal!"

That did not faze the photographer, he had an agenda of his own mapped out and ready to execute, so he kept on with the personal questions.

"What about your boyfriend, does he like when you do not wear bra and panties?" The man continued prodding.

"Of course, he likes to see me sometimes with nothing underneath," Henan quipped nervously.

"Henan, do you like model work? Do you want to be famous Henan? We can make this happen for you;" as the photographer methodically prods her for the unexpected carnage to come.

"What kind of model work?" Henan asked inquisitively.

"Maybe, say, just still photographs. Some with clothes on, maybe little-revealing poses here and there. It is good money Henan," he declared. Trying to get Henan to commit; as he continues baiting her.

Henan asked. "How much money does a model earn?"

He replied. "Maybe two hundred American dollars every time we take pictures."

"I don't know about this," Henan said. "I must have time to think about it."

The photographer decides to make his advance on Henan saying. "Henan, why don't you take your blouse off now so we can see? Maybe we will offer more money if you do that. You are nervous Henan, just take your time," he said with a smirk.

With fear and trembling noticeable in her body language, Henan hesitates and then asked. "You want just the blouse off?"

"Yes Henan, just your blouse. We want to get a nice picture of your upper torso," the photographer stated plainly.

Henan began nervously unbuttoning her blouse, fumbling with the buttons as it seemed like an eternity to him as he started to show signs of impatience waiting for Henan to finish disrobing. She was going to extremes as her fingers began trembling before she was able to finish. Once the blouse was unbuttoned, Henan sat on the bed with the shirt still on but slightly opened.

"Okay," Henan said, "it's unbuttoned."

The photographer walked the few steps to the bed where Henan was sitting and remarked. "Oh, but you have to remove the blouse completely so we can have a good look. Here Henan, I will help you."

Gradually, purposefully, he began to remove Henan's blouse while simultaneously his eyes' gazed at her torso. No longer content with his first demand, he then continued coaxing Henan into removing her dress. Reluctantly, out of fear for her safety, Henan pulled her dress down, prompting another reaction from the photographer, as he made sexual overtures to Henan's anatomy. Goading her like this was all an innocent fun game to him.

From this point forward, she was shoved onto the bed traumatized, as the photographer began raping her. He was forcing himself on her with little regard for her tears. "It was savage and brutal, Henan said." As the abuse continued unabated, the man with the video camera was capturing the entire abusive scene. He apparently had no desire to end this relentless assault on Henan. It was degrading and humiliating as the photographer forged ahead having his way for forty minutes.

Meanwhile, Henan could hardly contain herself from his onslaught, screaming uncontrollably, struggling to get out from underneath his powerful grip on her. "Stop ... Stop ... Stop!" Henan screamed, but the man would not let go. He just kept on and on. "It was painful. I was bleeding something terrible. He was a monster," Henan testified.

After he had finished his diabolical deed, the photographer remarked to Henan. "This was consensual sex, so you cannot report us to the police because you willingly unbuttoned your blouse and pulled down your skirt," the photographer boasted gleefully. "It is all on tape you see," he declared. Then added. "We know where you live. We also know who your friend is and where he lives." Then using blackmail as security, he said. "Should you have foolish idea to run, we will hurt your family, boyfriend, or anyone who is close to you," the photographer threatened. Then, adding salt to her wounds he raved. "Run, we will find you. By the time we are finished with you, you will wish for death," he warned Henan, shouting in her face.

"I had no choice and no way out Jim. I just gave in to them. It has been torture ever since." Henan concluded.

"Who gave you the name Henan?" I asked. "Where did the name Henan come from?"

"They gave me the name Henan to use as an email address," Henan claimed.

"So, how did you end up in Ghana of all places?" I inquired.

"Well, these two men told me to go tell my Mom, Dad, and boyfriend that I've been hired as a model, and they are taking me to the United Kingdom for location photographs. I was told to say no more than what they told me to say." Henan said. "They said they would get my passport and also said they would pay enough money." Henan went on to explain. "They threaten me if I told anyone what happened in the hotel room, so I stayed quiet," She concluded.

"Okay, how long were you in England then, Henan?" This just seemed too unbelievable to hold water.

"Seven-years," Henan informed me. "They let me have a boyfriend while I lived there, but he cheated on me. He did not like the photographers that were always around. They paid me some money but not what they promised. They always had their way. Taking advantage of my body when we went to sites and filmed videos and take still photos," Henan alleged with a sigh.

"How was it you came to Ghana?" I didn't share with Henan that there were reasons for asking question. Henan is getting impatient, as she says. "Jim, you ask too many questions. Aren't you ever going to stop asking questions?" she wanted to know.

"It might be helpful for me to know," I countered. "Maybe I can help you get away from that poverty-stricken country."

Seizing the moment, Henan replies. "Okay, these people tell me I'm supposed to be partners with them. I have a web page on the internet that people can find using, *www.carnalcarriexxx.com.* They call me a partner because they think we will make more money if we go to Ghana," Henan informs me. "We had trouble with the law in England, so we renewed our passports, and came to Ghana."

Then Henan pleaded again. "Please Jim, no more questions Jim sweetheart, okay?"

"Honey, this is perfectly fine with me, after all, I believe I've asked enough questions for now."

"I will talk to you very soon Jim darling. However, I'm so tired right now. I'm going to bed. I think maybe we will talk again tomorrow honey; okay?"

"Alright dear, get some sleep then, and we will talk tomorrow," concurring in agreement with Henan as the chat session ended. "Goodnight princess," concluding the messenger chat dialogue.

Henan's harrowing account of rape, if true, makes an honorable man want to hurl. Henan's description of what occurred to her at the tender age of eighteen by scrupulous evil doers was beyond civil. However, even if it cannot be verified, I recognize that this violent act of rape on women is played out on every continent in the world every day. It is an egregious, violent, and personal assault on the human heart, mind, soul, and body. This barbaric attack on female victims for the amusement of man's quest to satisfy some warped sense of gratification is shameful. A feeling of disgust was reinforced when I googled Henan's website page under her model site www.carnalcarriexxx.com.

You never know what you are about to see until you left clicked the mouse to open the video feed. Within ten minutes, tears began streaming down my cheeks, as the video depicted a rape scene. This isn't entertainment value material. This was by far too realistic … too authentic. Even the Hollywood elite could not have pulled this off without re-takes. The humiliation and degradation of the female anatomy went on for more than forty minutes. After twenty minutes, it was more than enough for me to witness. Becoming too distressed; tapping into every human emotion conceived by God, my tear-filled eyes' became droplets of rage as this scene kept playing itself out before me.

My initial reaction upon viewing this video was a resounding. "Woe! Woe! Woe!" Could this really be Henan at the tender age of eighteen?

Everything Henan described to me was happening to this young woman in the video. Henan was thirty-two-years-old now. Positive identification for the age of an eighteen-year-old was not verifiable to compare with Henan's current age. There were close similarities, but fourteen-years have passed and this was so surreal.

That evening I had to go over to my sister's home to get something. Still emotionally affected by the video, I reassured myself I could keep my emotions under wraps while visiting. Within five-minutes after arriving at Brenda's house, the tears began rolling down my cheeks as I began to weep uncontrollably. The more Brenda inquired about my sadness, the more tears that trickled down my cheeks; head hung low in shame and embarrassment. Blurting out a response, I remarked to Brenda.

"I do not know why man has to be so cruel and brutal Brenda. I am actually ashamed to be a man. I just do not understand this world."

Somehow, visual observation remains in the human psychic much longer and affects your view more so than reading or discussing a traumatic event. There was nothing pleasant about watching this vicious assault. It was pure torture for Henan by a couple of sick demented animals. I had become so incensed with this video that it disrupted my sleep for a week. How men view pornography and women in general is disgraceful. Women are not sexual toys to feed their alter ego, or to satisfy perverted desires. Woman are not sexual objects to still our raging male hormones.

God created a woman out of our rib. She is our equal, esteemed as a precious gift from God given to man as a valuable pearl. This video had affected me so, that I had to include and approach web-camming as a personal crusade along with scammer's, and fads.

Chapter 12

Leader's lead

*Euphoria, its opposite despair, indignant paired
with bitter, chagrined revels exploited.
Manipulate, stipulate, else hibernate; the indifference,
to be imprisoned ... isolated maladroit.
Eyes' peer forward in this whirlwind of fog; words
cascade with arrogance, intense pride.
Boast not in knowledge, rather lament on emptiness,
untruths sin; detest shameful lies.*
Jim Jacobs

This crusade has become more than personal. It was born out of the tearful ruin of the oppressed. An aggressive approach to immorality must take center stage. I need to engage in a tireless ... Endless battle against wickedness. Society needs to become part of the solution, and not the problem. Furthermore, since we are discussing immoral behavior, I'm getting off topic of sorts, as the Holy Spirit has led me to impart other nefarious activity, but still within the scope of the central theme. What is perplexing to the author as we branch out, we see seeds of melancholy concerning man's motives in the public arena of sensationalism and then we retreat back to old habits after periods of mourning have passed and the dust has settled. Furthermore, we have an influx of pundits who by their very nature, are skilled at stirring up discord.

Every time we have a manmade calamity, or tragedy as in the case of the twin towers on September 11, 2001, when thousands of innocent victims were killed. 343 first responder firefighters were killed in New York City. Hurricane Katrina in New Orleans on August 25, 2005, where the levee was breached and 80% of the city was under water causing mass casualties. Then we experienced the Loma Prieta earthquake fault that caused infrastructural damage to San Francisco on October 17, 1989; inflicting additional casualties. The planned and executed bombing of the Murrah Federal Building in Oklahoma City by Timothy McVeigh and Terry Nichols on April 19, 1995, with 168 casualties. We can report on any natural or manmade disaster that captures the nation's attention. Through these calamities, a unification process begins, as it brings people together and we rally around the flag.

We flock to the churches in droves. We call upon the name of God, hands raised … Praying … Seeking comfort, answers, and solace. However, when the dust settles we gravitate back towards old habits and we immediately stuff God into a suitcase until we need him again. "Where is the outcry for justice and a need for God 365-days a year, 24/7? Why do we do this?" We memorialize children and young adults victimized by drive-by shootings, wars, or we become a casualty in the hands of law enforcement officers during an attempted arrest. Voices cry out in the name of God once more, but as before, once we get the all clear, we dispose of God until we need him the next time.

And what do we usually hear from the parents, relatives, or friends? "He/she was a good kid, trustworthy person. They were kind, wouldn't hurt a soul. However, Scripture teaches in Romans Chapter 3: 10-12. As it is written, "none is righteous, (free from sin) no, not one; no one understands; no one seeks God. All have turned aside; together they have become worthless; no one does well, not even one."

In the author's opinion, what should be told when parents, friends, and family members speak before a national audience, is whether the victim had accepted the redeeming qualities of Jesus Christ; repenting of their sins with a sincere conviction of heart and soul. Did they walk daily with Christ during their life? "We have a people problem in America, and it is not just the children and young adults, but adults as moral examples. Furthermore, it is going to take more than a village to fix the corrupt state of affairs in America. Strength in numbers is what this nation collectively must engender to steer this country in the direction of moral and ethical behavior.

Direct your attention to people of great status. People whom, by their self-serving educational achievements, or status, exemplify leadership in their own eyes' for the sake of the nation. Louis Farrakhan Muhammad Sr. Louis Farrakhan is, as most American's are aware, leader of the religious group, Nation of Islam. The Southern Poverty Law in America Center describes Farrakhan as, anti-Semitic (hostility towards) and anti-white.

Farrakhan, however, disputes this view of ideology. (Concepts of human life and culture) In October 1995, he organized and led the "Million Man March" in Washington D.C., calling on black men to renew their commitments to their families and communities. To Mr. Farrakhan's credit, the one good quality that stands out about his character is that he is an outstanding orator. That is if you can get beyond the hate monolog in his speeches. Mr. Farrakhan is a man that has the potential to unify this nation, irrespective of national origin, and make a difference. Yet, what is the charge against Mr. Farrakhan?

Having had the opportunity to listen to Mr. Farrakhan during one of his tirades, I observed his body language, looked into his eyes', and searched his heart. The wormwood dwells inside this man's heart and soul. It is eating away at his insides. He is arrogant, prideful, and condescending. Mr. Farrakhan has the voice of hate speech spewing from his lips, which is contrary to the teachings of the Qur'an. Mr. Farrakhan has a greater calling, and that is to conduct himself in the image of God, rather than divide this nation. He has the potential to be a national leader. He could be a unifier rather than a divider.

To Mr. Farrakhan's credit, his leadership in organizing the "Million Man March" in Washington, D.C. to encourage black men to renew their commitment to family and community, took leadership and planning to amass that many people in one place on a date certain. His ability to articulate a message, and motivate crowds to respond is extraordinary.

Twenty-years after the "Million Man March," held on October 16, 1995, had this author questioning if a survey or follow-up by his organization has ever been conducted to determine how many of the one-million people in attendance took his message to heart. It is one thing to give a persuasive speech, yet another, to follow-up and tend to the flock.

Mr. Farrakhan could play a pivotal role in this nation in collusion with other renowned Ministers of the cloth to spearhead a mission to squelch immorality. I'm sure Mr. Farrakhan is aware of the drug problems facing this nation. Prostitution is a pandemic, the sex slave industry is thriving, pimps go about their business unabated, internet pornography is an incurable disease, internet scams mutate like an infectious virus, drive-by shootings is cancerous, drugs are smuggled across our borders in unprecedented amounts, and domestic abuse is rampant. Poverty is at an all-time high, and single parenthood is a national disgrace. Gay rights and abortion, have become an eye sore. Mr. Farrakhan could have a voice and critical role in silencing iniquity to a murmur. This is not the time for division. No! It calls for a United front with men of influence and leadership. Lead by example.

Alfred Charles "Al" Sharpton Jr. Now here is a household name most of us can identify with because of his activism. Critics describe him as a political radical who is to blame, in part, for the racial divide. Minister Sharpton is a Baptist preacher from Brooklyn, New York. President Obama said that Mr. Sharpton is, "the voice of the voiceless and a champion of the downtrodden. Of course, there is disagreement with the President on his assessment of Sharpton. This is not written to bash anyone. But I do want to outline some misgivings I have about the Reverend Sharpton, and what my eyes' have seen, and my ears have heard. The Reverend Sharpton's own words reverberate with indifference. Quote. "An activist's job is to make public civil rights issues until there can be a climate for change." Then let us get going Reverend! There is plenty on the platter.

"Wait; hold on; wait! With all due respect, Reverend Sharpton is no Reverend Dr. Martin Luther King. He will never fill Dr. King's shoes. The Reverend Sharpton lacks charisma, character, and understanding. First, and foremost, Reverend Sharpton has been ordained and called by God to preach the good news. Reverend Sharpton is to be held to a higher standard due to his position as a representative of God. Christ's teachings are about love, the seven fruits of the spirit, and salvation.

If one assumes the role of activist, then an activist represents all ethnicities and classes of people, not just one. The Lord makes no exceptions for bigotry. (Hatred and intolerance) The Lord does not distinguish between ethnic origin. The same wormwood residing in Mr. Farrakhan's heart also takes residency in Reverend Sharpton's heart. It permeates from his lips like a roaring lion. Let go of the past, and let the bitterness of heart receive nourishment from the living water. Climb out of the abyss and into the light. What is learned from Scripture is that we have been made in the image of God. The most powerful tool in your arsenal Reverend Sharpton, is Scripture. Use it in love. He is noted for marching and founding the National Youth Movement to raise resources for impoverished youth, but I cannot seem to wrap my arms around other notable achievements in your itinerary of accomplishments.

Let us do something bigger than all of us collectively, and I will be right alongside you on the front lines, shoulder to shoulder, hand in hand. It reaches every neighborhood and socio-economic class in this nation. We are talking infrastructure, living wages, fraud and Illegal border crossings. The list has a bottomless pit into the abyss. I'm not hearing anyone yelling and screaming in protest when pimps involuntarily beat women into submission as a means to implant fear and control.

They are brainwashed and too frightened to report their pimp to authorities about the vicious cycle of violence they are exposed to daily. "Is this not a form of slavery?" This requires executing justice on a massive scale … "Shock and awe," as former Secretary of State Colin Powell stated. Mr. Sharpton, like Mr. Farrakhan, can be a leader's leader in these areas of immoral degradation, provided everyone puts aside their egos by working to unify this nation. Help clean the streets of the criminals regardless of ethnicity.

Jeremiah Wright Jr., Pastor Emeritus (an honorary title given retiree) of Trinity United Church of Christ in Chicago, Illinois. Pastor Wright made several inflammatory speeches using the Lord's name in vain. You do not preach rhetoric from the pulpit regardless of your convictions.

You stay the course with God's word or leave the ministry and become an activist or whatever suits your purpose. Here is a man of the cloth who has two wormwoods inside him. There is one feasting on his heart while the other eats away at his soul. Pastor Wright; known for his controversial personality takes the podium with hate speech. Some will argue Pastor Wright was speaking out of jeremiad tradition that was preached in the U.S. going back to the Puritans. This was something that both, "black and white ministers have used since the 17th century in this country." The Jeremiad (prolonged lamentation or complaint) tradition dealt with "woe," promise, and moral failure not only in the church but in the nation."

Dr. King confided in Pastor Wright once concerning some U.S. activities. We're at the crossroads now where socialism and moral failure is at the doorsteps. Unless we begin to take a proactive response to this nations ill's we will have no one else to blame but ourselves. What side of the fence will Pastor Wright find himself? Bitterness, anger, strife and rage make for bad bedfellows.

Rush Limbaugh is a man who, in his own eyes' believes he is dignified, compassionate, iconic, and an intellectual. We have the Granddaddy of radio talk show hosts. A political commentator, Rush Limbaugh III, who now lives in Palm Beach, Florida, Rush is perhaps the most incendiary conservative of our time. A conservative, conservative, Rush is arrogant, prideful, verbose, (wordiness) hatchet man, insensitive, greedy, and idol worshiper of self. For a guy who signed a contract for $400-million over an eight-year span. Wouldn't you think Rush would have more substantive issues to discuss rather than spending a few hours a day, five-days a week, bashing liberals and their policies, while making demagogues out of Republicans whose record of accomplishments is just as tainted as the Democrats. The only bias is in his tunnel vision. When a man has wasted a large part of his life chasing after a father to gain his respect and approval, this suggests a need for a high level of emotional support.

Also, it is this authors opinion Rush is a very insecure individual who needs his ego stroked daily. What better forum than a radio talk show host with a brew for controversy to become an activist for all people. Rush's inflated ego makes him a poor candidate for relationships with the opposite gender. Rush is quick with the tongue to criticize liberal's yet he never has any concrete solutions to this nation's complex issues. He generalizes, waffles, huffs, and puffs like a villain hiding in the hedge waiting to see whom he can deflate with his quick-witted dry humor.

Limbaugh made an anti-Semitic comment about Donovan McNabb that caused him to resign in 2003 as an NFL commentator. Also in 2003, Limbaugh admitted he was addicted to pain medication and sought treatment. However, in April 2006, Limbaugh turned himself into authorities on a warrant issued by the State Attorney's office for prescription fraud. The only thing Rush and I are in agreement on is the abundant abuse of drug use in this nation.

This talk show conservative can get his message out by putting his boots on the ground. What has Mr. Limbaugh contributed to this economy other than a short run on ties he manufactured and marketed while married to Marta. Do you really think Mr. Limbaugh knows what it is to labor in factories or retail stores for minimum wage jobs that the ultra-conservatives argue is a living wage? Does he recognize how minimum wage devalues a person's self-esteem and self-worth? Does he or our lawmakers in Washington understand that minimum wage does not even come close to a living wage? Does Rush want to work towards the greater good of the country?

If he acknowledges in the affirmative; which is unlikely, because that would be beneath his dignity. But if his response is yes, he could galvanize his followers and join forces with other notable personalities to rid this nation of immorality. However, that could only occur if you've denied yourself from chasing after prostitutes as if they were your personal play toys. Step out of this comfort zone you've created, and do something productive and honorable for a change. That is, if you truly care about America.

Among notable members in the ranks of influence and name recognition, who have taken an oath to support and defend the Constitution of the United States, are officials like Governor Jerry Brown of California. United States Senator Harry Reid, from Nevada; practically a full-fledged light fixture hanging from the Capitol Rotunda in Washington.

"House Minority Leader Nancy Pelosi, also of California representing the 12th district." Furthermore, we must include the 61st Speaker of the United States House of Representatives John Boehner from Louisiana.

Representative Pelosi served as House Speaker from 2007 to 2011. The only woman to have served as the House Speaker and to date is the highest ranking female politician in American history. Every politician who takes the oath of office raises their right hand and repeats the recital by an appointed official. Before every session, Congress opens with a prayer given by the House Chaplin and is proceeded by the Pledge of Allegiance.

There is absolutely no reason why we cannot have complete representation on the moral issue's facing our nation. We have former President's Clinton, Bush (2), Ford, Carter, and the current President, Barrack Obama. Also included on the list are Governors, law enforcement agencies, and Ministers of the cloth. I have been known to be results oriented … All-inclusive. We have allowed this country to be swallowed up in the darkness of the abyss. Unless we commit to a vision, allocate huge sums of money, and a significant manpower contingency, this country will be pulled deeper into the abyss, and there will be no one to blame but the one looking back at you in the mirror.

"I pledge allegiance to the Flag of the United States of America, and to the "REPUBLIC" for which it stands, one Nation under, "GOD" indivisible, with "LIBERTY" and "JUSTICE" for "ALL." Congress ratified Article IV, Section I, Amendment XIII on December 6, 1865. Amendment XIII says, "Neither, SLAVERY nor, INVOLUNTARY SERVITUDE, except for punishment for crimes of which the party shall have been duly convicted, shall exist within the United States, or any place subject to their jurisdiction. I call the reader's attention to Amendment XXI, Section 2. The transportation and importation into any State, Territory, or Possession of the United States for delivery or use therein of intoxicating liquors, in violation of the laws thereof, is "PROHIBITED." This Amendment was "ratified" on December 5, 1933. At the end of each Amendment, it clearly states Congress shall have the power to enforce the article by appropriate legislation.

I pose this question to the reader. "What is the difference between intoxicating liquor and other mind-altering substances?"

Verily, verily, I say to you the reader, knowledge is for your edification and not for eyes' that are glazed over with impurities. Permit the author to embolden himself by filling the pages in this chapter with pardonable truths concerning some of our renowned public officials. There is a reason for every season! I will explain the rationale as best as I'm able. However, it will mean saber rattling and offending the proud, and arrogant. Criminals are afforded far more rights than victims who are victimized under our current system of jurisprudence.

As you know, I kept pounding home the state of affairs, and moral decline this nation is facing. Drug trafficking, prostitution, pimping, human trafficking, internet pornography, internet fraud. We also have Drug dealers, poverty, domestic abuse, white collar crime, abortion, illegal border crossings, drive by shootings, and so on. Under Amendment XIII, the question begs for more answers.

"Women who are controlled by PIMPS; is this not a form of bondage, and slavery?" You could make the case that law enforcement has trained task forces to perform covert operations to capture perpetrators involved in these heinous crimes. However, an argument can also be made that even as dedicated and honorable as their efforts are in bringing criminals to justice in this enslavement industry, they are barely scratching the outer layers of the abyss. Lord forbid, we should discover law enforcement is taking bribes and tainted blood money by looking the other way. There simply is not enough resource's, manpower and funding to neutralize this heinous crime.

"Let's define LIBERTY?" Liberty has four distinct definitions. (3) "An action going beyond normal limits." a. "A breach of etiquette," (prescribed by authority to be observed in social or official life), or propriety." (Socially acceptable) b. "risk ... chance ... variation from standard practice." (They took foolish liberties with his health) c. violation of rules, or a deviation from standard practices. The author chooses freedom because every Citizen under the Constitution is granted this right. The Constitution is interpreted as written: Our rights have been compromised by all the pervasive immorality mentioned in previous paragraphs. The Governor of California; Governor Brown, including all Governors, who take an oath of their respective States swear to defend against all enemies foreign and domestic. So let us break down the definition of the enemy. (One that is antagonistic towards another. One seeking to injure, overthrow or confound an opponent, something harmful, or deadly, a hostile unit or force.) Antagonism means enmity, and enmity we define as positive, active, and typically mutual hatred or ill will.

Governor Brown has been in politics as long as kindling wood has been in existence. A Governor is commander-in-chief of his state. He ensures that state laws are enforced. Governor Brown is the longest-serving Governor in the history of California. Truly, at wits end, there is a question why the Chief Executive of a California state government has not taken crime and immorality and given it the priority it deserves. Widespread bacteria are mutating over the entire country, spreading like the plague without a cure.

Governor Brown and Governors within the Continental United States have within their authority to deploy the National Guard, and Reserves to assist law enforcement agencies in stemming the tide of criminal activity that influences our liberties in this country. Why this is not given the attention it deserves defies logic. Governors, who profess to be "Born Again Christians," and believe Scripture to be the infallible word of God, should be ashamed. Why would they sit idly by, and allow their States to run rampant with corruption by prostitutes, drugs, pimps, (the lowest form of humankind) and other criminal behavior? Our States are being inundated with all manner of iniquity. The hour is near, the citizens are growing impatient, and it is time to make a statement on white and blue-collar crime.

Senate Minority Leader Harry Reid, who switched parties, and is now an Incumbent, did so to secure his long-standing seat in the Senate. He has served in the Senate since 1987. Senator Reid represents the state of Nevada. Senator Reid advocated outlawing prostitution in Nevada, but the bill didn't pass. He revealed to reporters that his niece is a lesbian. Reid also opposed legalization of online poker but recently changed his position. Some have argued Senator Reid came under the influence by thousands of dollars from Las Vegas casinos who contributed to his re-election campaign.

"Money talks, but we all knew that, didn't we?" Senator Reid earmarked a spending bill that would provide for building a bridge between Nevada and Arizona. This would make land he owned more valuable because the bridge would be on our near the real estate he owns. This Senator seems to rule the day in the House and Senate Democratic side of the isle. Yet, he cannot get a law passed outlawing prostitution in his own state! He can get his transportation bill passed by a bridge to nowhere that will border his parcel of real estate. However, when it involves prostitution and crime, his voice is a mere whimper. How the citizens of Nevada can continue to vote him into office, knowing full well he is the Godfather of cronyism, (pal, buddy) needs to re-examine their own moral compass. No one in the Senate hinders passage of legislation more than this controversial politician.

Nancy Pelosi is Minority Leader of the United States House of Representatives. Congresswoman Pelosi was the 60th Speaker of the House of Representatives until Congressman Boehner and the majority of House Republicans unseated Democratic rule. Pelosi was the first woman, first Californian, and the first Italian-American to lead a major party in Congress. The Human Rights Campaign for the 107th, 108th, and 109th sessions of Congress, Congresswoman Pelosi does not receive high marks because she voted in agreement with HRC's slate pro-gay legislative issue. She voted against the proposed Federal Marriage Amendment, which defined marriage federally as being between one man and one woman, thereby overriding states' individual rights to legalize gay marriage.

Pelosi voiced her opposition to Proposition 8, the successful ballot initiative, defining marriage in California as a union between one man and one woman. Pelosi stated her Catholic faith is behind her position on LGBT rights such as same-sex marriage. She goes on to say, "my religion compels me … and I love it for it … to be against discrimination of any kind in our country, and I consider the ban on gay marriage a form of discrimination. It is unconstitutional on top of that. Congresswoman Pelosi has to be listening to false teachers or she is illiterate in the word of God, who rules the day. The Congresswoman voted against the Ten Commandments being in public buildings, including schools. Now she opposes the interrogation technique of waterboarding.

Majority leader in the House, Congressman John Boehner is your typical, go along to get along legislature as echoes are heard in the hall's of Congress crying out for stalemate to end. Not much commentary to add about this elected official other than he is incapable of getting legislation passed, let alone agreed upon, even though they have the majority in the House of Representatives. To be truly honest, the author believes each person profiled also has wormwood infestation in their hearts. To put this in perspective, this has been a do-nothing legislative body for nearly two decades.

On June 14, 1954, President Eisenhower; based on a bill passed by legislators and signed into law stated. "From this day forward, millions of our school children will DAILY; proclaim in every city, and town, every village and rural schoolhouse, the dedication of our nation, and OUR people to the Almighty ... In this way we are affirming the transcendence, (being beyond understanding) of religious faith in America's heritage, and future. In this way, we shall constantly strengthen those spiritual weapons, which forever are our country's most powerful resource, in peace or in war.

In Proverbs 6: 16-19. "There are six things the Lord hates." Seven that are an abomination to him: Haughty eyes', a lying tongue, and hands that shed innocent blood, a heart that devises wicked plans, feet that make haste by running towards evil, a false witness who breathes out lies, and one who sows discord among brothers. I would highly recommend Congresswoman Pelosi, Feinstein, and other liberal politicians open their Bible's and read what God has to say about immorality. If these Congressmen and Senators can't tell the American people what is contained in the appropriations bill, other than the earmarks for their perks back home, our nation is in terrible straights.

Leviticus 20: 13, says. If a man lies with a male as with a woman, both of them have committed an abomination. Furthermore, refer to Leviticus 19: 29. Do not profane your daughter by making her a prostitute, lest the land become full of prostitutes. We are so vexed in the muck and mire of our wicked hearts it is going to require a unified effort to claw our way out of the abyss. A revival is what this nation needs, regardless of religious beliefs, or political affiliations.

Taking the opportunity at this stage in the manuscript, to enlighten the reader about what is weighing heavily on my heart by highlighting people of influence is a way of bringing awareness to the forefront. We are a Republic, as such; these men and women have an opportunity to receive retribution. Issues brought to the forefront are fixed and across all, socio-economic classes affecting our very survival. Everyone can make a difference if our leadership took a posture of honesty and genuine leadership.

Furthermore, the President of the United States, the House, and Senate, Governors, Christian's, and anyone who believes we have a serious problem on our hands should be taking a proactive position on these criminal social issues. Allow me to repeat for emphasis. "Our current policies to combat crime in all facets of society is minuscule in comparison to the high volume of criminal offenses committed throughout our country every day." We need to be taking a long hard look at ourselves and come into alignment with morality. I believe the day of reckoning is drawing nigh.

How many folks can say they have served in a battered women's shelter as a volunteer? Better yet, how many Americans have witnessed a pimp beat his property (women) into submission? Pimps, who by their very nature isolate they're stable of women using control and brainwashing as weapons. How would you like to be monitored twenty-four hours a day, seven days a week? Always under the watchful eye of the pimp? Forced to turn 10-15 tricks a day, or more 24/7. The prostitute is facing the fear of death every day. These girls have already suffered one death. These heartless evil doer's, have already killed the woman's heart and soul. Some pimps get their stable of girl's dependent on drugs to make them more compliant ... Easily controlled. They are trapped in a never-ending cycle of vicious treatment. "Where are her liberties? Has she not become subservient ... In bondage ... A slave?"

"Sorry, I blew up folks! Some of us just care too much about the oppression of the human soul and victimization. So if you don't feel immediate interdiction is warranted to rid our streets of pimps and drug dealer's, and you profess to be a Christian, then by all means, divorce yourselves from becoming an activist; saver of souls and stay the course. "And when the Lord asks you what you did for his creation…What will you tell Him?"

Chapter 13

Into the Abyss

Part II

Living in your lair, you turned against thee, that I should be shamed and broken.
From loftiest clouds beyond distant stars … lost lines, collectively spoken.
Growing pains weighty are the challenges; thus,
shall it remain, struggles to overcome.
Stigmatized and petrified, an unwelcomed sunset noted and vilified by some.
Jim Jacobs

We are now going to confront the experience Henan encountered during the brutal rape while under the control and influence of the photographer. Patience and perseverance in pursuit of the truth remain on the agenda. Should this pilgrimage demand the sacrifice of money and time within reason, so be it! I am determined to see this through to the end.

The eyes of the writer discover in each person a unique and irreplaceable humanity. While superior intellect seeks to control and manipulate the world, the spirit of the author bows in humble reverence to Almighty God. At every opportunity, we must run from the abyss and put away the gross immorality that leads us to it. Some emotions and feelings add depth to the adventures of humanity. One of the most notable occasions occurred on a Saturday during the early afternoon hours. I told Henan I needed to make a trip to Wallers for some personal items, so we parted ways.

Taking the cell phone with me before leaving the apartment, something I seldom do, it took about five minutes before I pulled into Wallers parking lot. I parked the vehicle and strutted to the entrance. As I entered the store, I hadn't walked more than fifty feet when the cell phone rang. It was Henan, or someone masquerading as her on the other end. The voice on the other end was muffled and sounded like an eight-year-old child. It was Henan, and she wanted me to do my shopping quickly and hurry on home so we could chat. This was not the voice of a thirty-one-year-old woman but someone much, much younger.

While Henan was still on the telephone I remarked. "You have the voice of a child." I could barely make out her syllables when she uttered her words. Henan repeated what she said before in this child-like voice. Additionally, her English lacked clarity. "You will come home soon so we can talk some more, okay?"

"Sounds good Henan." Acknowledging I understood.

Henan replied. "Okay then, we will talk later, goodbye."

Just as quickly as Henan appeared, she had taken flight like an eagle. "Bye Henan, I will be home soon," I told her in the event she didn't hear the first time, but I think she was gone.

The pictures of Henan and the voice that I heard on the other end of the phone were not similar. This was a red flag for sure. We are dealing with someone who practices her craft well and fosters deception with skill. Although Henan confessed to her role as a model, she continued to insist she was a student at the University. Henan expressed a fondness for entertaining her friends at her place for meals. She also mentioned trips to the lake with her friends and shopping. I ask you, the reader. "Does this sound like a woman in need, or enslaved?"

However, Henan's biggest fabrication came alive when she attempted to sell me on the notion she was attending church services on Sunday. This was a whopper of a story. I am sure this was said to stroke my ego because we talked about my faith. Sometimes it was better to go along, to get along while stringing Henan through murky waters. Then again, it may be the other way around. I wasn't sure at this point in our friendship.

Therefore. I posed as the gullible prince charming for a while. Henan was unaware I was going to her web page dissecting information of value in my quest to obtain her birth name, or any other interested parties profile who may be involved in this swindling scheme. Pinpointing her precise location would prove just as challenging as names. Beginning to unpeel the layers of our conversation, I would confront Henan directly after everything had been checked, and double-checked for accuracy. Only then, would I challenge her during our next chat session.

I interrogated Henan through rapid-fire questions as a means to garner information in pursuit of the truth. The great pretender would need to rely on current and future strategy. Learning the fundamentals of computer technology would prove challenging. Without mastering the technology, everything else would be useless. When Henan appeared on messenger to chat, the questioning would begin with a flavor of innocence. We are in the middle of May, six weeks into the intelligence gathering process.

"How did your day go Henan?" I asked, to get a feel of her temperament.

Henan responded. "I went to the University with my friend today; six hours of classes again."

"I see, and what time did school start for you today sweetheart?"

"Oh, we probably left at nine in the morning," she replied. "It rained a lot today," she added. Then Henan stated. "Tomorrow if it's a good day we will not have school, so my friends and I will probably go to the beach or lake." As an afterthought, Henan said. "You can come too, and then you can carry me on your shoulders and back," she said laughing.

"Henan, how hot is it there now; is it scorching hot there?"

"Yes," Henan replied. "It is always so hot here in the summer."

"How do you get to the beach if you don't have a car?" I inquired.

"Ahhhhh, my friends take me. We get lunch together in a basket," Henan explained. "Then we go to the beach and find a private place where it is secluded."

Being ever vigilant, I posed a question of a personal nature. "How come you never give me the names of your friends?"

Henan countered. "I didn't think it was that important for you to know." Adding. "They are just friends I know from University." She explained.

"Perhaps Henan, but your friends are my friends as well …Yes?"

"These are friends from all over the world I hang out with. They speak different languages." Henan insisted.

"Okay, so tell me, how are you able to communicate with each other, isn't there a language barrier?"

Henan was beginning to dig herself into a rather deep hole, the gateway into the abyss, as she painstakingly attempted to mislead me with one false answer after another. As long as I'm aware of her deceitfulness, it is tolerable for me to accept; at least for now. All I need to do is keep Henan engaged and let her folly do the damage.

Henan continued with her explanation. "We try as best we can to understand each other." Declared Henan.

While sitting at the computer reading Henan's answer, an epiphany came my way. If all these students come from different countries; then how are the students able to understand what the professor is instructing them in the classroom? Then another thought occurred to me about Henan's web page. Where does she find the time to develop all these different sites with her name posted all over them? Especially if she's attending school.

Responding to her latest explanation required a stern warning. "Honey, we have to come to an understanding very soon; like now!"

"What is the matter dear?" inquired Henan.

"Henan, I have never gone to your cam site. However, I did use *www. carnalcarriexxx.com* that you provided me, and I came to a host of Carnal Carrie referrals redirecting the user to one porn site after another. Furthermore, sweetheart, what caught my eye was an advertisement redirecting the user to a site named, Carnal Carrie updates."

Pressing forward I hinted. "Honey, my curiosity surrendered to the busybody must see, so I clicked on the site, and guess what my eyes' beheld?"

Responding quickly, Henan said. "No sweets what could it be?" she asked.

"Honey, after reviewing the update page, and considering what you just told me, it would be virtually impossible for you to be in two places at the same time," I explained.

Henan answered saying, "I don't know what you're talking about, Jim darling!"

"Okay sweetheart, let me explain it for you," so I continued. "Then tell me if I'm in error about what I saw, and what you said earlier about you girls' going to the lake, alright?"

"Sure," Henan replied. "Go right ahead and tell me, darling."

"Thanks honey."

I am about to open up an assortment of problems for Henan to navigate. As I explain. "This updated site that has your name associated with pornography is a site visitors are able to view and receive the latest updates of you webcamming in an assortment of compromising images. This does not bode well for you." Elaborating further on my interrogation, the evidence begins to mount. "Now hon, the specific dates and times you claimed to have been at the beach, shopping, or at the University, you were really quite active posing for pictures to put on your profile page." Am I right?

"I see," Henan said. "I was going to tell you, honey," then she added. "I was afraid you wouldn't want to continue talking with me as a friend," she said alarmed.

"Henan darling," I said. "This is the second time you used fear of losing a friendship if you revealed something sinister to me. However, I'm here to tell you I will discontinue talking with you if I'm being misled, or you are lying to me," I remarked.

This was in-your-face realism given the nature of my debut into Henan's secret world. It began to expose Henan and other potential criminal's associated with her, who defrauded Jim Jacobs and other victims. I was prepping Henan for an exclusive insight into her network. This was a top priority. There was much more to explore here that far exceeded the author's expectations. If anyone can have applications to use as a learning curve, this was the crown jewel that was revered and loathed.

Henan, after learning she had been caught in her own web of lies, came clean with her confession.

"Okay, so now you know about the many sites I have under Carnal Carrie, so I will be honest and truthful from now on," she insisted.

"But this is only after you are caught with your hands in the cookie jar. Why weren't you honest with me from the beginning? To date, you have been less than forthcoming sweetheart, all lies," I said.

Again, Henan countered. "You do not know the whole story and if I told you, I might get myself into trouble," she declared.

"I think I understand more than you are giving me credit for when it relates to our friendship Henan. Your memory is short in these matters," I uttered. "We are friend's. I am not the enemy honey. I'm here to lend help when it is practical to do so. However, you have to start trusting me sweetie," I concluded saying.

As if it were said in confidence, Henan replied. "If I tell you the truth, you will not tell anybody?" She pleaded. "Because if you do, I will get myself into trouble."

"I am here to listen and learn Henan, not condemn." Attempting to reassure her.

Henan then began to relate the same story she had recounted earlier, only with a few added twists. With resolute patience, my ears were attentive but guarded. And so, Henan went about the task of reliving her rape all over again. It was no less painful to hear the second time around as it was the first.

"So why can't you leave these people?" I asked.

"These are very dangerous people," Henan answered, adding. "They took my passport and gave me a small income for videos, and still shoots to live on," she claimed. "When my mother had surgery, I had to borrow money from property owner so I could send the money to my mother for surgery," She concluded.

"How much did you have to borrow from the property owner?" I inquired with a sigh.

Henan wasted no time replying, saying. "The surgery cost over seven-thousand dollars, but the landlord could only give me seven-thousand dollars," she concluded with this ridiculous assertion.

No sooner had Henan finished with this incredible story when I remarked. "What, are you telling me, you still owe your landlord seven-thousand dollars?"

"Yes," she said. "And he wants the money back very soon!"

"What about those men that took you hostage against your will?" I asked. "Won't they help you pay restitution to the landlord?"

"No, they said it is my problem," Henan stated. "I live in this apartment without an air conditioner while they live in a fancy home," Henan complained, then muttered. "These people are very stingy with money, they only give me fifty dollars a day for still shoots and one-hundred dollars for video's," explained Henan.

"Henan," I protested. "You have to get away from there!" Warning her with a sense of urgency while making it appear as though I was disparaged by her predicament.

"I do not have any money to leave, and the owner wants some money now," Henan insisted.

"I'm not sure what can be done Henan!" Adding. "There needs to be some thought given to this problem," I explained.

I knew what was about to come. Therefore, I had to give serious thought into this matter if I had any hopes of prolonging the inevitable. Money! This would be her demand. And money was a luxury I could not afford to give right now.

Just as sure as a cat meows, meow happened. "Can you send me some money?" Henan asked?

"How much do you think you need to pay the landlord just to keep him happy Henan?"

Henan's response was immediate. "He wants all of it now, or he is threatening to go to the police," she uttered. "He is furious right now because he was told the money would be paid back very soon," Henan alleged.

Aware of Henan's end game, I said plainly. "Honey, I do not have that kind of disposable cash to give you," I informed her. "Furthermore, I would have to save this amount of money in increments, or borrow the money," I complained.

"Okay darling," she said. "You think about it and we can discuss it tomorrow, but now I have to go do web-camming."

"Alright sweetheart," I acknowledged. "We will discuss this tomorrow."

"What time do you think you can be on chat tomorrow Henan?" I inquired.

"In the morning," Henan hinted. "How does 11:00 A.M. your time sound; is that Okay honey?"

"Works for me darling." I replied.

The following day, just as sure as frog's croak at night, Henan logged onto Yahoo Messenger eager as a lonesome coyote at the ready to tap into Jim's wallet. However, the script remains on course for now. Questions, questions, and more questions. I needed to get inside the operation. See who, if any of the players might be and begin gleaning names of any other co-conspirators associated with Henan, and this criminal entity where fraud has its name engraved.

"Ding. Ding." Henan is available to chat.

"Hello my darling," she said. Henan smothers her victims with words of endearment as she works her magic; perhaps thinking I'm naïve yet to wander in darkness, ignorant of the real agenda.

"Good morning honey," I greeted Henan. "After giving much thought about what we had discussed yesterday Henan. I have some additional questions I would like to ask."

Henan, having no recourse but to agree to my inquiries. She found herself in a difficult situation than perhaps even she may have expected when she came online.

"Very well darling," she replied. "Whatever you want to ask I will try my best to answer."

"Thanks, honey," continuing, I ask. "Can you tell me one more time how much they pay you for still photos, and how much money you receive for video shoots?" I asked. The stage is being set to trap Henan again.

Henan replied. "Fifty dollars for still photos and two-hundred dollars for all day video shoots, with unlimited retakes," she answered.

"And, how much is your monthly rent?"

"The landlord wants seven-hundred dollars monthly," Henan replied.

"I see, and what are your monthly expenses for water, electricity, and telephone bills on average you think, Henan?"

"Oh, maybe one-hundred-fifty dollars a month, she said."

"Okay honey," as I continue. "Now let's assume you pay two-hundred dollars monthly for all your utility bills, would that be a fair statement Henan?"

"Sure, that is fine" she informed me.

"Now groceries Henan, what is your best estimate on monthly groceries?"

"I think I may be spending two-hundred dollars a month, but if I entertain guests then a little more; say two-hundred-fifty dollars," she informs me."

After calculating Henan's expenditures, I then pass the total amount unto Henan, saying. "If we add all your living expenses; the total comes to thirteen-hundred dollars each month ...Yes!" Asking Henan. "Would you agree with this total?"

"Yes, okay," she replied. "So what are you getting at honey?" She asked bluntly.

"Patience darling, I'm getting there." Noting Henan's impatience growing, I get giddy. "Earlier you said you receive fifty dollars for still photographs and two-hundred dollars each time you do a video shoots," I tell her, adding. "In the worst case scenario, if you only did photo shoots, you would be earning fifteen-hundred dollars per month, more than enough to cover your expenses," I told Henan, as I continue.

"This does not take into account the two-hundred dollars for video's they pay you for each session," I said. "If you did one per day honey, you would be earning six-thousand dollars every month for video's, and this doesn't include your web-camming," she is informed. "Sweetheart, that's seventy-five-hundred dollars a month.

"True darling, but they don't always pay me," she countered, saying. "They keep most the money to themselves. They told me it was to help pay travel to sites, costumes, lunches, and other stuff," Henan insisted. "These are very mean …Greedy people … Very dangerous; no one to help. I am all alone." Henan claims.

"I really don't understand this at all Henan, I really don't," I said with skepticism. "I just don't get it," I declared.

"But you will help me, right sweetheart? You will help, please, right?" Henan begged mercilessly.

"Sweetheart, never in all my years have I encountered anything quite like your situation," I said. "It seems to me Henan as though you are being held hostage as a sex slave without any avenues of escape available so you so you can gain your freedom," I said.

"I cannot go anywhere honey," she whined. "They have my passport, I'm hopelessly stuck here," Henan insisted.

"You have a unique problem, Henan," I insinuated. "I am going to have to ponder how best to render assistance so we can get you out of Ghana," I stated. "This is no way to live your life darling," I concluded.

Henan layered her demise on pretty convincingly. The more she expressed how dire her situation was, the greater was my resolve to let her think how concerned and worried I became of her seemingly unending predicament. I don't know how much longer I can stall her."

"Honey," Henan stated. "I love you and want to come to the States to marry you," she said anxiously. "You are a charming person, I can tell."

Ignoring her sentiments, I said. "Still Henan, you must make enough money to pay your bills and other necessities right?" I asked, knowing what her answer will be.

"Not always, as they come up with many reasons why they keep from paying decent money," she declared. "When that happens, I get behind in rent," Henan said. "This is why I ask you to help me Jim darling."

Fast-forward to May 16, 2013. Continuing this chess match has made it tough. Henan's fictitious story compels Jim Jacobs to take this matter to another level. If I refused to assist Henan, this exhaustive research could blow up before my eyes' … Before I even have the opportunity to gather any information of value. Weighing the pros and cons was considered.

Furthermore, uncertainty was a reality. Unsure what Henan was willing to accept for gratuities to maintain the line of communications open while researching the plausibility of Henan's stories was becoming complicated. Guarding against becoming entangled amidst Henan's web of lies may be problematic. Human slave trafficking was nothing new. However, I reasoned in this case, captors of victims in organized criminal activity, as a rule, do not allow their captors that much latitude in communicating at will with their intended victims outside the parameter of the vigilant eyes' of their pimp.

The dilemma! Should one proceed with the money Henan is demanding, so she can get out from under the alleged misgivings of this fictitious property owner who has threatened to get the police involved. Is there a possibility of losing more money under the guise of these best-laid plans of hers that can, and do go awry all the time? Grrrr! It would be a win-win for Henan, with Jim Jacobs, caught on the short end of this rogue operation.

Enter boldly go I, as feet trek into the hornet's nest of fraud. Actually, as an afterthought, Henan doesn't have many options either. "Go for it … All in," I concluded. May 16, we are both signed in to Yahoo Messenger to discuss the hybrid stories Henan insists is the gospel.

"Henan darling, this assistance you are asking of me is more complicated than I first thought. "Do you think you could be patient, and wait until tomorrow for my decision?" I inquired.

Henan spoke immediately. "Jim my love, I really need the money right away," she said. "The owner wants the money soon, or he told me he was going to the police and report me for being delinquent in my payments," she exclaimed. Adding drama to her doomsday predicament, Henan expressed panic. "Ghana people are very nasty people as well, and the landlord is not very pleasant."

Henan was in no uncertain terms, projecting a sense of urgency, and the subsequent consequences for any delay in payments. "Stick to the original script," I told myself.

"Sweetheart, I am only asking for a little more time," I announced. "Promise you, honey," I insisted. "Besides Henan, disposable cash isn't lying around my apartment like decorated wallpaper. I have to see where I can put my hands on that kind of money. That is, if I'm able to get it at all," I declared forcefully.

"Okay honey," she said with reluctance. "But please see if you can get the money for me, and we will chat again tomorrow," she said, disappointed I'm sure.

"What is the least amount of money the landlord will accept in order to keep him happy?"

"I don't know honey, maybe two-thousand dollars," Henan replied. "I will ask the landlord tonight love."

"Great I announced, and then we will discuss this tomorrow honey," kisses I wrote.

Henan returned the compliment before signing out of messenger. "Hugs and kisses' to you as well honey!"

This allowed me more breathing room, even if it was for only a day. String her along until an alternative plan to divert Henan's attention away from money; if that is doable. Whatever decision is implemented; it has to be crafted before tomorrow. Desperate for a solution, I compromised my word to Henan about visiting her site. Using Google search engine to check her site *www.carnalcarriexxx.com*, it directed me to her web page. Once on this page, it had a caption that advertised; "Carnal Carrie Sexy cam girl and pornstar goes hardcore." Clicking on the captions it re-directed the user to her (official name is Carnal Carrie), webcam site. Before clicking the mouse to enter Carnal Carrie's room, her advertisement is highlighted with several choices for the user to view if they wished. "HOME, PHOTOS, UPDATES, NEWS, ABOUT, JOIN NOW, MEMBERS, and FREE WEBCAM.

Scrolling down to the bottom of the page, I came across what I considered the "mother lode" of leads. It hit me between the eyes' like a bolt of lightning. It read. Copyright 2013, *www.carnalcarriexxx.com*. All Rights Reserved. Clicking the mouse on FREE WEBCAM, it revealed, the licensed operator of the "OpenCamNetwork," Live Feed Chat Network, 18 U.S.C. 2257; Record-Keeping Requirements, Compliance Statement for *www.carnalcarriexxx.com*.

This became invaluable information. It put a completely new spin on the research and confirmed what intuition was telling me all along. Henan/Carnal Carrie was indeed a swindler and a webcam prostitute. It also clarified Henan wasn't doing this alone. Upon learning of this information, I decided to reverse course. I would employ psychological indifference with her until other identities and players were exposed.

How do we define copyright? "The exclusive legal right to reproduce, publishes, sells, or distribute the matter or form of something." (Artistic work) Self-control, more so now than ever before, would be required of me. This newfound discovery would take me into uncharted territory. Ever deeper into the abyss. "This is a human machine of deceit," I thought. The damned are rascals to the end. Later revelation revealed Henan has been in the industry for approximately twelve-years. As with most challenges that surfaced, they were uncovered the hard way. You can win the battle but lose the war. "What would it cost to continue in this game of chess?" I asked myself. Henan could be perceptive one minute, careless the next, or outright incompetent at other times.

The next day, at mid-afternoon on May 17, Henan signed into messenger. Sometimes waiting for Henan to appear was often a hit or miss proposition. However, were talking money, so she appears on cue. The small brightly lit dot on the screen signaled Henan had signed into Messenger. Type your message, hit the enter button on the keyboard or mouse pointer and . . .Walla; message appears on the screen for the recipient to read. After reading the typed message, the recipient responded to the message.

Henan begins the discussion with the customary greeting. "Hello, honey."

"Hi sweetheart," I replied.

Wasting no time, Henan gets right to the point. "Money … Money … Money!" This is her agenda for today.

"Darling, did you give thought to the money yesterday?" Carrie asked.

"Yes dear," I said. "I gave much thought to the money. However, I know I cannot send you two-thousand dollars," I told her.

Henan then responded. "Honey, I am in big trouble then!" Adding. "I'm afraid of what the landlord will do to me." Continuing, Henan comments. "He may go to the police today, and I will go before the Judge and he may order me to jail."

"Sweetheart," I asked. "You can keep him happy with a short-term payment until we can figure this out together, can't you?"

"Maybe," Henan said. "How much you think you can send me today? Tell me now please," she pleaded in earnest.

"Perhaps six-hundred dollars, but I'm not sure," I said. "There is some money," I reassured her. "Let me go to the bank and see if I can borrow some money. That's the best I can do for you Henan," I insisted.

"You are a very kind, and giving man Jim," Henan stated. "I will talk to the landlord and see if this is okay for a while."

"I pray it will Henan," playing the game close to the edge. "Handing over six-hundred dollars is the best I would be able to put my hands on," I informed Henan.

Henan then threw a whiffle ball in my direction. Frozen in a time capsule, her comment seemed to drop from the sky without rhyme or reason.

"I love you, Jim," Henan said. "Jim you are a very nice, gentle man and I want to have a baby with you, you and me together Okay?" She stated outright.

Pausing for what seemed like an eternity, bouncing this latest revelation around in the four corners of my cerebrum, I wondered. "What is Henan up to now, this is not good! Where did this thought come from?" I wondered.

"Henan, did you just say what I thought you said about babies? Is this a misprint, spelling error?" I asked dumbfounded.

Laughing, Henan replies. "Of course it isn't; why not," she declared. "I think it is a good idea when I come to you in the States," Henan said with conviction.

"Oh!" I replied. "And just how do you think you are going to escape the watchful eyes' of those two characters that control your every move?" I inquired...

Go along to get along, have to play her game with discernment now.

"We'll work together on this idea. I just know I want to be with you soon," Henan stress's.

"Gee Henan, I hate to burst your bubble, but need I remind you that I am old enough to be your father twice over," trying to dispel her wild idea's. "Secondly, I had a vasectomy three decades ago. This means I cannot father any more children," she was told, hoping to get off this subject.

"So! Get reverse then," Henan said outright. "And age is no big thing if a man is nice," Henan concluded.

"Henan," I said. "We will focus on one problem first before we entertain any preconceived notion of any other ideas. In the meantime, I'm going to see if I can get this extra money for you," then pausing briefly, I continued. "That is if the bank will lend me the money. If successful, I will send the money through wire transfer fromWestern Union; return to the apartment, sign into messenger and relay the information you need to claim the cash. Okay with you, Henan?"

Henan perked up when she heard the plan. "Okay, dearest, I will be here," she replied. "What time you think you will be back?" she inquired.

Apparently giddy at the prospect of receiving some money, Henan sends one of those "emo's;" as they are referred. (Short for emotions) The emos were large, loud sounding kisses. Henan sent four, or five in rapid succession. I would receive these kisses every time Henan stood to gain anything of value from me.

I told Henan I would return around 3:00 P.M.

"Okay honey, the men are coming here now so we can go look for our next photo site," Henan informed me. "Hope to return in time for you darling," Henan told me.

"If you're not back in time, I will leave the information on messenger, just as I said,"

"Bye love," Henan said, signing out of messenger.

"Goodbye, darling." Signing off as well. I headed to the bank in Braxton.

I wondered how gullible Henan thought Jim Jacobs was. If Henan is in Ghana, there is a six-hour time difference. It was 2:00 P.M. when I left for the bank. And Henan wants this man to believe she and her people are going out at 8:00 P.M. in search of sites. It has been my experience that if you allow people to talk long enough, and they are less than honest, they end up putting their foot into their mouth's. They fall, stumble, and cracks begin to surface in their stories.

Within minutes, a short-term loan was securely in hand. Once the formalities were completed, Western Union was next on the agenda. Giving pause to reflect on whether this was the sensible thing to do was a huge decision. Yes, six-hundred dollars was big money. However, what was unearthed after contacting Henan, was priceless. The hunter needed to peel away the layers of secrecy involving this network of swindlers, and I finally got the break I needed.

I knew Henan was lying. I had to remind myself that I was committed to staying on course now that I became the hunter, rather than the hunted; regardless of the cost. The dividends outweighed the money. This should keep her in the game for quite a while. That is, unless Henan takes the money and runs, ending this odyssey. I needed Henan to go to the trough so that I might savor the bitter herbs she has hidden from me. It is going to take time. Meanwhile, strategizing was a continuum, as I strive to remain one step ahead of Henan.

Chapter 14

Evil within our Midst

Breathe in this deep voice of arrogance and deceit.
Vocal cords reign in pride, evil, and foolishness.
You've entered the abyss without end;
and deep.
Fraud seeks its own path. It walks, talks, schemes; in sorrowful unrelenting crime.
Absolute power corrupts absolutely; justice always prevails in due time.
Jim Jacobs

From this chapter forward, we are going to use "Carrie" as the principal character now in lieu of "Henan" for the remainder of the manuscript. This is the username she chose on her web page, "Carnal Carrie."

At Western Union, I used the same address Carrie had given previously for the shipped items I sent her in April, using: Henan Asante, P.O. Box 14781. Adum Kumasi, Ghana. The form also required their phone number. (+2332267820517 or 233245798910) The only change would be a new password. Carrie or a mystery person called a mule would need this to collect the money. I chose "blue" as the password on this transaction. Additionally, an "MTCN" number was required to claim the cash.

Finished with the difficult decision to transfer the six-hundred dollars to Carrie, I left the Western Union lacking six-hundred dollars to my name. However, that was my choice. I returned home to pass on the information to Carrie via messenger. As fate would once again rear its ugly head, Carrie didn't appear on messenger that night. Fearful she had taken the money and run, I began to suspect Carrie had outsmarted me. Only time or measured days would validate or disprove my fears.

While waiting for Carrie to re-appear on messenger, I discovered some interesting facts and intelligence. While insignificant in substance, it was still helpful for me to be able to tunnel into the mind of fraudulent scheme practitioners. Often referred to as, "deceptive scammer's." The first thing a person of interest needs to know in this ever-increasing criminal organization is that individuals at any level of intelligence are vulnerable to deception by experienced swindlers. "Confident scammer's," exploit human weaknesses like greed, dishonesty, and vanity, but also, virtues like honesty, compassion, or a naïve expectation of good faith on the part of the scammer.

Just as there is no typical profile for swindlers, neither is there one for their victims. Virtually anyone can fall prey to fraudulent crime. Indeed, victims of high-yield investment frauds may possess a level of greed that permeates their need. Therefore, they believe what they want to believe. However, not all fraud victims are greedy, risk-taking, self-deprecating people wishing to make a quick dollar. Nor are all fraud victims naïve, uneducated, or elderly. Just the opposite is true. Many citizens are highly educated, family oriented working people.

Fraud, or "scams" is the practice of pretending to have an interest in a fraudulent scheme to manipulate the victim. The purpose of a "scam," may be to waste your time with small introductory chats that may cause the victim to reveal information, which can, and "will be used" later on to bilk hundreds of millions of dollars from victims. Sometimes, this can lead to victims committing crimes to raise enough money to feed the fraudulent schemes.

"Scam" artist often attempt to waste the victims time by pretending to be a victim themselves. (Sound familiar?) Baiting forums relish in particular bait they term 'safari', in which they attempt to persuade victims into traveling long distances to meet phantom victims. A standard method utilized by the scammers is to send money to the victim using money transfers the likes of which would be the Western Union.

Shannon Rossmiller is an American judge, serving in Montana, who has a controversial role as a vigilante online terrorist-hunter, who poses as a militant anti-American Muslim radical, hoping to attract the eye of those with similar mindsets. (Anti-pedophile activism) Perverted Justice is a well-known example of an anti-pedophile organization that aims to expose and convict adults who, using email or websites, solicit minors to commit sexual abuse. They often collaborate with law enforcement and television crews. (This is proactive, results oriented folks)

Some freely hosted blogs, claim to expose real or potential child sex offenders. Another initiative, Predator Hunter, headed by Wendell Krutch, aims to track down and expose the pornography-related activities of alleged 'sexual predators.' In 2002, Krutch disclosed the details of his activities in an interview with Minnesota Public Radio. Members of the subculture 'anonymous', have also been credited with seeking out pedophiles and collaborating with law enforcement.

Search the mind of a "scammer" through dissecting their brain and you will notice they have fallibilities that can be exploited as well. Critical thinking may be distinguished; yet not separated from; emotions, desires, and traits of mind. Failure to recognize the relationship between thinking, feeling, wanting, and attributes of the mind can easily lead to various forms of self-deception, both individually and collectively. When a person possesses intellectual skills alone, without the intellectual qualities of mind, weak sense critical thinking results. Fair-minded or strong sense critical thinking requires intellectual humility, integrity, empathy, perseverance, courage, autonomy, confidence in reason, and other mental traits.

Thus, critical thinking without essential intellectual traits often results in intelligent, but manipulative, often unethical thought. In short, the sophist, the swindler, and the manipulator often use intellectually defective but effective forms of thought serving illegal purposes. Critical thinking yields itself to analytical considerations readily, and may be considered primarily objective. Few humans notice the degree to which they uncritically presuppose the mores and taboos of their society and hence fail to discern their own "subjectivity and one-sidedness.

There is no simple way to reduce one's bias. There are, however, ways one can begin to do so. The most important requires developing one's intellectual empathy and intellectual humility. The first requires extensive experience in entering and accurately constructing points of view toward which one has negative feelings or perceptions. The second requires extensive experience in identifying the extent of one's own ignorance in a wide variety of subjects. Ignorance whose admission leads on to say, "I thought I knew, but I merely believed."

One is less biased and more broad-minded when one becomes more intellectually empathic and intellectually humble, and that involves considerable personal and intellectual development. To develop one's critical thinking abilities, one should learn the art of suspending judgment. Ways of doing this include adopting random orientation; that is, avoiding moving from perception to judgment as one applies critical thinking to an issue. Become aware of your own fallibility ... for we all have our biases'. The scammer can be in denial of their responsibility, but the train-at-risk will eventually hear the words, "Gotcha!"

It is not only swindler's, cams, and pornography that the social networking tools of the World Wide Web have been used as an instrument to easily and widely publicize instances of perceived anti-social behavior. Bloggers, (a website that contains an online personal journal with reflections, comments, and often hyperlinks provided by the writer), targeted a woman who refused to clean up when her dog defecated on the floor of a subway car, labeling her 'dog (expletive) girl'. Another passenger had taken a photograph of her and her dog and posted it on a popular website. Within days, internet vigilantes had identified her, and much of her personal information was exposed on the World Wide Web in an attempt to punish her for the offense. The public humiliation led the woman to quit her job.

In 2002 in the United States, Representative Howard Berman proposed the Peer-to-Peer Privacy Prevention Act, which would have protected copyright holders from liability for taking measures to prevent the distribution, reproduction, or display of their copyrighted works on peer-to-peer networks. Berman stated that the legislation would have given copyright holders 'both carrots and sticks,' and said that copyright owners should be free to use reasonable, limited self-help measures to thwart P2P piracy if they acknowledged the threats to the privacy of legitimate internet users. Those actions can invade privacy, such as metal detectors at airports. If I'm interpreting Representative Berman's proposal correctly, this legislation affords those involved in the porn and fraud business more liberal freedoms to do their evil, deceitful schemes without fear of retribution.

If I had my wear-with-all, anyone participating in online dating sites, pornography, fraud, and the like, a call for the enactment of laws forbidding and abolishing them from the internet, even though there are claims that some of these jump-start sites are considered quite legitimate. Yet, these same internet dating sites are also an avenue scammer's use to entrap unsuspecting victims into their lair to exploit money. I'm told an increasing number of these online friendships blossom into genuine long-term relationships. Many of these people have found life partners via relationships started online.

Sadly, however, scammers have managed to exploit this trend to further their own evil ends. Many people around the world have been duped into sending money to Internet swindlers posing as a would-be girlfriend, boyfriend, to separate you from your hard-earned income. The proactive politically correct solution to this problem is enacting legislation to disband dating sites and pornography on the internet. Wherever loopholes exist, they need revision sending a message to criminals on dating sites that this behavior is not tolerated. Whatever happened to the conventional way of dating? You want a Russian bride-to-be; go to Russia in search of that perfect woman of your dreams.

A typical internet dating swindle goes something along the order of applying subtle techniques at the onset. A person registers at an online dating service and creates a profile. The profile will include information, and possibly a photograph, of the person, along with a way for interested couples to make contact. It is not a question of if, but when the scammer will make contact. They make contact posing as someone interested in a phantom romantic relationship. The victim responds unaware of who this person is other than what the swindler has fed them in their phony profile. The two parties begin corresponding regularly. They may soon bypass the dating service contact system, and start communicating directly, usually by email, Skype, Yahoo, Facebook, or other mediums on the internet.

Over time, the scammer will slowly earn the trust of their potential target. They may discuss family, jobs, and other details designed to make the correspondent seem like a legitimate prospect who is genuinely interested in the victim. It is inevitable, photographs will be exchanged, adding further credibility to their standing. However, the swindler that the victim assumes they are corresponding with may suddenly realize this is an invented alias of the scammer. Then again, they could sink deeper into the web of misfortune. Photographs may not even show this to be the real person on the other end. The victim's apparent love interest may look completely different to the person in the photograph and, in reality, may not even be the same gender.

After the scammer has established the illusion of a genuine and meaningful relationship, he or she will begin asking the victim for money. For example, the scammer may claim that they want to meet in person and will request the victim to send money for airfare so that a meeting can take place. The scammer may also claim that there has been a family medical emergency (sounds like Henan), and request financial assistance from the unsuspecting victim. The scammer may employ a variety of schemes to entice the victim to send funds (Hmmm, that too sounds familiar). If the victim complies and sends the money, they will probably receive requests for more money for whatever the swindler manufacturers as the trumped up excuse. With judgment clouded by a burgeoning infatuation for the scammer's character and personality, they may continue to support their lifestyle with money.

Finally, the victim will come to realize that they had been played. Perhaps the victim will realize this after waiting at the airport for their lover, who will, of course, never arrive. Meanwhile, the scammer pockets the money and moves on to the next victim. In fact, the swindler may be stringing along several victims simultaneously. In many cases, the victim will not only have lost out financially, but also left broken-hearted, thoroughly disillusioned, and damaged emotionally. These scammers tend to prey on victims that may be especially lonely, shy, or isolated, and, therefore, more vulnerable. Some variations are using the same basic scamming techniques. In some cases, the scammers may be the one to create a profile on a dating site and wait for a potential victim to contact them (Crafty, and without shame). Typically, the profile will include a photograph of a very attractive young woman who will have no trouble attracting would-be suitors into her lair of deceit, lies, and shameful behavior by tracking their prey.

In other cases, the scammer may only send out random, unsolicited emails expressing a desire to begin a relationship in the hopes some gullible (just like falling far from the tree) victim responds. Alternatively, they may strike up a conversation with a potential victim via an internet chat room. "Oh, … No." In some variations of the "scam," the swindlers may not ask for money directly. Instead, they may ask their victim to cash money orders or checks and wire them the proceeds. These money orders will turn out to be fake or stolen, and the victims will see their hard-earned cash disappear, and quite possibly held responsible for receiving stolen funds. The scammers may also try to trick victims into revealing sensitive information such as credit card numbers … "Owee … Ouch!!"

I would suggest that if you begin corresponding with an unknown with the view of reigning in the woman of your dreams in a romantic relationship, that you remain vigilant even if the relationship shows promise. The scammers are very skilled at building trust and know how to make vulnerable victims fall in love with them. Regardless of any indifference, you may have towards this author, you should view any requests for money as highly suspicious.

If you do discover you are the victim of a swindler, you may be able to find information on a dating blacklist website. These sites publish information and photographs of known dating scammers. Internet dating fraudsters often use the same names, family details, and cover stories in multiple dating fraud schemes. You may be able to expose a fraud by conducting internet searches on names or identities used by scammers as well as key phrases they use from their emails.

An example of a dating profile would read like a who's, who in the rich and famous column of a newspaper, formatted to flatter and get the attention of the curiosity seeker. It would read something along this line. "A self-sufficient beautiful, happy, secure, self-confident, psychologically aware, emotionally, and financially stable woman. I'm a hard working person and very friendly. I do not have any children and have never been married. My father passed away when I was only eighteen. I will say my dad was the best man I have ever loved. He was so caring, loving, God-fearing, respectable, and a responsible father. I trust and believe in God, and I know God is doing things in His time, and in His own way. I have learned to be a strong woman … hard working. When I lost my father, I was working and attending school at the same time … that taught me to grow stronger.

I have never been in a relationship before. However, I am now looking for a God-fearing and responsible man to settle down with. That is why I'm here. So if you are interested, let us get together so we can get to know more about each other. In any good relationship, there should be trust, communication, understanding, and honesty (This sounds familiar, blah, blah, blah, blah). Life is a precious gift from God, and it should be lived with love and joy. I enjoy various activities such as bowling, swimming, skating, chess, checkers, bike riding, and fishing (ideal woman; I declare). Golf, tennis, camping, sports, etc. (Any takers out there?) It does not matter. I am a talented person … easy to please. I enjoy games. Keep smiling and take care. Hope to hear from you soon, and I want you to tell me more about yourself, … work, and complete family history (Give them your credit card while you are at it).

Yes, even women in pornography and live sex webcams have chosen fraud as a means of supplementing their income. Carrie is not the only alleged swindler on the internet searching for and finding victims to manipulate and coax as unsuspecting victims to harvest as trophies they display on their mantle. These swindlers are as vicious as a swarm of piranha that attack and eat flesh in a frenzy of feeding. The more blood these piranhas consume, the more vicious they become. The culprits, (scammers) inflict dangerous wounds to your heart and soul. They are heartless, cold, and evil. They leave in their wake destruction and financial ruin to their victims.

Many names can be associated with the same photo. One female porn star used twenty different aliases while using the same photograph over twenty-times. Those involved in this lucrative business of fraud will use Ghana or Nigeria as their mode of operation, while convincing the victim this is where they live. They know full well that if they tell you they operate in countries like Ghana and Nigeria, law enforcement has little success, or jurisdiction to bring them to justice because these countries are corrupt. If someone finally figure's out who their perpetrator are, and they are uncovered, the scammer claims Ghana or Nigeria is stealing their photos and using them to run their fraudulent operation. "Yeah, right!"

When a victim finally discovers they have been scammed, their reply to the swindler is not too polite as you can well imagine. This is just one response written by an admitted victim: "HERE IS MY EMAIL TO THE SCAMMER TO LET THEM KNOW THAT THEY HAVE BEEN "SCAM BAITED!" I HAD A LITTLE HELP FROM MY REAL LOVE, LISA MIDWEST." Oh yeah, I cannot believe that you sent me all those phony pictures of someone else. I know a scammer when I see one. I am sending you some examples from another scammer in Accra. Maybe you can learn something. Her name is Maggie and goes by the porn name Malinda. You are a sick little Yahoo Girl that cannot do an honest day's work to earn a living. Therefore, you try to bleed money out of hard working victims, and older men. Get a real job and quit trying to get me to send you more money … You swindling little (expletive) girl.

In this sleight of hand "scam", there is an appearance of role reversal involved. The swindler used a picture of a porn model as the photo of choice. The victim said he found it on, "Me on you"; and was also seen on, "Mitch Dot Com." He also provided some vital information about the scammer by providing their email address. pappkua_4tune@yahoo. com and using "Mandy," as her porn model photograph. The victim publically advertised the swindlers address, name, and phone number that the scammer voluntarily gave to him. "Janet M. Thoms," P.O. Box 13733, Accra, Ghana, West Africa. The phone number he was given was the twelve-digit number used by Africa, +233246489228. Many times if you are computer literate, you can run what is called a reverse email search, to get the parties IP address (Internet provider). This can prove invaluable in pinpointing the person's location. Everyone who has a computer and uses the internet has an individual IP number assigned to it. What this person described, appears to have the earmarks of Henan splattered all over the screen.

There was an anonymous person who expressed what they felt was the worst swindler of all time. The person in question is a dating scammer also using Accra as their place of residence. She goes by the name of Ester Anosmia. Ester preys on individuals who run ads on the internet. The only problem with her photograph is that it is the image of a mannequin. I have seen it, and it sure looks life-like to me at first glance. However, the longer you view it, the more you begin to see the imperfections. Ms. anonymous use's name-calling, such as "idiots," to chastise victims swindled through her web of deceit.

One last bit of information relating to dating fraud, before moving on to the next chapter. This involved an individual born of innocence who was not expecting multiple emails. This isn't a dating "scam." However, it is a "scam," none-the-less. I believe he was just letting off steam when the letter was drafted because he used uncharacteristically foul language. He begins his selection by saying. "What I would like to know is how in the (expletive) can the sender and the receiver have the same email and have it end up in my mail?" He continues on saying. "If they wait for me to send them any money, (expletive) will freeze over," Adding. "This is hogging ... Dog ... Camel, and just plain old bull." (Expletive) Continuing on, he said. "I hope someday justice is served and these lousy (expletive) rot in prison."

Who can blame him for being an unhappy camper? These experiences are placing a tremendous strain on all victims, with the same disdain for scammers as I do. Language notwithstanding.

Chapter 15

Into the Abyss

Part III

Awaken to the symphony of birds singing Ballard's in unison to all melodies, hear.
Fragile memories; as fate surrounds the sojourner.
No recompense this Life, too soon a blur.
This great divide, who amongst us can measure its significance, times its value.
Enter youth's gates on Wings of Eagles, for innocence known, suddenly devalued.
Jim Jacobs

Endeavoring to defeat feelings of agitation by disrupting Carrie's attempts to sway me with her cold demeanor, we have reached a pinnacle in our conversations where arguments challenge the flavor of hospitality. Rather than this becoming a mutual friendship, the more it evolved into something sinister. The more searches executed, the greater came the frustrations, but with it, lessons learned. The unknown maladies were beginning to occupy cognitive thinking. There were relentless virus attacks that continually infiltrated my computer's hard drive during and after Carrie's simple introduction, and while writing this manuscript. Another computer was reserved as a secondary backup in the event one of these computers was rendered unserviceable.

Their agenda was to hack into the computer and steal informational files relating to what was in my archives. Apparently, Carrie's clan of organized swindlers were intentionally using their technical expertise to disrupt and corrupt either computer, rendering them inoperable for brief periods. They were so effective in fact that chasing to Bargains for repairs became a regular event. Even the new Apple computer wasn't immune from their mischievous behavior. The more they tinkered with my computers, the greater became my resolve to fine-tune knowledge of computer software and its applications.

Yahoo Messenger conversations with Carrie turned out to be an invaluable tool. Records of our chat sessions, when practical, were placed in the archives. Henan/Carrie continued to insist she was from the continent of Africa in the country of Ghana. As June approached, evidence to the contrary suggested Carrie was not in Ghana but suggested she was either residing in the United Kingdom or operating within the borders of the United States. Exactly which of these two countries remained a mystery … If only briefly.

It was during this period of our discussions that Carrie was habitually attempting to blindside me with contradictory statements. Moreover, Carrie was accusing her partners of bullying her and preventing her from leaving Ghana. Our next online chat session occurred on June 4, 2013. Sometimes Carrie loved to make me sit at the computer and wait for her to log onto messenger. Perhaps a technique used to get on my nerves, I imagined. Especially if I had grilled her the previous day, or evening and she would log out of messenger pouting.

Carrie had not come online yet. However, Carrie would know immediately when someone came online to chat because it would display a small circular orange neon light that illuminated. The time had arrived to glean additional information from Carrie. The session proved very confrontational and contentious, as would most of our interactions throughout this intelligence gathering process now.

The moment had arrived for a full court press to differentiate lies from the truth. It came time to discover who her co-conspirators were. Forever evasive, Carrie has seldom been forthcoming on the truth meter, as one false statement after another dripped like honey from her unreliable lips. Her words were filled with dead man's bones. After all, it was probably painstaking labor for her to alternate between live webcams, and swindling during her life as a scam and webcam artist.

On top of all this busy work, Carrie had to remain consistent in her chat sessions with each victim if she expected to separate any money that may be clinging inside someone's wallet. We continue to be paired equally when attempting to outfox the other in this game of chess. Therefore, a continuous stream of flames containing words of flattery to stroke Carrie's ego became routine because I never knew when the lines of communication would be severed. She yearns to hear rainbow-colored words in the context of edification. "Sweetheart, love, honey." She absolutely craves the endearing words all women love to hear. "I love you" and "princess." Rhetorical compliments if you please.

"Good morning sweetheart, thinking Carrie had logged onto Yahoo Messenger, so I begin a conversation by mimicking her presence.

"Considerable thought has gone into our present dilemma darling," I confessed. "You deceived me again; you won't be coming in October as we previously discussed, regardless of any further financial assistance I may send," I said in disgust, adding. "The contract you signed with your partners in September of 2013 is a fallacy. You own the website, Carrie, assuming the position as an adviser. You never tell the truth," I growled.

Continuing to display my rage, I said. "You have as much if not more controlling interest in the daily affairs of your website than these criminals you call partners. You have been resolute in being evasive with me Carrie," I complained, and then voiced surprise. "I have doubts and suspicions relating to a person of interest living with you who may have taken up residency in your home," I announced. "Are my concerns legitimate or unwarranted Carrie?" Asking her to disprove my findings.

"What is this, what gives with the silent treatment? How come I feel like there are barrier's all the sudden?" Vocalizing my disappointment. It appears words are slamming against an imaginary wall only to return void. Carrie is not saying anything ... Dead silence; eerie. "Is she fuming?" Not to worry, Jim Jacobs will continue to move forward with my repertoire of facts.

"You never schedule times where we talk Carrie. You are more open to members on your website than spending quality time with someone you claim to love," as I express my viewpoint. "I have been waiting for you to log online, only to be disappointed," I chanted. "Carrie, I am ordering a cease and desist action. We rarely do live video or voice chat because you always have some fabricated excuse to avoid live video with me," I declared with impatience.

Long before this silent treatment, I compromised my word and visited Carrie's website with her knowledge to observe her while she was broadcasting a live session. She remained clothed until I left. A condition I made before I would enter her room. I was there to monitor traffic and observe the dialogue she was exchanging with her members. (Perverts) I left her site convinced they resorted to fraud with an equal flair because their site did not draw in a high volume of paying members. There is a graph showing moderate to low traffic flow for her website.

"Carrie," I said. There is just too much information you are withholding from me. You can "short message service," (SMS) me on the cell phone number you have when you are ready to come online," I declared. Continuing with my conditions, I said. "After today, if we cannot agree on substantive issues, then I would rather not talk with you until you are ready to depart Ghana."

This was a demand communicated to Carrie voicing my displeasure along with a twist of rebellion. Furthermore, I used this forum as a bluff. I was hoping against all hope this might weigh heavily on her guilt. I didn't want her taking flight just yet.

"Carrie, I'm tired of subjecting myself to this madness lately, I haven't had a normal life since I met you on Skype," I said dejectedly.

Based on the conversation between me, myself, and I, there was enough frustration to go around to the full for all parties concerned. Carrie's nonchalant clandestine no-show attitude was becoming a thorn in my side. She eventually logged on later that day at approximately 5:00 P.M. in the evening. The conversation begins to breathe life shortly after

Carrie Logged onto messenger. I was sure she read my tirade before making her appearance known.

The conversion started with a snide remark I made to Carrie. "How much time are you going to allow me this time, Carrie, and why are you doing this to me?" I said complaining.

"Hi love," Carrie opens her greeting, acting as if everything has been tidy over the past few days.

"Carrie!" I shouted. "Is this the reason you came online; to mock me?"

"No, to talk with you," Carrie announced unfazed.

"What!" "What do you mean, talk to me?"

Carrie, using a one-syllable word remarks nonchalantly. "Chat!"

"Chat about what Carrie?" I asked. Her response caused a knee-jerk reaction, as I sense Carrie is goading me, as she repeats the use of one-two syllable words.

"Anything, she replies."

Wanting to probe the depths of her sincerity, I again ask Carrie. "How long, and why are you doing this to me?" I inquired.

Carrie countered saying. "I guess until I fall asleep."

It was time to retaliate with another harsh reply. "Don't you get it, or are you just toying with me again?"

"What!" Carrie asked, appearing surprised.

Trying to be soft-spoken now, I exclaimed to Carrie. "With a world population of over five-billion inhabitants, you just happened to choose my name from an endless array of names on the internet, why is that?" Emphasizing my point, I asked Carrie one more time. "Why are you toying with me?"

Carrie, placing herself in a defensive mode rejects the notion she is toying with me. "Am not playing with you; why would I play with you?"

"You are gone all day without one word, and now you come online when you are tired and decide you want to chat with me, I asked tersely" adding. "And this is showing respect for me when you pull these no-shows on me?"

"No!" Just don't get enough time, that is why I cannot come online, Carrie confessed, using this opportunity to invent an excuse.

Denouncing Carrie with dismay, I said. "This is not the life I want," she is told. "You may want this, but this is not for me princess."

"Okay! I know things will change," Carrie assures me. However, at this point, I think it is only smoke and mirrors to cater to my ego once more.

To let Carrie, know where I stood, I appealed to her guilt again, as I continue with a barrage of self-loathing.

"Things will not change," adding, "you just keep stringing me along," I declared.

"Couldn't you just find somebody else, Carrie?" As I attempt to seduce something … Anything, substantive from her.

Carrie quickly replies. "Things will change, but you just do not believe me," she insisted.

No sooner had Carrie replied when I offset her reassuring response with my own answer by saying. "It will not, and no I do not believe you!"

Then Carrie equivocates, "No, I can't, and will not find somebody else!"

There was a ten-minute pause in our discussion for reasons I was unable to discern. Dead silence. Frustration was a common theme with Carrie. I was always fearful of her abandoning ship. The longer we remained in touch, the greater the possibility Carrie would accidently divulge bits and pieces of their profile regardless of how subtle or quasi the revelation. To illustrate the point about bits and pieces coming together, a rare event occurred quite by accident when Carrie agreed to video chat with me.

The camera was already activated on my computer, so while I was waiting for her video camera to power on, another piece of the puzzle was revealed. Mysteriously, I'm greeted by a photograph of a small black girl on Carrie's computer screen. She couldn't have been older than ten. At least coming from the view where I was sitting. Just as quickly as the picture appeared on the screen, it was gone. That little girl wasn't supposed to be seen. This girl's age was in accord with the girl claiming to be Henan from Ghana, whom I had talked to on the cell phone earlier while at Wallers.

Another lead that proved invaluable in the hunt was Carrie's Twitter account. This was another venue we used to stay in touch and send brief messages back and forth. While viewing Carries Twitter account one day, one word stood out amongst the others.

Apparently, one of their computer's was hacked into, leaving a nasty virus by a rogue hacker. It destroyed the entire history of Carnal Carrie's videos and photographs. She claimed they were worth hundreds, if not thousands of dollars. She was replying to a close personal friend who had tweeted her that went by the name @pattiputts, saying. "Yeah, Nate has been working on the computer for two days now, and boy is he ever." (expletive) Then she adds. "You would be angry too if you relied on those videos and pictures for your income," Carrie declared. The key word was "Nate." It suggested one of two truths. Either Carrie was married, and this was her husband or, as she would remind her followers, Carrie was single and this was her partner in crime who goes by the nickname, Nate.

Eventually, I would identify "Nate" through Google search. Whatever business took Carrie away for those ten-minutes seemed to have accomplished her intended goal, and so we resumed our discussion.

"Why is it Carrie, that you keep so much from me?" I demanded to know. "Am I supposed to be kosher with your secret world?" I inquired.

Carrie winged an unexpected remark I wasn't prepared to hear when she blurted out. "I did vomit today!"

However, I ignored her comment. I had my own agenda. "Your partnership with these pimps is right, yes?" I asked inquisitively.

Typical of Carrie's evasiveness she answers back, "not actually!"

Revisiting Carrie's brush with her vomiting episode, I commented. "Well if I had to perform unnatural things before the camera all day, I would vomit too."

"Hmmm," was all Carrie could blurt out. Uncertain why she reacted as she did is anybody's guess. But this I'm sure. It did not carry much weight, given Carrie's propensity to lie.

"Is hmmm, all you have to say, I asked?"

Taking a defensive posture, Carrie tries to solicit empathy with a disclaimer. "But I was feeling sick, that's why."

Knowing Carrie's comment to be erroneous, and untruthful I replied, "I don't know why," I said. "You seemed perfectly helpful, and playful in your other videos with men and women," I argued.

Finally, Carrie knowing that I knew what she had done during one of her video tapings she couldn't help but admit to her tryst with another (expletive) so Carrie had no choice but to admit to wrongdoing, as she replied, "sometimes!"

"You're also accommodating your friend Bernie's appetite quite frequently aren't you Carrie?" I said. Initially, I thought Bernie was a man residing in her home, but it was finally identified as her pet dog. "Bernie, the dog." Expensive little doggie at that.

"But you have not," … Carrie began and then stopped.

"There are certain things you cannot muddle your way through Carrie; you can't have it both ways. You can't be offended one minute, saying it made you sick and then the next time find it acceptable. Moreover, you don't think I have any inkling of what is going on with you. I am not the man for you Carrie! If you wanted to drop me altogether, there were many windows of opportunity for you to unhitch the wagon and go to another unsuspecting victim."

However, you stay, while this poor soul waits until November, is this right sweetheart?" I asked.

"Ahhhhh, forget it, you are either too tired or you're refusing to answer." Adding. "And this is the gratitude I get for hanging around the computer, waiting for you?" "You should find another friend Carrie. Games over. I don't understand," I concluded.

After babbling on for almost five-minutes endeavoring to glean information from the invisible Carnal Carrie and getting nowhere, a protest was fitting given the circumstances. Was I supposed to gravel at her feet by begging for quality time? I decided to hang around for a while longer, just to see if anything developed. This I do know, Carrie has me reeling on my heels.

Carrie, after a period of silence finally initiates a response. First on Carrie's agenda was the display of three "emo" happy smiling faces. Those three faces just served to fuel the fire burning inside me as I summon strength in this never-ending battle to entreat the truth from Carrie. In her own manipulative demeanor, Carrie could be very cunning during chat sessions. The thought occurred to me that someone might be looking over her shoulder, aiding and abetting her during our chat sessions. Continuing with our conversation, I opened my remarks with an apology, a strategic dressing.

"Sorry you had to vomit Carrie," I stated.

The event that made Carrie hurl, which I doubt ever happened, was Carrie's husband, Nathaniel whom I observed in one of her videos. My hunch would later substantiate my suspicions when I found some photographs of Carrie dressed in a wedding gown surrounded by the maids of honor during one of my searches. This meant, of course, Carrie had fabricated another lie about her marital status. The irony of it all was that there were never any photos of her husband in the wedding pictures.

"You need an understanding person. Someone who is patient. You didn't even answer my question the first time Carrie so I will ask again. "Did you say I will not see you until November or later; is this true? That is if I see you even then."

"What?" "Am I talking to me, me, and me again?" "Don't you want to defend yourself," I inquired. "No! Good, then I am continuing on with my life with or without you." Declaring to whoever may have been listening on the other end of the screen ... Perhaps an at large mystery man. I continued the lonesome dove conversation whether she was there or not.

"Carrie I'm making other plans because you only answer questions that you are comfortable with and I cannot have these unsettling toxic issues you burden me with remaining open wounds," I declared, adding. "It is unreasonable and selfish.

"Goodnight, I can't continue talking with me any longer," lashing out it seems, with no one in particular.

Putting on what I considered the performance of a lifetime, I was starting to believe my own frustration. From 6:15 P.M. until 7:05 P.M., there was silence. I didn't sign out but made a decision to keep messenger open and remain vigilant. I wanted to see if there was any likelihood Carrie would log into messenger before 9:00 P.M. If there wasn't any desire on her part by that time, I would log off and revisit this squabble between me, me, and me another day.

Evidently, Carrie was on her site web-camming for the past fifty minutes for her members and guests, because she appears online at exactly 7:05 P.M. as though everything were peaches and crème. Moreover, Carrie must have read the noisy comments while she was away because she immediately responds to the ranting and raving of bitter words.

"No love, fall asleep," Carrie alleges.

Continuing with this counterfeit blitzkrieg before Carrie conveniently falls asleep again, I wanted her to know I remained upset with her shenanigans, so I reply with indifference.

"Why even bother, you are so lethargic you're not even aware of what I'm saying half the time."

"Just woke up," Carrie insists.

"You were web-camming; making up for lost time," I retorted. "If you can't be truthful in small matters of the heart; how can you be trusted with greater things concerning the truth?" I asked.

Carrie replies with the assumption Jim is going to believe her fairytale lies again as she says. "I do love."

Some actions defy logical probabilities, so I spoon feed Carrie another question.

"How do you fall asleep, yet leave your imo application on sending smiles my way; how do you do this, are you a magician?" I demanded to know. Then I remarked. "How can I endeavor to say, "I love you," when you are unable or unwilling to be honest about something as simple as explaining the emo mystery?"

As usual, Carrie refuses to respond to the question. Then I ask Carrie a follow-up question.

"Are you still busy working on your site right now Carrie?" No answer.

"Forget it," I said. "Goodnight Carrie," tiring of her chess match, I surrender to a lost cause. Enough was enough, so I abruptly logged off messenger.

We didn't talk on June 5. I wanted Carrie to think I was in a state of indifference from the previous days' chat session. I would take advantage of this opportunity, using Google search engine to examine the sites for dating and romance scammers that displayed pictures and identities swindler's used to promote their fraud against innocent victims. Specifically, I was searching for Henan/Carnal Carrie's images. What I discovered left me startled, uneasy, and discombobulated at the magnitude of different names associated with this out-of-control woman and her band of misfits.

Oscar Wilde wrote a quote dealing with morality saying, "The books that the world calls immoral are books that show the world its own shame." Mahatma Gandhi had his own definitions on the Seven Deadly Sins. "Wealth without work, pleasure without conscience, science without humanity, knowledge without character, politics without principle, commerce without morality, and worship without sacrifice."

Whom amongst us believes we are sinful creatures? Dare I entrust this question to humankind to answer truthfully? "I am!" Unless you admit to yourself and the Lord with true conviction of heart that you are a sinner, and have a need of Jesus as your Savior, you will have no place in our Lord Jesus' kingdom when you breathe your last.

Identifying swindlers on these dating and romance scam sites revealed endless pages of female crook's including but not limited to Carrie, who unashamedly had hundreds of pictures, of alias' she used. But when asked about these, she insisted the pictures were stolen. Used by Nigeria, and Ghana, people to execute their fraudulent schemes against American citizens, she would tell me. Since Carrie blamed other countries, this diverted attention away from the true source. (Carrie and company) I know Carrie is untruthful based on material evidence gathered from searches that disclosed other co-conspirators associated with her.

I don't deny that some models and/or prostitute's photos are compromised and used by incorrigibles from Africa. However, to the degree that I have witnessed Carnal Carrie's name appearing time, and time again by other victims who have fallen prey to her fraudulent schemes is just not mere coincidence. Here are some references that parallel and illustrate this point.

One person writes about seeing a picture of Carnal Carrie, who had given herself the alias Jeanne Maples using email, hot.heat@yahoo. com. Jeanne claims to be from Accra, Ghana, age thirty-three, DOB:

05/12/1988. The man feels it is his civil duty to inform the public about other alias' Carrie uses. He drafts his letter based on the scammer's list found on the internet "I have chatted on social networks using chat bazaar, and I think this scammer girl from Accra, Ghana named Princess Jeanne Maple is a swindler." She sent me a copy of her passport, United Kingdom visa, and some photos by email. It is the same photo on your scammer list but now she identifies herself as Janice Troffer, using email hot.heat50@yahoo.com. It is the same location and the same age. Additionally, Jeanne had an account on Skype going by the username "Crispy fly." This woman has multiple emails such as crispyfly@live.com, and jeannemaples66@yahoo.com. This victim insists they are all the same scammer using multiple emails that run a secret network in Nigeria.

Next, let us examine a different format scammers engage in to snare innocent victims. This individual points the finger in Carrie's direction as well. The victim advertises his experience with Carrie via a love letter Carnal Carrie, aka, Cybil Jones wrote to him using email hooo_hum@ yahoo.com. In this fraud scheme, her age is 31, DOB: 03/13/1987. Carrie insists she resides in Accra, Ghana. She begins the letter that has the makings of a grief-stricken young women pouring out every ounce of affection for her dearly absent lover ... Very dramatic ... Almost believable.

Love,

Dear handsome lover, I love you so much sweetheart. I just cannot get enough of you. You have brightened my world in such a way that I cannot express how much love I have, and feel for you. I am overflowing with so much happiness that I'm crying, and they are tears of so much joy hon, and it is all for you, my love. You have lifted me from the grave ... dark shadows of loneliness, solitude, and doom that I thought my life would always be. Thank you so much for all you have given me ... a new beginning and a beautiful future to look forward too. I love you.

I cannot get you off my mind hon. You are in my thoughts every morning I wake up and then, I look at your picture and tell you good morning. As I stumble to the kitchen to make some coffee, you are there with me. When I take my shower, you are always on my mind. When I drive down the road, I sing to you and you occupy my mind as well. I cannot wait to touch you and feel your loving arms wrapped so tight around me. I want to look deep into your eyes' and show you all the love I have for you. I want to kiss your soft sweet lips forever. And I want to whisper in your ear; I love you hon.

Every waking moment I live, you are on my mind, and as I lay down at night to go to sleep you are in my prayers, and your picture is the last thing I see as I close my eyes' to dream. You are in my dreams, and they are so beautiful hon. You are my one true love, and my one and only. I will not love anyone as much as I love you. If I cannot have you, honey, I will lay down my life, as I cannot go on without you. I feel your love and I pray that you can feel my love for you. You are my inspiration and my reason for being. Without you, I could not exist.

Most scammers intentionally throw religion into the mix with the pre-conceived notion they will not be perceived as a threat, and, therefore, more apt to connect with their targeted victim. Feeling embolden, allow me to be a tad facetious and enlighten you with a smidge of my dry sense of humor.

"Wasn't her letter every man's perfect dream to receive a heartfelt love letter from Carrie? How could anyone reject this woman's touching sentiments to her one and only?" "Of significant interest; she vows to lay down and die because she is unable to live without her beloved." What is peculiar, neither the victim nor scammer has met the other except through photographs; how dreamy!

Carrie now mutates into another female feline becoming Yasmin Abib using an email address, seemstressalsum6@yahoo.com. She resides in Kumasi; Ghana and is now age 13, DOB: 05/01/1994. However, there is a notable flaw in a photograph dating back to 1997. Observing the picture and comparing it with other pictures, it doesn't take a novice photographer to realize this photo highly resembles a woman in her thirty's and not a thirteen-year-old. I paid particular attention to a high priced cross Carrie wears almost daily or while she is on live cam. I printed off this page on 6/11/2013. If the photo I was viewing showing her to be thirteen, with a DOB as 1994; then the math tends to favor a woman in the age group of 29-30. It is a very foolish decision on the part of Carrie to pose as someone younger than her actual age.

Anonymous brought this to the attention of the public as he reveals Carrie's Skype username as "Shadow. Malinda." The picture is Carnal Carrie at age thirteen. Victims are conned to her website to view; unbeknownst to them, the misfit's simple scheme. It is a rerun from a previous video. Everyone believed Carrie was in real time, as she disrobes etc., etc., Carrie asks the viewers to partake in the celebration, provided the members paid for the privilege. One member asked Carrie how she was able to dance in the background away from the computer with her hands waving while she is replying to messages on her keyboard. He went on to say, but there was no response. He then concludes by stating. "Whoever they are. they are always asking for money to fix their webcam because it keeps cutting out while she dances, or for some other strange problem, and it is a rip-off."

The person addresses Carrie as a porn star. However, I believe any woman engaged in this profitable industry performing as "flesh for money" sex is prostituting themselves, not to mention it is an abomination in the sight of God. "Call em as you see em, is all I'm saying."

To regard men as easily duped to the degree that they think hundreds of Carrie's photographs were compromised by groups of renegade Nigerians and Ghana residences from Africa just boggles my mind. With literally hundreds; thousands of models/prostitutes to choose from out of the myriad of photographs on the internet, it is precarious they just happen to single out Carnal Carrie's photographs. Also, Carrie and crew favor Ghana for their base of operation because they feel secure knowing our government will not send any investigator to those two countries. The majority of the time Carrie sends email's using Yahoo.com accounts, to entrap their victims.

Theatrics is an artist forte. Cloning herself repeatedly, Carrie goes to great lengths to make Accra, Ghana her residential operation center for swindling. Carrie assumes the alias name of Gail Mitchell, using email gmitchell8@yahoo.com. Gail is twenty-nine-years-old, DOB, 01/10/1984. Carrie, an active professional by now, is a law student from

Quebec Canada, who transferred to Ghana. Again, the victim asserts the picture he is seeing is that of a porn star. "Of course, it is!" It is the ultimate fraud to divert attention away from themselves even though they have their own websites www.carnalcarriexxx.com, using it as their secondary operation. Fraud is their meat and potato's operation.

One more registered a complaint, and we will put this puppy to bed. Carrie identifies herself as Helen Bailey, and she is using email, helenbailey@hotmail.com. Are we surprised to hear Helen is from Accra, Ghana, age twenty-eight, DOB: of 11/20/1984? This list foreshadows early photographs of Carrie. Under this alias, Carrie includes four separate photographs in different settings. The page, as it turned out, is the victim's account of his acquaintance with Helen.

His story begins by informing the viewer he had developed a relationship with Helen since July through Skype. (Here we go, Skype, Skype, and Skype) Anonymous goes on to say, Carrie asked for funds from him because she had been sick and needed these funds for medication. She had a job as a host at a restaurant, however, from there she moved to Accra. He had sent her a total of three-hundred dollars.

She was coming to me when her Dad died. He had an estate and sent me this certificate for five and one-half-million dollars. It was an authentic bank document, according to this person in every way except for the money. Much of the information she had gathered from me was from my chat video and resume', and my contacts there. Anyway, I have not heard from her since. I took the document to the bank for authentication. He ends his account of events here.

Behind the scammers mask is a con artist that gets infinite pleasure in "putting one over" on anyone who responds to the call of the swindler. The compulsion to swindle is so high that a scammer will produce a fraud even if they gain no money from it. Scammer's swindle each other. They are so obsessed with this form of crime that the big lie reaches out to another lie, leaving truth in the light and the lie nestled in the abyss.

Carrie and I had not talked to each other for two days now. The next opportunity came on June 7, 2013. I initiated the chat session again. It took some prodding to get Carrie's attention, but she finally appeared. At 10:28 A.M., I logged online expecting Carrie would be there. If she wasn't, I would have squandered the most valuable asset for information gathering. "Gotcha," would be in ruins in the corridors of this apartment complex. The first order of business was to see if I could use threats as a medium to tell Carrie there were consequences for bad behavior.

"Carrie today is the final day," I threatened. "If you don't chat with me by 8:00 P.M. your time, there will be no further contact from me," she was warned. Another feeble attempt to reach Carrie was made at 1:54 P.M.

"Where are you? Time will have its way," I muttered to myself.

Getting closer to the deadline; crunch time, Carrie makes her presence known, logging in at 7:14 P.M. Her behavior using the silent treatment as a weapon of choice during our last session was crude. What Carrie stood to gain by this radical maneuver wasn't understood. I hoped it would not rear its ugly head during this session. None-the-less, I counted it as all gain since Carrie did not abandon me and move forward to another unsuspecting sacrificial lamb. Admittedly, Carrie had me sweating bullets for a while. Carrie didn't express any remorse, and no apologies were forthcoming.

Carrie opens the discussion with her signature salutation saying, "hello dear."

"Do you know what I was just doing?" I asked lightheartedly. "Are you there Carrie?" I asked.

"I'm here," Carrie responds in typical fashion.

The first topic was going to touch on emails and Ghana briefly, so I fired off more questions to Carrie. "Since you never answer any of my email's, etc., I went blogging in Western Africa," I informed Carrie.

I told you about the problem with email," Carrie stated.

"No Carrie, you didn't tell me." Anyway, "I was researching Ghana for Kumasi, Ashanti Adum." Using the element of surprise, I wanted to catch Carrie off guard. However, it didn't go as planned, as Carrie replies, "Okay!"

Continuing unfazed, I remarked, "I looked into area police reports to see if you had ever been arrested." Carrie's response solicited a three-syllables reply.

Carrie answered. "Okay, cool."

"Not cool!" I uttered. I felt Carrie was making a valiant effort to get beneath the surface of my skin again.

"Okay!" She replies without much fanfare.

Nothing was working to get Carrie unnerved, so I typed an open-ended comment sent hurdling in Carrie's court hoping to get some resemblance of an intelligent response. "It frightens me."

That must have hit a nerve. I believe I have Carrie's attention as she says. "What is it?"

"They are getting serious about arresting people caught in the pornography industry," I explained.

"I see," Carrie remarked, using few words again.

Getting a flat response from Carrie, I thought to sprinkle a little spice into the conversation, so I tell Carrie. "I would hate to think you would go to jail over something like pornography," telling Carrie bluntly.

"This was in Kumasi?" Carrie asked. Carrie's interest peaked when Adum Kumasi was mentioned.

"Oh yes, especially Kumasi. It is because of some pervert earning ten-thousand dollars every thirty-minutes uploading homemade porn and sending it to the U. S." I inform Carrie.

Inquiring minds now want to know, so Carrie asked, "is it going to be out soon?"

"He was using women and young girls. Then they arrested a man for selling child porn. Also, it was a sting operation between the U.S. and Ghana authorities," I remind Carrie.

"That is bad, never knew about that," Carrie declared.

"No it's sick!" Came my response. "This is exploiting children. It's plain evil." I emphasized.

"Bad," Carrie repeated to herself.

Reversing course, I switch to another subject entirely. I intentionally asked Carrie about her departure status from Ghana. "How soon can you leave?" I asked.

"You mean leave Ghana?" Carrie inquired.

I repeated the question to see what departure date she might give, just to see if she might give me a date certain.

"About when do you think you can leave the country?" I asked.

"I am really not sure. Maybe no more than two months. That would be my guess." Carrie hedged.

I surmised I would never see Carrie, so I entertained myself with her cheap trash talk.

"That's quite a long time. About when your contract expires with GoDaddy.com., isn't it?" I mention GoDaddy.com in an attempt to force Carrie's hand by seeing if she will admit to being associated with GoDaddy.com server.

"Yeah," Carrie said in agreement.

"Well, sweetheart that is Mid-September, just a little over three months from now." I countered.

Carrie isn't going to be arrested for stretching her lungs, that's for sure, as she says, "yes."

Play along to get along again, as I ask Carrie. "So am I supposed to wait, and wait, and wait?"

"Yes." Carrie replies.

Spreading the icing on thick in order to gage Carrie's guilt, while appealing to her reasoning, I commented. "You're asking a lot, my darling."

"Oh!" Replied Carrie, sensing she was grandstanding or at the very least being condescending.

Remaining steadfast and not surrendering to Carrie's attitude of complacency was not going to occur on Jim's watch, so I continued bombarding Carrie with more questions.

"Don't you think so, I asked?"

"Yes dear," responded Carrie casually.

"It has been almost three months now Carrie and we began our friendship sometime before April Princess," I said, expressing a sense of futility.

This time, Carrie replies with a one-syllable word as she pointedly remarks, "right."

"How much longer do you think Jim Jacob's can wait, honey," I sheepishly ask while biting my tongue.

Carrie replied. "What do you mean?" At least, Carrie strung together four words.

Playing the trump card; my age, I answer. "I'm not getting any younger."

"Yes honey I know. We were to meet though." Carrie's words are given in broken English. Likely staged roleplaying like I frequently use with her.

Playing possum, I ask Carrie. "Are you saying we were meant to be together," just so we are on the same page.

"Yes," Carrie responded without hesitation.

It's time to switch to assertiveness mode, as I announce. "How do you know? All we ever seem to accomplish are these back and forth barbs we exchange towards each other!" I informed Carrie.

"Yeah, but I do know from my heart," Carrie confesses.

"But honey, you have to be truthful and honest with me. That hurts me something bad," challenging Carrie to get soft.

Carrie is compliant, acknowledging in agreement. "Okay dear."

I appeal to Carrie's sense of sincerity as I say. "I want to talk about our future without having to continuously nag you about truthfulness, princess," I said wanting to capture Carrie's undivided attention by using "princess" to stroke her ego.

"Okay," Carrie replied without hesitation.

"Carrie, there is nothing you do or have "DONE" that I'm not aware of concerning your adventurous life at this point." I then repeat the use of the word. "Done … Done … Done," for emphasis.

"Okay," she answers. Carrie has such a command of words, I thought, smiling. "Okay, okay, okay, okay!"

I continue using flattery to persuade Carrie to open up more. "Just be the love of my life, that is all I want honey." I insisted.

Carrie is in conformance saying. "So as I want dear."

"No more secrets then; please!" I pleaded with Carrie.

"Okay," replied Carrie. Does this sound familiar? Rather catchy, this word, "okay!"

"I have told you everything about me, which is boring, by the way," I tell Carrie.

"Okay dear," Carrie replied.

With dry humor over Carrie's lack of words, I spontaneously type. "Blah, blah, blah, blah."

"My sister and I talked about a Missionary Ministry in Ghana. This Minister has been to my sister's church on five separate occasions. He wants volunteers to come over there to do some work for the people of Ghana building pig sty's."

In Carrie's usual formatted response, the reader must be bored with her replies. "I see." She acknowledged.

"Although he did insist the individual had to rely on their own resources for airfare to Ghana. I thought maybe if I called World Relief Organizations, they could fund my trip." (Throwing out the carrot to see if I would get a nibble)

"Okay, sounds like a good deal." Carrie's response to the plausibility of a trip to Ghana didn't seem to have the enthusiasm I was expecting, "red flag" again.

"It's a Christian organization that wants to spearhead this project," I added.

"I see." Carrie blurted out in a rather flat-line response.

I wanted to "tickle" Carrie's ear, so I said. "If I get close enough to you during my free time maybe we could create the perfect reunion princess," I said in gist.

Carrie's reaction to this proposal. "Hum!"

"Not good, right?" As I put out feelers to assess Carrie's response.

"It is," Carrie replied quickly.

"I will check into it Monday. Call a friend who does mission work in Liberia. Maybe it's Libya or Sierra Leon," correcting myself.

"Okay," Carrie responds with her customary simplistic reaction.

I pinpointed the location for Carrie. Informing her it was in the Northern part of Africa.

Carrie replied in agreement, saying, "Yes."

"Anyway, we will see." Then I switched gears again saying, "so why the silent treatment for three days Carrie?"

That question hit a cord and Carrie was all over it like a high plains drifter.

"Okay love, I was seeing if you could get me the money for the rental because you never answered me when I talked about my need," Carrie responded with deliberate speed.

"Not now Carrie. I can't," I insisted. "You must be getting a significant income from your website." This was my position repeatedly, in defiance of Carrie's demands for additional money.

Carrie, becomes combative, trying to make the argument that it wasn't so, as she replied. "Not as you think, though."

"Honey, there was no rational in what you did by sending the seven-hundred dollars to your mother that was meant to pay your landlord," I reminded Carrie. Continuing, I let Carrie know that she was withholding another dirty little secret from me.

"You have three screens you monitor on your website," I informed her.

"She needed them," she claimed.

We approach the dueling banjo extravaganza again as I begin calculating the math for Carrie. I begin to break down the dollar amounts according to the information she had given me previously when we discussed her earnings. I haven't told her anything she does not already know. However, play the game I will.

"You earn between three and five dollars per minute chatting with paying customers, in addition to your token tips perverts contribute as a bonus for your coffers Carrie."

"There are partner's involved," Carrie said adamantly.

"Princess you should not be sharing tips you earn and giving it to them," I said. "Furthermore, you have "on-site" tapings, and "in-house" tapings at two-hundred dollars per video, and fifty dollars posing for photographs every day. Then you said sweetheart, you were doing videos and putting in longer hours, just to catch up for lost time. Isn't this what you said hon?" Badgering Carrie to concur.

"Yeah," she replied.

"In addition darling, there is revenue sharing when your videos are played, or sold on other sites in addition to all the other garbage you distribute on your web page." I wanted Carrie to know I knew much more than what she was giving me credit for.

"Yeah," was all Carrie could answer concerning these recent revelations.

"Every partner, including you honey, receives advertisement revenue that most everyone shares in that industry." I wanted to explain to Carrie how advertisement revenue works.

Carrie interrupts to educate me about her predicament saying. "Yeah, that is right. However, I am not getting as much as that," as she fervently attempts to educate Jim Jacobs.

"But honey, my figures suggest you should be receiving as a minimum, five-thousand to ten-thousand dollars per month," I insisted.

"Yes, but it is not what I'm getting." Carrie declares without hesitation.

Applying fatherly advice, I inform Carrie that she should be getting the lion's share of the profits. "You helped direct some of those films, and you recruit new models for web-camming," I declared. Also. "Are you telling me you are making little or nothing? This is difficult to wrap my arms around Carrie," I confessed.

"That is why I went to court," said Carrie attempting to drive home her point.

Knowing Carrie is in deception mode now, I decide once again to play along.

"But you are not there now, are you?" As I voice objection over her alleged court appearance.

"No," came Carrie's curt reply.

"Carrie, then what have you gained?"

Currie could do nothing but concede to this contrite scheme saying, "nothing good yet," she admitted.

I deliberately tell Carrie to give her partners a proposition. "Tell them your fiancée will charge them two-thousand dollars per month for the use of my computer. "If not, tell them I want it back," I insisted. "They can give you the two-thousand dollars."

"Okay love." Carrie is playing this game very well.

"My laptop is probably the best computer they have right now, tell me this is so." As I patiently wait to see how Carrie answers this question.

Carrie, after a while, said. "There are two."

Carrie did not answer my direct question, so I lean on her some more. "My computer is one of two; right Carrie?" I asked while waiting to see if she would admit to receiving the Toshiba laptop.

Carrie took a long pause before answering, however, as a lamp is unable to give light without a bulb, so it is with a confession. Without guilt, there is no confession of truth. Carrie finally gives her answer. "Yes," she replied.

Now that I have her admitting to having my Toshiba laptop, I forge ahead with another buzz-saw question. "How much do you think they stand to lose if they do not have that computer? Plenty I should think." With bravado and gusto in my swagger now, I feel splendid while probing Carrie with these questions as I end this segment of the questioning.

Carrie responds quickly. "I am not sure what they would lose, I would have to calculate," she concluded.

"Would you do that for me please darling?" I asked.

MBASE has all the figures (MBASE is an acronym for some kind of computer language or computer talk) they keep up to the minute reports on how much prostitutes earn each day.

"Somebody there knows." I said.

Carrie finally agrees, and replies. "Sure."

"Why not ask? If you don't want to, I will." Informing Carrie with boldness.

"No, everything is fine, I will ask them," Carrie responded quickly.

Manna will rain from Heaven the day I see this pulled off for my benefit.

"You be very careful Carrie." Letting her think, I was concerned for her safety. Although, bogus at best.

It appears Carrie is getting giddy about now, as she acknowledges saying, "Yes dear, thank you."

"I don't trust any of your partner's darling," I stated with contrived caution. "Look how many times they have corrupted my computers. Prowling about like roaring Lions seeking whom they might devour."

I decide to go all in, (my call to arms) by approaching Carrie and asking if she would be willing to get me in contact with one of her partners in crime. (Pimps)

"Princess, do you think it would be helpful if I talked to one of your partners," I inquired.

"Gee, I don't know honey. I don't want to get into any trouble," Carrie hesitated.

"Honey I won't get angry or threaten them. I don't want you getting into trouble either," trying my level best to convince her to reveal a name and phone number of a known associate.

Carrie relented too quickly, but she surrendered name and number none-the-less. "Okay, but do not call him now," she said. "You just want to chat with one of them; Right?" Seeking reassurance.

Lending piece of mind to Carrie, I replied. "I will talk to him as if I were your agent."

As an afterthought Carrie asked. "Why do you want to speak to them? Oh, don't call them now, I beg of you sweetheart!" Carrie said panicking.

"I promise you princess," trying to put Carrie at ease. Adding, "I just want to get a sense of their temperament, is all."

Carrie continues to seek validation as she again says. "You will later sweetheart, right?"

"Of course; at a reasonable time, honey," I remarked.

Carrie is finally at peace once she is convinced of my promise. "Okay!" (Where have we heard "okay," before?)

"I will speak very calm, and be reasonable with them," giving my solemn oath to Carrie.

Carrie pleads with me to be careful saying. "Please, okay?"

"If I'm getting nowhere, I will let him know most assuredly that I will find a way to fly over to Ghana and have a man-to-man talk with him ... Leave you out of it of course," I inform Carrie, grinning from ear to ear while typing the message.

"Okay sweetheart, that's good," she said, then added. "I'm feeling sleepy," she declares deceitfully.

"What time is it now?" I asked.

Carrie informs me it is 1:30 P.M.

I ask Carrie before she logs off for the big man's number, saying. "I will call and talk with him in the morning."

Carrie replies to my request for his number with a surprise response. "Nope!"

So much to say, yet; so little time, so I ask her again. "May I have his number before you go?"

With cell phone number now in hand, I will know in the morning whether the number is bogus or legitimate. (+233246619665) "Is this his cell phone number honey?" I asked.

"Do you have a name that belongs to this number sweetie?"

"Yes, his name is Allen Simple," Carrie informs me.

"Okay darling, thank you." Before letting Carrie go, I expressed praise for her courage and cooperation.

"Well princess, I missed talking with you very much, and missed you a ton," I said coyly.

Carrie, not one to miss a queue replies. "Miss you too sweetheart, and love you bunches."

Then, for Carrie's edification again I said. "I worry and pray for you always."

As we are winding down Carrie concludes the chat by saying. "Thanks."

Continuing to bombard Carrie with gushy, excessive flattery I tell her. "I will always love you Carrie, and will save a place in my heart for you."

When Carrie stated she was allegedly taking partners to court, I impressed upon her the importance of retaining her own counsel to represent her best interest in this joint pornography adventure. Even though one has to be repulsed by the very idea of encouraging anyone to get involved in this industry) It is clear by now Carrie is an accomplice to her partner's crime's. Carrie just about sold me on the idea she was living in sub-standard conditions while her partners were living the life of luxury some miles from her location. She informed me later in one of our chat conversations that she did indeed, retain an Attorney. Of course, the name was correct, but in reality, Carrie never consulted with any attorney, as I discovered later using Google search. There were some occasions where Carrie could be very convincing. This is why it is referred to as an ongoing chess match.

The following day, I was on the phone talking with Allen, who somehow has somehow managed to obtain a telephone number in Ghana. I must admit Allen's role-playing was done rather well. Not knowing what to expect, I proceeded with caution. Here was a man on the other end of the telephone using a cell phone (red flag) who spoke with an accent. I surmised he was either British or Canadian. However, as we progressed into the conversation, the accent favored more Canadian than British. The phone rings a few times before Allen answers.

"Yes, who is this?" The voice on the other end of the phone line asked.

"Jim Jacobs," I answered.

"Who gave you this number," Allen insisted on knowing.

"Henan Asante, also known as Carnal Carrie, as you well know Allen," I replied boldly.

"What does this have to do with me?" Allen demanded to know.

Not one to miss an open door opportunity I replied. "I'm glad you asked Allen. Say Allen, Carrie has shared with me some rather disconcerting injustices at the behest of you and your partner friends. This does not bode well if you are partners," I say, testing his demeanor.

"Why? What is the problem? Everything is good!" Allen insisted in what sounded like a Canadian dialect.

"First Allen, there is this business about a vehicle or lack of one for Carrie," I told him.

Allen gives what he believes to be a logical explanation. "Carrie had a car at one time, but unfortunately, she had an unfortunate accident and we do not have the money for another car for her," he alleges.

"I don't know about that Allen," I reminded him. "You seem to have plenty of money to live in luxury while Carrie pays for a sub-standard rental house. She is practically living in squalled conditions in Adum Kumasi, but you already knew that Allen," I announced. "She tells me the landlord is after her for back payments amounting to seven-thousand dollars," I inform Allen. "Then again, you know this as well."

Allen, alarmed, said. "Carrie never told us about this problem with the rent."

"That isn't the only problem we have Allen," expecting him to end the conversation at a moment's notice.

"What do you mean, not the only problem?" Allen asked bewildered, his tone hurried.

Hearing Allen's comment beckoned for brusque badgering. "Allen, Allen, I said. You folks have been cheating Carrie out of money that rightfully belongs to her," pressing him to get my point across. "Carrie has copyrights to her material and she is the licensed operator of her own sight, and yet, I find out you folks are feeding Carrie table scraps as income," I politely inform Allen. "Allen, I question your official dealings with Carrie in this phantom partnership you folks created," I declared.

I beginning to feel disdain for him. I know it's just another platform to try and con me with dis-information. I walk Allen through the same math formula I shared with Carrie, just so that Allen knows what I knew about income distribution. Especially, with Carrie's name attached to the products they peddle to their customer base in this smut-laden industry. Realistically speaking, I get agitated when women are viewed as a commodity or a piece of property and should have no part in associating with this industry of iniquity. It's men who dominate this age old industry, which is why I refer to them as "pimps in suits."

Continuing to express misgivings I have about Allen, I inquire. "Why doesn't Carrie have a generator for backup during power outages like you folks have in your upscale home?"

Allen, avoiding culpability, tries to pacify me by saying. "My other partners think Carrie doesn't need a generator."

I seize upon this opportunity to voice my strong opposition; sternly reprimanding Allen for his assumption by letting know he was misguided.

"Allen, how can you even entertain the thought of two different standards here?" "You use one set of rules for yourselves, and another for Carrie," I said in all candor. "And that is cruel and insensitive where I come from," I profoundly stated.

I wasn't actually arguing this point on behalf of Carrie, but in the outside realm of sex slave trafficking were women are mistreated and abused in this crude, unforgiving pay-for-flesh industry.

"Other partners have a say too, Allen argued in his defense."

"Look Allen, I began. In plain English let me tell you in no uncertain terms how I feel about now," I announced. "You have been very condescending towards me ever since we started this conversation, so I'm going on record to let you know I don't appreciate it. Furthermore, you should know that without Carrie, you would not be making any money off the flesh of other women like the leeches you are," I hissed. "Carrie is your meal ticket, and deserves better. By the way, she owns the company," I informed Allen.

"Here is what needs to be done," as Allen listened intently. "First you need to assist Carrie in paying down her debt to the proprietor's rental property. Next, Carrie should be given better living accommodations. I base this on what I have seen of Carrie's inadequate living conditions when we video chat. You still listening to me Allen?"

Allen's voice came in loud and clear as he replied. "Yes, yes, of course. I'm listening Jim."

Time for the meat and potatoes of our discussion as I continue voicing my displeasure, even though they may assume I'm gullible enough to fall for their counterfeit charade of mistreatment against Carrie. Both unaware I am onto this wicked roleplaying they've concocted to apparently convince me it was legitimate. The question is, "Which one of us has the upper hand."

"I believe it is justified, and morally conscionable that you and your partners compensate Carrie for the agreed upon wages based on the contract everyone signed." When you signed the contract with your other partner's and Carrie, it became binding when you put ink to the paper and it became a legal contract Allen."

Allen acknowledges in agreement replying. "Yes, yes, of course, you are right Jim."

"Why do you have Carrie's passport Allen?"

"We keep it safe here for us so she doesn't lose it," Allen claims.

"Allen, that doesn't wash with me. I believe Carrie is old enough and far more capable of managing her own affairs; don't you think? So why do you folks insist on keeping this from her?"

"Partner's think it is best Jim," Allen said, his tone becoming gruff and defensive. "But I will talk to partner's and see what can happen Jim."

"How can she leave Ghana, if you have her passport Allen?"

"Why does she want to leave Ghana, she has good life here with us," Allen protested.

"Perhaps Carrie wants a breath of fresh air Allen. Change of scenery, who knows."

"Okay, I'll talk to partner's, but I can't promise you anything now," Allen insisted.

"There is absolutely no reason why Carrie shouldn't have a wardrobe allowance, and subsistence for meals," I stated to Allen. "Furthermore Allen, you used a very lame excuse when you informed me you didn't have the funds to purchase a vehicle for Carrie."

"Of course Jim, I totally understand your position, and we will make changes, okay?" Allen assured me.

"If you don't uphold your end of the bargain, me and my military buddies will come to Ghana to pay you a visit. I don't really think you would enjoy seeing us intruding on your lives," I declared while continuing. "This also implies hands-off Carrie. I do not want to see bruises or marks on her body … No abuse…. No mistreatment, nothing Allen."

Allen quickly concurs when he hears the ultimatums. "We will take care of this problem Jim, you can be sure," Allen assures me.

Business finished, mission accomplished, I hung up the phone. I loathed talking to this person knowing he was bogus, however, if I was going to make headway, this introduction with Allen became necessary even though I knew it was staged. It would be to my benefit. Just the idea of knowing this person could speak English fluently, was enough for me, and that he had connections to Carrie.

I could have prolonged this makeshift discussion, but I felt it was pointless. Success already materialized when Carrie gave me the phone number and a name to one of the many parties that now comprise the missing pieces of the puzzle. This confirmed Carrie was not acting alone but had several people involved in this scamming operation. I was scammed, and I was certain they were not Nigerian or Ghana scammers. This was too well orchestrated and organized. So, I placed a period on my conversation with Allen.

My next session with Carrie didn't occur until June 9, 2013. It was very early in the morning for an old man such as I. The time was 5:53 in the morning. The only logical reason for being up this early was my inability sleep that evening. Who knows, I was probably thinking about the previous day's contact with Allen. I needed to concentrate on my next strategic move if I wanted to make any progress in the "gotcha" hunt. After all, I didn't hedge for a millisecond the encounter I had with Allen would feel so surreal. If this swindling group wanted to manipulate me through mind games, I would show them I was a most formidable opponent. The hunter is inching closer to identifying his prey.

Carrie and I begin another chat session after the previous day's discussion with Allen, even though I knew it was an exercise in futility. I have awakened from my slumber. Why was "instant messenger environment" turned off again?" I wondered.

Carrie is online and wants to initiate a conversation with me. "Hi honey, I'm very well today darling," Carrie announced.

I cannot understand why the environment is off but hesitate to bring it to Carrie's attention for fear she will give me the silent treatment again, so I welcome her greeting. "Good morning sweetheart."

"How are you doing dear?" Carrie asked. At least Carrie is stringing words together now.

Returning Carrie's greeting, I expressed concern for her safety. "There was no word from you yesterday," I told Carrie, attempting to show concern.

"Oh Yes! I was with partners," Carrie insinuated.

I intervene before Carrie can speak as I say. "You're with them every day!"

"No, Carrie replied plainly, not all days," Carrie tells me.

Carrie briefly has me unhinged, so I ask. "Then what …Why not let me know? .…Are you angry with me?"

"Nope, Carrie replies."

I wish she would not do this to me. I remain fearful of losing her before I get what I have labored so meticulously for these past few months. However, I knew why Carrie did not appear online yesterday, so I grilled her for the truth. (What's new?)

"Why not contact me then? Did you go out somewhere?"

"No, Carrie answered, I was with a friend."

"First you said nope, then no, and now you tell me you were with a friend. I'm feeling hopelessly confused Carrie. What do you mean princess?"

"I was out with a friend at her salon," Carrie alleges.

"This is classic mind games 101 as I want Carrie to think I've become combative. "I just asked if you went somewhere and you said nope, no, a friend, and now bar!"

"No, salon!" Carrie corrected me.

Still wanting to seem ignorant, I challenge Carrie with her use of the word "salon" asking for clarification. "What is a salon?"

Carrie finally straightened out my application of the word "salon" by correcting my confusion. "Salon is hairdressing, nails, etc."

"All right honey!" I said. "You caught me off guard there for a while."

"I came home late, Carrie admitted."

Always at the ready with another question, I wanted to know Carrie's excuse for getting home late. "Why late, was it Sally?" I inquired.

Although I was grasping at straws, this other person was just another piece of the puzzle coming together. Little did I realize it at the time that it was one of Carrie's Siblings.

"Yep," Carrie confirms seconds later. "I was with Sally."

Once again, I had to resort to grilling Carrie during this chat session. Initiating a little psychological cat and mouse game, as I plot to conceal my cunning and crafty wares. The ultimate objective was to solicit a confession about her deceptive behavior. I start the discussion with innocence as I begin to lay the foundation by grueling Carrie about yesterday's activities.

Commenting, I said. "You are awfully quiet. Apparently something is wrong that you are not sharing with me Carrie."

"Yeah, Carrie replies."

Trying to divert attention away from herself Carrie asked. "How is the weather there?"

"Cloudy," I replied. "But the real question I want to know is why you are so quiet, did the two of you do something wrong?"

Carrie adamantly attempts to deny anything is wrong. Her response. "No!" She said.

However, it is not setting well with my soul, as the discussion continues. "You must have honey, my heart aches so bad. You must have done something wrong. My heart weeps when something is wrong," I insisted.

Carrie questions this phenomenon as she asked. "How is that possible, how?"

"I really can't explain it myself honey, the heart just knows when something is not right. Maybe it is the indwelling of the Holy Spirit inside me that is warning me about something bad that has happened." I explained.

A twinge of nervousness comes from Carrie when she says. "Okay, okay!"

"Okay, okay!" That doesn't say much, so I said. "Okay what?"

Carrie is playing musical chairs with me because she knows very well what is about to come next. However, I feel Carrie is mocking her hunter right now, as the inevitable is about to be revealed.

"What is wrong dear," Carrie asked innocently?

"Something you did yesterday, it doesn't feel right," I reminded her again.

Again, again, and again, Carrie rephrases the question. "What is it, sweetheart?" Showcasing her bewildered state of mind.

"Carrie, you tell me," I demanded. "I just know you are not your insolent self."

She has to be testing my tolerance threshold as she states. "How do you know?"

For the umpteenth time, I repeat what I know. "I can feel it, even now princess!"

"Okay dear, have you had breakfast?" Carrie uses deflection as a defense mechanism from answering my probing question.

"Yep, when I talked to your partner Allen, I could discern instantly that he was lying to me as well," I informed Carrie.

"I see, about what dear?" Carrie seems eager to capture the details while knowing she was privy to the conversation between Allen and I the day before.

"What?" Parroting Carrie. "I talked to Allen yesterday. I knew when he was lying about the money. What he knew and didn't know. What he intentionally kept from me." That type of dialogue Carrie," I said.

Well, Carrie asked. "What did he have to say?" As if, Carrie didn't already know.

"Carrie, I said, Allen's demeanor is compatible to that of yours. I have to coax information from him. When he's cornered, he tells the truth … Bottom line honey."

"But darling, I am more interested in what he had to say to you," I impressed upon her, throwing it back onto her shoulder's.

"Allen said he was going to pay half of my rental costs," Carrie finally conceded.

Trying to extract additional information, I pressed Carrie ever harder. "And?"

Carrie added. "Allen might pay for half of the other stuff."

"What exactly is Allen willing to do?" I wanted to know. "Like clothing allowance, generator, additional compensation for taping pornography …How much more?" I inquired.

Carrie responded by throwing out a figure of four-hundred fifty dollars for videos.

"Did Allen indicate they were willing to pay the cost of airfare tickets to the United States?" I sat there waiting anxiously for Carrie's answer.

Carrie responded to the question as if she hadn't a care in the world, as she replied. "He didn't say that!"

Doing a 360-degree turn, I made a direct plea to Carrie by rendering her a word of caution. "Honey, I really wish you wouldn't do pornography because I'm fearful you will contact a transmitted disease. But no less traumatic, is the sin you are committing in the eyes of God." I declared matter-of-fact.

Carrie wasted little time repeating. "He didn't say that; he didn't say that!"

Something must have gotten lost in translation because I have no germane clue what Carrie meant, so I just rolled with it.

"Allen should, that's the way I understood it." Referring to my earlier statement about an airline ticket.

I haven't witnessed Carrie so energetic since seeing her for the first time on video chat. "Yes! Yes!" Carrie said jubilant. Why was she repeating, "yes?" This is the second time she has gone. "Air Jordan" on me.

Returning to my earlier comment, I repeated words of caution. "I really do not want you doing pornography. Contracting aids is not worth a life," I told Carrie.

Carrie must have been itching to get into the fray now because she brings in a new topic I didn't think was fitting, since she remains in denial, refusing to be open about what happened the evening before.

I doubt Carrie will ever admit to (expletive) violations of an immoral nature.

"Okay, Carrie begins, and you said I have requested help from you, and you do not like it, or feel unhappy about that. I will stop," Carrie boldly says. (I hope she will)

Not that I want to intentionally wound Carries heart, but I tell her forthrightly. "That's because they are making plenty of money that they should be paying you to meet your expenses, and save money. That is why I said that. Not because I don't want to help you," Carrie was told. Additionally, I said. "I told Allen you are partners with them, and that all the money should be divided equitably, but that you should get a higher percentage based upon you being the principal owner of the site."

"Allen said you will not help me with the rent so he needs to!" Carrie chimes in.

Reiterating my position with Carrie, I announce. "I shouldn't have too!" Making a point of this pointless squabbling. "Besides, I instructed Allen you were to be given the same living accommodation's they enjoy. They are to get you out of that rental property and put you in your own upscale home," I declared.

Lending creditability to previous comments Carrie discussed with me, we are going to dismiss her version of events. Carrie was at the salon where her sister Sally allegedly was employed. "Does this sound like a woman held prisoner against her will?" Confiding in me that she is indebted to a proprietor in Ghana, but when she receives the six-hundred dollars I sent her, she then forwards it to her mother! Her profile indicates she is married, but we now learn she is married. Carrie claims to be an only child, but we learn now she has two other sister's involved in this criminal entity. Later revelations will reveal the other sibling whose name is Debra. It will also tie close friends Patti Putts and Joey Money into the fray. But for now, we forge ahead.

"What are your plans for today?" Carrie inquired. Apparently getting bored with the information she was already privy too. I'm certain when

I contacted Allen, Carrie was in the same room with him or them. How they obtained phone numbers from Ghana to use in the United States is best left to the FBI or other investigating agency. We have to remember, they also have connections with another webcam network using their server, promoting the same smut in Quebec, Canada.

Purposefully putting in a plug, I tell Carrie. "I will be praying for you. I will also be reading Scripture to see if it speaks to me about your dilemma, and see if we can arrange to somehow fly you out of the country."

"Thanks, Carrie replied."

Carrie wants to reverse course now and redirect her attention away from Allen and gravitate towards another matter; "money." However, I was determined to distance myself from her pandering scheme's. If she were tiring of our discussion all she had to do was make an excuse to remove herself from messenger. After all, it bears repeating. They are all one and the same group of swindlers. Even if I did have an occasional flash of "hum," there wasn't any question in my mind I had the real perpetrators and they were operating inside our border's.

Carrie interrupts my next remark saying. "It's storming now." Masterful, there go my plans for a video chat.

"Might storm here too," I added.

"Okay dear, all right dear." Carrie yells, giving me pause to wonder. "What is all this brew-ha-ha?"

"By the way, Allen told me you have three computers, and he claims to have two of them in his home."

For a split second, this gets Carrie's attention. "What did he say?" As if this were a new revelation Carrie had not heard before now.

"Of course, I said, Allen alleges they don't generate that much revenue for you."

"Okay." Carrie must have breathed a sigh of relief with this piece of information.

Carrie must be sitting behind her screen laughing uncontrollably since being debriefed on all the details of my conversation with Allen by her cohorts in crime. By this time, I sensed Carrie wasn't listening, but she remained online I assumed, just to see if there were any discrepancies or extrapolated falsehoods I might have injected into my conversation with Allen.

Out of nothingness come words of anguish as Carrie's voice cries out.

"I'm feeling frigid, I'm feeling chilly, I'm, freezing, I'm freezing," Carrie continues to utter sounding as if in distress.

I'm confused by this sudden outburst, so I ask Carrie. "Why you cold, what is going on with you over there?" I wanted to know.

Carrie just continued repeating over and over. "Am feeling cold. I'm freezing."

Trying to get Carrie's attention, I ask. "What are you feeling cold from Carrie?"

Carrie continues repeating the same words, apparently in distress and without rhyme or reason. "Am feeling icy."

"Get blankets," I instructed Carrie. There was no validation other than the repeated anguish Carrie was feeling. "Am feeling frigid." Then it occurred to me. This is none other than a skit. Another ploy to get out of the chat session and go do whatever. Maybe out of necessity, she is going to swindle more victims.

Carrie goes on babbling with her apparent anxiety, saying. "Am feeling cold."

"Get some more clothes on," I told Carrie. By now, I'm beginning to feel helpless because I'm not sure whether to take Carrie seriously or if it is a collaborative effort to deceive.

On, and on, and on, Carrie verbalizes her discomfort. "I'm freezing."

"Go to the hospital, call an ambulance, do something, Carrie," I said with urgency.

Carrie wasn't listening. Instead, she verbalizes her discomfort like a broken record. "I'm feeling frigid; am feeling cold," Carrie complains in apparent agony.

"Blah, blah, blah, blah, what's new?" I then suggested Carrie call an ambulance again.

"Good," She replied.

"Now! I yelled you need an ambulance right now," I insisted again.

"Good idea Carrie said."

I love the intrigue, the game, its twists and turns. I tell Carrie. "Go to the doctors now, princess," I screamed through the screen.

"Good," Carrie answers. "What did you think Carrie would say?"

Exhausting my options, I declare. "Call a friend, somebody," I said. "Do you have chills? Can't stop shaking?" I Inquired.

"The connection is slow …The connection is slow …The connection is slow." Carrie now blurts out of nowhere.

Allowing Carrie to believe in her own misguided adventures by having her believe I'm concerned about her health, I tell her. "Go take care of you, we can talk later, okay?"

"Honey I want to have some sleep," she informs me. "Let's talk more about this later today." Carrie insists.

"Love you honey. Kisses, Jim."

"Love you, love you, love you!" Carrie is stretching this a bit much.

I embrace her words with skepticism as I return the compliment. "Love you always sweetheart!"

"Love you, love you!" Carrie finally gasped, and signed off.

Carrie and I spent about four hours on messenger that day. Keeping a tally of the one and two-syllable words Carrie used during our conversation is for your benefit as well as mine. There were eight, "yeah," "twenty-eight, "okay," ten, "no," eight, "good," "eleven, "am feeling frigid, icy, freezing, or cold," twenty-one, "yes," five "cool," and four, "I see." The point of this whole exercise was to make you aware that most swindlers, who engage in conversations with you for extended periods, reveal little about themselves. They tend to keep their responses' to a minimum. However, when they do engage in a discussion they use one and two-syllable words unless they are ready to hit you for money. Fraud artist prefers the victim do the talking. That is how they glean information from you.

"Loose lips reveal numerous tips." I appeared online at 4:13 that evening the same day. However, true to form, Carrie did not log on. There is an absolute certainty; Jim Jacobs is not amused. Swindlers typically work several prospective victims at a given moment. Before I logged off that day, I expressed my disappointment and disgust at her lying and unreliability.

"Honey, I don't think I am important enough in your life. I waited all afternoon for you to come and chat with me. It is 9:15 P.M. your time as I write this message. I told you many times, I do not want to be last in your life. My conclusion is that I'm exactly that … Dead last!" This, I concluded, was distinguished by your behavior this past week. So go and be happy. This is very wrong. Have your fun for the rest of the evening. You never fail to keep wounding and hurting me. Good night, glad you had a good day," as I close and log off messenger.

Chapter 16

The Hunted Becomes the Hunter

Aha! What a spider's web we weave, when we practice to deceive.
The weight of it all; fatigue, frustration; yes, souls' grief awakens spiritual reprieve.
Great pretender; sudden darkness without life,
and yet so hopeless, teach me insight.
Onward, forward! To what length empty offerings, surrenders to hindsight.
Jim Jacobs

Sooner, rather than later, truth prevails under the veil of secrecy and deceit. What has been hidden in darkness is revealed in the light. Dead man's bones are always there to explain mysteries of its immortality. Each one of us is prone to go astray to places that they dare not tread. Yet, whether one chooses to admit it, they find themselves going to the very place they are trying to avoid. It is a struggle sometimes for us to embrace righteousness. There exists some reprieve in life, but also trials. However, we soon realize the later will hold true. Why may you ask? The flesh is always waging war against the spiritual forces in this world. The evil one whose name is Satan, who roams about like a roaring lion to deceive you, exchanging the truth for the lie. Yes, there is occasional euphoria in a person's life, but our Lord doesn't have us here for mere enjoyment alone. We are here to glorify God, and shine the light of Jesus to a dark world in need of salvation. Lies wage war with your mind depleting you of energy. We live in a world where the eyes', ears, and heart are our most formidable enemy when differentiating between good and evil … And it is not God. Material possessions and the lust for the flesh have become our idols. The mentality of society today is a disease known as the "I" factor. "I want it and I want it now!"

As if we can dismiss the notion there are no consequences to this great deceit. "In its Simplicity, it's called. "Idol worshiping."

The author for one is just as guilty as the next man when it comes to idol worshipping. However, I'm a work in progress, and with the help of the Holy Spirit (Helper) working in my life, who is here to convict me of my sins; growing in conformance to Christ-like living, and increased faith, I can declare completeness. I pray we will all overcome the demons in our life, becoming more god-centered. It's vertical, thinking as opposed to horizontal wanderings.

The very purpose for this manuscript is to search where sin exists and attempt to disciple the lost souls of this world by bringing them to the redeeming quality of our Lord and Savior Jesus Christ. I didn't have to look very far. In Matthew; Chapter 9: 37-38, we read. "The harvest (sinners) is indeed plentiful, but the laborers (Christian believers) are few. Therefore, pray to the Lord of the harvest to send out laborers into his harvest."

Who should respond to the Lord's voice but I Jim Jacobs, who chooses to do the "Will" of our Father, who resides in Heaven Again, we turn to Isaiah; Chapter 6: verse 8. Also, I heard the voice of the Lord, saying: "Whom shall I send, and who will go for us?" Then I said. "Here am I! Send me." I have to admit, when I went to <u>www.LegofLambCams.com</u> for my research, I was met with ridicule and scorn as I tried to convey a message about the sinful nature of their immoral behavior. I found myself asking the question. "If not I, who? If not now, when?" Furthermore, if there is no interest in humankind's soul, "why not?" Moreover, "if not you Oh man, then who will bring to light the pervasiveness of pornography and the destruction that accompanies it? How do you find if you do not seek, and expose iniquity where it resides?" The hearing is not seeing. Seeing is the testimony.

I have committed unmentionable sins in my lifetime. Gossiping, speaking critically of others motives or intentions, harbored resentment, uncontrolled anger, selfishness, failure to trust in God during times of affliction, surrendered to materialism, even allowing sports to become the idol. Moreover, I have lusted after the flesh on more than one occasion in my lifetime. Echoing the Apostle Paul's Epistle where he confessed to being chief-of-sinners. I on the other hand, admit to being the commander-in-chief of sinners. John Newton said. "I am a great sinner, but I have a great Savior." That is our only hope. That is the only solution for my sins, and it is your only solution as well.

The Apostle Paul and John Newton said of themselves as sinners in the present tense. It's is not, "I was." They said, "I am a sinner." A persecutor of the Jews was Paul while Newton never forgot that he had been a slave trader. Over the years from their conversion to their death, both Newton and Paul grew more Christ-like in character. Over time, both Paul and Newton acted more and more like Saints they were to become at conversion. Nevertheless, that growth process involved, becoming more aware of and sensitive to the sinful expressions of the flesh still dwelling within all of us. Therefore, Newton could easily say, "I was, and still am a great sinner," but I have a great Savior. Just getting the lost to admit there is a God, and in need of our Lord and Savior Jesus Christ is a daunting task I have committed to carry on.

My objective in spending a page and one-half on the sinfulness of the flesh is to inform sinner's searching on the internet for pornography and those who are involved in hardcore pornography, that they are doomed to eternal darkness, and the light is not found in them. Criminals involved in prostitution, and misguided souls running "scams" using different venues to engage their criminal activity need to be forewarned. Pimping, drunkenness, slave trafficking, and illegal drugs has so moved my heart that I have committed to a personal crusade to eradicate immoral behavior.

I will expose those who chose to live in the darkness and where they take pleasure operating with impunity. You may suppose you are doing it under cover of darkness or closed doors, but it doesn't ever escape the eyes of God.

In II Timothy 2: 24-26. A servant of the Lord must not quarrel, but be gentle to all, able to teach, patient in humility, correcting those who are in opposition, so that they may know the truth, come to repentance, and escape the snare of the Devil having been taken captive by him to do his will. I had become a pawn of the Devil's trap for quite some time. At first, I was slightly stimulated by the images I saw on the screen until I began to see it for what it was, and what it does to women. It is degrading, debasing, self-destructive, and psychologically vexing on the human spirit to anyone associated with all the sinful behavior that now permeates society.

My focus is not on the physical, but the person's heart, soul, and mind. Just because a person assumes they are good, kind, generous, and above reproach does not guarantee these character traits are your ticket into Heaven. You had better think twice and read the four Gospels in the New Testament. Read what Jesus has to say about your assumptions. Yet, man is cold and stubborn by nature. Many have already rejected Lord Jesus. "Why would they accept Scripture?" Humankind is inherently stubborn and stiff-necked, relying on their own understanding. We do not like being told how we should live our lives.

It has been a few days since Carrie and I chatted. However, on June 10, 2013, at 3:30 P.M., I logged online to see if Carrie was on messenger. The last couple of days, I pursued my research on Carrie and her alleged partner's. "This is what Carrie calls them?" I wondered aloud. "Partners, and not criminals?" The research was beginning to pay dividends, and it was noticeable in our chat exchanges. Also, the dialogue starts to take on a new life of its own. However, to have this conversation take root and grow, I have to have a willing participant logged onto messenger first. The night Carrie was to log onto messenger and didn't, created a vacuum for me to continue searching for leads.

Again, for reasons I cannot explain, I was channeled to the Skype application to check and see if Carrie was using Skype that night. I was not able to determine with absolute certainty she was on Skype. However, I thought she might be on because there appeared two other usernames on the screen that I had not seen before, "Fundi," and "tulip girl." Why would she have those two names on Skype alongside her other alias Henan? This was a new revelation that needed explaining when I talked to Carrie.

The following day before logging onto messenger, I returned to Skype to make sure the names I saw the night before were still listed on Carrie's account. To my bewilderment, the names had been removed from her Skype account. Furthermore, it wasn't only those mystery names but my name was removed as well. I was quite taken aback and alarmed by this latest development, but it should not have come as a surprise.

It seemed every time I mentioned something about her web page or site, that might incriminate her or raise questions, it was deleted from her site or web page on their computer. In this case, however, I hadn't talked to Carrie about the two unknown names yet. The only thing I could conclude from this latest development was that they were probably tracking me, and when they found out I was snooping around, they deleted all the names to prevent me from learning more about their operation. This made me more determined than ever to get to the bottom of the mystery. When Carrie finally logged onto messenger, I wasted little time putting her through the gantlet of questions.

"The first order of business before we move on Carrie, is about two names that appeared on your Skype account the other night," I began. "What role do the names "Fundi" and "tulip girl," play in your life?"

Carrie replied. "Tulip girl" was a name her girlfriend gave her and "Fundi" was an alias she used years ago. Moreover, Carrie asked. "Where did you get those names from?" Nobody except her knew about their existence and she wanted to know where I saw them mentioned.

Either they became visible erroneously, or Carrie is playing me for someone who apparently lacked intelligence. She had to know I was logged into Skype at the same time she was using Skype online. Carrie sure wasn't talking to me, so I could only conclude she was targeting another potential victim using those two aliases'. When Carrie recognized I was online, she immediately signed out. I asked Carrie why she removed my name, but she never uttered a word. It was her silence that prompted me to question her motives. Carrie was methodically beginning to block me or delete material that might come back to jeopardize their operation. They were obviously becoming aware of me showing myself on their accounts and are getting suspicious of my motives.

Further intelligence revealed Carrie had accounts on Facebook, Myspace, Twitter, Pinterest, YouTube, and other suspicious accounts I have not mentioned. Carrie asserts she didn't use these accounts, but it was her partners who had access to these accounts and used them. If this wasn't a condescending remark towards my intelligence, then I need to examine my sanity. I don't know if Carrie is capable of telling the truth. All Carrie does is written in the context of deceitfulness or harmful behavior meant to deflect every emerging issue I bring to her attention and deny its existence. I'm becoming very annoyed with Carrie because I still needed to associate "Nate," to a birth name.

I became more demanding, accusing Carrie of being in collusion with her partners. She was just as much a full-blown player in this as the rest of these malcontents. Now I would turn my focus to the laptop computer, telling Carrie she had her own computer, the one I sent her in April, but she would remain steadfast in her denial. Finally, after much coaxing, Carrie admitted to having the laptop but said the partners share it. Carrie alleges she did not have time for me because the partners were forcing her to work long hours. My immediate reaction to this preposterous lie… "Right!" What Carrie wouldn't admit to at this time, was implicating herself in the swindling activity. Carrie was likely searching for new prospects to swindle or she already had a prospect they were already working on swindling. Usually, when they can't get new victims to bite on their scam, they will revisit some of the old victims.

Carrie does a flip-flop and brings up the topic of "money" again. However, I play possum with the "fox of scams" and divert her focus from money to how disrespectful she has treated me with her broken promises, especially when we would chat with me on messenger. Carrie clings to the assertion that she has been forthright and truthful. She insists the repeated power outages in Ghana continues to affect our lives video chats. She blames the power outages are at a crisis stage in Ghana. Carrie used Ghana's power failures to justify her absence from Yahoo Messenger. If it isn't problems with power outages, working long hours, or torrential downpours from storms; any excuse is employed to prevent us from live video chats. Often, I would verify the power outages and storms in Ghana using Google search during times Carrie swore outages were occurring. The evidence didn't support Carrie's alleged lie. "Lie, lie, lie, became the battle cry."

When Carrie used the power outages to explain away her absence from messenger chat, I informed her that most computers have six or seven hours of battery life, (as if she didn't know) even if the electricity was down. As mode-of-operation would suggest, Carrie had a ready response.

Carrie would reply by saying. "But I was playing games on the computer and the battery was weak."

I started to become more combative with Carrie, telling her that she was using me as a pawn. Secrets lies and evasiveness were all components that were dressing for Carrie's profile. I knew why Carrie didn't appear on messenger chat the evening she had promised. I was waiting for Carrie to tell me, but as was customary, she would conveniently evade the question. Tiring of her evasiveness, I finally decided to call her into account. Carrie needed to know she wasn't pulling the wool over my eyes'.

"Carrie," I said. "You were making a video the other night and that is why you didn't log onto messenger." Adding, "I don't think I need to tell you who participated with you in that video. You should be ashamed of yourself." Reminding Carrie it would be pointless of her if she attempted to lie her way out of it. I had become sloppy seconds in Carrie's busy swindling schedule. Moreover, I was letting Carrie know I was tiring of this madness. There had come a point where I did not want to make this my lifelong journey. She was slow in feeding me anything of relevance. However, I desperately wanted this mystery man's name with a passion. Usually, when I repeat certain words or phrases' that are carefully thought out and conveyed to her, I noticed an alarming trend develop.

Carrie would go silent when I was onto one of her lines of lies or when vulgarity would come into the conversation. However, Carrie could be just as calculating if not more so than I. If she becomes too receptive and relaxed; letting down her guard, she has a tendency to reveal information that wasn't intended for my eyes to see. What continues to puzzle me is Carrie's endless charade to "scam" me further. Carrie has been living the lie for so long that she believes the lie she is telling becomes the truth, and the truth is not in her.

These conversational sessions were rather informal as discussions go. After a while, you become immune and numb as you begin to separate the truth, from the lie. There were just too many inconsistencies in Carrie's behavior. I surmised Carrie was hanging around to squeeze me for more money.

During one of my search missions, I used Carrie's site www. carnalcarriexxx.com and typed in a keyword that would take me into another dark corner of the abyss where swindler's hide their identities and information. A typical keyword search would be entered in the search box. "What is reverse phone look-up?" Then you type in the phone number. Or, "What is a domain name," blacklist, tracer route, domain name server, Internet service provider, etc. The "What is," followed by the topic of search, is generally what is used for "keyword" searches. It was a learning experience for the author, but worth the effort. Moreover, it could be overwhelming, time-consuming, frustrating, and daunting as I had entered uncharted waters. There were volumes of information to review and digest; discarding what was irrelevant, retaining what had possibilities.

The next chat session on messenger occurred on June 12, 2013. However, rather than engage in bickering Carrie was now demanding something contrary to what I was expecting. Moreover, one never knew what Carrie would do from one day to the next. The first thing she wanted to know was if I was angry with her. I imagined Carrie was putting feelers out before Carrie confronted me with another monetary favor. When I informed Carrie I was moderately upset, she immediately seized the opportunity to reply.

"Dang, you are always angry when I talk to you," Carrie said complaining. "I don't know if you think of us as being together anymore or what," She exclaimed. And I do not know what you are feeling or what your intentions are… "My intentions are to be together," Carrie concluded. I believe Carrie will be making a plea for all the wrong reasons. Rather, I felt she was setting the stage for the big question. "Will you give me some money?" After reading Carrie's erroneous perception, I informed Carrie she hadn't changed the way she conducts herself.

True to form, Carrie wasted little time blurting out the big question, "will you!" We had discussed getting Carrie out of that forsaken country where she claimed to be living, but I knew she was not in Ghana. Now Carrie wanted to solicit from Jim Jacobs money to purchase airfare to fly to the United States. I, on the other hand, challenged Carrie with her false idea. The more probing sent in Carrie's direction, the more likely she would argue over which one of us should buy the ticket in Ghana. Carrie was not going to agree with my proposal to procure this ticket over the phone and arrange the reservations. Therefore, we remained at an impasse.

I wasn't about to be played as the gullible fool again, despite all the possible scenario's Carrie created. She even sweetened the deal by allowing us to have a live video chat, but as usual, it soon froze, and that was the end of the live video. When video didn't work, Carrie then played on my emotions, saying how her partners were treating her with indifference and withholding money. It must have taken them all but three days to arrive at a consensus as to how they might devise a plan to separate additional funds from my wallet ..." Notta gonna do it!"

Take it all in! You, who have invested your hard-earned income in reading this manuscript. As you can readily see for yourselves, a swindler or fraudulent criminal will stop at nothing to separate you from your livelihood. They will nickel and dime you out of house and home. Convincing you through various techniques and schemes that all they want is your friendship, even marriage may be indicated in your stars along with all the trimmings of flattery. Hardships are employed to gain your empathy.

Remember, this is their occupation. They do nothing but scheme, plan, and conspire 24-hours a day, seven-days a week using ingenious methods to convince their victims they are in a hopeless situation and in need. I compare their mind to one who has been given a life sentence in prison. All the criminal has going for them is plenty of time to entertain ways of escaping the environment they find themselves in, or they create problems within the penal system. These swindlers are crafty, perceptive, and evil. They lurk behind the faceless masks of computers. These Scammer's and their fake counterfeit identities just sit and wait at the ready for the next victim to appear.

It has been two days since Carrie contacted me. But on June 15, 2013, Carrie has logged onto messenger. The time is 4:30 in the afternoon and it ends a little over an hour later. This session allegedly pertains to an emergency crisis relating to groceries. Apparently, the airfare controversy has escaped Carrie's attention for the moment. The reader should have noticed by now that Carrie's speech is fragmented but still discernable. However, if the truth is known, Carrie has an excellent command of the English language.

However, she wants you, the potential victim, to assume she lacks the necessary tools to speak fluent English. That is because Carrie continued to insist Ghana was where she was held against her will while being treated inhumanely. She has seen me on video in her room, and yet she remains steadfast in having me believe she is in Ghana rather than the United States. I really don't know what kind of fool she has conjured up in her mind, where she continues to move forward unchallenged in her efforts to scam more money from Jim Jacobs.

When Carrie logged onto messenger, she was as pleasant as a proud woman who promoted her status as a victim of society, rather than her real occupation as a prostitute and swindler. However, that is part of Carrie's façade. Carrie continues in her own fantasy world thinking I will forward her money for the airfare ticket to the United States.

When I told Carrie I had been out by the pool tanning myself, she commented. "Great! I hope I will like tan."

"Yeah, I remarked. "Vanity …Vanity …Oh, what vanity." Humankind's obsession with aesthetics. Never content with self, always worried about how they are viewed and perceived by the public.

Twenty minutes into the conversation, just as though it had been script, Carrie changes the tone of the conversation to one of need and greed again. Should I be surprised? Not in the least. In this plea from Carrie, it would require compromising my debit card number.

"Is a hyena a scavenger?" Carrie has turned into a scavenger. It made me wonder if this group of misfits sits around during the day manufacturing ways to "scam" ordinary citizens. No matter, I was not signing onto this latest request. What she wanted was for me to be amendable to her request, bolstered by a complaint her partners were withholding the agreed upon lion's share of the income. She had the unmitigated gall to log onto messenger only to ask that I Google www. ghanamart.com, and give these swindlers my debit card information so she could artificially go to the Mart and purchase groceries.

Carrie stated. "It is urgent, an emergency." She alleges there was no food in her home. I asked Carrie why there was a problem obtaining monies from her partners.

"They will not give me money," she insisted. "They tell me they pay me money already."

I can't imagine where Carrie has her head right now. Has she become an Ostrich that buries its head in the sand. Her request defies logic, saying. "When I go to the market it is very hard for me. I get frustrated and frightened in grocery shopping when full of blacks," Carrie muttered.

Carrie kept insisting I do this for her, but I was determined to stand my ground and let her know this just wasn't going to happen. In the meantime, I continue to badger Carrie about getting on the laptop I sent her so I could make a positive identification, even though I already knew "Henan and Carrie" were one and the same person. I wanted her to admit she received the Toshiba computer. Eventually. She did confess to having my computer, but it was pulling tusks from a boar.

C. S. Lewis once coined the phrase. "It is one thing to see the land of peace from the wooded ridge, yet another to tread the road that leads to it." Carrie insists on being vague if not inherently stubborn. She is forever using meaningless gibberish and going off topic frequently. It isn't the ravenous lust that should tempt me about women, but that I knew of it for its temptations. Above all, I now knew peace and joy did not point in that direction. There is a clear distinction between having and wanting. To have is to want more, and want is to have even that you already have.

Therefore, such as it is to my dismay, that I discovered layer upon layer of the conscious and unconscious counterfeit ideology of humankind's inability to show genuine spiritual love. We are truly independent people …

Guardians of our own destiny, cowards at all points… Insecure … Empty and smug. Carrie and her criminal swindlers are of likeminded-disconnected creatures of society. Likewise, it should come as no surprise to the Christian that it is the "sin nature" in all of us where wants and needs are what we demand, regardless of the carnage left in its wake.

Deaf ears appear to be the norm for these misfits. They will only hear what will increase their bounty. Future chapters will contain email exchanges, and Facebook letters Carrie and I exchanged. The sandcastles of history will eventually produce a bounty of information on Carrie's account. Therefore, for the time being, I will let the mold on other Chapters of discourse become antique mirrors of creative wanderings for the reader. We are now engaged in another messenger chat. This time, I take Carrie to the woodshed.

"Whoever you are Carrie, you do not seem to get it, or you do not choose to," I declared. "You worship worldly things that rot, and rust, and waste away, it never lasts," adding. "It is paper funny money… Worthless." I then asked. "Is it worth the price, if you should lose your soul and be denied eternity in Heaven Carrie?" I went on to say. "Maybe you think there is no God … And that is your choice. However, there is a God and he does exist; this I have first-hand knowledge of Carrie, and you know this to be the truth. Every creature walking the face of this planet knows there is a God." I concluded.

As rainstorms, unexpectedly approach from the west winds, so Carrie can disappear without rhyme or reason, leaving me sitting there like a dunce. More often than not, when Carrie feels she is not getting anywhere with me, she will drop off the radar and perhaps move on to another potential victim. I knew Carrie would eventually reappear. It was just a matter of when, and what new scheme she would fabricate in her zeal to separate additional monies from me. Little did I realize Carrie would sit and wait this one out for ten days before making contact with me again. She had to be one unhappy camper. Never knowing what to expect, I always braced myself for the worst-case scenario. Rest assured I was not sitting around waiting for Carrie to reappear.

June 25, 2013, at 3:10 P.M. would close out messenger chat for the month of June. Unfortunately, Jim Jacobs will continue pursuing and persuading Carnal Carrie to allow me to view her on the laptop computer I sent her in April. Whatever springs forth new precedes images of the old. Words uttered and thus dispersed into thin air; does not the air return from whence the word had its origin? Since our attention span is suspect to waffling, then it must follow that once the spoken word departs our lips and passes through this great chasm, and disappears into a vacuum; only to have its tailings search the air for another ear to digest its significance.

Filled with indignation, I have met more than my match in the African nation of Ghana. However, she was not in Ghana as Carrie so adamantly defended from the onset. This was a certainty. Sometimes I felt out-maneuvered and out-flanked by the "who is who" in the Land of Oz that hides investments in the armor of evasion, carefully scripted by my adversaries. There is a supernatural force determined to guide me in another direction. I am the likes of a stubborn ass that needs prodding, pulled, and pushed to do the Masters Will. It is becoming a novelty and I'm stimulated by the mystery. I have totally immersed myself in the immense task that lies before me. The one strength I claim ownership of is determination. The Lord willing, this will catapult me in a new direction.

For far too long my whole focus has been on www.carnalcarriexxx. com, as the web page used for Goggle search. Now this supernatural entity was goading me in another direction. It has awakened my eyes' and drawn them down an entirely different path. I was prompted to my office where Carnal Carrie's binder containing her profile was kept. As I was thumbing through the pages of documented information, my eyes' were transfixed on one particular page. The title was "Carnal Carrie." Looking at the page, I thought there wasn't anything worthwhile that would be helpful until I felt my eyes' being pulled down to the licensed operator.

There it was, seemingly insignificant, but its subtlety painstakingly guided me into an entirely new dimension in this underground operation. www.carnalcarriexxx.com was incomplete. It was to read. www.carnalcarriewww.com.LegofLambCams.com, Video Net Operations. I was not sure where it was going to lead, but what did I have to lose. It was worth the effort. In our next Chapter, the reader will discover as I did, that it will reveal the pearls inside the clam.

Chapter 17

Blind Guides Leading the Blind

The lure of complacency cast into the sea, its bait beckons; what man can resist?
All riches and honor do you not see; cast in your lot
of prideful hate; Satan has no waiting list.
Hidden confessions buried behind closed doors. Man's
little secrets written upon the scroll,
Carefree, aren't we all? Stymie worry. What risks
agnostic, for you to shall surely lose your soul.
Jim Jacobs

This Chapter is reserved for women who made a free choice to become webcam models as their chosen profession. The only exception would be women trafficked, as human slaves displayed in whatever setting the Pimp dictates for the entertainment value of perverts, operated by these scrupulous criminals. The industry that promotes this abomination is referred to by the entity as "webcam models." The writer, however, has a different slant, and I'm not comparing apples and oranges. It is contemptible for webcam models to be seen in the same light as a model that poses' for clothing lines, and other merchandise. A webcam model is nothing more than a prostitute selling their flesh on the internet, or through the sale of their porn videos and photos.

Jezebel was the Phoenician wife of an Arab, who according to accounts in I and II Kings, pressed the cult of Baal, (any of numerous Canaanites and Phoenician local deities). Deity (One exalted or revered) on the Israelite Kingdom, but who was finally killed as prophesied by Elijah the prophet. Jezebel was a loose woman … A prostitute. If girls on

LOLC have a distaste for the label "prostitute," get out of this flesh-laden industry. Moreover, if the word "pervert" offends men, stay off websites promoting flesh-for-money entertainment.

An anonymous woman working in the prostitution industry wrote an article entitled: "Some things to consider when you think you want to prostitute yourself." There is a chasm between the ideas, "I have thought about prostitution" and "I think I would like to be a prostitute," namely the difference between wanting to make three hundred dollars an hour and wanting to do (Expletive) on strangers for a living.

Since Carrie chose diversity, meaning web-camming and swindling as her occupation of choice, the question thirsts for answers on options. "Why would anyone want to be in the pornography industry?" If the answer is "I want quick money," and it often is, I suggest you walk away and don't look back while you still have some dignity or worse yet, become a slave to the prowling pimps. This anonymous prostitute stated there was nothing inherently unhealthy about sex work, but there is something inherently delusional about get-rich schemes, and if that is what you think you are getting into, it is not a sound career move.

What anonymous neglected to tell its readers "while claiming that sex work in a community nominally accepted as a legitimate way to make a living." She is obviously deficient in her knowledge of Scripture and more than likely does not know her Lord and Savior. What does God's word have to say about immorality? Refer to Romans Chapter 8: 6-7, (6) for to be carnal, is death, but to be spiritually minded is life and peace. (7) "Because the carnal (relating to or given crude bodily pleasures and appetites, the fleshly temptations), the mind is at enmity (great wickedness, deep-seated dislike or ill will), against God; for it is not subject to the law, nor indeed can be.

Concerning soul and sin, we turn to the book of Ezekiel Chapter 18: 4. "Behold, all souls are mine; the souls of the Father, as well as the soul of the son, are mine; the soul who sins shall die. See I Samuel, Chapter 15: 23. "For rebellion is as the sin of witchcraft." Moreover, stubbornness is as iniquity, (a wicked act or thing), and idolatry, (the worship of a physical object as a God). "Because you have rejected the word of the Lord, He also has rejected you."

If you are in this male dominated pimping industry, you (the prostitute), may make enough money one day, but it does not mean you are going to hit the jackpot every night. There are lean days or weeks where there are no earnings. Not only is this morally wrong but if you allow "Johns" (perverts), to get into your head you will be broke more often than you realize. Working in hotels or massage parlors means perhaps hours of down time before you get an hour or two of actual work; whether you are making one-hundred or two-hundred dollars a session, it actually breaks down to a whole lot of nothing per hour. Wage notwithstanding, if the truth is told, you will not like your job very much. Eventually, if you begin to experience a cash flow problem, you will start to make bad choices … Let your guard down. Protection becomes a real issue when you unintentionally forget to screen your clients, or you begin seeing more clients than you can handle.

The women may find the word "prostitute," objectionable especially if they see themselves as strippers, escorts, or webcam performers. Yet, if it looks like a duck, quacks like a duck, waddles like a duck; it is a duck. Let us examine the word, "prostitute," and its definition. "It is an act, or practice of engaging in promiscuous sexual relations, for money." A State of being prostituted … Debased. (Debase, implies a loss of position, value, worth, dignity, debasing through sensual indulgence). Pundits can put a spin on this in any language that might make them feel justified to legitimize immoral behavior, and they will. However, if it looks like sin, it is sin; if you are openly displaying flesh in front of strangers, then you are sinning against God. It is not debatable. Simply put; it does not justify a debate.

Now, many within this corruptible business will defend their actions by aggressively defending it as an economic necessity that fuels them into the enterprise. Moreover, graduating college students who claim it is a quick way to pay back their student loans is considered by them acceptable behavior. Then you have Lowlife drug peddlers who sell drugs wherever the demand exists. As with the sex industry, they justify the pushing of poison because they earn more money peddling their wares than they might otherwise make working minimum wage jobs.

Our government is apparently treating internet prostitution, street prostitution, and drugs with indifference by placing these immoral epidemics on the back burner and redirecting their resources' to wars in the Middle East so more American soldiers are killed, wounded, or mutilated. I'm curious to know where lawmakers in Washington, D.C. stand on these issues … This mega social disgrace that is allowed to smother our liberties. Either our lawmakers are out to lunch, have taken the hands off approach, no political will, or just do not understand the scope and financial burden immorality undermines our economy.

A former prostitute claims there is a stigma that follows them around and forces many women to denounce their careers. She asserts prostitution is an emotional labor and they too deal with burnout. "Welcome to the real world!" In Genesis Chapter 3: 18-19, God said. "Cursed is the ground for your sake; in toil, you shall eat of it all the days of your life. Both thorns and thistles it shall bring forth for you, and you shall eat the herb of the field. In the sweat of your face you shall eat bread till you return to the ground, for out of it, you were taken; for dust you are, and to dust you shall return." "Why?" "Who was God talking too?" Adam and Eve, who disobeyed God in the Garden of Eden.

Disobeying God is a sin. From Adams seed, sin entered the world. This woman goes on to suggest that there is a common assumption that for prostitutes to take time off work means that you have the sense and ability to tend to your own health in a way that makes people very jealous. This has all the appendages of a broad statement that is replete without foundation. "What does this have to do with jealousy?"

Once again we must look to Scripture for time off, a day of rest? I refer the reader to Exodus Chapter 20: 8-11. Remember the Sabbath day, (Now the Lords day) to keep it Holy. Six days you shall labor and do all your work, but on the seventh day is the Sabbath of the Lord your God. In it, you shall do no work: you, or your son, or your daughter, or your male servant, or your female servant, or your cattle, or your stranger who is within your gates. For in six days the Lord made the Heavens and the earth, the sea, and all that is in them, and rested the seventh day. Therefore, the Lord blessed the Sabbath day and hallowed it. (Hallowed: to make "HOLY" or to set apart for Holy use). I do not believe I can stress this more firmly. Shame on us all as a people … nation … country to think we can trample on a day that the Lord

"Hallowed" by doing the exact opposite of his word, the least of which is allowing retail stores to continue operating in the name of profits.

That the "church of Wallers," and for that matter all retail stores, dare keep their doors open on Sunday. Sunday is a day of worship, the first day of the week. The day Christ Jesus was resurrected from the dead. "Does this day not reverence anymore?"

The prostitute asserts, when they become prostitutes, they accept the reality of the job, with its difficulties like any other; they should not have to face coercion into accepting the meaning and experiences written by others. Well, let us see what Gods word has to say about her opinion. In Hebrews Chapter 13: 4. "Marriage is honorable among all, and the bed undefiled; but fornicators and adulterers God Will Judge." Exodus Chapter 20:14. "You shall not commit adultery." Matthew Chapter 5: 28. "But, I say to you that whoever looks at a woman to lust after her has already committed adultery with her in his heart (the same applies if a woman lusts after a man). To be candid, prostitution is a sin. Therefore, it should not compromise God's moral law.

No doubt, thousands of women choose this profession. But there are many more who are forced to prostitute themselves as unwilling participants. Forced through trafficking, exploitation, and kidnapping by scrupulous pimps whom I consider the lowest form of an animal. They beat, coerce, brainwash, de-humanize, and imprison innocent young runaways into this flesh for money industry. These pimps often inject vulnerable women with drugs as a means of control. I have even read where some girls are no older than 15-years-old. And now pimps are branding women like cattle with tattoo's imprinted on their bodies so that in the event she tries to stray and is found by another pimp, they can identify whose property she belongs too so she can either be sent back to her master for punishment or to be killed.

Moreover, I want to address women who chose this business voluntarily. Some of these vulnerable women begin as cam models and before long are lured to places like Los Angeles, Phoenix, New York, and many other major cities where hardcore pornography is viewed as a natural and acceptable way of life. There is no shame, no fear, and no sense of right and wrong.

The face of global prostitution is the face of poverty and exploitation. I am convinced one of the ways to combat prostitution is to have boots on the ground, through legislation, and regulations banning this harmful practice in every state in the union. Putting stricter laws on the books for dealers arrested for peddling drugs. We need to reform sentencing guidelines for non-violent crimes. These same measures need to be applied to pimps who keep women prisoner. However, left to my own devices, the "pimp" should receive the harshest incarceration imposed and then some. Dangerous animals are kept behind structured walls so as to pose no harm to people. These are animals the likes of which are dogs, cats, and mammals that do not have a soul.

Law enforcement officials need to be given more latitude in arresting pimps and drug peddlers who seem to operate with impunity. Pimps are known to work truck stops, motels, vehicles, condemned homes, etc. with their helpless captives always within eyesight. There has not been a vision in this country since John F. Kennedy. Our government has failed to offer legislation to bring living wages in line with inflation. Lawmakers have allowed the minimum wage to fall so far behind the cost of living index the past fifty-years, it will never return to living wage equity.

Unless drastic measures are taken to correct this injustice, we may discover the hole we dug ourselves is so deep, that a rebellion by our citizens could very well be prime to explode into chaos. You are either part of the solution or part of the problem. Either abolish minimum wage altogether or raise it to a respectable living wage of no less than twenty dollars an hour without incrementing the increase in stages over periods of years.

We move forward and focus on an industry that has taken off like a swarm of locusts devouring everything in its path. I am speaking of "webcam modeling" (prostitution). It has taken over the internet by storm the past eight-years. It continues to grow in numbers and popularity. Companies that promote these sleazy websites do so by aggressive ad campaigns to recruit more and more prostitutes into this sea of immorality. These aren't only American prostitutes, but we now see prostitutes from every continent in the world. They have sold their flesh and souls on these websites, the author believes are without verifications in place. Some of these sites even have pimps planted right in the prostitute's room.

A typical advertisement may approach something nearing a glamorous career. A typical solicitation may appear in the following format.

"If you have ever given thought to a career as a webcam model, or looking for a way to work from home making money in your spare time, then this is the career for you. We will show you how to earn money as a webcam model, (prostitute) and we will give you hints and tips from the beginner to the experienced model. With this ad, you will be well on your way to making money in no time. The company will take a percentage of the money, however (I despise this word; "however," because it connotes a condition), to provide value to models such as promoting the model within the site, technical support, and training." They boast to the perspective clients by dribbling honey on the plate, adding. "You will find some studios that will pay just 20% of their earnings. They tell you this may seem low but that 25-35% is the industry standard. The majority of the earnings stay with the studio to help pay for credit card fees" … Yeah, right!

Most studios will send a check out every two weeks. Some pay weekly and some even pay daily through a PayPal account or other means. Before any of this takes root, they must prove they are 18-years of age. They are required to fill out forms, provide a photo ID, sign a contract, fill out a prostitute release form, and give their SSAN and address. It is all personal information on the girls they are hiring. Studios claim they will give the model (prostitute), everything she needs to succeed and offers personal representatives that will help her become successful.

The prospective prostitute is encouraged to choose a username that the pervert can identify on these websites when the pervert logs into chat. The agents claim that by the prostitute choosing an easy to remember username it will bring more customers to her room. Then the entity goes further to encourage that her username is conjoined to her Twitter account, and other social networking sites she may want to promote herself on. By doing this, the agent informs her; it will be easier to develop her persona by bringing new members to her webcam site.

These webcam entities almost hand-feed new recruits so they can get the maximum bang for their investment. So much so that they even go as far as to give instructions on how to establish the models (Again, models are prostitutes on webcams and not the typical model that works in the fashion industry) profile. The girls are instructed to upload high-quality pictures of themselves. The pimping entity actively encourages colorful pictures in quality poses', and taken from various locations to grab the attention of the perspective pervert.

Of course, we all know a picture can convey thousands of words, so the entity recommends the prostitute project a statement to attract its men of perversion. The tutor suggests the model have a minimum of seven pictures spread over three albums. The industry pimp (owner of the website), stresses to the model that they see time, and again the prostitute has attracted more visitors, and thus, made more money with higher quality photos advertised on their profile.

They use attention grabbers such as using their best picture as the profile picture. They stress again that they want the best picture for when the prostitute comes online. This they conclude will ENTICE guests into the prostitute's room. The prostitute is to fill out a detailed description of what she is willing to do on cam and in private chats while mentioning her kinks or fetishes. Therefore, guests who search for those specific kinks or fetishes will discover her. The tutor will even go so far as to inform new clients whose sites have the opportunity to place text at the top of the chat box. However, most prostitutes use their smartphones to text messages. The entity wants the new recruits to use this tool as a sales opportunity, telling her guests what she is willing to do and for how many tokens. "If this doesn't sound like prostituting and bargaining for dollars, wheeling and dealing for the best deal before trotting off to do a private show, someone needs to explain to me what wrong means and give me another definition of prostituting yourself.

The entity prefers the recruit use a high-quality webcam telling the recruit a 1-megapixel webcam works (Here's that word again; "but"), but the better the video quality (Here is more propaganda overstated; "money"), the more money you will make. Some sites list which models have high-quality cams, so they have more traffic in their rooms.

"Ooops, here comes the pitch!" A standard high-quality webcam accepted on all cam sites and used by many prostitutes is Logitech 720p Webcam Pro 900. Another is the Logitech HD Pro Webcam C910, known for its very high quality and HD (high definition). The industry pimp does not hesitate to hard sell the recruit on buying the latest technology as they claim demand for prostitutes with HD video streams is growing and the C910 delivers.

In the business of real estate, the emphasis by the real estate agents is, location, location, location! In porn where webcamming is used, the byword is, lighting, lighting, lighting! It is recommended they have at least two light sources but (there is that word again, "but"), three or four can help prevent their face from having shadows on it. They caution the users of lighting to make certain they are not lit up like a Christmas tree, stressing, too much light is not good either. The entity recommends having the prostitute maintain a clean area in their room, meaning clutter free. They do suggest some decorating to make the room attractive and inviting and set the mood, but they tell the recruit it is best to have the focus on them not the (expletive) in the surrounding area. This next advice is essential for the prostitute. They are to make sure any (expletive) or props used on their website are nearby.

Imagine all these subtle hints employed to allure prospective perverted or corrupted souls into the prostitute's room. (Perverts that cannot or refuse to turn aside or away from what is real, true, or morally right) Therefore, the entity stresses (expletive) and props are handy. They tell their recruits that they would not want to leave people waiting while the prostitute goes off camera to find an (expletive) to use during their show. They go on to say that if an (expletive) is within reach, they can show it to those viewing members to ENTICE them to take the prostitute private since they know you have it. A prostitute stands to make more money in a private or true private session than if she performs in a public forum.

More about this individual or "truly private" show request by the pervert later in the manuscript. Here is where the rubber meets the road ... Literally. Although the focus of this Chapter is on cam models, I do not want you to lose interest or think I have forgotten about Carnal Carrie. She is also a prostitute with her own cam site. We will be returning our attention back to Carrie shortly. Meanwhile, each cam site has its own, rules and expectations. However, the objective is prostituting human flesh for money. It is all about generating money for the pimps or entities who peddle their propaganda to entice young naïve recruits to sign onto their websites for the express purpose of enriching themselves and their bank accounts. "Do you really believe these pimps have these prostitutes best interest in mind?"

Our next highlight by the pushers of pornography is likened to roaches or gnats who invade home's living of garbage. Here, they begin to set the trap, as they prepare the stage for perverts visiting a prostitute's room. These no-name behind-the-scenes folks may as well be pimping on the streets. They want their models to be dressed in attire that is alluring while highlighting they're (expletive). Now, what do you suppose they mean by (expletive)? It is a structured Vista on display like an animal in a cage showing and revealing the prostitutes (expletive). "A wiggle here, seductive giggle there, (expletive) cajoling nearly everywhere."

These unscrupulous pimps of the worldwide industry want to corral as much money out of these foolish perverts for one reason only; to enrich their selfish motives. They allege some perverts like to (expletive). I ask you, the reader, "How demented can this get?" This is insane; the (expletive) can request they go private with the prostitute while other (expletive) join in to watch the show, or they can elect the costlier; "true private," where it is just the prostitute and (expletive). End result equates to more money for the prostitute and the pimp's coffers.

The recruits get coached to plan and scheme creative ways the perverts might demand on how the prostitute should perform to generate more tokens into the prostitute's room. Prostitutes should plan games or contests they may want to play with the members in their room. This, constructed in such a way as to garner more tips. It is common sense to be well groomed, and the pimps are cognizant of this vital, pressing need for personal hygiene to sell the PRODUCT. (She is now given the label "product," without an identity.) Again, they stress that the better one is groomed, the more money they can make. What is actually implied here is; the more money we, the pimp's can make.

Even minute; trivial matters, such as taking a deep breath and imploring relaxation techniques that are coached, does not escape the pimp's attention to detail formula. If they are not relaxed, their nervousness will show up on her cam. Over and over the emphasis is on taking deep breaths and relaxing. I cannot help but laugh at these so-called finer points to detail. The pimp reassures the perspective prostitute that first, and foremost that while appearance is stressed, they do not need to have super model looks. The important thing was their personality. "Do not be afraid to be yourself," the pimp stresses.'

Granted there are prostitutes throughout the internet that have joined these webcam sites by choice and do so without a moral conscience. They reject the notion that this is an abomination to their creator and Lord. Many have thumbed their nose at the mere suggestion they could face eternity in Hell, or what is known as the abyss in Scripture. Romans 5: 23. "For the wages of sin is death, but, the gift of God is eternal life." Also, refer to I Peter 2: 11. "Beloved, I beg you as sojourners and pilgrims abstain from fleshly lusts, which war against the soul."

There is audio in every prostitute's room where you can hear them speak live. However, the pervert must type out his chat message to the prostitute. The prostitute can choose to mute her audio at any time. However, the pimp tells the recruit that guest prefers to hear the model speaking than typing. Also, they claim, the prostitute can talk more with the voice since they can use different tones. Guest will be able to hear them giggle, whisper, and the big attraction for the pervert; (expletive). The pimps again exaggerate the drama by telling prospective prostitutes.

"This is part of the package the perverts will want to pay for!" Yet, here is the biggest drawing card of all.

"Always, repeat always," be friendly and polite. If there is any disruption in the room, politely ask the violating party to stop. If they persist, do not get into a confrontation with the offending pervert." The Pimp offers the perfect solution when he instructs the recruit. "Kick, or ban the offender out of your room," they tell her. Getting into a verbal altercation will only take away your attention from those who want to pay for your attention, the pimp stresses. These vicious creatures never miss a beat when playing on the words pay, play, and increase income with such a callous disregard for the female; as a precious human creation of God.

Continuing on this topic makes me want to hurl. However, for informational purposes it may prove valuable to an audience that may not have any inkling about this very destructive, dehumanizing occupation these young girls get themselves into. These impressionable young women are "brainwashed," and "spoon fed" on the "do's and don't" in this industry that is run by men for men. The pimps of any entity highly recommend that the prostitutes online acknowledge and chat with everyone. Those who are paying members or customers (perverts) on these polluted websites should get priority attention because frankly, they will tip more tokens.

Pimps caution the prostitute that guests, … Perverts, who are not in member status can often turn into paying members. Therefore, these greedy pimps tell the prostitute not to ignore anyone. Names are a viable instrument for the prostitute to learn. Namely, members who regularly visit her chat room. The assumption; the more a guest or pervert feels like the prostitute knows them personally, the more likelihood the pervert will return to their room, and ask to take you for a private session. However, they must also be vigilant in welcoming other perverts into her room. They too could ask to take the prostitute private. "Money … Money … Money!"

These folks have mastered the art on how they want their prostitutes to conduct themselves and what is permissible when asked by perverts about a prostitute's personal life? "How would you like restrictions on what you can say?" For that fact, what you should not reveal about yourself. The prostitute is matter-of-fact, coached to tell her paying perverts that she is not married, but single when in reality she may have a husband. Then again, what kind of man allows his spouse to degrade herself? The theory of this ideology is to create a fantasy in the member's mind that someday the two of them could become involved in a relationship. Of course, it doesn't happen according to the jackals, but the fantasy could keep the member's around as a paying (again, and again, and again; it is all about the money) regular pervert.

These websites also attract what the industry defines as, "beggars." These include perverts who are guests, and who literally beg prostitutes to do something in free chat. Sometimes it involves displaying a part of their anatomy or perhaps performing an (expletive). Perverts may even promise the prostitute they will take them to private session after she fulfills his request, but he never does. Then, when all things are said with indiscretion, the pimp encourages the prostitute not to be timid about making use of the (expletive) she has at her disposal. Also, these lost souls persuade the prostitute to allow perverts or guests into their room so they can see for themselves what (expletives) are available.

The thought behind this brainstorm idea is that it could lead to the likelihood of private sessions. (Long and the short …You guessed it…" Money.") All this boils down to idol worshipping of women and money, not to mention the sinfulness of this abominable immoral conduct. These money grabbers maintain that because the schedule is so important, they claim this will eventually make the prostitute a top model prospect. Moreover, it is believed they will spend more time online in paid private sessions instead of in free chat. These Pimps do not stop here. They want to take this a step further by insisting in the most stringent terms, that the prostitute opens up a Twitter account. Using this method, it allows perverts, to follow favorite prostitutes. At the start, the pimp recommends no more than forty-tweets per eight hours.

These pimps of the female flesh have all their bases covered down to a science. Just like Satan, it does not take the novice observer to know what is behind this evil industry. Coach, coach, and coach even more! Now she receives instructions on how one actually manages their Twitter account. The recruit gets one-on-one instructions on her Twitter account. They want to have an absolute certainty she has a picture of herself on Twitter to encourage people to visit their room on cam. It is encouraged that they tweet often. Furthermore, they are to show their personality on Twitter. They should tweet when they go online such as pictures of themselves, what they may have done during the day, what you like, and on, and on, and on. "Blah … Blah … Blah … Blah." Prostitutes and recruits should also promote their profile. Again, this is accomplished by twitter or other social networks.

"What we have here, is a failure to com-mun-cate."

It is a given that every webcam site has similar rules and guidelines they use to run their pimping operation. Everyone in this business has as its primary goal, the need for greed. To make as much money off the backs of women and young girls without regard to human decency and what Scripture, has to say about this abomination against their creator. Moreover, it is a fact the majority of women who choose this degrading occupation, will end up on drugs … if they aren't already, or, become alcoholics. I can only register my objection on how distressed and grieved I am for the souls of all who participate in this corrupt industry. Furthermore, I echo the words of our Lord Jesus, as He took His last breath on the cross for sinners.

"Father forgive them; for they know not what they do!" I hate the sin, but love the sinner, and pray they will come to a saving grace and knowledge of Jesus Christ. The prostitute is required to create a web page to promote their profile, highlighting what the prostitute does on her website. Yet, they caution the prostitute not to include any information that might give away their location. If that were not enough, these fools tell the prostitute to make sure they get "privacy" for the domain so nobody can look up their information. By building a website, it would increase traffic from Google and other search engines. Not only will they get traffic this way, but it also allows the prostitute to have another place to interact with potential perverts. We are not quite finished ladies and gentlemen. They are capable of inventing more ways than a squirrel foraging for food so they can put more money into their pockets.

We can move onward and forward as this group of lowlife's guide their prospective prostitute to Facebook. Here they want the recruit to make a Facebook fan page of all things. Again, there is a tendency to avoid linking it to the real Facebook account. The thought behind this idea is that the prostitute can react with other potential clients as well as turning the innocent into regular perverts by steering them towards their webcam room. They can also promote their online times as to when she will be performing.

These people never miss an opportunity to draw folks to their sin-site web page. The prostitute is to make use of all the webcam sites features. Some, they insist may have fan clubs, (That would be an anglers' dream catch) which gives the prostitute more ways to make money. Most sites even allow the prostitute to sell pictures and videos. They are to take advantage of these opportunities and promote them on their social networks. This, in reality, is all about looking after number one; the pimp; who cares little about the long-term damage it does to these women. They flaunt their self-importance and control women with fear by the rules they impose on them.

This is the Granddaddy of all instructions I have researched thus far on prostitute web-camming. It tells the prostitute different ways they can get at the pervert's wallet. They inform the prostitute that there are numerous ways at separating perverts from money. They tell the prostitute most men will tip her because they like her. The pervert will tip with tokens to have you do something specific in your public room. The prostitute can extend an invitation for the both of them to go private. It is a set rate per minute that the room is open. They claim the prostitute can change this rate at will later. However, the greedy pimps suggest she wait until she has more experience and becomes more familiar with her perverted lust seekers.

After spending thousands of hours researching information for the manuscript, I discovered to my utter surprise that I must have overlooked the hidden needle in the haystack. I was enlightened by a former prostitute who claimed female prostitutes contract HIV at a slightly lower rate than women who do not work as prostitutes. Because, as she states, they understand the importance of safer sex and know how best to put it into practice. Of course, she asserts some women think they are safe because they charge three-thousand dollars for (expletive) sessions and have fewer clients. This anonymous prostitute also made the statement, which in the authors mind is a misnomer.

"The choices we make with our bodies are our own."

Here is where I must take a step back and see what Scripture has to say about the body! Romans 12: 1. "I beseech you therefore brethren, by the mercies of God, that you present your bodies a living sacrifice, Holy, acceptable to God, which is your reasonable service." I Corinthians 12: 27. "Now you are the body of Christ, and members individually. Finally, we refer to Ephesians 5: 29-30. "For no one ever hated his own flesh, but nourishes and cherishes it, just as the Lord does the church." For, we are members of His body, of His flesh, and of His bones.

I am a great supporter of and believe in apologetics (a branch of theology devoted to the defense of the divine origin and authority of Christianity). "God said it, and that settles it!" Whether pornography, the feminist movement, pro-choice, or the gay rights activist. Your body, your very life is not your own. It belongs to your creator. I Peter Chapter 1 14-16. "As obedient children, do not conform yourselves to the former lusts, as in your ignorance; but as He (Christ) who called you is Holy, you also be Holy in your conduct," because it is written, "Be Holy, for I am Holy." (Holy is one who is exalted, or worthy of complete devotion, as one perfect in goodness, and righteousness ... Divine).

Nowhere, in this anonymous prostitute's article was there the slightest mention of Scripture in her written orientation. Rather than writing and discouraging women from this abomination, she appears to take a neutral position. Actually, prostitutes or, "wanna-be" women of the evening, come to her for advice on how to avoid the pitfalls of prostituting themselves. To summarize Chapter 17; I implore the reader to be open-minded about the contents contained on these pages. Realistically speaking, whether we are addressing a stripper, webcam model, prostitutes, or porn magazines, and videos, the end result is the destruction of the soul. Whether it is a man or woman participating in the flesh-for-pay industry; where money is exchanged for lust, then in the opinion of the author, it is prostitution. Prostitution, is prostitution, is prostitution. God does not approve of immoral behavior, and neither should we.

Chapter 18

Shades of Shame

Steadfast and stubborn, they snicker in collaboration saying what it is you did.
Haughty lots they are who never say who I am.
Heart and soul; it's never been hidden.
We are but strangers to strangers. Yet, the Lord
knows us all. Are we all not the same?
Man clings to the mortal soul but it too belongs to
the Great I Am; God is his name.
Jim Jacobs

The first week in July proved to be challenging and overwhelming as I became adamant in my quest to get Carrie to produce the Toshiba computer in her room. As desperately as I wanted to get her on live video cam the more she resisted. We spent the majority of our time haggling back and forth on messenger chat about the Toshiba laptop computer I sent to her out of compassion. Furthermore, I was still making an effort to obtain Carrie's whereabouts. She was now getting short with me while outwardly showing another side of her demeanor, as foul language became one of her package deals while words freely rolled off her tongue like maple syrup poured from the bottle.

Our next session began on July 2, 2013, where I dominate most of the conversation. We no sooner log onto messenger when I start the discussion by inquiring about the laptop computer.

Where is my Toshiba laptop Carrie?" I demanded to know.

"There is no laptop, why are you arguing?" inquired Carrie.

Rebuking Carrie's denial of the facts, I inform Carrie with indifference. "Because I saw the maroon Toshiba laptop on your desk when we did a live video, and you so much as admitted to having it in your possession the last time we were chatting."

Carrie replies. "There is no laptop here."

However, I remain steadfast knowing Carrie has it in her possession. "I saw it. How did it disappear?" I demanded to know, and then I repeated. "You just finished webcamming on it, I am done playing games with you and your pack of misfits!"

Carrie was livid as she said. (Expletive) "You don't love me, huh?" she stated.

I am not in a position to be intimidated or surrender any time soon with the laptop so I press on. "Go on the laptop," I told Carrie.

Carrie responds, remaining in a state of denial. "There is no laptop or I would go retrieve it," she declares.

Carrie is trying her level best to wear me down, so the ploy was to concede defeat. "I guess you win this argument," I announced with a sigh.

Carrie quickly replies. "Nooo, but what would be the chance if there were a laptop, I would go with it so we could video chat together."

"No you wouldn't." I protested. Then I reiterated the facts informing Carrie. "You have two there now, and by the way, we know where you are, and isn't Kumasi," I informed her.

Carrie refutes this information, as she says. "I am in Kumasi," (expletive).

"Carrie, you are in the United Kingdom, you and your partners," I hinted, not really knowing for certain. However, research still favors the U.S.

Carrie resorts back to her one-syllable replies. "Nooo!"

"Now it is just a matter of time for us to find your location in the United Kingdom," baiting her. Additionally, we may have information that suggests something else Carrie. You never left the U.K., you just changed locations," I said, bluffing. And, you obviously do not read my email's either; do you," I said sternly. "Now, go on the laptop," I demanded with earnest resolve.

Carrie becomes spunky towards my demands as she replies, "Maybe!"

I mimic her remark with my own. "Maybe?" "Your partner's fingerprints are all over my computer," I inform to Carrie. "Furthermore, you are giving me other subtle clues … Amateurs. I'm not as dumb as you think Carrie," I concluded.

"So you think I know what they are doing?" Carrie asked.

Now that was really a dumb question. What did she believe I was going to say? "Of course you are all in this together," I insisted. Unbeknownst to Carrie, she has just verified there are numerous partners in this colony of swindlers.

Carrie. ("Expletive.")

I reveal to Carrie that I know how their scamming operation works.

Carrie counters with what has become her signature potty-mouth reply. ("Expletives") "So you think I'm a scammer?" she asked with indignation.

"Yes," I replied. "You are in the U.K. with them, how could you not know? You are up to your neck in this criminal activity, as are your partners," I declared. "If I fly anywhere, it will be the U.K.," I said. "You didn't know my niece was married to a British citizen did you?" I informed Carrie. "It is always good to have connections in the right places," I declared; rubbing salt into her wounds. I was basing my presumptuous accusations on photographs I had seen on her site. The landscape appeared similar to that of the U.K. However, I was merely grasping at straws. Furthermore, there were indicators on searches I conducted mentioning the U.K. Thus, I used this as a possible location. It would later prove unfounded, but I would withhold this information from Carrie that I had been mistaken.

Carrie remarked. "I am not in the United Kingdom."

"Stop lying Carrie, the game is up. The best thing for you right now is to run. I have never lied to you, and I have always been straightforward and honest," Carrie was told. "Now you know why I said your partners picked on the wrong person to swindle because sooner or later mistakes are made and this becomes a "Gotcha" moment for me," as I keep the rhetoric coming. "Now we at least, have a general idea where you are and it isn't Kumasi."

"You have "mules" …Carriers. They pick up the money and deposit it in bank accounts over there, and then funnel the money back to you in the states," Carrie was informed.

"Now, go get on the laptop, please. You have a chance to get away and leave the U.K. before the law catches up with you sweetheart," I declared.

However, Carrie remains defiant saying, "I am in Kumasi."

"Nope," I replied.

"Okay, if you don't believe," Carrie stops in mid-thought for some unknown reason.

"I am not conceding defeat in getting you on my computer Carrie, now once again, get on the laptop; I dare you to prove me wrong!"

"I have shown you many times," Carrie protested.

"So you say, but here is how you can make me believe in your truthfulness Carrie," I insisted. "Take the laptop outside with you, and we will see if I am wrong. This is how you prove it. Go out on Santasi Street," prodding her. Apparently, without rhyme or reason, or merely discouraged, Carrie decides it's time for her to log off Yahoo Messenger, unwilling to cooperate with my wishes. Therefore, the session ends abruptly on July 2, 2013, at 5:11 in the evening.

I want the reader to understand that I am not advocating Carrie's behavior. Nor was I approving of her involvement in the industry of pornography. Neither do I endorse their alleged swindling activity. I was merely playing the role of advocate, giving the appearance that I believed in Carrie's dire circumstances. It was evil bedding with the enemy. These sorts of behavior patterns most always pit one side against the other. So I continue role-playing the ignorant patsy. When dealing with evil, you know you are in the belly of darkness when lying becomes the norm. Then it becomes necessary to "hard sell" yourself until you're convinced all avenues of discovery have been exhausted. Only then can you know if you've escaped the abyss successfully.

The following day, July 3, 2013, at 6:24 A.M., Carrie logs onto Messenger for a chat session. She acts complacent. This became Carrie's mode-of-operation throughout our friendship. She leaves angry, returns like a blooming rose. It has got to be a request for money.

"Good morning," Carrie said.

I was surprised to say the least to find Carrie logged on this early, as I asked. "Are you on?"

"Yes," she replied. "And how are you doing today?"

"Just in the process of waking from my sleep," I told Carrie. "I'm still in bed."

Carrie responds. "Okay, I see, and how is the weather?"

"I don't know, I haven't wormed my way out of bed yet," I told Carrie.

"Okay, I see," she acknowledged. "What have you been doing?"

"Sleeping already," I snapped back. "This is the second time I've told you Carrie."

"Okay," Carrie acknowledged without much fanfare.

"I had a very long sleepless night, so I'm crabby right now," Carrie was informed.

Carrie is too uplifting and candid with me thus far. Nothing good can come of this as she comments. "Oh, I see dear."

"I 'm going to leap out of bed and bring the computer to the desk, so give me a minute would you please," I asked. Sitting down at the desk, I remarked to Carrie. "This computer must have a nasty virus in it yet."

"Dang it," Carrie noted. "Sorry, I don't know where it came from," she said.

"Sure Carrie, now it needs to be taken into the store. More than likely your partners infected it."

"I am ninety-nine percent unaware of what mostly you are talking about Jim about what partners are doing to your computer," Carrie stated.

Alarmed and a little unsure of myself right now, because out of nowhere I said. "Maybe I'm not talking to the real Carrie."

Carrie wastes little time trying to soothe my fears by telling me, "it is me you are talking to honey."

Taking a little comfort in what Carrie just said, did nothing to ease the unsettling state of my computer, so I blurted out again. "Maybe it is Nate I'm talking too."

"You're talking to me," Carrie insisted again.

Continuing to dig in my heels, I share my suspicions with Carrie. "It was about a week ago I began to raise some questions about the authenticity of the language I was witnessing. The wording was different," Carrie was informed. "It was crisp, structured, typed in complete sentences using three and four syllable words. Much different from your style of writing," I concluded.

"You what? Are you sure?" Carrie asked.

It bears repeating that when Carrie is aware I am onto her, she has a tendency to become stoic, speechless, and suddenly quiet. In this case, she did respond gingerly by muttering the sound. "Hum mm."

"They were too self-assured, yet, their words contained too many contradictions," I stated. "It was not as we speak. They were complete sentences. The English, pure and concise, not broken as you are accustomed to typing," I said.

Carrie answers, "I see."

"Carrie you usually use one or two syllable words which I have come to expect from you. But this other discussion was very different." "When you comment, "I see," it is a dead giveaway where you become aware I am onto something sinister," I implied, attempting to get Carrie to admit this was a rogue partner of hers. "You not only see, you know, so let's stop the nonsense and tell the truth, Carrie."

"Okay, Carrie replied casually without any apparent concern."

I find myself continually having to coax every scintilla of vowels and syllables out of this woman, so I plainly said. "I am ready to hear your side of this mystery person, Carrie."

However, Carrie, the deceptive con artist that she is, takes the discussion in another direction saying. "I just want us together, but you have been screwing all that we planned earlier when we first met," she charged.

"It's because you never tell the truth that's why," I declared. I want to resist allowing Carrie to drift off topic, so I redirect, and pose another question to her. "Have you read the story about the man running through town yet? It was sent via email."

Carrie nonchalantly replies. "No, I never read that."

"Where is it then," I inquired. "I went through all my old emails and none of the emails I sent you were ever returned to me."

Carrie is beyond stubborn and would rather address what is on her mind. "I am in Kumasi. I told you that when you wanted to come here. My partners ran to U.K., but they are back now," she said.

If Carrie expected me to believe this "Rudy-to-dee fresh-n-fruity" version, then I surmised she was exercising her right to be condescending. Reacting in defiance to the battle of the wills I return a rebuttal of my own. "No, you are all still in the U.K." I insisted.

"I am in Kumasi. Believe me and stop what you think is right," Carrie demanded.

Undeterred by her denials I bring up an entirely different subject matter saying. "Why do you keep doing videos then?" I inquired.

"I do it for the work," she remarked without shame.

I counter her response by declaring. "Then they never left the U.K. and you are all still there," adding. "You better read my story Carrie," I remarked.

Carrie remains indifferent, holding onto the same old song and dance routine. "No, I'm not in the U.K.!!!" Carrie belabors her point. "I have so." (Meaning now she claims to have read the story.)

"You just told me earlier you didn't read the story, Carrie!"

Carrie appears slightly confused as she asked. "Did you email it to me now?"

"What did I say?" I'm getting a tad short with Carrie. "I emailed it a week ago," I said, getting impatient with Carrie.

Carrie replies as expected. "I never got it sweetheart."

I quipped. "Somebody did!"

Carrie, now interested in the email asked. "Who do you think?"

"Yes Carrie, please let me know," I plead. "Who else has access to your email?"

"No one I know!" She claims. "I just got your email and it said I should return all your stuff, and money!" Carrie exclaimed.

Replying back to Carrie I announced. "It didn't come back here undelivered; so someone has it."

"No, I never got such email," Carrie claims.

Since Carrie is adamant in her denial of ever receiving the email, I asked. "You do not remember the words. "The sky is falling ... The sky is falling?"

Expressing disappointment, Carrie responds. "Dang, I never got that email."

"Someone did!" I replied in disbelief again.

Carrie characterizes' this debacle by asking. "Dang, you got reply back?"

"Never," I said.

As an afterthought, Carrie asked out of curiosity. "So why do you think I got the email?"

For the umpteenth time, I find myself apparently talking to myself; disappointment written all over this page. "Because Carrie, if you didn't receive the email and it was accidently sent to the wrong email address it would have been sent back to me, "returned to sender, address unknown."

All this bickering back and forth is obviously for not, as Carrie still insisted. "But I never got!"

"Then you better talk to your partner's," was my recommendation to Carrie.

Determined and convinced she never received the email Carrie commented. "Dang, no one has my password."

I informed Carrie what I thought might have happened to the email. "You said "Nate" is computer savvy, didn't you?" Adding. "Anyone with head knowledge and experience can hack into a computer and obtain passwords."

"Yeah, Carrie said," finally coming on board in agreement with my viewpoint.

"So go and ask the little man," I encouraged Carrie.

Carrie responded. "Okay."

I needed to challenge Carrie over an observation that just occurred to me. "If everyone scattered to the U.K. like you said, I don't know how you can shoot videos if he was able to gain access to your computer."

"Nate can get into the computer," Carrie finally admitted.

With complete candor, I question Carrie's sequence of events. "How can "Nate" be in two places at once?"

Carrie echo's her previous replies. "I am in Kumasi!" Now she is beginning to irritate Jim Jacobs.

Repeating like a parrot who masters one or two words, I bluntly ask Carrie. "How can your partners be in two places at one time?"

"They aren't in two locations!" Carrie snapped back.

"Before, you said they left for U.K and then came back."

"Yes," Carrie acknowledged.

"But you were shooting videos while they were gone Carrie, how can this be?"

Carrie justifies the sequence of events with a vague answer. "Sure, in Ghana we were doing video shoots." Carrie is confident she has it right, but it only begs for more answers.

Responding to her version of events, I said. "Not if they were in the U. K. like you claim."

Carrie tries using sweet-talk with me as she says. "Yes, we did dear."

"Then they never left."

Carrie briefly responds. "They did."

"How can they be gone while you continue to shoot videos," I continue to ask.

Carrie is definitely circling the wagons with her story. "They did leave, and yes they are back now, she said."

"Then how did you shoot videos on site while they were in the United Kingdom?"

Carrie, not one to be out-done said. "I did with HQ equipment."

"You did this yourself?" I asked in disbelief.

Carrie, deciding to bolster her argument and give it creditability said. "We planned it, so I needed to do it."

"Who planned this for you?" I inquired, adding. "If they are in the United Kingdom, how can you plan any video taping's?"

Carrie and I are at an impasse as she said. "I planned it together with them. We planned it when they were with me, she alleges."

"You were doing video taping's while your fellow cohort's in crime ran off to the United Kingdom … Highly unlikely Carrie," I argued.

The gist of that whole exchange was to determine how Carrie could shoot solo videos on her own while she was in Ghana at the time she claims her partners had taken flight to the U.K., supposedly hiding from me while Carrie was left behind to shoot videos on her own. The crux for the line of questioning was that these video tapings couldn't have taken place as she described the sequence of events because it was impossible for Carrie to do this on her own. It amounted to another fabricated lie.

Following the video controversy, I reemphasized how we differed significantly using her timelines and reliability during our friendship. I remained steadfast, continuing to insist Carrie had two laptops in her possession. So we continue to be at odds about these laptop computers, as the lines of questioning continues.

"What about those two laptop computers Carrie? I know you have at least one, mine,"

"No I don't!" Carrie insisted on saying.

The truth has to be somewhere beneath these layers of lies so I asked Carrie a second time. "What happened to the two computers?"

"One is with someone, and the other is broken."

"Who is that someone, this mystery person," I asked Carrie.

"A friend," Carrie answers without hesitation.

This didn't sit well with me either, as Carrie is told. "You know what I want you to do?" You need to show yourself to me and prove you are in Ghana," I remarked. "You have some nerve leaving it with a friend, and if true as you have said, it tells me you are not serious about us," Carrie was informed. "Are you absolutely sure you gave the Toshiba to your friend, I asked?"

I intentionally mentioned Toshiba to bait Carrie into acknowledging for a second time, that she did, in fact, receive the Toshiba I had mailed to the P.O. Box number in Ghana she had given me.

"Yes, she needed it for school work, and she has not returned it."

"Then, why don't you go get it?"

"I had it, but she asked me if she could use it again.

"Then why isn't Nate working on the broken one Carrie? There must be a lot of video's and photographs on there that cost money." I reminded her.

The question stymied Carrie briefly because the only response she could utter was a murmur, "Hmm, okay, I see."

Carries answers to the computer status posed a dilemma in my view, as I asked. "Then what are you using for your two daily cam shows?"

"Camera and desktop, Carrie replied."

This is a contradiction Carrie. "The desktop is the main screen on the computer when you power it on, and you and I know this Carrie." Adding. "So why are you in denial about not having a computer?"

Unfazed, Carrie responds to the question with a simple remark. "No!"

Ignoring Carrie's remark, I respond with irritation. "No!" I declared. "Okay, let's do a live video chat then."

While writing these conversations on paper as outlined in the context of he said/she said, I have decided that while it may or may not make for interesting reading, I concluded that for me to continue at this pace, the content would likely generate an eight-hundred-page manuscript. That said, I have decided to do a summation of our conversations in the remaining Chapters. However, if I feel the conversation has significance, I will revert back to dialogue again.

335

I extended an invitation for Carrie to join me on live video chat and she accepted. "What a surprise, I murmured to self. But more than likely Carrie will use the antiquated computer that is known to freeze mysteriously after one or two minutes. So if past behavior is any indicator of present behavior, it will hold true to form that my suspicions would likely come to fruition.

I was certain this was a preemptive strategic plan on their part to prevent me from viewing the surrounding work area for any hint of evidence that would further implicate them. When I was able to see Carrie and the room, I noticed they added another desk and chair. Within a minute, I saw a shadow in the room where Carrie was broadcasting. After repeated demands to bring this mystery person into view of the camera, Carrie would remain resolute in refusing my request. All she would say was that it was her friend Lillian.

Since Carrie alleges she never received the email I sent, I was going to use Yahoo Messenger to tell her about the man who went about the village screaming, "the sky is falling." I would wait until Carrie logged off messenger. She would be able to read it when she logged in the next time. The story is written to enlighten Carrie about the pitfalls of deceit and lies. If their behavior persisted, it would eventually lead to negative consequences. It may be worth the effort, but until Carrie reads the story, it is too early to predict what if any impact the story would have on future behavior from her.

A well to do respectable man who lived in a quaint small town was well known and respected by the town citizens. Now, everyone in town was going about his or her business. It was a slow day. Warm with a breeze blowing from the west. The only excitement that would raise any awareness would be the occasional train that passed through at different times of the day. One day this well-respected man who the town citizens viewed as someone whose character shown itself as trusting, generous, and likable. He wouldn't even harm an ant, to the degree that he would avoid stepping on one as he walked along the sidewalk.

Nevertheless, this day, the man did something you might consider abnormal. Like a bolt of lightning coming down from the clouds. This man began running through the town streets frantically screaming at the top of his lungs. "The sky is falling; the sky is falling!" Well, with the unexpected outcry and the terrible sound of the man's voice and warning, the town citizens without a moment's delay, began to take cover to protect themselves. Scrambling to find what shelter they could for protection from the falling sky. They darted to the nearest safe haven they could come upon. After all, who wanted to be afflicted, or injured by a falling sky?

Therefore, they stayed secluded in their shelters for about four hours or thereabouts. They were somewhat puzzled when they came out from hiding and noticed the sky had not fallen. Why did this man say such a thing? What was the point? Why did he lie? You can imagine the town citizens were quite upset about this. Therefore, they gathered around and discussed what to do with him. They agreed they would just leave it alone and not approach the man, passing it off as maybe he was losing some of his right thinking. No one was hurt, but it did alarm the people in the village. Yet, they forgave his annoying behavior.

After two weeks had passed, the town citizen's soon forgot about the man's earlier behavior. Wouldn't you know, two weeks to the day, here comes the man again. Once again shouting in a deep voice; even more frantic and neurotic, screaming uncontrollably: "The sky is falling, the sky is falling!" At this, the town's people once again scrambled for cover to protect them from the falling sky. They were frightened, expecting the worse. So again, they waited several hours, but nothing happened. So one by one they slowly creeped out from under whatever shelter they could find for protection and began to resurface.

After the initial shock had passed, they realized this same man had once again been responsible for his misleading and deceitful lie. Once again, the citizens of the town held a meeting to decide what to do about this man's unusual conduct. The consensus was, they agreed, not normal behavior. What to do? They began to quarrel about what action should be taken on this man. They were very irritated and upset by this time. Surely, they could not allow this man to keep deceiving and lying to them. So far, no one was hurt. But the possibility that people in a panic, or who are in a panic and who are frantic to find shelter... why; it would just be a matter of time when ... if people were in a hurry to seek shelter, by this man's continued behavior, could eventually cause some of the citizens to slip as they run for cover. The person or persons who slipped and fell would be trampled.

Now the citizens thought what the man did was wrong and dangerous, but they again decided to give him one more chance to redeem himself and passed it off as a prank, or the man was just a compulsive liar. Perhaps if given time, he would see his mistakes and the consequences and effects it had on other innocent victims … He would stop his lying. All in the town agreed to give him one last chance. "Surprise … Surprise!" Three weeks later, the man pulls the same stunt with his deceit and lies. Darting through the streets and alleyways with the same uncontrolled panic as before; the man, his pitch filled with urgency to it, yelled. "The sky is falling; the sky is falling!"

This time, though. The citizens of the town did not take cover but ignored the man's plea to take cover. Furthermore, everyone went about their business, as usual, paying the man no mind. However, the old man sought shelter. The outcome was different. The sky did fall and in the process, it killed all the citizens of the town. Only the man survived. So I asked Carrie to give me an explanation of what the story was trying to convey.

"What does this story suggest to you Carrie, and what do you think my reason is for having you read the story?

"In the beginning, of our friendship when we first crossed paths, I made an all-out effort to believe everything you told me. Then after we were into the details of the conversation, I would immediately get suspicious of what you were telling me. But I gave you chance after chance to redeem yourself. As time went on, I realized most everything you said had as its element an orchard full of falsehood."

"Carrie, my dear princess, the moral of the story is this. If you cry wolf too many times, people will not trust you any longer because your reputation will become tarnished by your blatant lies. So now, when you tell me you are truthful, I cannot believe you because you have cried wolf too many times. Maybe this story example will impress upon you the consequences you face for bad choices."

The next time Carrie was on messenger I asked her if she had a chance to read the story. She told me she did. Then, in the next breath, Carrie claimed she hadn't read it. We went back and forth, about whether she did or did not read the story. Then Carrie would abruptly change the topic. I would question whether, or not I was actually talking to Carrie, Nate, or another of their partners in crime. It was when the name Nate was mentioned that Carrie would become agitated and defensive leading me to believe he was her husband.

Mentioning the name Nate also solicited unkind words that spewed from Carrie's mouth like poison. She would re-direct the conversation to another subject entirely. I informed Carrie I was arranging to travel to Ghana to pick her up. She was pleased with this surprising bit of information, but I knew better than to chase to no man's land, even if I knew she was in Ghana. Since Carrie's hopes were high, she wanted a smart phone bought along.

Not on this man's watch, I thought to myself. Everything is so slanted; I don't know what or who to believe anymore including status of my laptop.

Carrie interrupts my thought process saying. "Dang, you didn't trust me the first time that's why."

"Carrie," I said. "You are always walking all over me. I am not some puppet on a string you can manipulate when you decide it is going to profit you."

Carrie commented with sleight of hand. "That is because you are so arrogant," she remarked.

"Look here Carrie, first you say you sold the computer. Now you're telling me you loaned it to a friend; who is walking over whom?" I asked, searching for a valid answer.

Carrie feels it is fault finding time. "You been thinking and searching for my mistakes since we met," she stated with anger.

"Did I just lie, or is it the truth Carrie?"

Carrie countered with her own read of our current relationship. "When I told you it was sold you didn't believe me, so I needed to lie to convince you. That's what I said." Adding. You want to be lied to before you will believe me," Carrie said.

Moving forward on the trust issue, I inform Carrie that she put herself in the position I was in when she wanted a favor from me for an alleged emergency. So we revisit Ghana Mart where Carrie is beside herself because she had no food or money to buy groceries. Carrie wanted me to go online and give Ghana Mart my credit card number so she could buy groceries. I refused her request because I knew the real sinister intent behind her scheme.

It was late at night, 11:00 in the evening Ghana time when she calls me up to tell me she is afraid to go out to the Mart at that time of night because, one. There are no streetlights, and two, she was scared of the black men. I then reminded Carrie that it wasn't too long ago that she was faced with the same situation with buying groceries. Time and circumstances were identical and you didn't have issues buying groceries at the Mart then. She was to log onto messenger when she returned home, but it never happened. Thus, I told her there were two inconsistencies in her request. Therefore, I was not about to give my card number to anyone and I sure was not going to send money through the Western Union.

After this chronological order of events had been explained to Carrie, she had nothing else to say.

Because it was July 4, I informed Carrie I was going to Stout Lake for the fireworks and a picnic, so I discontinued throwing darts with questions attached to them and tried to have a civil conversation with her. That got me all sorts of "honey's" and "dears" from Carrie. Especially when I reassured her, I was still coming to Ghana. I asked her if she prayed before going to sleep and she informed me she did. (?) We discussed how she needed to heal her wounds. "It would require a specialist, I told Carrie." A physician once told Jim Jacobs that if one member of the family was sick, then both partners required treatment.

"When you come to Ghana, bring me a phone Okay, sweetheart?" she asked. "My phone screen has a crack, and ink is on it now," Carrie alleges. "It sounded as if Carrie was in panic mode, but I knew Carrie had more than one cell phone if not more in her arsenal of disposable "burn phones." Carrie is bent on having me get a reverse vasectomy. What an evil; cruel request coming from a scammer who apparently has no conscience, and who loves victimizing their victims over and over. Sometimes that procedure can be very painful either way you go.

My mission; to attach names to other players. Before Carrie logs off, surprise, surprise. I am asked to top-up her cell phone. One-hundred dollars is her asking price. I told Carrie I could not because someone had attempted to compromise my checking account and everything was frozen. Carrie claims she is broke all the time because she sends money to Sweden where her mother Fadi Svennson Asante resides. Another irony crops-up in the red flag group. This was not the name Carrie gave me initially when I emailed her mother.

The following day July 5, 2013, I take off my kid gloves again to begin bombarding Carrie with more questions.

"Carrie, when are you getting that laptop back from your friend?"

"I sold it, Carrie replies, without going into further detail."

"Now you're telling me you sold it?" I demanded to know. "you just loaned it to your friend, what is going on with you Carrie?"

"I first told you I sold it and you were still messing with my head," Carrie implies.

With all the care I could muster without seeming overly spiteful, I said. "Here is the deal then. Until I see you live on that laptop, and I am in charge of directing your movements, there will be no cell phones." I reminded Carrie that there were just too many inconsistencies in her discussions with me.

(Expletive) "Jim, you ask too many questions, Carrie remarked."

Making it entirely clear I said. "I want to be able to guide you on every move on live cam, it is that simple Carrie."

(Expletive) "That is (expletive), what are you thinking," Carrie stated.

"For someone who swears she loves me, yet refuses to honor one simple request asked of her while insisting on making this a big issue makes me very suspicious indeed," I told Carrie. "By the way, there is additional findings I happened to discover," telling Carrie. "Bernie the dog and his playmate are terriers I believe, right?" Carrie refuses to answer but remains silent.

Apparently I Triggered a hot button as Carrie says. "No, if you love me, and believe me, why would you suspect I am not real, or what?"

"That is exactly right, it goes both ways, Carrie," making it known where I stood.

"Whatever!" Carrie replies with a hint of frustration in the atmosphere."

I begin to goad Carrie because I sense her indignation. "A terrier dog is an expensive breed," I informed Carrie.

Carrie is beginning to become unhinged as she repeats her previous comment. "Whatever!"

I continue to brand Bernie into Carrie's memory bank, saying. "They are not cheap, and Africa does not breed Terrier dogs because they are very expensive dogs… Carrie, you are not in Africa," I concluded saying.

Carrie falls into a defensive mode again coming back with a rebuttal; "I am."

"Intelligence gathering information tells me you are not," I told Carrie with absolute confidence.

Carrie continues to insist; she is in Ghana despite the overwhelming evidence to the contrary as she says. "But I am."

"Then prove it!" I insisted. And I mean business!"

So Carrie replies. "So, I should do something to make you happy?"

"No, you do it to confirm that you are where you claim to be Carrie."

Carrie launches her objection of sorts saying. "I am in Kumasi! (Expletive)."

"Then you will have no problem proving it to me," I said. "You folks must think I'm really a gullible imbecile, a weak fool, dumber than dumb," I said without shame. "Who knows, maybe I have all these traits," I jokingly replied to Carrie." Carrie, not one to be happy lately, sends a rebuttal. "If you want to be serious with me, stop the (expletive) you are talking (expletive) and contact me, Jim. I want to know you as I have known you from the beginning," Carrie insinuated.

I reprimand Carrie on how distasteful her vocabulary is getting lately and voiced my displeasure. "I think that it is about enough of your foul language Carrie. I suggest you get control of yourself."

Carrie can be in denial all she wants. Every time Carrie speaks in opposition to the evidence I have on her, the foundation beneath her feet becomes more insecure. Where once there may have been hairline fractures in the foundation, what now emerges are huge gaping hole's leading into the abyss.

From July 5 through July 12, 2013, there was no contact from Carrie. She was punishing me for lack of care to caress her needs. This did not prevent me from logging onto messenger to leave snippets of wisdom. There were times I noticed Carrie had logged onto messenger. However, she never uttered a word. She just logged on to let me know she was around. So I extracted versus' out of Scripture with the expectation Carrie would receive fulfillment from its discourse and have it weigh on her mind, heart, and soul.

Here are the soul attesting words from God, I left for Carrie's eyes' to see. To the people of King Solomon's day when the Lord said to them, "if my people who are called by my name will humble themselves and pray and seek my face and turn from their wicked ways, then I will hear from Heaven and will forgive their sin and heal their land. (Household as well) Now my eyes' will be open, and my ears attentive to the prayers offered in this place. "Woe." "Woe." "Woe;" to those who hear, and do not see or listen.

Whether Carrie accepts or rejects the message is a choice only her or anyone of her cohorts in crime have to make. Sixteen days had passed without any effort on Carrie's behalf to contact me. Not even a peep was ere heard. I wasn't sure if she expected me to grovel at her feet and surrender to her demands. Perhaps she realizes the scam with me has come to an abrupt halt and they finally decided they couldn't squeeze any more money out of me. Therefore, it was time to move on but that was just pure speculation. If you recall, Carrie and I had discussed travel arrangements over to Ghana to get her, and bring her back to the States. We went to great lengths talking about these plans. However, all that amounted to was a precursor to solidify my suspicions that I was on course to get what I came after.

The date, July 21, 2013, Carrie, after being absent without leave, finally signs into messenger where travel arrangements are discussed.

"I think we should forget about this whole arrangement Carrie," I suggested.

"I see, but you are the one I want." So says Carrie.

"Then why can't I make the arrangement for your airfare from here? Must I come there?" I attempted to convince Carrie my proposal seemed more practical.

"I wanna, but I am here by myself," Carrie insinuated.

I am not sure what you are implying Carrie; what you mean? You have your partners and girlfriends, what do you want me to do?" I inquired.

"Buy ticket here," Carrie insisted with complete candor.

"Not a good idea Carrie, especially when I can purchase it here at a discount."

Carrie thinks she can hoodwink me said. "So as here, I can."

I am way ahead of Carrie's evil intentions. "Why do you think it is better for you to buy it in Ghana, rather than for me to purchase it here"? Using reverse psychology, I play on Carrie's emotions. "Please don't make me sorry for falling in love with you."

Carrie, not one to be upstaged, replies. "It is better because I can schedule much and know what I'm getting into." Continuing to apply pressure, she argues her position. "It will give me much faith and hope about leaving here."

Challenging Carries thought process, I try to reason with her. "Why can't you have faith and hope and allow me to purchase the ticket. Don't you trust me?"

Carrie is determined to come out of this exchange victorious, but she seals her own fate. She can be predictable and unpredictable all in the same breath; if that's possible. Carrie is relentless however. Defending her position to purchase the ticket in Ghana. Her explanation and justification are never clear.

"When I go to buy it myself, it is a sign of good loving and a big sign telling me I am leaving," Said Carrie.

"You know I'm not lying to you, Carrie. You always make me feel inept, princess."

Carrie being Carrie continues to butt heads with me. "Not a good sign," Carrie implies. I don't even have courage about that. That is why I still want to buy it myself," Carrie insisted profusely.

Of course what Carrie said is nothing more than psychobabble, so I question Carrie's motive. "If you don't have courage now, what makes you think you will have courage if I send you the money to buy the ticket," as I challenge Carries truthfulness.

"When I get the cash, I will surely have and buy it." Carrie tries to assure me."

Carrie and her crew of misfits live for the scam. I sometimes wonder how naive they think I am. It is true, I was had in the beginning, but now? Give me a break! Does she not realize I am with her and that group of malcontents? Nobody from Ghana, or Nigeria in the swindling business is going to dialogue with any targeted victim for months without receiving dividends for their efforts. This is why I am convinced Carrie and her cohorts in crime are operating within our borders. The question remains; where in the U.S.? To get the location of these faceless warriors of the internet, I will need names.

Entertaining Carrie with a suggestion I introduced as a bogus teaser, I proclaimed. "Maybe it would be best if we left Ghana together."

"You mean we live here together?" Carrie asked.

"No, came my answer, we leave the airport together honey."

Carrie, perhaps employing the same mind techniques I use gave me pause, if ever so briefly on how best to respond to her question as she asked. "Can you live here?"

Given the nature of her question, I decided to concoct a fool's reply. "I might have to live with you a little while should it become necessary," Carrie was told.

"Good, then we would be staying in the hotel all the time, or my home?" Carrie asked. Then Carrie must have reconsidered, saying. "It is too dangerous here. Why don't you just get me the money to buy it? I will buy it," I promise, Carrie steadfastly assured me. As an afterthought, Carrie added. "Yep," she said. "I wanna leave here, and don't want those partners to know about this."

I interrupted Carrie by inquiring. "What about Bernie?"

Carrie replied. "I May leave him behind."

"I think you are too close to him. I could see how you interacted with the little guy. Probably the closest thing you have for love and affection." I remarked, putting Carrie to the test.

Carrie acknowledges with understanding. "Yes, my dear; Sure."

Carrie and I were on messenger for the better part of six hours that day. I posed many different scenarios to Carrie. Challenging her sincerity and truthfulness using every adjective, noun, pronoun, verb, and syllable in the English language. The result produced one contradiction after another. By the time I had finished, I had accumulated nothing but a basketful of enunciated lies. The only reason for lingering around this group of misfits is to reap at least one name. If I could just get a name; especially the mystery man Nate. I felt it could put me in the driver's seat. So patience continues to be my mainstay, holding Carrie on a string hoping her tongue will misstep. Carrie says plenty, but not enough to blurt out want I so desperately need. I wanted to hear the battle cry. "Gotcha."

The next time Carrie made an appearance, July 23, 2013. She wanted me to use the debit card again. Carrie wanted me to use the internet by going to, www.Ghananetworks.com. I informed Carrie I would have to purchase a gift card for the fifty dollars she wanted to scam me out of additional money by telling me she needed to top-up on her minutes so she could call Mom in Sweden. The gift card would not do, it had to be the debit card. She remained adamant about the debit card. Well now, there was no way this man was giving out his debit card to anyone, so she dropped that idea like a hot potato. Finally, after much haggling, Carrie agreed to a Western Union money order. Rather than taking a chance of losing her, I made the choice to send her the fifty dollars, praying it would be well worth the sacrifice in the end, so I asked Carrie for the address to send the money.

"Is it the same P.O. box as before?"

"Yes, P.O. Box 14781, Adum Kumasi, Ghana." Carrie typed on messenger page.

This would be my last donation in the name of this swindler. Carrie or her gang of criminals wasn't going to squeeze any more monies from Jim Jacobs.

On July 25, 2013, I had not heard from Carrie as promised on July 23. I went into a rapid descent calling the entire bunch on the carpet. Using messenger as a sounding board to vent my displeasure with the whole lot. I held nothing in reserve.

"What kind of pure evil are you trying to pull on me now Carrie?" You fledgling liars; all. There isn't an ounce of truth in the pack of you. The only sickness you can claim is your compulsive lying, cheating, stealing, and conniving. You bunch of deceitful children of the Devil. You are a band of malcontents destined for ruin; if not now, then the day of judgment. You have manipulated me one too many times, you lying pack of wolves.

"Hide behind the screen you children of darkness; scammers all. "Love, what is love?" "You are pitiful cowards with hardened hearts having evil inside as your companion. Now read this … I challenge you to come here and confront me! I know you misfits can see this message. The scammer will be scammed. I am going to expose the whole lot of you before this is over. I'm not threating you, I am challenging all things honorable that are absent in the abyss.

"Your days are numbered. You picked the wrong person to scam this time. You, folks, know what a pit bull does when it attacks? He grabs hold and does not let go. I'm that vicious pit bull you agitated. I do not dismiss evil intent quickly.

There was a picture taken of Carrie standing by her truck outside a mall. The license plate had blue lettering on a white background. Now I know Ghana does not have plates in this design, so it allows me to narrow the location down to a select few states.

Rather lavish truck for someone who claims her partners are cheating her out of money. As it were, there were several vehicles in the lot with the same color plates. They were right in our own backyard I thought. Carrie was right, they are not in the U. K. Pretty soon I will be close enough to identify them and their location that I'll be able to shake their hands.

Carrie decides to log onto messenger after a long absence. Out of the starting gate, I tell Carrie I knew she and her misfits in crime have read how dissatisfied I was with their renegade conduct. Nothing fazed Carrie though. It seemed Carrie wasn't reading the words or she was in a stupor because she replied. "I got the money you sent, though."

Grrrrr! How frustrating can this saga get? Carrie does have a coat of many colors indeed. I Remind Carrie they have chosen the wrong person to confront in this game of chess, as I say. "What does that have to do with anything? We are discussing an entirely different matter right now. The rules of engagement have changed. "Money isn't important right now. I told you money is just a medium of exchange … It rots its funny money," I declared angrily to Carrie.

Carrie apparently was not in the mood to hear my ranting and raving, so she went off the radar screen. While she was absent, I penned some more gobble-de-gook for them to chew on. I figured they were probably getting bored, so why not stir the pot for these busy bodies and give them something newsworthy to chew the cud on.

"I am getting closer my dear. You were right. I am closer than I thought," I declared with confidence. "On second thought, you are so close, I can smell the dirty river." "Does IP 98.116.217.103 ring a bell," I asked? "Tell me, who is the mule over in Ghana for yawls," I wanted to know? "Who is it, that sends the money back here, or deposits it into an account under a bogus name for you to claim later," inquiring minds wanted to know?" "do you think it could be that little black girl who appeared on your screen by mistake?" "Boy! Did you ever do a Houdini on that image fast," I stated?

Wanting to tighten the screws, even more, I added. "I think I will search the color of those license plates. I believe it has blue colored letters and numbers with a white background, after all, there are only a select number of states with that design," I informed Carrie. "I found a picture of you on the internet about ready to get into that big black fancy truck of yours." There was a vehicle behind yours with American plates as well Carrie," I told her. "If you give someone enough time, they will eventually dig their own grave."

The remainder of the month was spent having a conversation with myself. Carrie was either logged on and just sat there and read the chat messages while I gave my assessment of how events were unfolding, or if she was there she chose not to respond. I kept repeating how I had been lied to and deceived. I suggested that if they wanted my funny money they could have it.

I was inciting them to action hoping I would awaken them out of their hibernation. "You want money guys? Fine, I will give you the money. Just come to my place and it is yours. Stop trying to think you and that bunch of misfits are getting anything over on me," I boldly announced. "So, how much money do you want? It is yours for the taking and you can divvy it up between yawl, and boy toy," adding. "Come visit yawls, yah hear?"

Carrie must have been getting impatient, or offended by my words because she finally responded by saying. "I never played you, I was forced to," she alleges. "I don't know why you do not believe what I tell you," apparently anguishing over my comments. "You never believe me even if I speak the truth."

"It didn't sound like anyone was forcing you last night on your website," I told her point blank. "How is it you have taken away every method of communication from us except for messenger, and your personal website," I asked. "I could observe you clear as a window pane without anything freezing. Your voice was clear without any interruptions, so tell me Carrie, who is forcing you?" Adding, "For a change, I would like a truthful answer from you."

Carrie responded, shifting blame. "It is your fault!"

Carrie never told me how she could justify blaming me, but it didn't really matter. Nothing else of significance occurred on July 25, and so, the month ended with a whimper. However, the Month was not a total disaster. I was able to discover that these folks were operating somewhere in the Newark, New Jersey area along with some other subtle clues. I still needed Carrie to be around. I am still searching for the last name to one of these misfits. I have been patient this long, I continue to take a wait and see approach.

CHAPTER 19

Truth, what is Truth?

The Heavens is the keeper of time, as time is the adversary of humankind.
Love blossoms and can have beautiful liberties. Yet,
its fullest affection; witnesses' life's decline.
Morality oblique with iniquity, dispenses much chaos,
trampled asunder on hallowed ground.
Arrogance, pride, sin, envy, strife, greed; man owns,
but Jesus Christ possesses the crown.
Jim Jacobs

The truth is a contentious adversary to just about everyone who walks on the face of the earth. We avoid the truth for several reasons. We are fearful of the consequences should the truth be revealed. It is skewed quite frequently in the arena of politics, covert operations, guarding the public image. In the process, we may have created for ourselves an unwanted monster. Truths Thunder has become an abysmal ineffectual minute burst. Let's look then, at Webster's Dictionary and the definition of truth. Then we will search Scripture to see what God's word has to say about truth.

Webster's defines truth as, Fidelity, Constancy, the body of real things, events, and, facts Transcendent, fundamental, or spiritual reality. A judgment proposition or idea that is true or accepted as true, the fidelity of an original, or a standard. Truthful, an adjective, it means telling or disposed to speak the truth.

What does the infallible word of God tell us about truth? To the Christians familiar with Scripture, and to those who may have seen, "The Greatest Story Ever Told." When Jesus was before Pontius Pilate, and just before Christ crucifixion you read in John Chapter 18: 38. Pilate asked Christ. "Truth; what is the truth?" Christ answered Pilate with these words. "I am the way, and the truth, and the life." In Scripture, there are thirty-four verses or references to the word "truth." Additionally, there are five verses on the use of the word truthfulness, truthful, and truths. What this suggests to me is that God takes honesty very seriously and not some whammy mammy byproduct humankind needs to take lightly.

Citing a few passages of Scripture on truth. If you feel a thirst for more, get a Bible. It is the best investment you will ever make. After all, we are talking about the destination of your very soul when you breathe your last breath. It is Jesus' promise of the Holy Spirit in John Chapter 14: 15. Jesus said. "If you love me you will keep my commandments. And I will ask the Father, and he will give you another Helper to be with you forever, even the spirit of truth, whom the world cannot receive because it neither sees him nor knows him. You know him, for he dwells with you, and will be with you."

We are orphans, therefore, if you have not been born again, you will not receive the indwelling of the Holy Spirit. It is only after accepting Jesus Christ as your Lord and Savior of your life. It is only with true repentance in your heart, and asking Him to come into your life, and rule over it, can you receive the Holy Spirit. Unfortunately, too many folks have a problem with this, because they do not want change, and they do not like being told how to live their lives. John Chapter 14: 6. Jesus said to him. "I am the way, and the truth, and the life. No one comes to the Father EXCEPT through me." 2 Timothy Chapter 2: 15. "Do your best to present yourself to God as one approved, who a worker who has no need to be ashamed, rightly handling the word of truth.

Dr. Sproul of Saint Andrews Chapel in Sanford, Florida would enlighten the congregation with the metaphor that took refuge in my brain like a flea taking residency in the coat of a dog. "Power corrupts; absolute power corrupts absolutely." Additionally, I continue to be reminded of the movie classic, "Cool Hand Luke," starring Paul Newman. In one scene, the warden of a prison chain gang where Newman played the role of a prisoner; escaped briefly from prison, and recaptured after experiencing a brief taste of freedom until the law caught up with him. All the prisoners gathered out into the prison yard to see Newman singled out as the topic of the warden's cryptic remarks directed at Newman's escape. Before announcing punishment on Newman, the Warden declared.

"What we have here; is a failure to, "com mune cate." That is what our state of affairs resembles in society today. What we have today is not the truth, but we choose to harbor iniquity in our hearts and indulge ourselves in worldly temper, chasing after things that perish.

There is an article I came across written by Ronald Weitzer that lends insightful declarations about prostitution. I cannot accept credit for the article because I am unlearned, learning from the learned. I have elected to use this article because I believe it complements the discourse of the manuscript. Although sometimes romanticized in popular culture, prostitution is more often portrayed as intrinsically oppressive and harmful. How accurate is this image? Well, since I desire the reader to be all-inclusive in this journey, I ask you to join me, and we will see what we can learn; shall we?

Mr. Weitzer begins the article with an observation after mentioning the exposition of prostitution to a friend: When I raised the topic of prostitution to my friend recently, he said. "How disgusting, how could anybody sell themselves?" A few weeks later an acquaintance told me she thought prostitution was a woman's choice, and can be empowering." It once again bears repeating in case you overlooked it previously. I do not want to burst anyone's bubble, but she is wrong on both accounts.

Ownership of the body belongs to God. It was in the beginning, at birth, death, and the finally the judgment. The body is the temple. It has value. To be seen as a precious pearl. Those opposing views reflect larger cultural perceptions of prostitution, as well as much academic writing on the topic.

A growing number of scholar's regard prostitution, pornography, and stripping as "sex work" and study it as an occupation. Exploring all dimensions of the work, in different contexts, these studies document substantial variation in the way prostitution is organized and experienced by workers, clients, and managers. These studies undermine some deep-rooted myths about prostitution and challenge writers and activists who depict prostitution monolithically. The most monolithic (huge, valuable) perspective is that prostitution is an unqualified evil. According to this oppression model, (weighted down) exploitation, abuse, and misery are intrinsic to the sex trade. In this view, most prostitutes faced physical or sexual abuse as children; which helps explain their entry into prostitution. Most enter the business as adolescents, around 13-14-years of age; most are tricked or forced into the trade by pimps or sex traffickers, or drug addiction. Customer violence against workers are routine and pervasive; working conditions are abysmal, and legalization would only worsen the situation.

Some women go further, characterizing the "essential" nature of prostitution. Because prostitution is defined as an institution of extreme male domination over women, these writers say that violence and exploitation are inherent and omnipresent-transcending historical time periods, national context, and type of prostitution. As Sheila Jeffreys writes, "Prostitution constitutes sexual violence against women in and of itself." And, according to Melissa Farley, Prostitution is an evil institution" that is "intrinsically traumatizing to the person being prostituted." Many writers who subscribe to the oppression model, use expressive language (sexual slavery, paid rape, survivors, and so on) and describe only the most disturbing cases, which the present as (typical-rhetorical tricks) designed to fuel public indignation.

The Declaration of Independence has its preamble that fuses together the Bill of Rights, Constitution, and Declaration which begins with the statement. "We hold these truths to be self-evident, that all men are created equal, that they are endowed by their Creator with certain unalienable Rights that among these are Life, Liberty, and the pursuit of Happiness." Observe the word "truths" in the Declaration, and the words Life, Liberty, and Happiness. I want someone in government to explain to me how women who are trapped in sexual slavery, paid rape, human trafficking, and kidnapping by pimps as being afforded life, liberty, and happiness.

These are women I empathize with. Apparently, our State and Federal government does not sympathize, or more would be done to eradicate this disgraceful practice. Anyone who is in bondage or held captive, have a constitutional right to be free. Otherwise, our lawmakers and governors are deficient in upholding the Declaration they swore on oath to uphold. "Truth; what is the truth?"

Street prostitution differs sharply from indoor prostitution. (No less inclusive, it should include webcam sites on the internet.) Many problems associated with prostitution is actually concentrated in street prostitution and less evident in the private sector. (Has anyone checked the internet lately?) Many street prostitutes work under abysmal conditions and are involved in "survival sex," selling sex out of dire necessity or they're supporting a drug habit. Some are runaway youths with no other options. Many use addictive drugs; risk contracting and transmitting sexual diseases; are exploited and abused by pimps; are vulnerable to being assaulted, robbed, raped, or killed, and even socially isolated and disconnected from support services. This is the population best characterized by the oppression model.

Other street prostitutes are in less desperate straits. Some work independently, without pimps. A Miami study found that only 7% had pimps, but the percentage differs significantly from city to city. Regarding the age of entry, the oppression model's claim of 13-14-years is clearly not the norm. A recent study by Marianne Hester and Nicole Westmarland found 20% of their sample had begun to sell sex before age 16 while almost half (48%) had begun after age 19. Childhood abuse (neglect, violence, and incest) is indeed part of the biography of some prostitutes. However, studies that compare matched samples of street prostitutes and non-prostitutes show mixed results. Some find a statistically significant difference in the experience of family abuse while others find no difference. HIV infection rates are highest among street prostitutes who inject drugs.

What seems to get less attention is the hidden world of indoor prostitution in venues such as bars, brothels, massage parlors, tanning salons, or in services provided by escort agencies, or independent call girls. (Can't allow a free pass as it must include webcam prostitution, and youths behaving badly.) Indoor prostitution accounts for a large share of the sex market. Indoor prostitutes have lower rates of childhood abuse, enter prostitution at a later age, and have more education. They are less drug-dependent and more likely to use softer drugs (marijuana instead of crack or heroin). Moreover, they use drugs for different reasons. Street prostitutes use drugs or alcohol to help cope with the adversities of the work, whereas private workers use them for coping, and as part of socializing with customers. (Hmm, seems to me there is plenty of alcohol and drugs consumed on these internet webcam sites.) Then you have to ask yourself why this is so. There is a shame, pain, guilt, and a lack of self-worth.

We create in ourselves something we desire and say; it is I. Present, all blessings are mine, absent all sorrows. But justice soon gives into foolishness when you finally experience that rendezvous with destiny. As you peer into the mirror, you see the monster you have created and begin to feel the guilt and truth, subdued by iniquities past and say; "I at last." Should any prostitute tell researchers or anyone else that has an ear to hear that they get greater job satisfaction; even if compared to their street-level counterparts, they are lying.

Truth does not reside with the unrighteous, but with the righteous. Dig deep enough and you will discover a problem. For every action, there is a reaction. It goes without saying. Everyone has guilt, and sooner than later, it will rear its ugly head. Researchers can classify their findings as oppression model and replace it with a polymorphous model Scripture. God's infallible word tells us it is an iniquity, abomination, and a stench in his nostrils.

Talk of legalization in the riddled porn industry, some pundits strongly believe this is the solution to this sin when all they will be doing is creating another Sodom and Gomorrah like the cesspools in Nevada, California, New York, and Phoenix. If anyone thinks they are going to lighten darkness without God's judgment, probably needs a reality check. The report goes on to say that although many Americans consider prostitution immoral or distasteful, a vast majority disagree. (This tells you where this country has been and where it's heading.) In the 1996 General Social Survey, 47% (52% men, 43% women) agreed to disagree that, "there is nothing inherently wrong with prostitution, so long as the health risks can be minimized. (Surveys can and are skewed) If adults agree upon exchanging money for sex, that is their business." (This is plain Ludacris, its Gods business, He created you, and He will condemn sin)

Isn't sin in anyone's vocabulary anymore? Doesn't any human soul in the last two generations fear the Lord's judgment? Better yet, does anybody read Scripture? Better still; just keep God in the closet until you need him again. But then, you may have waited too long and He will reject your pleas for help.

Moreover, some sizeable number favor alternatives to criminalization. (Yes, we call it abstinence, or marriage.) A 1991 Gallop poll found 40% of the public, thought prostitution should be legal and regulated by our government. (This is all dichotomous thinking. We've become a dysfunctional country.) In 2001, the State Department created a new unit, the Office to Monitor and Combat Trafficking in Persons. This office has endorsed the same extraordinary claims made by the anti-prostitution coalition. One example is the State Department's excellent website, The Link between Prostitution and sex trafficking, which contains these nuggets:

"Prostitution is inherently harmful. Few activities are as brutal and damaging to people as prostitution. It leaves women and children physically, mentally, emotionally, and spiritually devastated, and prostitution is "not," the "oldest" profession, but the "oldest" form of oppression. (Just creating a new unit in and of itself, to monitor and combat trafficking does little if you do not have enough boots on the ground to eradicate this morbid behavior. The idea has credibility and bears resemblance to God's truth, but much still needs to be done.) "Truth; what is the truth?"

Former President Clinton deserves some credit for taking a proactive role by signing into law legislation that would stem the tide in child pornography. President Bush, on the other hand, receives praise for funneling three-hundred-fifty million dollars into international and domestic organizations fighting prostitution. These groups received funds to conduct research, operate rescue missions, and engage in other interventions. Other organizations that provide these services but do not formally condemn prostitution are denied funding. Victims of the sex trade industry see little of life before they see the very worst of life … an underground of brutality and lonely fear. If the government took this seriously, and I believe they already know the cost, that would be needed to clean house on illegal prostitution. It is going to cost huge sums of money. However, no one has the political will, or desire, to right this wrong.

"Truth; what is the truth?" To answer any naysayers wanting to legalize prostitution, commercial sex, pornography in any forum, indoor sex via webcams, escort services, brothels, or any form of immorality, you must always refer to Scripture and God's breathed words. And what does God have to say about sin and its consequences? In the first book of Genesis, Chapter 18: 16, we read. Then the men, (angels sent by God) set out from there, (Abraham's home) and they looked down towards Sodom. And Abraham went with them so to set them on their way.

The Lord said, "shall I hide from Abraham what I am about to do, seeing that Abraham shall surely become a great and mighty nation, and all the nations of the earth shall be blessed in him. For I have commanded his household and his children after him to keep the way of the Lord by doing righteous and justice so that the Lord may bring to Abraham what he has promised him." Then the Lord said. "Because the outcry against Sodom and Gomorrah is great and their sin is very grave, I will go down to see whether they have done altogether according to the outcry that has come to me. And if not, I will know." You heard right! God knows. Nothing, nothing, escapes the eyes of God. He is all-knowing, always present.

So the men turned from there and went toward Sodom, but Abraham still stood before the Lord. Then Abraham drew near and said, "Will you indeed sweep away the righteous with the wicked? Suppose there are fifty righteous within the city. Will you then sweep away the place and not spare it for the fifty righteous who are in it? Far be it from you to do such a thing, to put the righteous to death with the wicked, so as the righteous fare as the wicked! Far be it from you! Shall not the judge of the entire earth do what is just?" And the Lord said. "If I find in Sodom fifty righteous in the city, I will spare the whole place for their sake."

Abraham is not content to leave fifty righteous to save Sodom and Gomorrah, so he begins to bargain with God. So Abraham said to the Lord. "I am but dust and ashes. Suppose five of the fifty righteous are lacking. Will you destroy the whole city for lack of five?" And God said he would not destroy it if he found forty-five there. Eventually, Abraham had talked the Lord into saving the two cities if the Lord found only five righteous in the city. The story concludes with the Lord unable to find five righteous souls and as a result, of the pervasive ... evil wickedness in Sodom and Gomorrah God destroyed both cities along with its inhabitants with fire because of their immorality and shameful wickedness. "Truth; what is the truth?" God and His words are trustworthy and true ... That's truth!

When thine eyes' have seen clouds of darkness overshadow the light, love retreats from my presence as I witness the abyss exhibiting its deficiencies fast approaching. What becomes unmerited, unwarranted, and undeserving are many excuses and extenuations having the passion for overcoming gaping wounds of brokenness. I had read some time back about a man whose name was Sean Dunne, who was the Director of a one-hour documentary about "Cam Girlz" who performed unnatural acts online for live viewers. (Dunne was interviewed by Rachel Giese of CBC Q, British Columbia, Canada) Mr. Dunne got the idea for the documentary while he was watching porn. It's quite apparent from his interview with Ms. Giese that he is pro-porn. And he has the mental aptitude to acquiesce his visible rational.

In his statement, Mr. Dunne is quoted as saying: "Specifically women who challenge the establishment and social norms." He goes on to say, "the most powerful way, of course, is to fight the power and to challenge social norms by reinforcing the socially acceptable patriarchal notion that women exist for male pleasure. It's the safest form of prostitution a person could possibly do, and when I hear anyone speaking out against it I'm so confused ... like, who's getting hurt here?" Dunne said in an interview with Vice.

Clearly, this man and many perverts like him need to get grounded in Scripture. Enough psychobabble has been spoken with an air of arrogance and wretched ideology. I'm going to educate you on what these pay for flesh websites with their godlessness promote. Then decide for yourselves if this engenders empowerment by prostitutes.

Since I allowed other folks their five minutes of fame to voice their opinions in this chapter, it is only fitting that I be allowed equal time in opposition to prostitution, pornography, escort services, or any form of self-degradation, humiliation, or acts of iniquity. I have drawn the line in the sand, here I stand. I can do no less. With great sorrow, to glean information about this manuscript, it was necessary for me to invest time and money to accomplish this research. All I ever wanted in this life was to live in peace and harmony with God's created order and, what seemed best to enable me to serve God in this world. If, by exposing immoral behavior I am able to lead one person to Christ, I shall count it as all gain … My efforts will not be in vain. I take no pleasure in looking at or observing women who are being carefully monitored by someone outside camera range.

How do webcam models; otherwise known as prostitutes by the author, get paid when they come online for show time. We will use www. LegofLambCams.com, as our link to this discussion. For any model to receive compensation, she must first draw perverts to her room where they can view her as a member, or guest. Unless you register with a username, password, and valid email, you will not be able to purchase tokens. Tokens acquired by the member, (pervert) is what he uses to tip the prostitute. If you insist on remaining a guest indefinitely, you will not be able to interact with the prostitute. There can be consequences the prostitute can impose on guests such as ignoring the guest as if he had the plague. Guest's cannot go private or truly private with the prostitute. And guest's are excluded from many other so-called perks. The only benefit the guest derives from remaining a guest is to sit, watch, listen, and sometimes interact with members. A guest is free to join anytime they wish. All the pervert has to do is pull out his wallet and buy tokens.

On LOLC, the pay center gives the buyer three (3) options for purchasing tokens.

- $19.99 will buy 200 tokens

- $49.99 will buy 550 tokens

- $74.99 will buy 900 tokens

Once the purchase is verified using your debit, credit, or pre-paid card, you are now in good standing with the prostitute. She is able to observe how many tokens you have remaining for tips on your screen. Whomever the prostitute, whose room the pervert visits, she will know immediately how many tokens she can take away from the pervert. Tokens are something like gambling chips; they have value when cashed in by the prostitute. The prostitute is not there to look gracious and cute for you. Generally speaking, most prostitutes begin their session with what is referred to as a "topic" with a set goal of tokens that she must receive in aggregate amounts before the next phase of her act moves forward.

Most prostitutes who set a time limit on a topic and do not reach the intended goal will sign-off LOLC network and may log online again at their discretion. But the "topic" starts from scratch again. Now the prostitute sets the topic amount. She may say to those in her room, "the topic will be set at 2700 tokens. Once the 2700 tokens are met she removes; say her shirt or brazier. 2700 tokens equate to $224.97. She also has the option of putting a time limit on the topic, which most do. Once the topic goal has been reached, she then moves on to topic number 2, raising the stakes a little higher. She may set this topic at 3500 tokens and a sixty-minute time goal to reach the 3500 tokens to remove her (expletive). 3500 tokens equate to $289.96. If she gets through this topic, she will move onto the last and final topic. She may set this topic at 4000 tokens to perform. 4000 tokens equate to $340.00, with sixty- minutes to complete the topic goal. If everything goes smoothly, and the topic goal is reached, the prostitute stands to make approximately $854.00 for say, two-three hours' work. To be divided 30% for prostitute and 70% pimp. (Entity)

After she reaches the final tier of the topic and begins to go into her performance routine, the tips often continue to flow into the prostitutes and entities account to be tallied at the end of a prescribed cut-off time.

Even then, she may not be through. She could have arranged for "true private" sessions where only the member and prostitute go private for whatever amount of time the two parties agree upon. True privates are charged per minute. This is where the prostitute makes her bread and butter money. The entity also encourages the prostitute to engage men in groups and privates for a fee. For example, a member may ask for a "private session" with the prostitute. Here the price is less than a "true Private." The downside is that other members may also choose to watch with you for a minimal fee pre-determined by the prostitute. A member or members who wanted a group showing from the prostitute need a minimum of two other members before the prostitute accepts or reject the request. The prostitute has exclusive rights to refuse any or all shows.

Other shenanigans prostitutes use to get at your money, is the promise of adding members to her friends list. The amounts range from 250 tokens to the greedy prostitute who may charge 500 tokens. For this generous contribution, they get unlimited private messages. They can text her, and she will respond in like manner. Next, they have the potential to increase their earnings by use of the cell phone camera aptly called "snap chat" into the coalesce, charging members 400-500 tokens for the lifetime privilege of receiving snapshots of the prostitute posing in various degrees of photo settings. Raffle tickets is another tool prostitutes use as a moneymaker for both prostitute and LOLC pimps. To grasp the wickedness of man, the prostitutes (expletive), are always in high demand. Perverts are willing to pay a high premium to have the (expletive) mailed to their home, (expletive) were next in demand. This, in all its repugnant behavior, takes the sinner, "From Light into the Abyss."

If prostituting yourself in front of a viewing audience were not scandalous enough, prostitutes take it to another level by creating a "wish list." The contents of the wish list can range from the mundane cheap gifts to clothing apparel, expensive electronic equipment, or personal erotic merchandise. This is the most gullible disgusting vulgar, disregard for human decency ever played out in a public forum as far as this author is concerned. The pervert is so smitten by the prostitutes role-playing to the audience, that their naïve enough to buy them products off their wish list and have them sent to the prostitute's secret P.O Box.

Another "scam" the prostitute entreats her members to, and systematically increase's the coffers of her pimps operating LOLC, is a proposed date. To entice the member's participation, the prostitute will offer to the highest tipper for the week, bi-weekly, or monthly a reward for their generosity that may include a special date with the prostitute; with restrictions of course. Prostitutes also offer time with her by raffling tickets as well. I have seen perverts tipping a prostitute 55,000 tokens in one lump sum to a her. To put 55,000 tokens into perspective, this would amount to approximately $4,400.00. There are hundreds of perverts just like this who think nothing of tipping 10, 20, 30,000 tokens in one visit. Who has this kind of money? "Pimps, doctors, lawyers, politicians…. You tell me because I sure don't know!"

Look to Proverbs Chapter 12: 15, where it says. "The way of a fool is right in his own eyes', but the wise man listens to wisdom."

There are perverts on, "LegofLambCams" that tip anonymously. They do not want anyone to know their names, so they address these types of tippers as behind the scenes "Ninjas." One Ninja has come under scrutiny in the authors view. This particular Ninja I single out appears to have very deep pockets as he meanders indiscriminately from one room to the next distributing gratuities very generously to every room he visits.

Without fail, he seems to be around every evening repeating the process over, and over again. Wherever his wealth is coming from, I find it difficult to believe his pockets are as deep as a bottomless pit. I know one thing for sure; it isn't coming from honest employment. Prostitutes who are on the receiving end of Ninjas generosity just worship the ground he walks on.

Some websites on the internet advertise free tokens for these sites. However, you're required to fill out an extensive survey and commit to certain products as a prerequisite for the free tokens. But I question the legitimacy of these sites promoting products in return for unlimited tokens. My hunch is this Ninja is peddling drugs or he is a pimp. But this is an opinion only and since I don't have the proof. However, spending trends can reveal plenty when profiling behavior. Another plausible scenario may have more merit than the other examples.

How much is a piece of property worth to you? What are you willing to spend for a product? Anyone who has ever attended an auction has knowledge on how the bidding proceeds. A piece of property is brought out to be seen and then bid on by the participants. The Auctioneer begins at a set price. His speech starts out slow and gradually rises in tone and pitch. It is intentional; deliberate. He works the crowd getting them to increase their bid on the piece of property up for bid. Before anyone realizes what is taking place the auctioneer has used emotion of the moment to get the prospective bids to rise, increasing the value of the property. You have now bid more than what the value of the item was worth, but you leave victorious, because you outbid everyone to own this piece of property that you felt was worth the price.

What has this to do with LegofLambCams? Now, that's a good question. Since LOLC operates from a position of secrecy the author doesn't think it is a foregone conclusion to have LOLC tip the balance and affect the outcome in a prostitute's room when generating tokens into her topic. Using the auctioneer as the catalyst, what if you have pimps in the entity who selectively visit popular prostitute's room contributing tokens in large amounts to incite unknown members to start tipping. Before long you have a frenzied group of members tipping, starting a domino effect that contributes to the prostitute's topic goal. After all, when you begin to see trends, at least in my view, I begin to question how members can sustain a marginal lifestyle when they are tipping 1100 tokens every few minutes for a few hours every night a prostitute is online. And to repeat this behavior each time she is online makes one wonder. This pervert has to be contributing over $4,000.00 every time.

Just thought you would like to chew on this for a while. Some things, like Carrie, when adding two-plus-two it doesn't add up to four.

LegofLambCams.com boasts itself as the number one, largest online webcam network connecting men and women from ALL over the world through high-speed live video chat. Here is what they claim makes them different:

- Commitment to their models. (Prostitutes) They collaborate with their models as partners, and their models earn a larger percentage than other sites. (Not)

- Their (pimps) commitment to the members. (perverts) Doing their best to make sure members are satisfied. From technical issues to developing new features on the site. Committed to listening to members, and making them happy. (Not)

- Commitment to technology. They claim to be computer geeks. (pimps) They build a website that is the most technically advanced on the internet that allows much more personal interactive experience. (Questionable)

- Commitment to FREE. They claim they offer more free features to the guests and members than any other webcam site on the internet. Spending money on tokens is always optional. (Questionable)

"Truth, what is the truth?" I hasten towards an hour when the truth will be unveiled in the four policies mentioned above. Each representation is very wrong, or at best deceptive. It is true, guests (perverts) are allowed to visit any prostitutes room. However, guests cannot chat with the prostitute. Even when they are able to type in a remark or comment, the words appear tiny. The prostitute seldom if ever acknowledges the guest verbally, but ignores the guests like the plague. Guests are not able to purchase tokens unless they become premium members

When prostitutes begin a topic, her room may have 50-70 viewers at any given moment and who may contribute towards her goal. After all her topics have been met, her room could easily mushroom to 300-1500 members and guests. How word spreads at warp-speed to other guest and members on this website, is a mystery. Regardless, this whole business is tricky; but the legislative body in Washington needs to make it disappear.

As if what is mentioned above isn't wretched enough, the envelope is pushed further when LegofLambCams.com features (expletive) in some of the rooms and you witness a population explosion by perverts, as they flock to the prostitute's place in droves, reaching in numbers exceeding 2300 perverts. You have the abomination of Sodom and Gomorrah all over again. At any given time, you may observe between 1100-1300 prostitutes online representing not only American but foreign prostitutes as well. LOLC claims that after expenses, nearly (this is a catch phrase; "nearly") all of the money spent on their website goes to the prostitute. (Not even close) LOLC asserts their competitors pay their prostitutes as little as 20% of their revenue, and spend the rest on advertising campaigns.

One other thing about truly private that requires a little shoe polish. When a pervert requests a "true private show," the price for an individual show will cost the pervert approximately 80-tokens per minute. Perverts have been known to spend an hour plus, in truly private with the prostitute where it involves only the two parties. Simple math: 60 minutes, X 80 tokens per minute equals $480.00. LOLC again asserts the higher rate helps offset the money lost by the prostitute since no one else can pay to spy on the show. Ninja has done this on numerous occasions and still makes his rounds tipping other prostitutes.

Here are the hypocritical bywords LOLC prints for users on their site. Warning: Please DO NOT post any inappropriate pornographic, violent, offensive, or disruptive images. Please do not post pictures over, and over. Do not post images that are irrelevant, or disrupt the flow of the chat or annoy members of the chat. We have added this feature so everyone can have more FUN and EXPRESS himself or herself. Please do not make us suspend your account due to abuse.

Now if that isn't a mouthful of cotton that lends itself to duplicity I need a better command of the English language. I have heard some of the most profane language coming from the mouths of both parties that I could write my own dictionary. Yet, it is the insensitivity of the men (perverts) that troubled me most. My ears would seek peace for all disquietude. To humiliate, degrade, and utter all caricatures of filth drooling from the tongue of perverts that causes' me to be ashamed and identified with the same gender as these perverts. Images perverts posted on the chat screen didn't bode well either. Bottom line; evil has encompassed prostitute, pimp, and pervert alike. Whereby they have gone from light into the abyss. They have "exchanged the truth for a lie. "Truth, what is the truth?" I know that these folks do not seek the truth.

Have these prostitutes lied? Of course they have, every prostitute who is on LOLC has lied. As has all women working on the thousands of webcam sites on the internet. And it is not limited to single prostitutes, but expands the horizon to include boyfriends allowing their partner to engage in this debauchery. It is husbands with their wives, boyfriend-girlfriend, Lesbianism, homosexuality, and self-abasement. It runs the gambit of all manner of wickedness on the internet.

It is expanding to the point where society doesn't feel there is no right or wrong anymore. An estimated 90% of prostitutes have tattoos located somewhere on their bodies. It makes me wonder if I'm seeing the mark of the beast. Also, we have prostitutes drinking all varieties of alcohol and smoking some form of mind altering chemical, whether its hashish, marijuana, or some other form of the Cannabis family. Alcohol consumption by the prostitute is another tool employed to separate the pervert from his tokens. If a prostitute is caught sleeping while she is online, she is banned from LOLC indefinitely.

This is big brother watching over the shoulder of his property. Cam scores will be the last feature discussed concerning web-camming, except when we return to Carnal Carrie. LegofLambCams.com rates Cam Score grades on prostitutes. Cam Score is calculated based on the performance of each prostitute on the site over an extended period. (Month) The pimps update it several times a day. All prostitutes start with a Cam Score rating of 1000, which is the average Cam Score for all models on the site. Prostitutes can improve their Cam Score by earning more TOKENS. "That's right, you heard me correctly ... TOKENS.

It is money, money, and, more money flowing into the coffers of the pimp. First, LOLC's formula and calculations are skewed. I cite this for a variety of reasons. Not all prostitutes are favorable on this site. Your typical pervert tends to be drawn to the more attractive prostitute, the more likely are perverts as a rule who will gravitate to rooms where the prostitute's performance is raw and soiled. Perverts have their favorites (prostitutes) where performance rewards come in the form of token gratuities.

What LOLC, has done by instituting Cam Score competition amongst its prostitute's amounts to creating a cutthroat rivalry where the prostitute is often pleading, if not begging for perverts in her room to tip her tokens. The rationale behind her scheme it is assumed because the prostitute wants her Cam Score to be high enough at the end of the month so that she will be among the top 100 of the 3000-4000 prostitutes employed by LOLC to receive recompense from the pimps. Going into the end of the month you will see a flurry of activity for prostitutes to win you over and get you to part with your tokens (Money).

The stakes could not be higher because these prostitutes not only follow their Cam Score, but they also keep track of their competitor's scores. If the prostitute is in the top five, and closing in on the number one position, she will likely approach members in her room to pony-up more tokens in exchange for whatever she decides to bestow upon her loyal following. Placing first, will award her the crown for the month along with a $1000.00 bonus check from the pimps at LOLC. I believe finishing below number five pays the other ninety-five prostitutes $100 dollars. Two through five receive more than $100 dollars but certainly not $1000. Furthermore, 1st place prostitutes receive additional benefits.

There is no fountain of delight in researching webcamming as some might repose. There was self-examination of myself applying my heart to vigilance and the folly of man. The discoveries were uncharted waters, entering into repose, I concluded there were no ill principals or motives shown on my behalf while researching the declining immorality this nation and the world is harvesting for itself.

Chapter 20

Irrational Behavior

Flint ignites sparks; sparks create fires, and fires under fire end in destruction.
A man goes about the people's business; insists on
justice, yet engages in carnal seduction.
Disrupted under wings of controversy, Gloomy
diversions trickle within torrent streams.
Condemnations laden with burrs; humankind filled
to the full, misguided empty dreams.
Jim Jacobs

As I embarked on this raging river of internet fraud, I never envisioned how prevalent, and extreme the tentacles of evil reached. Unaware of the impact this irreprehensible act of imputed wickedness has evolved boggles the mind. What affects me, even more, is the troubling if not disturbing awareness that it touches every socio-economic class in America, and around the world. It has become an epidemic with wings creating an unchastised blemish on American civil liberties. Limiting the book entirely within the scope of fraudulent activity would not do this book justice.

Satan loves darkness and deception. The light of the world is methodically being snuffed out by a Republic out of control; answerable only to self. We have pornography on premium channels, notwithstanding pay-per-view pornography. Television programs use vulgar language and suggestive out-of-control scenes comprising a monopoly on the airwaves. The movie industry promoting too many gruesome and violent movies; webcam pornography on the internet used for monetary gain for pimps and prostitutes alike … A list that goes on.

"Who among us, does not think we are going to face the wrath of God soon?"

Growing pains for the disenchanted, displaced, the disenfranchised moral fiber of our society has long since been a bridge of discontentment for countless years with this author, and now it is time to redress the demons within us all. Yes, prostitution has been around since God created man. We may accept this behavior as the social norm, but God has never given His approval of this immoral behavior since creation.

On the contrary, God views this SIN as detestable; a stench in His nostrils. Should we rebuke women who engage in prostitution? Do we apply the one shoe fits all mindset? May it never be! "How or what steps need to be taken for women under the tyranny of pimps to taste freedom?" What about human slave trafficking, and the flourishing escort service, "flesh for profit," while it becomes mere statistical data in some governmental agency report. Moreover, we are not going to sugar coat beaten, battered, and abused women in abusive relationships. What the author calls, "The Closed Door Silent Crime." Are we, as a nation, going to continue down this wayward path frequently traveled … Leading to mayhem?

To have a vision requires commitment, money, and resources. Our government is fully aware of these wicked problems. Perhaps they even did a cost analysis and determined it would not be in their best interest to squander THEIR money on social reform. After all, to commit to a vision would require clinics, doctors, food, lodging, trained psychiatrist and psychologist, nurses, medications, job retraining facilities, dentists, clothing, and any other needs associated with getting the walking wounded healthy again.

So what is the answer for you and for me? For those who have ears to hear let them hear "You are either part of the solution or part of the problem." Who among us will acknowledge these egregious atrocities, and become pro-active; advocating change for in-house slavery? Why do I not hear the call to arms for a million-plus man march on the

Washington Monument over these atrocities? If Louis Farrakhan can do it, what is stopping people from representing the voice of the voiceless?

I used the beginning pages of this Chapter as a staircase if you please because fraud is not the only crime affecting America. It is immorality in a packaged deal. It covers every minutia of dysfunctional behavior known to man including but not limited to administrators to the complaint process I undertook using the tools of letters, forms, and contacts involving organizations fraudulent scamming activities.

Since the complaint process was conducted on or around November 2013; there has not been one law enforcement official who has made a concerted effort to contact the author or show interest. No phone contact, no one-on-one, … Nothing, except an email or letter. And those proved to be of little or no value. To suggest that I'm livid and disappointed by the lack of interest in these matters would be an understatement. This then is our tax dollars at work in a bloated Federal Bureaucracy.

The first complaint submitted referenced Henan Asante, also known as Carnal Carrie. A complaint was lodged against Henan Asante on June 12, 2013, to "IC3," (internet crime complaint center). When the five-page complaint referral made its way over the internet, it was consistent with the information I had available to me and wasn't meant to mislead or compromise the legitimacy of the report. I did not have the computer knowledge or skills necessary for an accurate well-documented summary in the first report. As such, I accept full responsibility for being too hasty in my initial decision to submit information I thought to be accurate. Whatever its outcome, I continued to forge ahead with my intelligence gathering report.

The complaint form warns the complainant when filing the form that the information provided by the victim is shared with appropriate law enforcement agencies. As with any government bureaucracy the individual is required to fill out certain personal information: (Name, age, gender, address, etc.). Once all the formalities of your personal information are completed, the victim then provides information about the individual/business victimized. For Henan Asante, I listed her address as Santasi House, Block 10, Plot 17, in the city of Adum Kumasi, from the country of Ghana. Henan used a P. O. Box14781 for money orders sent to her by her victim. Internet Crime asked for phone numbers and email addresses' the swindlers used. Additionally, they wanted Henan's website, IP address, IRC server, chat room name, internet newsgroup, and any other miscellaneous information.

I provided IC3 the information I had gathered on Henan. When looking back now perhaps it would have been prudent to withhold what information I had on Henan until I had additional concrete and verifiable evidence. Internet Crime Complaint Center (IC3) wanted specifics in describing the incident by providing the dates of the transactions. Furthermore, a description of any item's that were not delivered or were counterfeited, any transaction numbers (EBay, Western Union, PayPal, etc.). Also, any other pertinent information that would assist them in identifying how I was victimized. Moreover, IC3 wanted to know if I had received anything by U. S. Mail, FedEx, or UPS. Did I send cash, money orders, or use any debit/credit cards in any of the transactions?

Finally, internet crime complaint center asked for the dollar amount of monetary losses from the incident in U.S. currency. Although I felt the report contained substantial information, my primary objective was just as important. There was a sense of urgency to curtail this criminal operation and hold them accountable. Also, there were other agencies, departments, and a member of the Senate, who I contacted concerning this swindler and their fraudulent activity. It appears that when the report was sent over the internet to IC3 some material was encrypted, so if label numbers don't look quite right, or words and sentences seem confusing; I believe it is due to the encryption.

Before I address other reports, I have chosen to elaborate a little bit on how, (IC3), internet crime complaint center functions. On May 14, 2013, they released a summary report of fraudulent activity, including data and statistics. The IC3 receives and processes 289,000 complaints annually, averaging more than 24,000 complaints per month. Unverified losses reported to IC3 rose 8.3 percent over the previous year. A new section of this year's report includes charts for each of the 50 states, detailing demographics, complaints, and dollar loss data.

Additional content includes frequently reported Internet crimes, case highlights, and graphs that explain the lifecycle of a complaint. The most common complaints in 2012 included FBI impersonation email scams, various intimidation crimes, and scams that used computer "scareware" to extort money from internet users. The report gives detailed information on these and other commonly perpetrated "scams" in 2012. The IC3 works to educate the public and law enforcement about fraud trends.

IC3 is in partnership with the Federal Bureau of Investigation (FBI), the National White Collar Crime Center (NW3C), and the Bureau of Justice Assistance (BJA). Since its start in 2000, IC3 has become the mainstay for victims reporting Internet crime, and a way for law enforcement to be notified of such offenses. IC3's service to law enforcement communities includes; Federal, State, Tribal, Local, and International agencies that are combating Internet crime. Internet Crime Complaint Center receives, develops, and refers criminal complaints of cyber crime. IC3 gives victims a convenient and easy-to-use reporting mechanism that alerts authorities of suspected criminal or civil violations. For law enforcement and regulatory agencies at the local, state, federal, and international levels, IC3 provides a central referral mechanism for complaints involving online crime. This sounds so crisp and clean, but here we are, two-years in since my first report and nothing. This is very disconcerting to any victim when reaching out to agencies who have been put in place to combat crime, but can't because of budget constraints.

As previously mentioned, the first report to the Internet Crime Center, (IC3) was drafted on June 12, 2013; approximately six weeks after Henan made her first request for help. By the way, June 12 is the elapsed time before realizing I had been deceived through malicious intent to defraud. On April 22, 2013, I sent via express mail a Toshiba computer, model number 775, using customs label, E1238989085US, and customs form, CW577227120US. Shipment costs came to $95.25. On April 25, 2013; I used USPS label number, 4205690191589010 077054009017561, and customs label, E1876651291US along with customs form, CW354540449US. Out-of-pocket expenses' to ship these packages' came to $100.60. In addition to the computer, speakers, Sony Camcorder, tape recorder, and miscellaneous items were sent.

On May 3, 2013, Henan informed me she needed extra money to pay additional customs fee charges where the packages had been sent in the Southern city of Accra. A Western Union money order, number MTCN-094-379-1588 for $275.00 to defray these bogus expenses were wired to Henan so she could claim the cash. A password, (pepper) was wire transferred to Henan.

Western Union sent the money order to P.O. Box 14781, Adum Kumasi, Ghana. Henan had to provide a phone number for the money order to go through, (+2332267820517). There was yet another Western Union money order, MTCN-401-518-8141 using password, (blue) same city, and phone number for this transaction. Henan told me her property owner had insisted on payment for past due rent. Henan informed victim the proprietor had demanded the full $7,000.00 past due amount, or he was taking her to court. I told Henan the best I could do to assist her would be $600.00. That was sent using the Western Union. The computer and other hardware that preceded the money, I freely admitted having been deceived by Henan. The $600 was my way of keeping Henan engaged because I was going to pursue this on my own since there weren't any indications other agencies in the government were pursuing my complaint. I have no regrets giving her the money because it resulted in what came known as: "I Gotcha," rebel yell.

Some aliases' Henan Asante is known to use are, Carnal Carrie, Henan Asante, Fadu Anlouni, carnalcarriexxx.com60, halo spirit, and a myriad of other known aliases Henan used on other unsuspecting victims. Initial contact with Henan was via Skype beginning around April 2013. Henan said she had arrived in Ghana from the United Kingdom to attend nursing school several years ago. She told me she was looking for online friendship, and that was the impression she left me with for the first two weeks into our friendship on Yahoo Messenger. After two weeks of open dialogue, Henan complained about her old antiquated computer freezing. Henan emphasized there was no money available for her to purchase another computer. Henan claimed her mother resided in the Netherlands, and was recovering from back surgery and could no longer fully support Henan's schooling. Later, after much-conjectured prodding, Henan informed me she did part-time modeling on the side, but it was not sufficient to absorb all of her expenditures.

It was at this, Henan posed a need. "Would it be possible to get her a computer?" Giving thought to Henan's request, I responded after hours of soul-searching. Even though I felt uneasy about the request, I relented, and gave Henan the benefit of the doubt; trusting soul that I am. My core values and character that Henan's situation was nothing less than factual I moved forward and sent the merchandise.

Hindsight, as we know, does not mean you are entrusted with doing something stupid. Days and weeks followed. I still felt in my heart that something was not quite right, even after I fool-heartedly sent Henan money orders. Therefore, I began to do research on the internet based on the information I was gleaning from Henan. "a slip of the tongue here, a slip of the tongue there!"

NOTE: I had told Henan during one of our chat sessions that I had hired a private investigator in Ghana. I told the investigator to be inconspicuous and keep track of any suspicious movements Henan made. That is if she was indeed living in Ghana. He was then instructed to report to me. However, this had no effect on her. It then suggested to me that Henan was not in Ghana. Although I did contact a PI firm in Dallas to inquire about fees and services should I decide to proceed with their firm to assist me in tracking Henan's whereabouts.

Henan was a consummate liar. Even coaxing half-truths from her was work. When Henan told me about her modeling work, I assumed it to be within the scope of innocence and good taste. However, additional intelligence, and headstrong manipulative perseverance I would eventually get Henan to confess that her modeling was in reality, pornography and webcamming on her copyrighted network, www.carnalcarriexxx.com. She was under contract or registered by GoDaddy.com. The contract was due to expire September 2013. She recorded her site using (URL) Uniformed Resource Locator http://registrar.godaddy.com. Henan informed me that after the contract had expired, she wanted to come to the United States to live with me.

Through time, I was able to cajole additional intelligence about the identity of Henan that I believed to be genuine and accurate. Sometimes we allow ourselves to be blindsided by the mystery of events, as such we lose all sense of direction, accepting another person's word as

"Gospel," when all the while we are spoon fed "Fools Gold." Henan/ Carrie came forth with new revelations that she was co-partners with others who accompanied her from the U. K. She began the business in "soft porn" at the age of eighteen she informed me during one of our chat discussions. Allen Simple was CEO, or head manager and was controlling Carrie and her activities, including the use of the computer. Allen Simple might be a fit somewhere in the organization, but not as CEO as we have learned in previous chapters. Thus, there is some half-truth to what Carrie tells me.

"These are very evil people, and I must do what they say, or I get myself into trouble," Carrie alleges. "They give me $250.00 for on-site live videos that have me doing pornography, and $100.00 for my website camming," Carrie said.

On the complaint form, I let the Internet Crime Center know I wasn't sure about their involvement in any child pornography. However, Carrie claimed at times to be 14-years-old on some of her sites, and some girls on her site appeared to be underage, but it could not be verified. Carrie also passed herself off as a 13-year-old in some of her photographs even though she was 32-years of age.

Seldom were their live video feeds when we talked. When we did do live video, the visual effects were reduced, and audio was worse yet. However, when you googled, www.carnalcarriexxx.com, Carrie's website, the visual came in with clarity and the audio feed was crisp. When I addressed concerns about her having a male companion around, she would say it was just a friend going by the name of Bernie. Only later was I able to learn "Bernie" was actually Carrie's short haired terrier dog. How Carrie knew of "The Tulip Hotel" located in Kumasi remains another mystery.

Carrie confessed that her friend who was allegedly getting married sent a wedding invitation to Carrie to attend her wedding at the Tulip Hotel where the ceremony was to take place. The other scenario I gave any creditability to was the possibility of them having connections in Ghana who they use as "mule's" Carrie could have visited Ghana, but I have no proof and no access to her passport, which would probably reveal plenty about her travels.

Henan said she had a friend over in Ghana, who went by the name of Sally, who worked nearby in a salon. Carrie admitted they have (expletive). Again, further intelligence revealed Sally was a sibling of Carrie. Whether they (expletive) should be left unsaid. Carrie said she enjoys the lake or beach that is nearby her home (Is it ever). While Carrie claimed to be in Ghana, she said she was without a vehicle and had to rely on public transportation or her partners. Carrie currently has blonde hair but has been known to dye her hair black. Again, research suggests Carrie was born with black hair and is a descendant of Poland. What is distinguishable about Carrie is the diamond cross necklace and I believe a rather large diamond necklace with the word "ANGEL." She wears both frequently as well as some rather large circular earrings attached to her lobes. She has a scar in the middle of her forehead … slight but still noticeable.

Each time I saw Carrie, she appeared appropriately dressed. She is photogenic and has an air of confidence when performing in front of the camera. Carrie's demeanor can have an outward impression of innocence. However, she can reveal an explosive temperament as well. Most notable is the childlike conduct she skillfully role-plays to cover her real character and personality.

The report concluded by apprising IC3, that when Henan initially introduced herself to me, she claimed to be a nursing student. However, within six weeks, reality set in leading me to believe that she was not attending nursing school at all. Henan/Carrie was not in need of assistance, nor was she burdened with financial hardships. Henan wasn't kept prisoner against her wishes. I informed internet criminal complaint center that I was more concerned with the victimization of others from this group of criminals than I was about myself.

I added. "This is a consortium of organized criminals that needed to be reined in before more hearts were broken, and their finances and assets whisked from them by these "scam" artists. Boldly professing my ignorance, IC3 needed to know that I fell into this web of deceit from the onset.

As I put the final period on this report IC3 was told. "I pray that the perpetrators would call upon the Lord for Salvation and forgiveness over their sinful behavior. The next Chapter will consist of email communications between Henan and me as I attempt to disciple her and Nate.

After I had written my complaint, the Internet Crime Center then asked for other pertinent information about the incident that required brief answers to more questions they had, and then the document was digitally signed and sent on its way.

On or about June 25, 2013, IC3 replied with an e-mail assigning a complaint identification number and password to my initial report in the event additional details surfaced. With this ID number, I could forward any additional information that might be helpful in the investigation. They provided a link to download and view my original complaint. In their reply, IC3 told me their mission is to serve as a vehicle to receive, develop, and refer criminal complaints regarding the rapidly expanding arena of cyber crime. IC3 aims to give the victims of cyber crime a convenient and easy-to-use reporting mechanism.

Immediately before or after this report, I contacted the Federal Trade Commission in Washington, D.C. by telephone, and gave them a verbal account of my grievance's similar to the Internet Crime Center relating to cybercrime. It wasn't as detailed as IC3's report, but the critical and essential information within the scope of rendering names, dates, and places were released to FTC in the event they decided to take the necessary steps to investigate this incident as well. As of this writing, I have not, and may never know the outcome on what if any action was taken, because nothing out of their agency has ever reached my eyes'.

On or about July 25, 2013, I reached out to (ICS) investigations, clients, and services founded in 1967. They provide private investigative services worldwide. Their policy is to secure their future through the development of long-term professional relationships based on a philosophy of earned trust and mutual respect. When I called their eight-hundred numbers, the call was immediately redirected to their Texas office. Once connected to a private investigator, I explained the dilemma I had found myself in; asked for suggestions, comments, or professional help. Mr. Murdock Hewitt was an excellent listener, patient, and professional. After giving him the facts, he indicated they would be willing to get involved; however, it would cost one-hundred dollars an hour to do the casework. I spent a good half-hour on the phone with Mr. Hewitt, who was very accommodating and very helpful in answering all my questions. Nevertheless, I let him know immediately, I didn't have the funds or resources to have them take the case.

We ended the conversation. However, Mr. Hewitt offered to keep the lines of communication open. Mr. Hewitt emailed a confirmation of our discussion in regards to my recent inquiry into their investigative services. Mr. Hewitt wanted to schedule a time for one of their investigators to call for a consultation. The day I received the email; as it turned out, would be the same afternoon they could have someone available to discuss the case. They looked forward to hearing from me and would follow-up with another phone call if the email was not received. This precaution was taken because it had become evident these alleged brood-of-vipers were intercepting my communications and hacking into my computer stealing files, and infecting it with viruses,' rendering the computer unserviceable for a couple days.

ABC News was next on my "hit list" of contacts, as I emailed them on or about July 25, 2013. The same scenario applied to ABC News. I wanted to know if they would have an interest in doing a piece on cyber-crime. Their reply came back to me seven hours later. (They didn't waste time on this email)

Their correspondence was brief and to the point. "As you can imagine, we receive thousands of messages a day from our viewers and while we appreciate you taking the time to provide feedback regarding our programming; we are not able to respond to each one directly. We encourage you to continue communicating with us! ABC News sent a set of guidelines with instructions on where to send questions and comments including what links I should sign into if I elected to pursue suspected fraudulent activity.

I soon found myself waffling. Now it became a matter of prioritizing. The manuscript had to take precedence over peace-meal information to a news organization; at least for a while.

Before August 12, 2013, I had been in contact with the Braxton police department by telephone on several occasions to alert them about some trouble I was experiencing with my landline and computer. First, it would involve interruption of the phone or the modem. When it wasn't the telephone, then the computer became the target of intrusive viruses'. I had mentioned earlier in one of the chapters that I was continually making trips to have the computer repaired by the Geek Squad at Bargains. These work orders accumulated quickly. One such work order kept my laptop in service for over a week.

"Suspect received a random virus; "avas" on the machine. Says it is a pop. D & R under gsts, remove all "avas" on the computer. Install Webroot, a security program that would remove any viruses.' This was not the same Toshiba laptop sent to Henan. It was taken into Bargains on 08/01/13. Because these incidents were becoming a nuisance, I wanted to make this a matter of public record so I would contact the Braxton police department hoping they would initiate some type of written report.

Finally, after several calls to the police department in Braxton, a female officer came to the apartment one evening after receiving a call from me. I registered a complaint about the telephone landline going dead. I suspected it was this criminal entity I was researching that hacked into the modem, phone line, or computer, disrupting services. The games they were playing with me began to wear me down. The female officer did not offer much to assist me. She certainly didn't take any notes while she was there. All the office had to offer was a call to my carrier, AB&C technical support. She had wasted my time and hers. Now I am beginning to question my sanity.

"Doesn't anybody care?" I wondered. "Is anyone taking me seriously," as my mind was wild with panic? "Who, if anybody out there, is going to help?" I wanted to know. "Psst."

By August 12, 2013, I had had enough. After being deprived of sleep for a couple of days, I decided it was time to make my physical presence known to the Braxton police station. Late on Monday afternoon, taking along three thick binders of information on this criminal organization fraudulent activity, I drove the five miles into the downtown district of Braxton. Arriving at 3:36 P.M., I parked alongside the metered parking area of the police station. Putting approximately thirty minutes' worth of coins into the parking meter, I walked the ½-block down the street; turned the corner, and entered the front entrance of the station expecting to do the people's business.

Approaching the thick glass protective area of the central offices, I asked the receptionist if I could talk to a detective about internet cybercrime. After trying a few extension numbers on her phone without much success, I was told to wait while she went into the back section of offices to see if there was an officer around that could provide some assistance. A short wait later, she reappears and informs me there is a shift change. I was instructed to take a seat in the waiting area, and when the new shift arrived, she would have one of them assigned to discuss my complaint.

At 4:13 P.M., thirty-seven minutes later, an officer approached from inside the contained offices and asked what was on my mind. Before we even touched on the reason for my visit, I told him I needed to go check on my vehicle around the corner. I informed the officer the parking meter time may have elapsed. Without hesitation, he told me that after 4:00 P.M., no parking was permitted. He said if I kept my vehicle there it would be towed away. The officer suggested I park it in a different location, and he showed me where to park. Turning the corner, just as sure as there are night and day, the vehicle was gone.

Like a vulture seeking its prey, so it was with the Braxton Parking Enforcement unit. In less than thirteen minutes, they had their prey in view, and a parking citation issued, the vehicle towed away. It seemed every time I went into the hub of the city I have been given more parking violations … and they are not cheap! Entering back into the police building, I apprised the officer of what had happened. He shrugged his shoulders and said. "We'll deal with that later," he said.

All the people's business was conducted out in the hall. We never went into a private office; standing instead as I explained my case to him. Like his female predecessor, he too never took notes. Didn't appear to have any interest in what material evidence was inside the binders. He offered his sympathy with the research project, "BUT" … There's that

BUT again! Time, workforce, and financial constraints limited their effectiveness to get involved in cyber-crime.

This did not sit well at all with me. With the conviction of dueling emotions, grief, and chagrined defeat, I was beside myself. Lack of sleep and the officer's indifference in offering assistance to my expressed concerns and pleas for help; produced floodgates of tears and emotions overwhelming this stoic facade I had once shown …I would characterize the officer's mannerism as detached and aloof. We could not come to a gentlemen's agreement on what constituted priority. After internally rationalizing further cooperation from him, I asked the officer to locate my vehicle, and I would be on my way.

It was time to seek other avenues to voice my concerns. Adding insult to injury, the court let stand the parking citation, saying it was irrelevant whether I was doing the people's business. There were clear and legible signs next to the parking meter showing times when a vehicle was authorized to park in the area. The court consented to disregard the towing fee charge; however, the parking citation stood, and a forty-five-dollar fine levied. All efforts to reach out for help seemed in vain. I would have to go it alone. I resigned myself that this crusade was going to be done apart from others willingness to reach out and dirty their hands. I was on my own.

A report written by the officer I visited on August 12, 2013, confirmed my suspicions. The language in the body of the report may as well have said Mr. Jacobs is imagining these events. It is questionable at best … A fabrication.

"Thank you very much for your help officer!"

On August 14, 2013, I submitted a written report to the U.S. Postal Inspection Service, with a Mail Fraud Report. This required downloading their Postal Service form 8165, a two-page form. This mail fraud complaint asked that the victim describes the area of concern. In this case, it was "scamming" with deceitful intent. I went about stating that I have been following Henan, aka., www.carnalcarriexxx.com, along with hundreds of other aliases' she had been using for the past ten-years. I have chronicled four months' worth of information on Henan and her cohorts in crime to this point. Since obtaining discoveries on this entity, they have been consumed with preventing me from gathering additional intelligence about their location and operation. My computer had experienced viruses' on two separate occasions where services had been disrupted. However, this wasn't going to deter me in my unrelenting crusade to have their operation dissolved and the guilty parties brought before the criminal justice system for prosecution.

The postal service wanted to know how the perpetrators contacted me. They wanted almost the identical information IC3 asked for on their form. They wanted websites used if any, as a kind of contact, telephone numbers, email addresses, and (IP's), internet protocol. Postal service asked for any other miscellaneous information I could provide; the Western Union would be helpful. The postal service also needed the dollar amount of loss, and personal effects sent. This was essential information but deemed necessary if I was to receive any hopes of retribution. To acknowledge the dollar amount lost, you would think I was utterly incompetent. (Yes, I'm still beating myself up over this)

Next in line was the New York Times. I drafted an email to them on October 2, 2013, giving a brief teaser about an ordeal I encountered with a group of "scam" artist. This was more an inquiry than a request as I began by saying. "I'm curious to know why no one in the news media or law enforcement agencies were taking cybercrime on the internet seriously … that is, to the next level?" I have spent the past seven months following and researching one such criminal element operating out of the Ukraine (Later revised to New Jersey), scamming innocent victims out of their money. This criminal enterprise uses their website as a forum for the big catch… "Swindling." This site features Carnal Carrie as a porn model and her partners in Crime, Nathaniel Raja, a Romanian by origin, and other alleged perpetrator's in the United States who employ sophisticated and elaborate schemes to deceive, lie, and steal from hundreds if not thousands of U.S. citizens every year. Not only does it involve swindling, but internet web-camming on a scale unprecedented in the history of the United States and the world.

"What is with these People? Do we extend liberties with a license to steal from American citizens without the full force of the justice system bringing the guilty to answer for their crimes?" Workforce shortage you say! Unavailability of resources; is this your defense? I take exception to your free approach. "Hire! Employ Shock and Awe." If you can afford to go to war in foreign countries and sacrifice our men and women, you can allocate monies that encumber our economy and free us from obstruction, the guile and corrupt transparency permeating our homeland.

I have amassed over eleven volumes of informational material over the months in hopes that some law enforcement agency would be in pursuit of these malcontents. They apparently think they are immune from the long arm of our legal system. After all, it is alleged they have been involved in this brutal crime spree for nearly ten- years and counting. "When is someone going to take me seriously?" I too am a statistic of their fraudulent activity. "Yes, I, Jim Jacobs!"

The next day, October 3, 2013, the NY Times sent an email reply. Thank you for taking the time to write the New York Times. We do understand your frustration and we will gladly assist you with that. We value your readership and welcome any feedback that we can use to enhance our customer experience, products, or service features. If there is anything else; we would be happy to help you. Please email us at http@nytimes.com or call us at the NY times. Ms. Jerica James was the online customer service representative who responded to my request. I felt, they had accomplished more for my morale than all the other agencies combined. It was a positive step in the right direction. I just needed the time to commit to the information they wanted. Time was a luxury I could ill-afford to sacrifice at the moment. Completing the manuscript was my primary focus and priority.

I waited two months for a response back from the postal inspector, but apparently, nothing was forthcoming. Using Yahoo email, correspondence was transmitted to the U.S. Postal Inspector on or about October 29, 2013. The big question remained.

"Can anyone provide me with an update on the fraud complaint which I submitted to the U.S. Postal Inspection Service on August 14, 2013? Has anything been accomplished? Does your department require information that is more detailed?"

I am becoming very suspicious and concerned that there isn't anyone in the government or elsewhere whom I have contacted that has had the decency to acknowledge my correspondence to your department. There are strong feelings of detached parties interested in pursuing my complaints. Attempts to raise awareness and action with various agencies are but futile and vain.

I for one, have taken fraud as a personal crusade to stop this criminal entity from doing further harm. There have been countless victims affected by this unforgiven travesty of fraud by this and other criminal organizations. I cannot count with accuracy the number of times my computer has been hacked by these spiteful con artists. They disrupt and prevent this author from gathering additional history on their activities and their person. I'm now eight months into the research, amassing eight binders full of information. I feel I have been abandoned in a vacuum where no one is listening to my pleas. I asked the Postal Service to confirm receipt of the email, but of course, if you ignore anything long enough, you hope it will go away.

"Poof!" It was this authors expressed desire to inform and involve as many independent agencies, organizations, and persons who were results oriented … or so I thought. The next candidate on the roster was the Honorable Senator Tammy Baldwin. On November 13, 2013, I sat down and drafted a letter to her staff office in Braxton. I had prepared an initial letter to Senator Baldwin on or about mid-October 2013, requesting assistance. I asked Senator Baldwin if she would use her position as an elected official, to contact the FBI, FTC, and USPS. I wanted her to have these agencies contact me with any updated information they may have accumulated during their investigation. If any material existed on this fraudulent entities status since I had submitted these written reports. However, before Senator Baldwin could begin the process, I was required to fill out a Privacy Act Release Form and return it back to her field office. On October 28, 2013, the form was completed, signed, and returned along with a letter dated November 13, 2013.

The opening letter begins with a reference to the attached "Privacy Act Release Form," and your letter dated October 23, 2013. Contained in this letter is additional information in support of my concerns. I

385

apologize for any delay in corresponding with your office sooner. The delay was a result of an unexpected move to a different residence because of health. In support of my conclusions, which I feel justifies this letter to you, is the realization that it is rather disconcerting to me for some reason.

When I contacted your Braxton office, grave concern was voiced along with severe disappointment over the agencies noted on the privacy act release form. Your staff was given a brief overview of the research, which is marked by excessive cybercrime on the internet over the course of many years. For the last eight month's I have been accumulating data on one criminal entity that has been singled out over the myriad of swindling entities preying on the innocent; surreptitiously without permission from the victims; their money and merchandise. Outward signs suggest they are using www.carnalcarriexxx.com, as a forum to conceal or lead people astray into thinking this link names the business sole proprietorship, when in reality, they hide behind this webcam site while swindling money from the American people.

Other indicators allege this group may be active in illegal trafficking of women, drug use, and quite possibly their own escort service on either the East or West coast. (Not substantiated or verified to date) Recently, I learned Nathaniel Raja is the go-to-man, operating behind the scenes in this very assertive and secretive organization. Additionally, information was provided to Senator Baldwin, alleging where this couple lived on the shores of New Jersey. Moreover, I could provide their street address if needed. I also discovered their home was listed on the market. Carnal Carrie; aka., Henan Asante, as I have come to know her over several months, is just one of countless models who "Cam" and "Scam." Obviously, swindling is a very lucrative enterprise for them. They have used applications with accounts on Skype, Facebook, LinkedIn, Rabbit, Myspace, Twitter, and various other websites to trick unsuspecting victims into their web of deceit.

Nathaniel Raja is of Romanian ethnic origin while Carrie is of ethnic Polish origin as previously mentioned in other correspondence. Almost every server they are registered under shows, they have been in the web-camming industry for nearly thirteen-years. They have been flying under the radar from law enforcement officials since setting up shop thirteen-years ago. I had been in contact with the Braxton City police department on five separate occasions. It happened once at their downtown station, three by telephone, and once at the residence.

I expressed concern for my welfare and safety. The other call I made ended up having me rerouted to a female lieutenant. The basis for the call was to see if anyone from the station, or perhaps patrolling nearby in their cruisers would drop by my apartment to hand over what I considered relevant information on this group of criminals. The Lieutenant blatantly refused. Not only did she refuse but she had terrible bedside manners … Rude prude if you will.

I informed Senator Baldwin about IP addresses, hosting sites, trace routes, and sites Carnal Carrie was known to sponsor or have her name associated with on an individual site. Reports I had submitted to various agencies. Name and address were mailed to Senator Baldwin identifying suspected collaborators. Also, Senator Baldwin was apprised of my reasons for contacting the regional FBI office in Vicksburg by telephone, while, on another call, the call was made to their Washington D.C. office. Thus far, I had not received any confirmation by these agencies, nor am I aware of any action taken by the FBI to look into these concerns.

I communicated to Senator Baldwin about cybercrime. How it was becoming an unmanageable epidemic on the internet. I told Senator Baldwin that I was aware workforce and resources were limited; and those who remained to do their uppermost to curtail criminal activity on cybercrime. However, unless more resources are engaged, our attempts are but futile, as we try to reduce the ever-increasing numbers of victims affected monetarily and emotionally.

The criminal investigation service center of the United States Postal Service finally responded to my mail fraud report. On November 26, 2013, Mr. Carl, Acting Manager of USPS, inspection services wrote to inform me that the information I provided would be reviewed to determine if there was any violation of the Mail Fraud or False Representation Statutes within their jurisdiction. (Jurisdiction is the key word used here) Mr. Carl went on to remind me how important it was to realize that their investigative efforts in foreign countries depended largely upon the willingness of that country to cooperate since their jurisdiction in these matters generally ends at our borders. Mr. Carl also wanted me to know they may share the information I provided with other agencies when there is a possible violation concerning their jurisdiction. I replied to this criminal service center on December 14, 2013, with updated information more accurate and helpful than previously.

Senator Baldwin's office forwarded me a response they received from the Department of Justice; Federal Bureau of Investigation, dated December 24, 2013. In his letter, Deputy Assistant Director Joseph Caldwell wrote Senator Baldwin, stating in his letter that I had written to her office and reportedly said that I contacted their bureau on three occasions in regards to alleged fraudulent activity. Mr. Caldwell went on to say I submitted a complaint regarding this matter via the Internet Crime Complaint Center (IC3) on June 12, 2013, but had no further record of my contact with any of their field offices. (Maybe the FBI should have taken copious notes because Mr. Caldwell is in error.)

In the Directors letter to Senator Baldwin, who in turn forwarded his letter to me, I internally questioned Director Caldwell's reply to Senator Baldwin that resulted in a final question.

"If there are no records as to when I contacted the field office by phone; given its serious nature, then why were there no copious notes taken?" Name, date, time, the subject matter of the call. I thought the FBI records all calls. My name has to appear somewhere in their databanks. If no notes were documented during these calls, it would make sense then, that there would be no record. Had Mr. Caldwell taken this a step further and contacted the phone carrier, I am sure they would have discovered my phone number to the Vicksburg office. I had a record of the initial contact with their Vicksburg office. Unfortunately, some of my notes were misplaced during my relocation moves; otherwise, I could have provided names and dates this regional office was contacted.

Mr. Caldwell defended their inaction by stating. "Due to competing priorities and limited resources; the FBI is unable to address all of the white-collar fraud schemes that target our citizens. However, Mr. Caldwell went on to state. "Complaints are essential collection tools which allow the FBI to gather information into the repository wherein it may be aggregated and reviewed to assist in prioritizing their efforts."

What was told next is the perennial in-your-face commentary from Mr. Caldwell. Director Caldwell said. "We recommend that Mr. Jacobs review information published by the Federal Trade Commission at www.ftc.gov." This information concerned fraud schemes, and how best to avoid becoming its victim. This summarization as to that action needed to be taken by victims of cybercrime is richly deserving, the "duh," factor!

Put any spin you want on this epidemic; it is not part of the solution. Apparently, the dollar amount is not significant enough to justify pursuing. I think it is a safe bet that for the FBI to pursue crime, it has to be a bank robbery, white-collar crime in the banking industry, or Wall Street corruption involving big money.

In the month of January 14, 2014, I sent a follow-up letter to Senator Baldwin in response to a letter she had sent to me dated January 8, 2014, with an attached FBI response to her inquiry on my behalf over concerns relating to, but not limited in scope to cybercrime. I began the letter expressing apprehension about the previous correspondence from the FBI, which I had felt, contained extraneous fiery indignation towards Senator Baldwin's most recent informational message. It lacked substance and favorable outcome. I was left feeling ill at ease, disappointed, livid, and stirred to the point of indifference about how callous and misrepresented my complaint had been received and handled by parties involved in the due process.

In my view, this had been handled as though I had nothing more productive to do with my time and life than to waste the taxpayer's money on frivolous oblique allusions of insignificance by infringing on their time." Within the imagery of insightful indignation, I virtually "spoon fed," every State and Federal agency having authority, or jurisdiction over crimes of immoral and criminal intent. To receive the wrong facts, and findings by Director Caldwell is not only irresponsible but also incomprehensible.

On April 18, 2014, I had one more influential person I wanted to coral before surrendering to lamentations. President Barrack Obama. Subject: The Exploitation of Women and Criminal Abuse on the Internet. To date, the President who resides at 1600 Pennsylvania Avenue has not come home yet. I do not know if he is on a prolonged vacation, he is lost, or my letter wasn't important enough for him to acknowledge receipt of my three-page letter. I have come to expect this treatment from our government. This letter contained almost the same information other governmental agencies were given. A word of advice, if you intend to send any correspondence to a do nothing bloated bureaucracy, expect nothing in return unless you are of nobility.

Mr. Water's, an employee of Senator Baldwin's staff; was the point-man in some controversial letter's I had written. "I'm not a man of noble ancestry." I have little or less than superior intelligence. I am not diluted with pride or arrogance. I do not cater to special interests, nor am I a lobbyist, a man of influence, and power. Rather, what defines my character as a man; who served his country honorably for over eighteen-years is my heart. I'm not just a hearer of God's word, but a doer also. You are either part of the problem or part of the solution. How many times must I repeat this?

I remember a eulogy given by Senator Edward Kennedy during his brother Bobby Kennedy's funeral. In the eulogy, Senator Kennedy said.

"My brother need not be idealized or enlarged in death beyond what he was in life, to be remembered simply as a good and decent man, who saw wrong and tried to right it, saw suffering and tried to heal it, saw war and tried to stop it. As he said in many parts of this nation, to those he touched, and those who sought to reach him:"

"Some men see things as they are, and say why. I dream things that never were and say why not."

This was certainly true of Bobby's life. Robert Kennedy's eternal flame for a better tomorrow has been effectively snuffed out by melancholy, pessimism, immorality, and evil. It permeates across all ethnic barriers. We need more Dr. Martin Luther Kings and Robert Kennedy's of this world.

It was not until August 15, 2014, when I felt confident and secure that I had identified the criminals in this fraudulent "scam" operation, that I felt comfortable enough to write the manuscript. There remained no second-guessing about their location and the names associated with this entities involvement in defrauding thousands of dollars from victims over the years. I am so convinced I have identified the appropriate body, that if they were ever brought to trial and found innocent of these crimes, I would voluntarily spend time in prison. Furthermore, if it was determined that I willfully and with intent, caused grave harm to them by falsely alleging these misfits of their internet shenanigans, that I would surrender my freedoms. What does not square with the author is the question of their professed innocence to me. If I'm in error, why haven't they sued for defamation of character? What remains in this long-standing relationship with the abyss of evil as we descend deeper into darkness, is yet unknown. There is a host of questions needing answers, but they will perhaps never be forthcoming.

We have reached mid-summer; sixteen months since my initial contact with Henan Asante began. It is the Month of August 15, 2014. I had enough valid information to submit one more report to (IC3, Internet Crime Complaint Center). Same outline, same basic questions, and finally the description of the incident. The only change was the validity of information that was updated to their agency. I felt very comfortable in what I released to them this time around. I had begun this process as a child learning to walk and was now mature enough in computer usage to develop the intelligence gathering to another level. The folks I have identified would love to pirate my information, wish nothing more than to make me disappear, or that I would just go away. Since I have little confidence in the government, I am hoping the manuscript will get published and distributed in every corner of the world so I can unnerve criminals like these. The manuscript is my weapon of choice!

"If you act the fool, talk like a fool, and live the fool … You are the fool!"

Interpol, (International Police) is comprised of approximately 193 member nations throughout the world. Currently in Lyon France, it has another central headquarters located in Singapore, China. I contacted Interpol on or about October 13, 2013, via the internet to alert their agency that I had suspected Henan and Nathaniel as possible operatives in Fraud, possibly located in one of the European countries. Which country I wasn't very certain because they showed a different IP address every time a tracer route search was done on them. There was Ireland, Germany, Spain, France, Sweden, UK, on, and on without any recompense. Finally, I discovered they were perhaps using bulk packages of Internet Service Providers (ISP), or Virtual Private Networks. (VPN) This is where multiple servers run simultaneously to prevent pinpointing someone's exact location. In the end, I was making myself look rather foolish and incompetent. This was nothing new to the author. Learning independently was always a monumental undertaking since I can remember ... Trial and error.

Interpol places tremendous amounts of resources and labor in the human sex trafficking industry. It is a multi-billion-dollar form of international organized crime, constituting modern-day slavery. Victims are recruited, trafficked between countries, and regions using deception, or coercion. Stripped of their autonomy, freedom of movement and choice, they face various forms of physical and mental abuse. This is the silent crime we as a nation fail in providing safety. There are three main types of human trafficking:

• Trafficking for forced labor;

• Trafficking for sexual exploitation;

• Trafficking of organs;

Pick one of the top three and put yourself in their shoes! "Lose your autonomy ... Lose your identity. Lose self!" This is my calling. There is no greater cause. It is the right thing to do. The war is here. The walking wounded is amongst us. Where do you stand?

Chapter 21

Gotcha

The ostensible language of symbolism reverberates until exact is no longer absolute.
An array of endless colors entombed within the
kaleidoscope, its brilliant images no one disputes.
Fanciful solar flares projectiles of sudden brief
outbursts of energy; ascertain its route.
Its sum is anemic, contagious, prevalent, humankind's
destiny, his nature but the sinful pursuit.
Jim Jacobs

"Was it not I who stirred up this hornets' nest of intrigue and evil?" Then it is only right and proper that I should begin to divulge how; through trial and error and what I honestly believe was Divine intervention, which produced a successful outcome to this hunt. I am convinced the conclusion would never have come to fruition had it not been for the Lords direction and guidance into organized scamming operations. I've exposed these criminal's identities by putting names to these secret, elusive, and heartless souls. This sojourn has taken eighteen-months of research, money, and cataloging for this manuscript to come alive. I would be remiss if I did not concede with a humble heart, that this journey has touched me emotionally, financially, and physically. However, I would do it all over again if I could expose one more scammer, pervert, or prostitute and prevent these lost souls from spending eternity in Hell.

Why do I have a passion for justice for the oppressed, beaten, battered, and sexually abused men and women? When you have been a byproduct of these despicable offenses, the scars inflicted are permanent, a lifelong open wound. As such, disdain towards immorality is the fixture. As I indicated early in the manuscript, it is devastating enough to be sexually molested once. But when it occurs on three other occasions in the span of a lifetime you retreat into a cocoon, and a wall is constructed. Trust becomes the dirty man. The remainder of life is spent being vigilant; the body always tense and rigid, unable to relax until you are in secure familiar surroundings. Unfortunately, men are most often the perpetrators.

What path was it that took Jim Jacobs from light into the darkness of the abyss? Too many unexplained occurrences happened during the journey that, had it not been for the Lords timely intervention, I would not have uncovered the muck and mire of immorality contained in this manuscript. Also, because of this experience, it has changed my view of humankind.

I do not profess to be perfect by any stretch of the imagination. Repeating for emphasis; I am the commander-in-chief of sinner's. I own sin. I have strived on numerous occasions to live a godly life to glorify God, but I fail miserably at times. However, when I accepted Christ into my life, the Holy Spirit without fail, has been there to convict me of my sins and radically change my behavior. It is living a life of vertical thinking in opposition to horizontal thinking." It has put me back on the straight and narrow path to righteous living and godly choices. I have a few ordained ministers of the cloth to thank for my transformation.

At present, it is a day of small things with me. I have light enough to see my darkest side. Sense enough to feel the hardness of my heart. Spiritually sufficient to mourn my want of a divine mind, but I might have had more, I ought to have had more, I have never been straitening (to make strait, or narrow), in thee, for you have always placed before me an infinite fullness, and I have not taken it. May my will accept the decisions of my judgment, my choice is that which conscience approves.

The Valley of Vision

To be fair to the reader, I cannot assume everyone who reads this book is going to have technical knowledge of computers. I for one have to admit when I first began this journey, I was computer illiterate. As a result, I was forced to learn as I went along, with some of the credit, whether I care to admit it or not, going to the swindler who relentlessly created havoc with my computer. As I progress through this chapter, I will attempt to clarify the computer language. The best way to accomplish this task is to start from the beginning explaining the basics.

Before anyone can lend legitimacy to accessing the internet (An electronic communications network that connects computer networks around the world), the first order of business is to get the hardware necessary to connect to the internet. This requires a "modem" (a device that converts signals produced by one type of device, from a computer to a form compatible with another; as a telephone). The modem is used in conjunction with a device called a "router," (this routes a device that mediates the transmission routes of data packets over an electronic communication network, (as on the internet). Generally, the internet service provider, (ISP) such as AB&C, Charter, etc., provides this equipment for you and will set up and activate the service for a minimal activation fee. However, there is a monthly fee before you can access the internet. You can purchase your own router. If you forego buying your own router the provider charges a minimal service fee.

How do you connect to www? (World Wide Web) The phone company usually assigns the customer, a Dynamic IP (internet protocol) number. A Dynamic IP addressing is for one customer per one IP address. Dynamic IP addressing assigns a different IP address each time the ISP customer logs onto their computer but is dependent upon the internet service provider (ISP) because some ISP's only change the IP address as they deem necessary. If you have Static ("IP") addressing through your website host, it means you are sharing an IP address with several other customers. Static IP addresses are more reliable for Voice over Internet Protocol (VOIP). The downside of static IP is that it can become a security risk because the address always stays the same.

The biggest advantages of Dynamic IP addressing are that they do not pose a security risk, as the computer is assigned a new IP address each time the customer logs on. The software that comes with the router allows for Dynamic Host Configuration Protocol (DHCP) setup and assigns each computer attached to the router an IP address automatically. It is used for families that have more than one computer, or by a small business owner who has a home office. An example of an assigned IP becomes your permanent number, (example 186.168.23.45.) When the phone company connects your service, they will likely wire your network for wireless, or wired, or a combination of the two. A wired network usually gives you a more reliable and faster connection but requires that your PC's, (personal computers) and devices be in a fixed location. For small home and work networks; wireless is usually the best option overall. It is laptop friendly. It is mobile and light enough to accompany one just about anywhere. Every computer connected to the internet has an assigned unique number known as an internet protocol (IP) address. Since these numbers are assigned in country-based blocks, an IP address is often used to identify the country from which a computer is connecting to the internet.

The information technology age has arrived. I hope this was not overwhelming to those unfamiliar with the terminology. I cannot stress the word internet protocol (IP) enough, and the important role it plays in the use of computers. For readers who may need assistance defining a protocol, prescribing to strict adherence to correct etiquette and precedence. Internet protocol is what the author made use of on a regular basis, using Google search for specific locations, and or persons. (Using URL) Uniform Resource Locator, or web address, is a particular character string that constitutes a reference to a resource in most web browsers. Especially when used with (HTTP://) hypertext transfer protocol. It is a set of rules for transferring files, text, graphic, images, sound, video, and other multimedia) on the World Wide Web.

Now that your modem and router are connected, you can now access the internet. The next step is to ensure you have browsers that serve as search engines, allowing the user to connect to the world wide web. Some free browsers that come with the Windows operating system and are found on most computers the consumer purchases include Google, Google Chrome, Yahoo, MSN, Bing, Etc. Other browsers available for download include Firefox, Opera, Safari, etc. These browsers are optional downloads and are left at the discretion of the user.

Most people purchasing a computer use Google, as their browser of choice to access the world wide web. There is another piece of information that is helpful. It is what we define as social networking accounts. Examples of these would include. Facebook, Myspace LinkedIn, YouTube, Twitter, Blogger, Pinterest, and Snapchat, etc. I used Google as my browser of choice and as my default homepage because it afforded me the opportunity to go directly to the source. Google has people search, translate, web search, toolbar, and images. Etc. You can also access your email from this browser.

If a user decides to use the social network accounts, you are required to register your name, establish a username, password, age, and assign a personal email account preferably different from your Google email account. Your email account is the most dedicated record on the Internet. Always be careful when opening any email from people or advertisers you don't know. Email is the easiest way for malicious hackers, (a person who uses computers to gain unauthorized access to data on your computer) phishing, (the activity of defrauding an online account holders posing as a legitimate company) to get access to your computer, and infect it with a virus. Malware, (software intended to damage or disable computers and computer systems). I have encountered every form of mischief by this entity of misfits who worked tirelessly in their efforts to prevent me from gathering evidence on their scamming activity.

Google uses, server logs that automatically record the page requests made when you visit their sites. These server logs typically include your web request, Internet Protocol address, browser type, browser language, the date, and time of your request and one or more cookies that may uniquely identify your browser. A cookie is a small file containing a string of characters and is related to your computer when you visit a website. When you visit the website again, the cookie allows the site to recognize your browser.

I have just given you a brief overview and insight into the basics of getting onto the internet with applications. There is additional advanced technology for the use of these computers, but for our purposes, my intent was to inform you of the necessary tools the author used to obtain information. As I indicated earlier, Google was my main browser as the go to for searches. It served my purposes quite well. However, it was not without growing pains, stress, and disappointments. In brief, when I finally have something to go on in the hunt for the co-conspirators there will be some more technical terms that I use.

In the beginning was Skype, and Skype produced this protégé who went by the name of Henan Asante, aka., Carnal Carrie, aka., Jean K. Stepnoski, her maiden name. These names in addition to the myriad of other known aliases' she used are endless. However, I did not know the model username she used, "Carnal Carrie," until a couple months later. Jean Stepnoski I discovered on my own after I learned of her husband's name. However, Jean unwittingly supplied information from the coffers of the unknown into the known. It is ironic that from May through August of 2013; perhaps longer, the clue I needed was within my grasp all along, but there was a disconnect for some reason, and I allowed it to get past my sight.

Before I could obtain Jean's maiden name, since she was married, I needed desperately to get her husband's name. Getting his first and last name proved the biggest challenge, taking upwards of nine months I believe, before putting it all together. Her husband remained a mystery for the longest time. No pictures, no profile, and no email address that I was aware. Finding an image of him proved nearly impossible. It presented many obstacles and hurdles to negotiate. Patience and perseverance would finally pay dividends. Eventually, light reveals that which resides in darkness. Jean's husband was well versed in computer technology, and I said as much to Jean on Yahoo Messenger chat. Yet, given enough rope, criminals always think they are smarter and craftier than their adversaries. Knowing this, they become sloppy, slothful, and think they are invincible. However, all too often, sooner than later they get careless and get entangled in the spider's web themselves.

However, for now, our focus is on Carrie. I will reveal how I learned of Carrie's significant other after we finish with Henan/Carrie. I had said earlier, I needed her husband's name to get to Jean's maiden name. It wasn't until many months later that I learned Carrie was married.

When I searched one of the social networks using Carnal Carrie's name, I found a picture of Jean in a wedding gown surrounded by the "Maids of Honor." Carrie's husband was absent without leave … Missing in action … A deserter. He was "Nada" in any wedding pictures. Finding Nathaniel Raja's last name made it a priority of choice during the hunt. Carrie was not divulging her husband's name freely so I had to figure out a way to best go about searching for him.

Without any warning, as I'm sitting in the chair stretching my brain, an epiphany took root. I had heard that if you have difficulty finding a topic or subject on a search engine, it was suggested that you type, "keywords" in the search engine and your success rate will increase dramatically. It is like the domino effect. If you don't find what you're searching for on the first page, it will generally refer the user to another link or page until you either find what it is that sent the user searching, or you start over using another keyword about the subject. It occurred to me that the key to solving inquiries was sitting right in front of my screen all this time for months. How could I have missed it? Carrie was the pivotal player. She had given me the solution to my problem all along. I did not need to prod her anymore because she had already provided it for me, "you're silly Jim!"

I finally realized I could use the social networks like Facebook, YouTube, LinkedIn, and Rabbit. Also, for more detailed information there was DNS, (domain name search) MyIp, database download, sneekin.com, reverse address lookup, Alexa, ARIN, (American Registry for Internet Numbers) domain ownership search. The possibilities were endless. I only mentioned a few to give the reader an idea of keywords. For example, if I wanted to find information on domains, DNS. Domain name search, you would type in the Google search, who is, <u>www.jimjacobs.com</u>, or what is DNS? DNS is like a telephone directory of domain names that translates domain names into Internet Protocol (IP'S). So what was it that escaped my eyes' all those months?

"<u>http://www.carnalcarriexxx.com</u>. I had her domain name ever since she gave me permission to go to her website. I didn't know what to do with her name until I believed Divine Providence interceded on my behalf, and when it did, I never looked back. It was fast forward from that point on. Don't misunderstand me, it was hard work, but through the process of elimination, I was finally able to obtain the name of Jean's husband.

Since www.GoDaddy.com is a domain registrar provider and web hosting company boasting fifty-nine-million registrar domains making it the largest ICANN, (Internet Corporation for Assigned Names and Numbers) accredited registrars. I was directed to run my search there. Typing my query using keywords I typed in the search box. "www.who is carnal carrie?" This was my best-laid plan to-date. It turned out to be pivotal, as it opened the doors of opportunity wide. It was a methodical process; time-consuming, but on August 18, 2013, I discovered the crown jewel of alleged internet scammers, "Nate" was Jean's pet name for her husband, Nathaniel Raja. I typed in the search box, which is track IP address.com on what was www.carnal-carriexxx.com. It gave me the following information. Registrar-Tucows Inc. It is the Ultimate Collection of Winsock Software. The server, Tucows.com., Administrator., Nathaniel Raja registrant; www.carnalcarriexxx.com; address, 8236 play money St., Summersville, N. J. 50309. Contact-swindler4$@yahoo.com. Date created: 06/21/2000, updated: 03/15/2010, Expires: 11/09/2015. IP: 65.271.132.09

The reader has to keep in mind that the information given above on Carnal Carrie and Nathaniel Raja did not appear on my computer screen on the first attempt at "who is." They have literally thousands of different IP addresses' and domains that are registered. They use VPN (Virtual Private Network), which means it will show an IP address you think is their location when in reality their home base of operation may be located elsewhere.

I had to get VPN to prevent them from finding my IP address when going online. Nathaniel intentionally remains as elusive as ever, using aliases', just like Carrie on different servers, false registrar names on, or he willfully leaves identity column empty. He changes email's frequently and lists fake addresses. Nate is the behind the scenes "little man," choosing instead, to link Carnal Carrie's name on everything that requires a legitimate signature. When Jean webcams, he is off to the side in the same room. When Nathaniel knows I have logged onto Carrie's site, he either cuts off the broadcasting or he will put a ban on my IP to prevent access to her site.

What self-respecting man would allow his wife to expose herself to perverts and swindle victims from their possessions? "From Light into the Abyss," is the darkest most loathsome coexistence partnering with evil and Satan. These are people without a heart, and soul. They lack moral character, and a conscience like the pimp Nathaniel, Carrie, and the other as yet named family of swindlers; who, by default belong in a penal institution. Now that I have Nate's name, I Goggle checkmate. This search engine asks for a first and last name; location; age, and gender of the person you want to identify. Checkmate is a fee for service site. Through the process of elimination, I was able to narrow it down to the right Nathaniel Raja. His name was all I had to go on when I began the search. From there I was able to glean Carrie's maiden name.

The background report revealed Carnal Carrie's name as Jean K. Stepnoski, aka. Stenoska; residing at 8236 Play Money St., Summerville, N. J. 50309. Phone number, (intentionally left out) as was her date of birth. She is of Polish heritage. This is where Nathaniel Raja lives. How do I know this? I have pictures of the interior of the home with still photos of Carrie/Henan in different parts of the house. They operate her webcam site mainly in the basement of their home. I was finally able to take an on-screen photo of Nathaniel, and there is reliable intelligence these criminals have placed their home on the market; asking price, $650,000 dollars. I just discovered they lowered the price to five-hundred-fifty thousand dollars.

If the reader will recall earlier in my manuscript, Carrie gave out the name, "Nate." This was the person of interest she mentioned on her Twitter account. She was retweeting a reply to someone who had tweeted her (Twitter account), voicing her agitation about the virus that shut down their computer. Carrie had made the comment, "and boy is he ticked." Carrie stated, saying. "Nate has been trying to fix this computer for two days now, and he is fearful he has lost thousands of dollars in photographs and videos."

I could not have been more pleased to hear Nate could be facing lost revenue as a result of a virus temporarily shutting down his empire. I also did a domain name search on Nathaniel using "network action," which Jean is the licensed user of that domain, and who they have partnered with Cutthroat Network.Alone.Com. David Sommers is from Canada and president of CTNA. I've always suspected Sommer's and Nathaniel Raja were partnering with this scamming organization. The domain registration lit up like a Christmas tree with Nathaniel's fingerprints all over one of three pages.

Just to cover my tracks for positive identification, I went back to my home page and googled; "who is domain registration domain availability?" On this inquiry, I discovered two pages were associated with Raja's name. It contained a list of domain's Nathaniel was selling at a discounted rate. For example, rajanathaniel.net, $4.88 a year, rajanathaniel.pw, $1.88 per year. The highest priced was rajanathaniel. info for $8.88 per year.

Nathaniel and wife Carrie intentionally use aliases' and different accounts, IP's, etc. to thwart would-be victims from trying to trace their location. When they are "scamming," they will never use their assigned IP address, 65.271.132.09, and 65.272.112.24. Rather I suspect they use VPN numbers, TCP/IP, or bundled packets of IP's for a cost. To prevent law enforcement from detecting their location they use burn phones, also called cell phones, or smartphones, because they are difficult to trace. There was an apparent falling out. I believed this to be a stratagem to mislead authorities, between David Sommers, ("sparky,") an assigned nickname because he's a shifty character. www.cutthroatnetwork, com, and www.carnalcarriexxx.com, are cooperatives with Nathaniel Raja ("Tinker Bell, his assigned nickname).

"I am not using CTNA any longer because David Sommers, the owner is a lying scumbag who stole thousands of dollars from my shows. I'm going to publish much more information about this in the coming weeks including detailed conversations. I will also be creating a new website containing all the information to warn others who are planning on doing business with this, (expletive) liar. Carrie continues her relentless tongue-lashing of Sommers, saying.

"If you are a webmaster or a prostitute that plans on using him or may have considered using his crummy network, be warned. DO NOT BELIEVE ANYTHING HE SAYS! If he promises you anything, he does not intend to keep his promise. If he makes you a deal, know that he DOES NOT HONOR HIS DEALS. He will walk away with thousands of dollars that you earned. The "guy" is cocky, full of himself, and the most arrogant person we have ever met. HE will NEVER admit to doing anything wrong, regardless of what kind of evidence you present, or how right you may actually be. YOU will always be wrong and he has an answer for EVERYTHING.

Cutthroat Network Alone is a known (expletive) scammer. NEVER USE IT PERIOD. There are many other options out there. Contact me if you need advice. "Whoa!" David Sommer's is A SCAMMER? Whoa! Look who's calling the kettle black! There is a saying in these illegal manifestations that arise out of troubled waters. "Evil begets evil!" Here we are, three months to the day Carrie posted this scathing report about David Sommer's and Cutthroat Network Alone, and Carrie has yet to publish a facsimile follow-up on her web page. It is another rogue people. These foolish people live, breathe, play, and have there being as one. There partnering again!

Carrie loves to deflect bad behavior away from her and the spotlight when the charade of scamming has been uncovered. My voice and allegations are not the only voice echoed against Jean Stepnoski. As a minimum, twenty other victims have gone viral on Jean's Twitter account registered as, @TheCarnalCarrie. Other users with Twitter accounts also identify Carrie as the responsible party for swindling them as well. However, Carrie will always short circuit and tell her accusers the scammers are from Ghana or Nigeria.

The following two paragraphs is a verbatim account written in Carrie's handwriting. So what does Carrie do to draw attention away from their illegal activities? She masquerades as an activist against internet swindlers as she writes on her web page.

"It is important to know that I do NOT use messenger, EVER … EVER … EVER! If you saw me on messenger, it was 100% a scammer using a recorded video from my website. It is not magic. They turn the sound off and cut off the logos. Then they say something like. Oh my sound doesn't work, so you cannot hear me, which allows them to let the video play without you questioning why they are not answering your question."

"If there is no sound, it's a dead giveaway. It is a pre-recorded feed." Carrie has been known to do this on numerous occasions, especially when she and I had ended our traditional game of chess. You can also be sure Nathaniel was involved in this folly. These are "Knights of the Round Table," forever planning and scheming to remain under the radar.

"Scams," using images of Sally, her sister, are very popular according to Carrie because she has so many pictures on her site including cam vids and photo images. "These criminals reside in Ghana. Unfortunately, they are difficult for us to stop," Carrie declares in a self-professed statement. "The country is far too corrupt and the criminals pay off the local authorities to get away with it. It is no different than other Ghana scams like ones that claim you won money and have to claim it." Did Carrie or Nate ever submit an internet criminal complaint report? (IC3). My belief is they have not.

I guess this is good enough to keep law enforcement at bay. And the Oscar goes to Carrie!" For her complete involvement in the fraud industry. Nate and David receive one for production and special effects. The supporting cast won an Oscar for behind the scenes silence.

In this section of the chapter, I need to make it entirely clear the author in no way endorses, promotes or encourages young users to visit sites that have been mentioned in this manuscript. The purpose and intention of mentioning, or listing sites is to make the public aware of the myriad of undesirable websites on the world wide web that avail themselves to the public. You could spend endless days exploring these obscene spores of destructive parasitic indecencies. I would highly recommend adults of children monitor their child's activities while using the computer. The porn industry has made getting onto their sites readily available using deceptive ads to guide users onto their websites.

Examine for yourselves how prevalent pornography has impacted morality the effect it has on society to the degree, it is becoming an epidemic and a disgrace. A report, conducted by the United Kingdom entitled; U.K. Online Porn Ban: Web traffic analysis of Britain's porn affair written July 27, 2013, and published by Daniel Buchuk. Mr. Buchuk reported that U.K.'s Prime Minister David Cameron announced that online pornography should be blocked by default in the U. K. What this means is that folks will be obliged to declare whether they want to maintain access to online pornography. (NOTE: Step in the right direction, but does not go far enough).

Using similar website data, the author wanted to dig deeper into the subject to find out three things: First, how much of the United Kingdom's web traffic has been affected by the corroding influence of pornography. Second, see how the U. K. compares to other countries when it comes to adult content, and finally, understanding what the demand for online pornography in the U. K. encompasses. "No surprise to this author!" Porn traffic is bigger than all social networks combined." What is troubling to the Author is how Pay-Per-view pornography has made its way onto premium television channels.

Mr. Buchuk analyzed the U.K.'s web traffic in June and broke it down by category, finding that an astonishing 8.50% of the U.K.'s web traffic in June 2013 took place in adult sites. To put this in context, traffic across all social networks combined accounted for 7.30% of U.K.'s web traffic in June compared to shopping 6.06%. He, the author, heard that porn was big on the web, but not more significant than Facebook. Only two categories surpass porn regarding traffic Volume-Search Engines and Arts & Entertainment (thanks to YouTube) which accounted for 15.65% and 9.59% of the U. K.'s web traffic in June.

Germany takes the crown regarding use on website's containing pornography consumption with 12.4%, followed by Spain with 9.58%, U. K. having 8.50% with the United States ranking number four, coming in with a cougar's share of 8.31%. Ireland, France, and Australia were not far behind. The worldwide average share of adult traffic is 7.65, nearly a point below U. K. (8.50%). Fact, most of the time people do not just stumble upon adult content, they search for it. When analyzing Google U. K.'s outgoing traffic over 3 months, we see that 8.19% of searches led to Adult websites. The top 20 sites receiving traffic from Google, 5 out of these 20 sites are adult oriented. Pornhub.com is the biggest gainer and even makes it to the top ten, or 1.16% of Google U. K. outgoing traffic ended up on "Pornhub." That is a lot of traffic. To put this into perspective, the top five adult sites combined receive nearly as many visits from Google U. K. as bbc.co.uk does.

Porn is a big part of the internet. Not just in the U. K. but around the globe. Filtering porn sites is not an easy job. The Mr. Buchuk spent four-years perfecting the best, adult detection technology. Yet it ultimately comes down to what people search for and what they want to see. The quick and easy access to pornography is indeed a phenomenon that the internet accelerated, but we live in a multi-device society.

"Where there is a will, there is a way." The fix is simple. Ban all forms of pornography and eliminate the overwhelming temptation for the weak, to peek their curiosity, (out of sight, out of mind mentality).

I viewed the analytical report on October 17, 2013. The statistics affected this author to the point where I felt compelled to comment on his statement about my own experience on a pornography website operated by Carnal Carrie. I addressed my remark to Daniel Buchuk that I had witnessed a disturbing video of a young woman raped viciously and violently that was showcased on Carrie's site that traumatized me for weeks.

"I am pleased to hear someone is doing analytical research on the denigration of the female anatomy. I have been involved in investigating one particular site on the terrible misuse of the Internet for eight months. This included internet pornography and using the internet for the purpose of defrauding unsuspecting victims of their money. I mentioned Nathaniel Raja and his partners in crime as allegedly involved in "scams" for thirteen-years. They do not just use pornography, but Nathaniel and Carrie are allegedly involved with defrauding victims while using their business of web-camming as a legitimate business.

This may mislead law enforcement from investigating their fraudulent activity. They have multiple domain servers, package IP's, and VPN. A VPN ensures privacy through security procedures and tunneling protocols such as the "Layer Two Tunneling Protocol" (L2TP); Data is encrypted messages. There are no longer any secrets between Nathaniel Raja, Carrie, and myself. I know where they reside, and they are well aware of my location. I believe there are many more players involved in this enterprise who are aware of or involved with stealing from victims that associate with Raja.

There are not any hindrances in place for anyone who is determined, to gain access onto any porn site. Once you have gained access to one of these websites, the possibilities are endless, as one web page may lead you to more web pages on the site, or it may lead you to another link altogether that has nothing to do with the web page you started out with in the beginning. Never-the-less, wherever you go on the internet, you are likely going to be exposed to pornography. In the example, I will use Carnal Carrie as the prop. We will use the browser Google as our search engine. Once the user left clicks internet explorer, it will open the page on the desktop where several desktop tiles containing browsers and applications come into view. Left click on the desktop tile, and it opens to rows of icons in which to choose. Internet Explorer icons should come into view. Before you click internet explorer, you must move your mouse to the right of the screen and click on the power to get online access to the internet.

If you are using Google as your homepage, once you click on internet explorer, it should then open up Google browser. You will use Google to type in your search. In the example, I am going to use Carrie's website. Typing, www.carnalcarriexxx.com, will direct the user to her site. For those who may not be up to speed; "xxx" signifies adult content. Once on her website, the first thing that is visible is the number of results for this name. This day it shows 701,000 results. Image looking for 701,000 different pages where Carnal Carrie may appear. You could spend the entire day on her site and never get through the web page. What will follow are ten different strings or sites the user can visit on this website. Some titles read as follows:

"Carnal Carrie Sexy cam girl and pornstar hottie, seen hardcore."

"Welcome to my new site."

"Gallery/Carnal Carrie cam girl and pornstar hottie, goes porn."

"Tag Archive for Carnal Carrie Sexy cam girl and …"

"CarnalCarriexxx.com, –Girls Released."

You get the idea. After the user scrolls down the first ten choices, they can then drop down to the end of the page where more opportunities await them, numbering one thru ten. Additional selections follow after exhausting the first ten numbers. Occasionally you will see at the end of the page, DMCA. (Digital Millennium Copyright Act.) This only means: In response to a complaint we received under the US Digital Millennium Copyright Act and we have removed one result(s) from this page. If you wish, you can read the DMCA complaint that caused the removal by typing, chilling effects.org.

Approximately two months ago, some pundit had given the rating by URL score of 2.25. www.carnalcarriexxx.com was registered 1 year and 11 months ago. It has an Alexa rank of 610,979 in the world. This site has a Google page rank of one-tenth. It has an estimated worth of, one-thousand-two hundred dollars. It has a daily page view of 1,574, with a daily unique visitor representation of seven hundred and eighty-seven. Their hosted IP address is 651.272.132.09, but I repeat, they also use other IP addresses' with this site. There (WOT) "Web of Trust" is ranked destitute. Privacy is indigent. Child safety is inadequate.

Chapter 22

Fallen Diva

Our tongue; yes, this tiny vessel of a muscle. Lucid, and miserably untamed.
Quick is the warrior his reverberating words;
unleashing its thunder of boastful acclaim.
Truth shows character, but man's desire to wallow in
the muck and mire; all shades of darkness.
Indifference matters little to man, your moment of choice.
Is it Jesus or Judas, is left this question mark?
Jim Jacobs

Since I now have what I've been tirelessly searching for, "is this the end of the odyssey? Can we stamp it parcel post, and send the manuscript to the publisher, and hope for the best?" No, no, no my friends, we have much work to do before we entertain the present. I have more business requiring my attention before I am satisfied all possibilities have been exhausted in my arsenal of inquiries. If you recall in the last Chapter, some pundit had given www.carnalcarriexxx.com a rating by (URL) Uniform Resource Locator, a score of 2.25 out of a possible 4 rating for their site. The evaluation suggests the middle of the road reliability. There (WOT) "web of trust" is ranked marginally. Privacy rated very poorly, child safety ranked very poorly. What this means is that I have more work requiring my attention on this website of deception. This site cannot be trusted. It is a soiled blot, one of many sites containing blemishes full of evil and darkness.

If you will recall, I had a strong suspicion Carrie had two other siblings, (girls) employed (used loosely) in the same demonstrated occupation as

Carrie. They are alleged to be involved with Carrie in fraud. This has embroiled itself in a secret closet family affair that leads to the front door of Nathaniel Raja. What did my follow-up search reveal on this secret group? It appears someone went to great lengths to erase one of the sibling's information from the radar. Therefore, I was only able to obtain information on one of Carrie's sister's residence using Spokeo and Checkmate.

Public records revealed the following: (1) Kelly Stepnoski, aka., Smitten Angel; 581 Payton Place, the Bronx, N.Y. 21301. DOB: 08/12/85 (2) Isabella Stepnoski. Aka., Debra Dare. 501 Water Blvd., Salem, New Jersey. (3) Carrie Raja Stepnoski. Aka., Stenoska, 8236 Play Money St., Summerville, N.J. 50309. Their mother, Nan, or Nancy also from New Jersey. There was no mention of husbands for her two sisters. I decided it wasn't worth the monies to verify whether divorce or deaths come into play. Nancy, I positively identified because she had the same phone number that Carrie and Nathaniel use with US Cellular as a landline. Nancy had another phone number listed but it had been disconnected. Nathaniel's DOB: is 02/21/87.

His behavior and conduct I define as that of an unruly teenager.

Carrie, Kelly, and Isabella have been seen webcamming on www.legoflambcams.com. Carrie's two sisters suffer from anxiety disorder. Kelly is the twin sister of Isabella. Kelly was prostituting herself on a website called www.peppers.com. Nathaniel's mother and father are also located in the New Jersey area. They are alleged to be divorced. Cathy is Nathaniel's mother, and is currently living in a house listed under Nathaniel and brother Bobby's name. Their mother's home is located at 1303 Denver Way, Summerville, N. J. Nathaniel's father's name is thought to be that of Yankovic Raja, also from New Jersey.

As previously mentioned, Nathaniel has one sibling I was able to identify. His name is listed as Bobby Raja born in 1980; and is also believed to reside in New Jersey, making this quite a family affair. To verify Cathy was Nate's mother, I called the residence listed under her son's name to confirm this was his kin. I barely got my name out to identify myself, when Cathy was all over me like cat eyes' prowling the neighborhood. The very first words spoken in utterance, putting the stamp of guilt on her tongue as I listened to the hiss of an angry Badger.

"You people leave my boy alone! You just call to see if my boy is swindling. You keep bothering me and I am going to call the police and tell them you are harassing me," Cathy angrily stated.

Undaunted by Cathy's idle threats I asked. "I just want to know why Nathaniel is listed as living there, that's all Cathy."

Cathy had not finished her ranting and raving, with a few choice words in between. "It is none of your business! You just call to get information. You call here again and I'm going to put a warrant out for your arrest, you hear me, mister," she threatened.

"Cathy," interrupting her ranting. "I challenge you, no I encourage you, better yet Cathy, I dare you to call the police. Do you want my address as well?" I inquired.

"You trouble maker, you no good," as her final words to me vibrated my ear drum while I hear the phone slam down on the receiver.

It wasn't until some weeks later that I discovered Bobby lived somewhere in New Jersey as well. Documents indicate Carrie's mother, Nancy Stepnoski owned the home at 8236 Play Money St., Summerville, N. J. but sold it to her son-in-law Nathaniel and Carrie on 05/31/2005 for approximately $340,000. This is a twenty-five hundred square foot home with a finished basement. The home features three bedrooms. I mentioned bedrooms for a particular reason because one of the bedrooms caught my eye.

Carrie and I talked about the bedroom briefly. As the questions became more pointed, Carrie decided it was in her best interest to move on and discuss other topics. I could not get this room off my mind, wrestling with various possibilities why this room seemed to stand still in time. Encapsulated, neatly preserved, pink adorned the walls. The bedspread overlapped the bed with Mickey and Minnie Mouse imprints. Ruffled curtains extended the width of the window, pale pink with white lace curtains for a backdrop. Pictures placed strategically on the dresser and small end table. A Palomino Horse with pink mane for hair and tail was situated at the end of the chest.

This puzzled me because none of the sisters had children of their own and remain single. Contemplating why Carrie would go to such lengths having a room painted Pink and not use it was something I could not let go. I began to put together a sequence of events that may; I emphasize MAY, account for the possibility of this room being displayed as a memorial for a baby female child. The first clue came on October 29, 2013, when I downloaded pictures Nathaniel had taken of some cemetery headstones. The first thought that came to mind was a photo of names on the granite marker to choose a prostitute's name for Carrie because some clearly had the name "Angel" inscribed on the grave marker.

Then it occurred to me. Could there be, can it be, is there a remote possibility Carrie could have had a still-born birth, miscarriage, abortion? After all, who goes around taking pictures of headstones if there in the web-camming/scamming business? Did I ask Carrie whether this had occurred? This was not something I would hound Carrie about at first. Identifying her and the group as possible scammers is one thing. delving into something that may be very personal is another. However, I felt this was critical to further the research so I sent a Twitter message to Carrie inquiring about the empty bedroom. I was blocked from tweeting her. Needless to say, it won't be the first nor will it be the last time I was blocked from her Twitter account. I bypass block simply by establishing a new Twitter account.

Although I have what I consider crucial information on their criminal enterprise, I intentionally played the role of a classical buffoon when chatting with Carrie during the month of August 2013. I told Carrie what my most recent discoveries had revealed "Nate's" nickname was actually spelled "Natty." Nathaniel was up to his old irritable shenanigans again by planting a virus into my computer. All Carrie would say. "I see!" She kept insisting she was in Ghana, but I countered, suggesting she might be living in the Ukraine.

However, I also hinted she could be in the United States. Carrie was asked if she knew a person who established a Twitter account with the name, @jeremyfamou$187. I explained to Carrie that I was turning the computer over to the authorities the day we chatted which was 08/01/2013. (Bluff) Carrie's reaction. "Okay!" They were beginning to scale down my options for contacting Carrie. I was banned from her Twitter account, emails were being returned, and I could no longer access Carrie's website. Of course, Carrie denied any culpability for these latest developments.

August 6, 2013, was the next time we were online chatting. Carrie decided we should live video-cam to see each other while we talked. This usually was a sign Carrie was about to beg for something that had a monetary value attached to it.

First I see you then I don't. That's how our video session's often went.

What it did disclose during one of our meetings in relatively elaborate detail upon further observation was an expensive necklace. It was likely handcrafted of diamonds inscribed, I believe, with the inscription, "Halo." Carrie wore this often with a pair of favored earring's that were the size of a half-dollar dangling from her ears. Faithful to my suspicions, Carrie asked about the new Galaxy 4 cell phone I was supposed to send to Ghana because hers was broken. We went back and forth on the number of cell phones she had in her possession. The final result of our discussion ended with the comment.

"Deny, deny, deny!" I told Carrie that when she was willing to give me her real location, I wasn't going to send her anything.

I asked Carrie if she knew @katyperry. "Yes," Carrie said. However, there was no longer any communication between them. She acknowledged knowing Allen Simple. Then I asked Carrie about @jeremyfamou$187. She acknowledged him as well. We will get to @jeremyfamou$187, and the pivotal role he and his wife play in this circle of criminal activity. Not quite finished with the questioning. I then asked Carrie who the skinny guy with glasses and short-cropped blonde hair behind the camera was while she was doing a lap dance. He was sitting on the couch. Scrawny fellow, I thought.

"Oh, that was Harry," Carrie replied. "And who was the prop for the dance?" I asked. "Yeah, that was James," she told me.

Carrie comes up with a cockamamie tale about the webcam girls and friends on her site. "Jealous of us," Carrie would tell me. Especially when Carrie was told I was going to put her on my insurance policy. "Not!"

"You mean Cali, and those other girls?" I implied.

"Yes!" Carrie confessed.

"You mean they're jealous of you, is that what you are saying?" I inquired.

Carrie remarked. "No. Of you. their jealous of you!"

Carrie is eager to return to the smartphone topic. Additionally, Carrie complains that she will have a difficult life until I leave for Ghana, Ukraine, or wherever her fairytale location happens to be at the time, before she is brought back to the U. S. with me. I plant a teaser for Carrie's benefit just too wet her appetite. I answered her previous complaint about having a difficult time until I arrive by saying.

"You're all getting along well," I implied resolutely.

"No." Carrie declared.

Ignoring Carrie's response, I continue. "You are all living well. All of you must be eating well. It appears you make exquisite meals. You are always dressed in appealing attire and have a modern kitchen with great cookware. Carrie, you are nestled in a beautiful home, with three spacious bathrooms. Looks like you have great plenty to me Carrie." I also tell Carrie she has been at this model and scam work for nearly thirteen-years now." The statement was meant to goad her into giving soliciting a response from her.

Carrie wasted little time in answering my summary. "You trying to research, and all that gets you are third problems," Carrie angrily proclaims. Carrie goes back and forth with her insistence that she resides in Ghana, but I won't be sold on that or the smartphone Carrie adamantly claims she needs.

We briefly discussed Carrie's website. I told Carrie about a visit I paid to one of the prostitute's rooms on her site. This prostitutes room no sooner granted me access to her room to get a visual on her, when as if on cue, this woman began performing in front of me without receiving any gratuities. "She was bone dry naked," I told Carrie

"They all need you!!!! Jealousy will kill them," Carrie declared.

"Well, when they begin this theatrical performance, I scoot out of the room. This is not for me Carrie," I announced to her.

Carrie answered. "Okay, good!"

I asked Carrie if she had any answer as to why there is a lot of jibber-jabber in their rooms, leaving the viewer with the impression they are chatting with someone when I'm the only person in the room on free chat.

"I don't know why Carrie replied."

Continuing the conversation, I told Carrie. "They're in cubicles, they're not shown in an open space like a living room, or bedroom with window's. It's just a bed, chair, and their (expletive) and skimpy outfits. Something like a hospital drape is used as a partition," I informed Carrie.

"Hmm," was all Carrie would utter.

But I replied. "So why do you get to roam around your house in wide open space?" I asked Carrie that challenged her to reply.

Carrie complies by answering. "Because mine is different from there's." Carrie cuts me off complaining the questions were giving her a headache. Was it a headache or did Carrie just now realize she had a slip of the tongue? She knows about the other women, and readily admits she operates at will around her home while the other women are networking through cubicles; their movements restricted.

To uplift Carrie and give her some hope, I told her I would come and pick her up in Ghana. However, even this gesture would lead to more questions. When we got to the arrangements for the trip, I asked Carrie.

"Who is picking me up at the airport?"

Carrie enlightened me by saying. "I will pick you up in Acura."

"Do you have a car?" I asked.

"No, I will get friends car, or will take a taxi," she announces.

Following up on Carrie's answer, I could not dismiss the facts and findings, as it spoke for itself. "You just sent me a picture of you next to a white vehicle, yes?" Carrie stated. "That car is not mine."

"The BMW is not yours either?" I inquired.

"Was mine, but don't have it now," Carrie claims without an explanation.

Then I asked. "Who owns the truck?" Carrie answered. "It was mine but I sold it. Have to sell, as no one will help me."

"What happened to the Corvette with the tinted windows?"

"Sold." Carrie replies.

The previous discussions occurred on Aug 6, 2013. When I began addressing the vehicle's Carrie owned, Carrie apparently tired of the questions, disappeared off the radar, leaving me stranded. Never-the-less, I was content with the information I was able to learn from this chat session. Carrie attempted to get in touch with me the next day. However, I thought I would ignore her this time around. Carrie logged online August 8, 2013, and I acknowledged her presence.

The first thing on my agenda was her web-camming. She had said she was going to stop. However, their Carrie was that evening, live video web-camming. I would not allow this opportunity to slip through the portholes of deception, so I asked her if she was web-camming the night before.

"No!" Carrie tells me. "I went to bed early."

It was time for a wake-up call as I said to Carrie. "I believe I mentioned this to you once before Carrie. I am tired of hearing myself talk. Sometimes the person asking the question already knows the answer to the other persons response before it is communicated to the person receiving it; just to see if the truth is being told."

Carrie just kept digging a deeper grave into the abyss, claiming she wasn't aware she was going to be on. But, when I had Carrie boxed into a corner, she finally admitted. "Okay, am sorry for not telling you."

Then Carrie wanted to know why I was not on messenger for two days. I informed Carrie it was confidential. Now it was my turn to withhold secrets since I had become the hunter. Added to this chain of events, Carrie or Nate, (tinker bell) were toying with my computer again.

Carrie was going to give me some welts with another emergency request.

"What's the emergency Carrie?"

I felt scorn reverberating through the computer screen as Carrie insisted. "I told you I need six-hundred dollars to repay my friend who I had borrowed from some time ago." Carrie declared.

"Do you want me to tell you what was told verbatim relating to a statement you made on YouTube?" I asked Carrie pointedly.

Carrie paid no mind to the threat. Instead, she rattled on. "Because it is time to pay, and I have no time to waste. I thought you got my email," Carrie asked.

My rebuttal came swift and clear. "No honey, this is another scam," I countered.

The tables turned rapidly, Carrie's reply was not very cordial. "This is not a scam!" Carrie said adamantly.

I rebutted her denial, informing Carrie. "I will not tell you what or how I know, but this I know for sure. You and your criminal partners are all in on this," I insisted. Then as a reminder, I mentioned YouTube again. "Remember YouTube, what you said?"

"So you think I am a criminal and want to trick you just for money????" Carrie said, obviously quite upset that I dare accuse her of such a crime.

"Yes," I replied.

Carrie became feisty, answering with determination. "I want you, and I want us together."

"Not!" I countered. "You want to scam me for more money."

Carrie ignores my allegations. Instead she chooses to rattle on. "I need your help in this emergency."

"The only emergency is greed Carrie," I said.

"Okay!" Carrie replied as if she were defeated.

Moreover, I informed Carrie. "Who do you think controls the girls on the website you own and operate using the internet as soiled entertainment?"

With a curt response, Carrie lashes out, saying, "God (Expletive)." And she was gone.

Carrie tried to touch bases with me the following day. However, I once again elected to ignore her on messenger. Matter-of-fact, I didn't have a discussion with Carrie the rest of August. Instead, I directed my energy towards gathering additional information to incriminate this evil entity. The next time we spoke to each other was on September 5, 2013. The gist of this conversation was about "Tinker Bell, (Nathaniel) rendering my computer useless with his viruses' again. Carrie for some unknown reason wanted to exchange photographs with me and text her using +233245798910. Further, she wanted my email address. Carrie was informed that I had seven volumes of information on their activity, and it was growing.

Carrie replied. "You are such a wicked person! I am getting upset talking with you."

To this, I stated. "You all have everything to lose by keeping tabs on me because I am not going to quit my intelligence gathering information on your fraudulent scams."

Carrie did not take comfort in my remarks at all, as she typed her own rebuttal. "Hey! If this is what you are going to talk about, then get out of here." And so I did.

On September 7, 2013, I intentionally left a message for "Tinker Bell." (Nathaniel). "If what you just did to the other computer is going to slow me down, or affect how I am going about identifying you, (even though I had his name and location already) think twice buddy! Your nothing more than a pimp with an attitude. Tinkerbell, you need to put your talents to better use instead of stealing from your own citizens. You folks should be ashamed, but I know it is business as usual with the lot of you," I concluded.

Carrie tried on one other occasion to get in touch with me. The date, September 12, 2013, but there was not anything else to say to Carrie unless she was willing to mend her ways. There were no more conversations for the month of September.

October was similar to September. October 28, 2013, was the only time we talked. In this conversation, I informed Carrie I was about to shut everything down. She insisted on an explanation. She wanted to know the reason for such a hasty departure. I told Carrie I had sent her an email explaining my reason. It was written using as many syllables per word that were in my reserve repertoire of the English language just to frustrate her. As we were talking, Carrie hinted that she did not understand the words; "mission accomplished." Carrie kept asking many times over.

"I don't know what you were trying to say!" Finally, I apprised Carrie that my research and intelligence gathering on their scam operation was finished and I was now in the process of being written as a manuscript involving their alleged illegal activity, which Carrie denied. I also informed Carrie that since she craved riches and fame, that should there be a demand for this book, I would make her a household name. Carrie and her group have been keeping surveillance on me ever since I made this declaration.

Carrie allowed us to have a live video chat. She saw the hat I was wearing and said. "I like that hat, why didn't you send it to me?" She stated how healthy I looked; whatever that meant, and that every time she saw me on her video camera, she got happy.

However, I quickly responded by telling Carrie. "You can't have me!"

"Why?" Carrie wanted to know.

"You are taken, and I'm too old for you," I said emphatically. "I have a longstanding relationship with Jesus. There is no possibility of a relationship with someone who is not a Christian."

We discussed Nate and his ongoing determination to interfere with my computers. Carrie vocalizes her input on this matter saying. "I understand and I do not know why he really does that. Maybe because you said you are going to help get me leave Ghana, and they are trying to get rid of you," Carrie asserts.

I cautioned Carrie by stating. "That would be irresponsible of them."

Carrie replied. "I know; Nate is just tired."

"Tired of what?" I asked.

"He is tired of trying you. He knew he cannot get rid of you no matter what he does." Carrie declared.

Carrie claimed to have taken drugs in the past. She also expressed a desire to be rich and well known.

"You will be well known Carrie. In fact, you may even become a household name someday." Then I added. "It wasn't Allen Simple I talked to either, but "Sparky," David Sommers, from Canada." I remarked to Carrie.

No sooner had I mentioned their names when Carrie logs off messenger. Nothing new. I was used to these quick exits by now. We didn't have contact with one another for almost six weeks.

On December 12, 2013, we had another conversation. Either she wanted more money or her conscience was beginning to trouble her. I favored the money option.

When Carrie alerted me that she was on messenger, she wanted to know why I didn't want anything to do with her. I was baking cookies at the time for the upcoming holiday. I began to disciple Carrie trying to find out where she was in her walk with the Lord.

"Because I still see hope for the two of you. All souls are worth saving," Carrie was informed.

"What do you mean the two of you??????" She asked bluntly.

"You and Nathaniel and the other misfits," I replied.

Sensing Carrie was about to hint of another gratuity; however, before she could ask, I reminded Carrie about the black fancy truck she had, although I found out it was recently involved in a fender bender. But she used the disclaimer that she didn't have a truck. Faithful were my instincts. The big question pierces the air like an out of control tsunami.

"I want you to get me something for Christmas," Carrie asked.

"Oh, what are you going to buy me?" I asked.

"Anything you want!" Carrie replied.

"Yeah, and my name is John Henry."

Unexpectedly dropping a bucket of bolts on my lap, Carrie said. "I want you to get me some money."

"Ok!" I agreed. "I'll bring it right to your doorsteps before Christmas. Then we can all sit down and break bread together," Carrie is informed.

"Okay, when will it be?" Carrie asked.

"Do you really need a set time Carrie?" I inquired. Suggesting a different plan instead, I offered Carrie a proposal. "Why not surprise you?" Furthermore, I asked Carrie. "Are you going to put me up for the night?"

"No!" Carrie replied.

"Why?" I asked. "You do have a spare bedroom, or better yet, I can sleep on the couch," I said.

"Yes," Carrie remarked.

Then we talked about where I should meet her once I arrived at the bus terminal. Who was going to meet me, what was the cost? Before I could finish my inquiry Carrie logged off.

On December 13, 2013, at 5:00 o'clock in the evening. Carrie decides to reappear on messenger. I immediately asked her what it was she wanted me to do. (As if I didn't already know) We were still on the topic of money as Carrie once more stipulates her need for money, but I cut her short.

"I said I would bring it to you Carrie."

"No," she said. "Send it!"

We haggled over how she was supposed to receive the money. (Not that she was ever going to get it from me.) When I told Carrie I had watched "Jesus of Nazareth" the night before, that captured her attention.

"Oh, do you believe in Jesus Christ?" Carrie asked.

"Yes Carrie I do believe Jesus is our Lord and Savior. He is the great I Am. They are three in one. He is God the Father, God the Son, and God the Holy Spirit. Jesus came to earth in the form of God/Man in the flesh to suffer and be crucified. Dying on the cross for our sins." I told her. "We are stiff-necked sinful creatures. Sin originated with Adam and Eve, who were commanded by God not to eat of the tree of knowledge of good and evil, for, in that day you surely eat, you will surely die."

"Humankind has been sinning ever since Carrie."

"Yes," Carrie acknowledges, adding. "Can we talk later?" It was as though Carrie was racing in the Formula 500. She became swifter than a gazelle and she was gone again!

The last time we officially talked on messenger was February 7, 2014. Our conversations came to a halt on February 10, 2014. On February 7, Carrie was on again, off again, without remedy. When Carrie logged onto messenger, I commanded most of the conversation. There came a time when I asked myself who it was I was chatting with. Could've been "Tinker Bell" attempting to get a location on me, or perhaps disrupt my computer. Finally, I said to Carrie.

"I guess when or if you are ready to have a lively chat you will let me know, so I will just go about my other business for now." Carrie quickly answered, saying.

"I'm here, I'm here."

"What exactly would peak your interest about now," I asked sarcastically. "Yah wanna smartphone, money, computer, what exactly?" I inquired. However, there was no response. "Are you playing hide and seek with me?" Voicing indifference.

That prompted a response from Carrie as she asked. "What do you mean?"

"One minute you're here, and next thing I know, you disappear."

"Carrie, if you think staggering your responses will eventually lead me to divulge information I have on you and your husband involving illegal activities, you can forget that idea … Never happen."

This comment prompted an immediate response from Carrie, as she said. "You're not serious, you're not ready for me!"

"I know more about the two of you than you know about yourselves," I said adamantly.

Carrie then answers. "You may be right, but you are not worth spending time with because you are just wasting my time … Not serious … Not ready for anything. I need you but you are useless right now. You just want yourself. Don't want to share yourself with anybody."

What I was observing was absent some of our previous conversations. Carrie was stringing complete sentences together rather than the usual one or two syllable words. At least now she is engaging me.

I informed Carrie how she had betrayed, lied, deceived, and used me for their personal gain. She had made me the brunt of their amusement … A fool … A laughing stock of their round table jokes.

On February 8, 2014, Carrie logs onto messenger with a well-versed script prepared.

"Jim, if you actually want me, then just be up to it. However, if you are writing to disturb, or annoy me, please leave. I don't have any intentions of messing with your computer. You have accused me of so many things, which happened to you. But you know perfectly well that is not me. So if you are not going to be serious, and ready for anything, so be it. In that case, you will not have me anymore," Carrie concluded.

After reading her dissertation, it caught me off guard … Not for its literary content, but for the length of the message. This was her longest substantive expression of cantankerous feelings by far. Not one to let this escape my attention, I respond.

"I don't understand how I can be wasting your time Carrie. I have invested over ten months of my life with you, and it has always been for the greater good Carrie."

Carrie conveniently shows signs of dementia. "And what did you invest?"

"I have spent time and money attempting to right a wrong for the fraud and abuse you impose on other victims through the misuse of the internet as you swindle victims out of their hard-earned money," I informed Carrie.

Carrie, while in denial, morphing into the great deceiver that she is, responds. "No way am I involved in anything wrong. You just got yourself into something bad and some hackers, hacked you, and you blame me." As Carrie attempts to implant doubt in my mind while continuing her tirade. "No way is Nate or whoever getting into your computer. I know well and you do too!! You better stop saying it," Carrie demands. "You were involved in entering this new website you tracked and hacked into. Then you blame the hands of Nate," Carrie expressed to me. "That is (expletive) I think, and I know better," Carrie snapped.

"How many times did I accommodate your needs when you asked me to send you the computer and money to Ghana?" I asked.

"What is wrong with that? Did that cause you any pain? Did it hurt you by sending the computer, speakers, and money?" Carrie counters trying to justify their criminal behavior.

I responded with internal displeasure. "Yes, because it was done through deceptive means. You could have been open and honest with me," I declared indifferently.

"No Way!" Carrie replied. "It was done right and it was proper. I have been honest with you, and you never wanted to believe, and I know anytime I am honest you think it is a lie, and that made me never to tell you anything." Carrie concluded, thinking she is somehow making headway with me.

"But Carrie," I said. "You made me send it all the way to Ghana when all the while you were living in New Jersey, across the river from Staten Island."

Carrie, with no remorse and apparently unware she has been implicating herself said to me. "Yes, you are right, and there is nothing wrong with it."

I answered. "I know you live at 8236 Play Money Street in New Jersey."

"Okay, and do you know I travel?" Carrie asked.

Without hesitation I said. "Of course you probably travel. You have "mules" in Ghana who pick up the money sent through Western Union. Along with computers, cell phones, and whatever else you can "scam" from victims. They, (the mules) keep their portion as a commission, and the rest is probably deposited into a bank account over in Ghana under an assumed name for you to withdraw without having to leave the States."

Carrie appears unaffected by the brief just laid out before her. "Whatever," she said. "If you're not ready… I wanted you as a real person, but you never want me like that. So if you are going to talk about organizations, computers, then better we don't speak. I thought you came along with some good news for me." Carrie concluded.

I simply respond by replying. "What does it profit a man if he gains the whole world, but loses his soul? The good news is here; you're just not looking for it." I remark to Carrie.

It seems to me; this is getting to be old hat with a period as the final indentation to Carrie's quick departure from the chat session. Could have hit another nerve, and it's too heavy a burden for her to hang around any longer.

Her departure happened around noon on February 8, 2014, around 12:30 P.M., Carrie decides to come back online to leave another imprint in our talks. I thought to myself, what ammunition is she prepared to welcome me with this time? Apparently, she must have read what had been said after her quick departure.

Carrie corrects me. "No, I didn't go away. You're just not ready to talk. You are not normal," Carrie informs me.

"What do you want to talk about then? And what makes you think I'm abnormal?" I challenge Carrie to elaborate.

Carrie was apparently not happy with the last part of my second question, so she forged forward. "If you are going to talk about that, (abnormal) then you just go and let me be restful." Then she added. "I'm sure you know more of me; that is right, and I hope you accept me being myself and are ready for me," as she gives me a mouthful of venom.

Carrie said she had to leave to make a phone call, even asking permission to go, as she said. "Do you agree, and do you accept me to leave and we'll talk later? Then when I'm on, I want you to be the man I knew when we met." Carrie concludes.

"You have said numerous times we would talk later, but you never come back Carrie."

Carrie replies tersely. "I do not want you to be like a computer tech looking after the system. I want you as a man."

Before Carrie excused herself for nearly three hours, I had mentioned in passing that when doing some additional intelligence on some of her other known sites, I had noticed escort service on the page. I asked her if they were involved in this bad service as well.

Carrie replied. "Shhhh, that's going to get you into trouble!"

So I wrote out a warning to the evil empire that read this message on messenger. "It would be ill-advised that we do not do something foolish; such as sending guns for hire. It could get very messy, just say' in."

It was an awful long phone call. Carrie reappears on messenger at 6:00 P.M., and seems frantic, as she repeats. "Hello. Hello," seven consecutive times. Finally, Carrie asked. "Are you there?" she asked. "I promised you I would be here, and where are you?" Twenty-three minutes later, I wake from a nap. I had apparently fallen asleep. Surprisingly Carrie was still waiting around. In the beginning, the discussion was small talk. Finally, I asked Carrie why she had deceived me."

She replied. "I didn't deceive you, you wanted to be deceived. You never listened to me." Carrie professes'.

"But," I said. "I was listening, watching, seeing, and I sensed," I told Carrie.

That said, Carrie stated. "You just did what you felt like doing, and that deceived your own soul," She claimed. Carrie hinted she was tired and was going to bed. It was 7:02 P.M. That makes it 8:02 P.M. in New Jersey. What Carrie intentionally neglected to mention, was that it was now, "Showtime for the little lady, not bedtime." Carrie usually did her web-camming for two hours. Eight until ten o'clock. She is back to the same old habits as before. Just as a dog returns to its own vomit, Carrie continues to perform for her loyal gathering.

Time and patience have a way of revealing the true nature of someone's heart. Our discussion was to be centered on us, but it soon took a different path as Carrie was now promoting her own charity for an orphanage in all places; Ghana, Kumasi. Yep, were going back into the abyss again on the continent of Africa. When I began questioning her about this noble project, Carrie called me a traitor when I rejected her plea to contribute to the orphan fund. However, it nothing more than another scam.

Carrie accused me of always being a negative person and now a moron. Officially, Yahoo Messenger had seen its last days between Carrie and myself. That does not mean they were not using aliases on other social networks to keep track of my business.

I have not forgotten about @jeremyfamou$187. You will be reading about him and his motley crew in an upcoming Chapter.

Chapter 23

Subjection Rejection

What is truth? What is the truth? What is trust? Who can discern truth?
You hear; yet do not listen. Or listen, therefore, do
not hear. What then does it profit us?
Are you of little Faith, some Faith, no Faith, much Faith; or high Faith?
Horizons bitter herbs life despaired; lack of holiness dead in Faithfulness!
Jim Jacobs

In this Chapter, you will find a compilation of emails written between Henan/Carrie and me over the course of months so that you, the reader can be enlightened by the nature of the dialogue ... To be sure, most of the emails sent between us were exchanged around the latter part of May 2013 through November 2013. Some were complimentary while others were rather; shall we say, manipulating and contentious. Moreover, a couple emails were meant to address Henan/Carrie and co-conspirators about salvation and repentance as I attempt to disciple them about the sinful nature of their criminal behavior.

Dear Henan, Subject: Postal Service

I do not think you should have given the money to the customs agent at the Post Office in Accra the other day without getting the package to take back with you. No money should exchange hands without getting something back in return. You informed me you handed this money over to some Postal Agent. I hope you, at least, received a receipt for the money you handed over. From the time I sent those two packages until it arrived in Accra by express mail; each person who were in receipt of those packages signs their name assuming ownership of the items before they left the postal service premises. If you had to sign something acknowledging they were in customs, it would at least assure it was there when you returned. Since the U.S. Post Office in Trenton was the point of origin; destination Accra, this Post Office knew Accra was its final destination. "I hope for your sake Henan; you know what you're doing!"

Dear Henan, Subject: Return money and computer

It is checkmate or stalemate as this email is drafted for your eyes to see, along with your partners in crime whom, according to unreliable sources has you located in the United Kingdom. You heard sweetheart correctly. Liverpool, Scotland Yard, and the FBI are closing in on your dirty little scam setup. It is just a matter of time now and the walls of Jericho will come tumbling down over the whole lot of you nasty, heartless, greedy, deceitful workers of iniquity.

Known to all, as the Devil and his legion going about like a roaring lion seeking whom they may devour. You have the address Carrie/ Henan, Allen, Bernie, Nate, and all the other misrepresented aliases' you all assume to prevent detection. I strongly suggest you return the computer and other hardware in addition to the money you stole from me. It isn't, "if," but "when" you are arrested and brought before a court of law. I pray you may receive mercy upon sentencing for your crimes.

Dear Henan, Subject: Dependence

Outwardly, this pilgrimage has proven unpredictable. Still, to a lesser degree, unidentifiable. What should we ponder as we continue on this path of the mythological order of malingering acronyms? What defines abbreviations with any logical conclusions? It stymies subsistence; characteristics of bonding, and all that manifests itself in favorable objectivity. This then, darling is the defining moment when smitten by the bite of a rabid bat; attenuation of greater symbolic adoration should, and can be employed. Distinctive flavors of an individual category contemplating factions to, well; somewhere along this plateau of dialogue, obscured by every failed attempt to advance the intended expressed agreement that was within the purposeful heart. Consider for a moment; the wonder of wonders, as we contemplate and consider in your fanatical imaginative mind, what lessons were to be learned from your coming in and going out. Yet, you were hindered, and eyes' obscured by a childlike behavior. Giving thought to what could have been, but its potential lay barren in waste.

Gather then, under the folds of the feathery wings of Mother Goose, who gives her paddlers a sense of comfort and security. Newborn Goslings, as you know, have a tendency to act mischievous from time to time. They scatter about straying further from the protective instincts of their mother, whose job it is to protect and nurture baby Gosling. As baby Gosling strays further from its mother, supposing he would do well without the scrutiny of Momma Goose, whose eyes' are ever vigilant. Always one in every family is baby Gosling. A hardheaded bird that thinks he is able to strut his bold and cavalier nature. In some respects, people are like baby Gosling, going off on their own, separating self from society by leaning on their own understanding.

Soon, however, soaring high above the midnight blue sky was scavenger Eagle with his keen eyes'. The eagle's sights at the ready, it zeros in at the intended target … its prey; hardheaded baby Gosling. Before Mother Goose is able to react, the Eagle came swooping down with breakneck speed, grasp the unsuspecting Gosling in its powerful talons, and whisked it away, assuring the Eagle of another day's meal.

"What does this mean for you and for me, and this clan of misfits, Henan?"

Sometimes men and women allow themselves to be deeply entrenched caught up in the moment to where they lose their bearing. The concept of common sense is frequently cast aside in place of our overwhelming need for greed and desires. There is a want, desire, and a choice to become the typical "scam" artist. As a result, we choose reaction rather than the more common approach godly obedience.

The long reach of your swindling has afflicted many victims with the tentacles of your selfish motives. You have enjoyed banquets you never paid for except with the victim's money. You have grasped the goslings at will to feed your craving for greed and a luxurious lifestyle. You are accustomed enjoying the finer things in life at the expense of others. Your wickedness will soon meet its end. "Fools don't rush in!" No. No. No. Counseling, planning, security, and preparation, they all gather under the folds of Mother Goose's wing to hide from laden fingerprints suspended over troubled sinfulness.

Eliminating foolish pitfalls, and matters of a precautionary pretext; I would conclude whereby if one expects to be successful in the mission statement, there is only one person who oversees' your destiny. Expect me to do nothing all-be-it, unless it is the council of God the Father. I need discernment, and wisdom to know the truth. Since I cannot do anything on my own, God has directed my path. I would not have chosen this odyssey if it were not for the Lord's designed purpose to place me in the way I should go for a reason. To this end it is to put an end to your shady swindling practices, God helping me!

Dear Jim, Subject: Love

I know we have not been around each other that much lately and you doubt my ability to keep our relationship together. I want you to know that I love you so much, and I will be here and there whenever you need me. Our love will always keep growing for each other day by day. I told you today I need six-hundred dollars for an emergency. I need this money to pay for my friend, which we were in terms with when Mom fell ill. I have to remain true to myself and pay this back or break my word, and promises we made. I want to let you know about this, and if you can help Jim! I would be gracious and thankful to you.

I want you. I love the feeling when you are patient; when you express to me, and that is a feeling no other man in the world can ever give me. I love you with all my heart. Just know that I will always be faithful. I know I lied to you. For every notable thing, there is a failure. But I won't leave, because I am yours, and no one else's. No one could ever give me what you and I share because our love is special even though we are very far apart, (not that far if you live in New Jersey). I want us to do everything together. I love you Jim, and I will be yours forever.

Dear Jim, Subject: Miss you, sweetheart

I just want to know what is wrong. I have not heard from you in days now. I hope everything is well with you. Love you. Send an email and let me know all is well Jim. Have a blessed day. Love you, Henan.

Dear Henan, Subject: Miss you?

What is the meaning of this darling? You have not missed anything! You know and I know everything that's been going on the past couple of days. After all, you were there when "Tinker Bell," put some more viruses' on both my computers to prevent me from obtaining information about your highly organized and sophisticated criminal enterprise which has its tentacle's reaching across all continent's and boundaries in the world. All "Tinker Bell" is accomplishing is a short-term interruption. However, he cannot stop me from exposing the truth about the nasty, sinful adventures of exploiting women for financial gain against their will. Keeping women in captivity to perform over the internet is the lowest form of human dignity one can stoop to ingratiate their need for money and greed. Not to mention your active participation in scams.

I find it dispirited, immoral, heartless, and disgusting. Frankly, Henan/ Carrie, it makes me want to hurl knowing you are a partaker in this unclean exploitation of a woman's anatomy. I will stop at nothing to see this activity through until something is done to put your criminal entity out of business. The more I discover, the greater my resolve to disrupt and hopefully lead the authorities to the locations where these women are staged like cattle to be used as subjects of entertainment to satisfy the male libido.

You may be able to slow this man down, but in the process; I am gaining more and more intelligence, and insightful feedback into this criminal organization. Tinker Bell may well continue to disrupt, and write programs to obtain access to my computers, and infecting them with viruses,' but in so doing he is allowing me to advance my computer literacy. They may very well discover that I too am able to play their games. The rope cuts on both ends. Mine remains secure on my end, what about yours? Do you think you can continue doing this without impunity Tinker Bell, and you Princess? An emphatic No! No! No!

Dear Henan, Subject: Reality, decisive moment

Princess, as I compose this email, I expect no less a response from you. I have come to terms that you are under the authority and control of your pimps and that they are doing their utmost to disrupt and prevent me from learning, and obtaining information on their criminal entity. Just so they are entirely clear on this matter, I am not operating as a lone wolf in the wild, as it shall be made perfectly clear to everyone. The problem as I see this unfolding, there is this notion that they think they are far more superior in intellect than the rest of us clodhoppers. They have this mentality that they are untouchable; immune from the long reach of law enforcement. It is a foolish man's way of thinking. Worse yet, is the perception that I am working alone.

History is clear. The greedy, the proud, and the egocentric always get caught in the end. This is a time consuming, information gathering process that focuses on illegal activities by one entity. The mission statement is to get the elite players. When the appropriate time arrives, the dominoes will begin to collapse, and history will prevail. It is unfortunate Carrie that you and others could very well be pawns in their evil schemes. We are very disturbed, and disgusted by the information we have amassed during this investigation of Raja and his cronies. These heartless criminals need to be in prison for the remainder of their lives.

I have always thought very highly of you Princess and wish we could end this nightmare as I speak. However, we must be thorough and concise before we move. Everything communicated to you has its purpose. Sorry if I offended you in the process but it is all part of the master plan.

Dear Jim, Subject: Reality, decisive moment

Thanks for everything you have been doing. I am happy you asked for forgiveness for some things you said in the past. It is always a pleasure to hear from you. I hope you have a wonderful time. I have missed talking with you and have always tried to be connected. Hope you have a good day, and email me anytime and I will get back to you.

NOTE: Some of my emails to Carrie were designed to keep her guessing, hoping, and confused as other players in this collaborated entity. They never had merit other than as a strategic tool to keep Carrie engaged so I could continue gathering information on them. However, sometimes it appeared Carrie had sensed a possible vulnerability during chat sessions and would exploit it, using it as a bartering tool to bait me for additional monetary gains.

Dear Carrie, Subject: No more "scams" from where I stand

That which is hidden in darkness; will ultimately shine in the light. Secrets buried for a time however, the Lord discovers all thoughts, and deeds at His Sovereign pleasure. Carrie, you may have succeeded for a brief interlude playing on my emotions with all your empty words, but my heart eventually reveals all. The material goods you so deceitfully and skillfully swindled from me, and the expenditures used to process these items to send to your rogue location is not considered a loss as far as I am concerned. You did not steal, lie, and deceive me, you did these wicked things to God your creator. God will become your Judge when you folks face Him on that final and dreadful day to give an account of your sins. True repentance is by calling upon the name of Jesus Christ as your Lord and Savior. It is the ONLY thing that stands between you, Heaven, and Hell. You are evildoers. Lord forbid when he says to you on that day. "Depart from me evildoer of iniquity, for I never knew you." And He will cast you into the lake of fire where there will be wailing and gnashing of teeth; tormented for all eternity.

Dear Carrie, Subject: The Long Goodbye

The title is most fitting for the occasion. I trust you received my Twitter message. I told you I was going to email you later this afternoon. I am a man of my word. After tomorrow, you and Raja will not be hearing from me whether it is on your website, Twitter, or Yahoo Messenger. It will be a time of rejoicing for everyone I'm sure, as freedom comes knocking at your door. As far as I am concerned, my job here is finished. I will be offline for quite some time. It would be nice if I could tell you of my plans, but it is a foregone conclusion that it will ever happen.

However, I am going to give you a summation on our long-standing journey together. I may be able to suggest without equivocation that in some circle's you may become a household name. After all, this was your goal was it not? Wasn't it an obsession of yours to become famous someday? You are already knee deep in other people's money. However, to have worldwide recognition would be a whole new realm. As for Nathaniel and his band of evil obstructionist; he has left an imprint engrained in this memory of mine, or so it would seem. Manipulation of the mind that employs tactics such as delusions and deceit becomes the lie, and thus the sin. Your fight is not with me, but with yourselves. Beginning inside where everyone has a heart and a soul.

The apparent gratification you and your husband seek by defrauding victims, and your guiltless involvement in pornography, along with your group of misfits is illegal, and duly noted as evil. Everyone believes in a God. However, the question begs for an answer. "Which God are you serving?"

Joseph Henry Hankins was a crying preacher. As he was preaching one Sunday, he noticed a young man in the upper balcony of the church opening and closing his hymnal as they were singing. After Joseph had completed his sermon, he asked those who were not saved, to come forward, and receive repentance and the Lord's grace. The young man walked out of the church while others went to the front of the pulpit.

A few weeks later Pastor Hankins discovered the young man who had left the church early, was gravely ill. Knowing of the young man's illness, Joseph went to the man's hospital bedside to visit him. He asked the young man. "Why did you not come forward to confess repentance and receive God's saving grace? The man looked at him with a determined look, and replied, "I'm dead inside!" "I chose to continue serving the pleasures of sin, instead of surrendering my way of life; rather than serve and trust Christ as my Lord and Savior." At hearing this, the preacher began to weep and pray for the man's soul until he died.

Without a remedy, there are no second chances. Without a remedy, destiny awaits us all. Without repentance, man will find his eternal destiny in pain, anguish, and separation from glory. "I can already picture in my mind, (perception excluded) Nate's response and his merry band of thieves … and let's not forget you, Carrie." Seems the majority of folks think time is on their side. Not!

"Someday, but not today," you say. "I got plenty of time for that Jesus stuff," you say. For sure, there is right and wrong. Many probably do not know they are dead in their sins if, and unless they have Christ Jesus. Moreover, wisdom along with discernment trumps the foolishness of Man's heart. You do not answer to me, but someday you will answer to Jesus Christ.

Dear Carrie, Subject: Clarifying the Long Goodbye

Although I am disappointed, and I have been affected by this pilgrimage in more ways than I care to embrace, I realized from the onset that it goes with the territory. The last dot in this Chapter of my life has seen its days. Carrie, I am of the opinion that certain phrases or words in the initial email where you had trouble interpreting the meaning. Well, I fear you have not taken my words very seriously. As a result, you may think all Scripture Jim is preaching to me means nothing. If that is the consensus of the group, then you are to be most pitied. I know you are smart and intelligent Carrie, so don't scream incompetence as a defense. When I told you, it all begins inside the body… Your thoughts, words, and deeds; all have their beginnings stemming from the heart and soul of a person. From the heart, our tongue speaks. Often, when our heart has not corresponded with the brain, we find ourselves getting into trouble.

If you do not believe that there is a higher authority; a Creator, who breathed life into you, gave you form and gender. If you are not in agreement that a higher power created you, then I have breathed these words in vain. However, believing there is a God who controls everything in the universe, including good and evil, and since He is the potter and we are the clay, God has it within himself to do whatever His will is for his creation.

437

He has known us from eternity past. God knew beforehand what you and Nate were going to do. It's true for all his creation. Since man was born into sin, he/she has that sin nature in them. God does not make you sin. He gives you that choice. Therefore, you have two options. Do "good" or "evil." Christ came into the world as God and man. (In the flesh) He was without blemish. (Sin) He was the perfect sacrificial lamb that died on the cross; subservient for all humankind, making atonement for man's sin.

Jesus covers the sins of all humanity who believe in Him. He who Confesses' with his tongue, that he is a sinner and in need of the Savior Christ Jesus for salvation. (Deliverance from the power and effects of sin) If your heart is pure in confessing your sins before God, the Holy Spirit will enter your body and begin good works in you, making you more Christ-like.

So you see Nate and Carrie, I take saving soul's very seriously. Should Nate decide to make light of my words that is fine. He is not rejecting me. He is only hurting his own cause with his stiff-necked wickedness.

Dear Jim, Subject: Clarifying the Long Goodbye 2

Well, thanks for such a mentally and spiritually challenging message with words of truth. I am pleased Jim. I will copy this message for Nate so he can read it. Who knows what will happen after he reads it? Only God knows! Well, I'm sorry that I was dishonest. I didn't really want to. I just didn't want you to know what the truth was because I really like you and was falling for you.

Jim, one last thing I wish to ask you and that is to help me with eight-hundred dollars. Please do not say that I am rich, and don't think too much. I need this to pay for a car from that accident I had. I crashed into someone's vehicle. Dear, I'm pleading with you to do the best you can to get this. I really need it now, so please do for me. I know I may be crazy not feeling depressed to ask, but you are the only one I feel I can ask this from, and I am not testing you either. Just do the best you can for me as you can right now.

I am a sinner and with you, some bad habits of me have been abolished. I know with you I can change for the best, but it is all the matter of time with you, Jim. You say such wonderful Biblical words which when I read, sometimes I feel like tearing. I regret some things I'm doing, but I'm sure in time I will be with you. Things will change for the best. I am Roman Catholic but have not been to church for a very long time. I still pray. Well, I just want to say thanks for being in my life and teaching me with what you know. Changing from worse to bad, I'm sure I will be from bad to good with you.

Dear Carrie, Subject: Another Scolding

"That was a rather quick exit from messenger this morning without a peep. The other thing left on the platter was the email I never received from you. You or Nate are playing this to the bone. You are both cautious, and very cunning to say the least. By now, I realize the games people play. Always have, probably always will. Nevertheless, the game will be taking other paths here very shortly. My dear Carrie of many names, and identities over these past months. "For shame. Shame on you!"

Carrie, I am not a Saint. Far be it for me to insult my Lord with such a proclamation. As the Apostle Paul wrote in Romans, "I am the chief-of-sinners, wretched man that I am." The difference between Nate and me is my total and complete dependence each day on the redeeming features of Jesus Christ. I am continually in prayer asking for mercy and forgiveness. I must be mindful as well, that I must grow and change my ways from the temptations of sin. Nate and his band of alleged criminals know the wrong they do, but refuse to change.

God will surely harden their hearts, even more, thereby missing God's grace and receiving an invitation to live in Paradise for all eternity. Their soul condemned to Hell, existing in total darkness, separated from God. Their idols are apparently pleasure, greed, money, and corruption. You have sold your souls to Satan. Why? For things; things that rust, rot, and disintegrate. They lose value over time. Your ears have obviously been sealed shut by our creator. You think you are wise in your own eyes', but your feet run to do wickedness; always!

Dear Jim, Subject: The Long Goodbye

Yes, darling, the last time on my site, Nate was in charge, and he was the one who did not allow you in my room to talk with me. I had no choice. And, no I do not want you to send the money to New Jersey. Why will you not send it to Ghana? I know you have so many reasons, and I know how much you care about my safety and my welfare these past eight months. I really do sweetheart. However, please change your mind and get me some money. Do your best on this journey for me Jim. I do not want to beg you for the money because it is just bad. I know you Jim and I sure know you can do something better for me now. Hope you have a good weekend.

Dear Carrie, Subject: The hoax

Today, I find myself in a rather awkward position in some respects. I dread writing and submitting it via email. However, under the circumstances I concluded, it was most fitting and proper to do so. Carrie, as you are aware, I have been following, and monitoring you, Nate, and other evildoers for the past nine months. Convinced I was being scammed by you and your organization. I felt you were a willing participant. Today, some government officials visited me from the local FBI office and IC3. They stayed about twenty minutes or thereabouts; explaining to me that I had been mistaken.

Further, they told me I am investigating the wrong people. They informed me that they had completed surveillance on you and your husband, and determined you were reasonable people operating a legitimate website. The FBI told me what I was mistakenly observing were pictures of Nigerians and Ghana scammer's who stole video's and images from your site and were using your profile pictures and video's as a diversionary instrument to swindle victims, including me of course, out of money and material goods.

Honey, to say I am sorry in my feeble attempts to smother you with apologies would not do justice to all the insults and accusations I brought upon your reputation. Including Nate, Jessup, models, or anyone affiliated with your business. To reach out to you with some sense of comfort would be inadequate for all the pain and disappointment I have caused you, your husband, and his circle of friends. I am very disgusted, and ashamed at this point in my life for the insensitivity and behavior I subjected you to as this is unforgivable. I should have listened to you. "I'm very sorry Princess."

NOTE: There wasn't an ounce of truth in that email. This was sent to Carrie to serve a twofold purpose. To see if she would let her guard down, and perhaps by using the cause and effect ahead of time, see if Carrie would solicit more money from me. I had all the information I needed anyway so you could say I was playing mind games with her. She will ask for a smartphone Galaxy S4 around Christmas to be sent too … That's right, Ghana.

Dear Jim, Subject: The Long Goodbye

I am pleased to receive your email. (I would be happy too) I knew why you wouldn't understand when I told you, and explained things. It is magnificent now that you are back with me. I have forgiven you. I hope you have a splendid day. We will talk again soon; Okay?

Dear Carrie, Subject: Deceiver

Did you really believe I would be insulted by you for your lying, deceiving, and dramatics yesterday, even though you made a brief appearance on video thinking I'm talking to you in real time? Your evil, conniving crime family used an old video shoot of you to leave the impression that I was talking to you to live and in real time. "Not, not!" I mimicked. "Who do you think you are dealing with here? Are you convinced I am an unskilled "clippie-the-clown?" If you believe this to be true, your nautical compass of morphogenetic genes is defective. You are nothing more than morsels of human evil. You folks are not even worthy to occupy my time and space. There is no hope for the hopeless. You have offended my God, who is the Father of Abraham, Isaac, and Jacob. You stiff-necked, rebellious children of evil will surely come to ruin."

Then, to circumvent the notion that I am irresponsible, dumber than dumb; knowing full well how you use these smartphones. You have just proven how brazen and foolish the depths to which your collaborators have sunk. There isn't one of you misguided and misaligned characters who will have dominion over me. Your acts of deceitfulness are disposed of semantically idiomatic expressions filled to the brim with judgment. "Do you want the smartphone?" Fine, I will come to New Jersey and give it to you personally. Then we can break bread together like one happy family. Look, listen, and learn, or deal with the impending storm.

Chapter 24

Guilt by Association

They all call me by name that I am; yet am not!
Employ resources; untangle this web of mystery these scheming plots.
Fantasy, deception, deceit … No matter; you're on radar; you're in sight.
Cunning criminals awaken with subtle eyes'. Seeking as when the vine is ripe.
Jim Jacobs

Who among us could ever fathom average American citizens swindled by tech savvy computer thief's bent on separating innocent victims of their personal possessions and money! However, they've been here for years, and unless there is a pro-active effort by our government, and law enforcement agencies, this evil … mean-spirited activity is going to continue unabated. The author is not implying that police are not doing anything to apprehend the influx of scammers. However, they currently do not have the workforce or the resources to do surveillance and undercover operations to slow this unsavory trend.

I for one would be curious to know what our government on Capitol Hill and the President are doing about this pandemic. Educating the American public on how to avoid this fraudulent activity is not working. Is it feasible to think they have no understanding of the information technology age? Rather than commit resources; namely our Armed Forces in countries which dislike us. The money we have spent and continue to support these countries could be put to better use to combat drugs, illegal border crossings, human sex slave trafficking and scamming, rather than taking a reactive approach employed presently. We've taken one step forward and two steps back far too long now.

The government insists that by deploying troops overseas, it creates a sense of security. I beg to differ with this do-nothing legislative body. We have a National Security problem right here, right now; the wounds are bleeding profusely.

The illegal trafficking of drugs and drug use in this fruit cocktail of moral decay has, and continues to be on the rise in the United States. When women have to resort to web-camming on the internet to pay their college tuition, suggests there is something amiss. When women profess to earn more money undressing in front of the camera flaunting their anatomy to a group of perverted males, than they can earn at minimum wage jobs, then this is shameful and unacceptable. Something has gone awry, and disproportionately wrong with how the government derives at a minimum wage scale. This is a very contentious; legitimate grievance, and should rally American's to voice their protest against injustices such as this.

I propose we all live in Appalachian, slums, be homeless, kidnapped, and sold as human sex slaves under the control and authority of low-life pimps. Maybe then, we as a society will better appreciate the plight of those who are prisoners against their will.

This hits a nerve every time I've had to vent my disappointment and sadness at this countries state-of-affairs. Leaders lead. Stalemate stagnates. Legislators legislate. Our Creator entrusted our lawmakers to govern with wisdom. They are to use the gifts given to them by God to accomplish what he has ordained. Congress is held to a higher standard as are all elected officials "Everyone to whom much was given, of him much will be required, and from him to whom they entrusted much, they will demand the more." Luke, Chapter 12: 48. Self-interest results in self-destruction. Is Washington the solution, or part of the problem? Most Americans would say they are the problem. I am inclined to agree with the majority opinion.

The words imparted in the previous paragraph are meant to ruffle feathers. They have a greater value; becoming a mouthpiece for victims victimized through internet use. After all, isn't this just one of many reasons our elected officials were voted into the Executive, and Legislative branches of our government? To preserve and protect the Constitution of the United States, and its citizens, from foreign and domestic threats. But our voices have been silenced by special interest groups and lobbyist. Money fuels the foolish while wisdom works its will. When the legislator's, (Congressmen, Senators, and the Presidential candidate's begin campaigning for office next year, I will be listening with great interest what main topics will fuel the debates. Will cybercrime, and internet pornography be on any of the candidate's agenda? Does anyone expect human slave trafficking or spousal abuse to be on the front burner of any candidate? Of course, I would not be replete without mentioning abortion, and same-sex marriage. Our founding Father's governed this country using Gods moral laws. Without Gods Word as our moral compass, we are headed in the direction that will destroy this nation. God's wrath will be swift, and certain.

Sin is a sin. Right and wrong is alive and well. "The Word," is the Divine, Holy inspired word of God. You cannot put a spin on the written word of God to accommodate special interest's agenda. You cannot add to it, or erase God-breathed Holy Scripture. Was I obscene, obstinate, or ostracizing women liberators, and gay rights folks? On the contrary. Keep in mind; despite what one may think, or believe, your body is "not your own," but belongs to the Father, who created you. Moreover, God didn't sanction fornication. It has always been, and always will be an abomination in the Lord's sight. If you have an issue with this, take it before your Father who is in Heaven. I worship Him and Him only. You don't have the right to murder babies. These babies were designed and created since eternity past.

I want to include a little more history on Carnal Carrie's two other siblings, Isabella, and Debra. Sometime around May 2013, there was a model contest called, "wheels and deals" involving Debra and her sister Isabella, aka. Sally. All three sisters encouraged their fan base to vote for the two girls. They were able to convince some of their fans to vote over, and over ensuring a lock-in for the grand prize of five-thousand dollars, for the most beautiful models of the contest. One of their die-hard supporters was somehow able to stack the deck for them to assure they won. If memory serves me well, Nate Raja took photographs of the girls in different wardrobes and poses, with a vintage automobile serving as the prop. Their efforts paid dividends and the women won the contest and the five-thousand-dollar prize. I informed the reader previously that Debra and Sally, twins, who suffer from anxiety and panic disorders, are prone to migraine headache's preventing them at times from web-camming. Debra was web-camming on www.pepper.com while Sally's site was unknown until I saw her on www.legoflambcams.com.

While I was continuing intelligence gathering on the internet, webcam prostitute's at www.legoflambcams.com had been gaining in popularity. As I was scrolling down row upon row of prostitute's, I came across a model who had assigned herself the username, "Sally." This name and face looked familiar. So I went to her room and had a little chat with her. When her video cam opened, she was on her smartphone talking to Nate. I didn't know this until I typed her a chat message. The first question I posed to Sally started out with an innocent question so as not to raise too many eyebrows.

"Do you know Carnal Carrie?" I inquired of Sally.

She interrupted her conversation briefly with Nate to answer. Sally had audio on so I was able to hear her reply.

"Yes, I do. As a matter of fact, I am talking to her husband right now. I just saw her this past week," she said.

"Is his name Nathaniel by any chance?" asking Sally innocently.

Sally, like quick draw McGraw said. "How do you know his name?" She inquired out of curiosity?

By now, I'm getting an adrenaline rush. Thinking I may have hit another "mother lode" to include in the manuscript. With renewed energy, I tweaked the conversation up another notch. Responding to Sally's question, I said. "Nathaniel Raja and I are close, friends, good buddies," I informed Sally.

When Sally saw the last name Raja typed on the computer screen, her eyes' opened wide, and with a gasp of surprise and wonder; cupping her hand to her mouth, she wasted little time in asking me a follow-up question.

"Where did you get Nate's last name?" Sally anxiously asked

Moreover, she is relaying this information back to Nate while she is awaiting my response. I am about to raise the bar another level before Sally decides she's had enough and ban me from her room. Therefore, I took advantage of the opportunity in the event I was banned.

"Sally, if this is the same Nathaniel Raja who resides at 8236 Play Money St. Summerville, N.J., then, yes, I have known him for about a year now." Plastering Nathaniel's address on Sally's chat room page sent her into orbit like a rocket taking off from the Kennedy Space Center. She went into a fit of rage.

"You stupid (expletive) whoever you are! Why did you put his address out there for all to see? You haven't the brain or common sense of an idiot," Sally shouted.

I replied. "What is all the fuss about? It took me nearly eight months to locate him."

Sally was back on the phone with Nathaniel, I expect, to inform him what I had said. Nate, without any prodding, must have told Sally to turn off her cam and leave. Since that brief encounter with Sally, I have only seen her and Debra together on LOLC during a few other occasions. The sisters look very much alike, and they should. After all, I did say they were twins. This places all three in the pornography business doing live video cams, but not everyone knows they are siblings. Guilt by Association. I allege all three are involved heavily in internet fraud while Nate calls the shots.

I also observed that folks who follow Carnal Carrie on her Twitter account, also followed Debra and Sally. I am not familiar with Sally's username for Twitter. However, I do have Debra's username for Twitter. @DebraElly. Of equal significance, as I was reviewing some of Debra's twitter messages, I came across Dan Terror, @danterror who continues to inspire (don't take this literally) me with his bold claim to have married Carnal Carrie. A follower of Debra, Dan reminds her of a photograph where Dan informs Debra.

"Here is another photograph for you Debra, you are on the right and the original Carrie is on the left, or don't you remember this picture with the original Carrie?" Dan says, mocking her. "Notice the "T" on Carrie's necklace sweetie," he said. On Debra's Tweeter, account there is displayed a group picture of all three sisters' with brimming faces. Debra runs with a couple close friends named Alley and Jenny. She mentions Jenny's name frequently because Debra had mentioned the two of them were going to share a place together.

Debra accidently backed her car into a wooden fence resulting in extensive damage to her car. No problem though. She just went out and purchased herself a new Ford Mustang. In April 2012, Debra was ranked 5th and eventually took top honors as "Pepper's" number one webcam prostitute. Debra boasts of being frugal when purchasing groceries. Using coupons, Debra claims to have received an eight-dollar return from the cashier after one of her shopping sprees. She also claims to have been on the Jackie Farrow show dressed (expletive). After the show, the two girls stepped outside to have a picture taken with Jackie.

Let us examine the last few paragraphs together. There was never an agenda on the author's behalf to glorify, approve, or otherwise endorse this sinful lifestyle. Rather, the manifestation is a manifesto declaring the intentions and motives of three radical women publicly. Beauties and the Beast shall we say! Here we have three sisters, Carrie, Sally, and Debra. Sally and Debra are about five-years younger than Carnal Carrie. I ask you the reader, what the odds are of all three sisters stepping into the arena of pornography. Furthermore, what is the probability all three girls could be involved in an elaborate scheme to defraud victims on the internet? Then, what is the probability friends they socialize with, may somehow be involved in this high-stakes internet fraud activity? Is it too far-fetched? If true, this would probably make for good news and a movie tastefully done.

Carnal Carrie's website does not generate enough income to sustain her website, so how do we offset our losses? The way their operation is set-up, it would be nearly impossible to determine their criminal intentions had it not been for "Providence" becoming an ally for the author. Much of the intelligence was based solely on trial and error. I never allowed myself to get too discouraged but encouraged only. Because there was always a voice in this soul of mine, telling me to move forward full throttle.

Going through my notes and pages upon pages of Carnal Carrie in numerous locations, settings, and poses, I still found it incomprehensible that people in Ghana or Nigeria would single out Carnal Carrie from the myriad of models posted on the internet that the African countries could use in their scams. Another search site I used to identify scammers was found on, www.delphifaq.com. This search engine shows Carrie and Sally in tandem as swindling victims? What is surprising is the absence of Debra's picture. There are claims they were stolen from scammer's located in Nigeria. The question then begs for reasoning. Why didn't the Nigerians take her most recent pictures as well? I'm certain Carnal Carrie will have a logical answer for this epiphany, but I think not.

There is a model, (very generous with the word, "model") who goes by the name of Patti Putt. Patti is attached at the hip of Carnal Carrie. They have made video's together in the past. Patti is on the scammer's list as well. Patti's name is mentioned for obvious reasons. Other victim's, who use the internet, allege that they too had been swindled by Patti Putts. It appears I am not the only person who has been scammed by women using their occupations as models to "scam" innocent victims. A man, who preferred to remain anonymous, wrote an untitled letter meant for Patti exposing personal information he discovered about her and posted it on the internet. Since it has relevance, I have chosen to share this message with my viewers.

Who is this Mrs. Valerie Pamelosa? aka. Patti Putts, pornstar, cam model, married to Jimmy the money Pamelosa, Cedar Springs, Illinois? You have the nerve to try and have someone arrested and prosecuted because they revealed your real name and information. Like their obligated to protect your alias. You question their right to do so. Well, what gives you, and your husband the right to make a video about this person you're trying to prosecute without his permission, and then calling him crazy, bipolar, and dysfunctional? This person never released your identities until after you and your husband made that video. Did you forget the apology letter you sent this person apologizing and regretting that you and Jimmy made it? That you felt ganged up on, and you just wanted to tell about the people involved? How about this person ganged up on by you, and your husband?

And not just the two of you, but your pornstar friend Carnal Carrie, Allen Simple, H VandePots, Claytin7, Adam Lemon, and countless others. Right, but it's all about Patti. You were asked on October 3, to remove it, but you did not do it until Thanksgiving, and only then for your benefit. You asked him to remove all tweets and postings; indeed! You started this, but you want the court to think you are the angel … an innocent victim! Who in your group made those two accounts, attempting to impersonate the person you were trying to prosecute. Well, this person went to the FBI, and the account was deleted very quickly. You and that husband of yours know who was behind this. Was it you, Carnal Carrie, your husband, Allen Simple, H VandePottjes, Claytin7? Really! That is the crime, and you know who did it! Take it easy, Ms. innocent!!!

The author intentionally excluded the objectionable language the letter contained for obvious reasons. This letter was a re-blog from the originator whose name shall remain anonymous. Patti Putts has approximately 24,000 followers, 10,000 tweets, and a following of 104. When you have a ratio of more followers than following, this usually indicates she is operating in secrecy.

Therefore, with well-intended virtuous contemplations, made known with definitive new acclamations, I report to you, that Patti Putts, aka., Valerie Pamelosa, and her husband Jimmy the Money, as persons of interest. For it is not just I who should boldly announce their convoluted encumbrances affecting the liberties of the blameless, but other voices have reverberated through the corridors of time and have charged her with alleged criminal intent to defraud them of their monetary funds through the use of the internet. Here is what we shall reveal about this couple through discovery.

The couple resides at 107 Tomahawk Hawk Lane, Cedar Springs, Illinois 51081-9013. Jimmy's age is listed as between 35-39 while Valerie's age is unknown. People search has listed Englewood, Lake Shore, and Stone Brook, Illinois as the previous residence's'. Valerie has one child. Jimmy, Patti's husband, also known as Jimmy stumblez, is believed to operate two websites, www.sloppygirls.com, and www.blacksin.com. Each features adult sexually oriented content. Jimmy needs remedial education in English. When language is immersed in expositions of disgusting filth originating from the heart; then Jimmy has a problem. It doesn't allow for a normal conversation. Jimmy's profile suggests an individual who is proud, arrogant, and callous. Apparently he seizes' every opportunity to humiliate the opposite gender.

When I surveyed the extremes of advertisement in the adult sex industry, a typical ad would point undeviatingly towards the glamorous and sensual desires of the female anatomy. As an example, many ads would read something along this venue: "Multi-Model Site, MeArt. com: What can be more erotic than for beautiful teens posing naked. A site full of them, that's what! Meddle captures this niche perfectly with high-resolution photos that show every beautiful curve and every innocent face in stunning quality while all movies can be displayed in four different forms. Jimmy the Money placed this on the website and received forty-eight-hundred plus views by sick individuals.

Under the categories of "sloppygirls.com," it boasts of four (4) Adult Websites, Solo Model Sites (3), Multi Model Sites (1), Affiliate Sites (1), and Movies (36). Whoever endeavors to remain in denial about what we as a nation are feeding our children who are in the possession of a computer with access to the internet, will, in all likelihood see popups appear on the screen tempting them to one of these sites. Within the boundaries of human inquisitiveness of different desires and our sinful fleshly invitations, children will venture into the abyss. When this abominable sex industry willfully influences the mind of young 18-19-year-old adolescents to disrobe in front of cameras with empty promises, this is merely playing on emotions by pimps. To falsely suggest this is a lucrative future in the entertainment (smut) industry while we slumber in complacency is inexcusable. To remain on the sidelines, where manifestations ultimately fueled with what is viewed as reasonable, quickly degrades to unreasonable.

Let's allow for some abnormal genetic correlations into the mindset of degrading, unacceptable behavioral traits of one, Jimmy the Money Pamelosa, @jeremyfamou$187, aka., Jimmy Pamelosa, as he describes the women he prostitutes out on the internet and who knows where else.

This then is Jimmy/Jeremy and the rest of his marauding pimps who associate with him. And don't lose focus on Jimmy for his interest in www.sloppygirls.com. Jimmy/Jeremy uses his Twitter account to keep his followers up-to-date on websites to log onto, names of models, and a brief description of what the pervert will be feasting their evil eyes' upon.

Jeremy tweets to @kinkytstainpink. What an (expletive) on this (expletive) babe! Cute smile, great (expletive)what else could you ask for? Next Jeremy tweets another one of his girls. @meetmelady. Toe Tooting Misfit looking sexy in her short shorts, bikini top, and cowboy boots. But don't (expletive), @pattiputts. Jimmy, the husband of Patti, describes her as, (expletive) Imagine how corrupted humanity's heart has fallen to pimp your own wife for perverts to lust with passion over the female anatomy. It reeks of immorality. This is in direct opposition from what is good, true, and morally righteous.

Happy Halloween; (expletive) excite Patti! Tight latex pants and (expletive) is bound in (expletive). Jimmy sends a tweet to @sassysins, Happy Halloween sexy Sardine dressed up as a sexy rabbit for Halloween. Cam show is live now! See her on www.manymany.cams.net. Jimmy hints to his followers about what, @kellypain is now wearing. Sexy black dress… Hot and (expletive) blonde Kelly is looking so beautiful in this dress and she wastes no …

Tall Red Boots. Satin looks so (expletive) Sexy with those tall boots while wearing glasses with that tight dress. Red Beach Girl, Teen Tabitha in her red and black bikini shows off her feet, and (expletive).

Body Double: What an (expletive) mess pimples has created. Paint covering everything on this teens body. Who is Jeremy? Jeremy is @ jeremyfamou$187 mentioned in an earlier Chapter.

Within the mechanics of sensibility, while gravitating towards discernment, it was purposeful, given the nature of the strange language used by Jimmy to refrain from the inclusion of noxious substance emanating from a heart void of ethical standards. Jimmy is only one of hundreds like him who are actively pursuing the sex industry that they have become desensitized to. They have become as dead soul's lacking any understanding of right or wrong. Deficient in decorum, Jimmy regards women as property. A reminder to the author of the actual autobiography of, "twelve-years a slave."

Women are nothing more than an object of his and other like-minded men for their uncompromising selfish will, to lust after, use, and inflict low self-esteem on the female soul. A "cash cow," that does no more than increase Jimmy and Patti Pamelosa's wealth as they prey upon, and seek young teens to do their bidding. If I were the parents of these two misguided souls, I would be duty bound to hang my head in shame and do everything within my power to close down this foreboding pimping empire and remove the child from their home. How parents allow their children to continue in this abomination to thrive unabated raises a multitude of red flags.

We've indulged ourselves with an informational overview of Jimmy, so now we will redirect our minds and venture into another realm of the Abyss by focusing our attention on the other half of this wicked enterprise; model Patti Putts, aka., Valerie Pamelosa. Several victims have identified Valerie, as a person of interest affiliated with organized fraud along with her husband, Jimmy the Money. With this information availing itself to us, I most assuredly cannot rule out others in Jimmy's circle as team players. The left hand always knows what the right hand is doing because they are paired like doves.

I created a bogus username so I could twitter Patti Putts. I choose @ rajacatnip as my twitter username. On September 2013, contact was initiated between Valerie Pamelosa and I about what was discovered relating to their suspected and alleged illegal criminal activity according to other like-minded Twitter users.

@pattiputts. "How is the "scam" business doing Patti? Money must be hard to come by. You and Carnal Carrie are involved in defrauding innocent people. Most if not the majority of the models on your website have "scams" going because there is too much competition, and you are not earning enough money." Refer to www.scammerslist.com, and see if carnal Carrie isn't shown on the scam listing over 100 times. Are you going to tell me that all these people are lying about your "scam" activity? Even your husband is using another Twitter account. He goes by the username @jeremyfamou$187 and has his greedy paws on this operation. This puts him front and center as an accomplice. I see where you also use several different Twitter accounts. @pattimoney. Almost like Jimmy with the money symbol at the end of jeremy$.

Patti's Twitter supporters were in denial, suggesting how I am mistaken about her and Carnal Carrie as "scam" swindlers. The only interest driving them in this whole affair that benefits the pervert is protecting their favorite cam model from being exposed and their operation shut down permanently. Or, they are part of this swindling group protecting their interests.

Patti re-tweets a return reply to me, @rajacatnip, as she initiates damage control. "It's like if I took YOUR picture and posted it under a profile I created, and said it was me in the photo, and my username was Billy Bob. What is so hard to understand about this? Carnal Carrie, the real person, the actual girl in the photo is NOT the scammer. But, the people USING her photograph ARE! It's not because we are the scammers, but to show you what photos and information the scammers are using." Patti suggested I Google romance "scams" and see how many of them include her name and pictures because people USE my stuff too. "Carnal Carrie is also on the list because she is one of the models PEOPLE USE PICTURES OF! "Say, Raja, don't you have anything better to do than create an account to spew ignorant (expletive)?

Continuing with the people's business I, with all worthy and honorable intentions made a calculated decision to twitter Carnal Carrie to vent the disdain cluttering between the pages of my mind.

@carnalcarrie. "You can forget messenger chat as well; all who harbor criminal intent in your wicked souls. All you do is lie, lie, and lie some more! Cheat, steal, deceive, destroy; you vicious, heartless creatures that you are. Henan/Carrie, you are even more contemptuous than first thought. You do not have a desire to seek salvation, so I reckon you will end up in Hell suffering in agony for all eternity.

"Satan the evil one has you on a one-way ticket to the abyss. It is not if, but when you and Nate breathe your last here on earth. Thumb your nose at God now. Suffer torment later foolish people."

"Hey, Tinker Bell, (addressing Nathaniel) you think you are going to continue getting away with all these evil shenanigans? Not on my watch you don't! I am more determined than ever to see you both brought to justice. Do you really believe blocking me from Twitter is hurting my feelings? … Get a life son! Oh, and the offer remains Tinker Bell. Come to my residence one and all. You are never going to escape the clutches of this outstretched arm while I'm still living.

You have all done me dirty and nasty! You are all heartless, evil, scheming children of Satan. It is shameful! And Tinker Bell, you and your pimp friends will have to do better than the changes you installed on Apache. Apache.ht access compared to the "URL?" Come; come! Not even a mark of cleverness on your part. Carnal, why didn't you tell me Nate was relocating with a 301 redirect? We continue keeping dirty little secrets and lies … At the very least you are consistent in that category. It was nice chatting with everyone on Twitter.

Robin Fletcher, @hatefulman38 was very direct with Patti in August 2013 when he tweeted Patti about their alleged scamming activity. His tweets are brief but to the point. Now if I could format and condense my tweets like Fletcher, I could have a talent in the making.

@pattiputts. "Yes, I have looked at a lot of them, there are two. @ladyparlor, @centralcasting. Amusing! I have pictures of her that are not on any website, what proof is that?" Very easy to solve this; send me a note on Facebook. It is called the second amendment. It is "Freedom of Speech" not harassment. Just like that one. You can alter pictures all day long. The ones you sent are very blurry. The easiest way to prove you are her husband is to produce a marriage license … And you call me stupid! Look in the mirror. We shall see when the FBI investigates your whole operation.

Carnal Carrie and Patti begin a Twitter exchange after Mr. Fletcher was finished with Patti. Carnal Carrie is the first to initiate the conversation to Patti.

@pattiputts. "Oh my God! They are doing it to you too. It is the same "scam!" They are trying to make us look like bad people! Crazzy! You have any more Twitter accounts harassing you too. Apparently, he put Nate in prison, and I'm next. So Nate doesn't know about me and the FBI hat, guy. Lol. (Lots of laughs) It looks like this criminal group of scammer boys is doing the same to all the models. Look at the person doing it to me! @dignity. He is doing the same thing! He has to be a scammer himself posing as a regular person."

Patti Putts replies to carnal Carrie.

@carnal carrie. "Yes, all the time! This guy, I've been dealing with for three weeks … He is convinced I am Valerie Pamelosa. Jimmy and I set up a whole site called, notattiputts.com, dedicated to fakes.@ hatefulman38, made a new account under, @sucker11, to harass Jimmy. No one else on Twitter lately, but where there is one there is always more. Hahaha, Right! The UPS guy was all like, "Ummmm," Illinois? Like I was crazy! Seriously, it is hilarious! Ha-ha, thanks! I could not take it anymore. I had to give it one last chance. Once you tell one lie, you have to lie more to cover your tracks! Liar's always get found out."

This was quite the prophetic statement made by Patti. It could come back to haunt the whole lot of these rascals. Be careful whom you trust, the Devil was once an Angel! Patti may be sticking her foot into that mouth of hers. What was disturbing to the author was viewing pictures of these homes, unaware of just how lucrative this swindling business is that perpetuates the flow of money into their coffer's affording the lifestyle these misfits enjoy. Once you locate an alleged scammer's address you can use an application called; "Google Maps."

With satellites, circling the earth above, you can zoom down to the target home using their address, and it will reveal the latitude and longitude while giving the viewer a bird's eye view of the house. Let me tell you, folks, this so-called swindler bunch was living the life of luxury at the expense of the victim's they intruded upon. I noticed on Valerie

Pamelosa's twitter page where she had just purchased a state-of-the-art treadmill. Their home was located in the northernmost suburbs of Illinois. The interior of the Raja residence was something the middle-class citizen could only dream about.

One room where she did her shows is the same room Henan Asante was resurrected to pull off her fraudulent activity. When the subject of Carrie's room became the object of a quasi-inquiry on Yahoo Messenger, I asked Carrie about the correlation regarding the décor and color of the places appearing identical to another living area, Henan showed me in Ghana, where she appeared to me on video chat. "The rooms are identical," I said.

"I'm in Ghana now, and we made this room look exactly like the room in New Jersey."

"Oh really," I said surprised. "That is really quite unique how everything can be an exact replica; walls, desk, the whole works, in two separate locations."

Carrie replied. "Yes, it wasn't very difficult to do."

Although brief as discussions go, this one was planned well in advance. I needed confirmation that what I had suspected for some time now would, in fact, seal the envelope with indisputable proof that they indeed were involved in fraudulent activity. Once I could get Carrie to commit and say she was in Ghana as Carrie and have her repeat it numerous times, only then did I request we video chat. Once Carrie opened up video for me to see her live and survey her room, I knew I had just caught her in a lie. Carrie and Henan are one and the same person.

As this operation is enjoying impunity with impure, lewd, and unchaste evil, this gang of thieves continues to go unnoticed, and unchallenged by law enforcement officials. How can this be? Are all their accusers in error? How is it that these invisible scam artists in Ghana and Nigeria; with the hundreds of thousands of model's around the world prostituting themselves on the internet, and elsewhere; choose to single out Patti Putts and Carnal Carrie video's, and photographs, as the models of choice for their scamming operation?

As Patti would tell Carrie. Once you tell one lie, you have to lie more to cover your tracks. Liars always get caught in the end. What a profound statement Patti made. Little does she realize, the very thing that comes forth from the tongue, has its beginning in the heart. As for touching up or doctoring photographs and video's Carrie accuses the Nigerians and Ghana people of pirating, is without merit. These people are not as sophisticated in technology as we are. Especially, if the scammer chose to use videos in their operation. If anyone is guilty of manipulating photographs and videos, it's these folks mentioned and branded on the pages of this manuscript.

Chapter 25

Live Video Networks

The word ... It is God's spoken word ... Words!
What is this word, word? Is it not life itself?
A slave to things of this world, you have rejected the word; merely dust on the shelf.
One sow's deceit, another murder's devoid of remorse ...
For others, evil resides in the soul.
Liberties went astray; freedoms foundation withers
away; cursed these grave sins toll.
Jim Jacobs

In big bold lettering, the introductory page announces its latest Search Engine at Varify.com, www.Cutthroat.Networks.Alone.org, sets up another sophisticated Web Instrument by Elisha Thomas on the internet June 10, 2013. With many years of video, and picture archives in their long-standing list of what they aptly call the worse, of the worse, dirty little cam girls under their belt. It didn't take "sparky," David Sommer's casting himself from "many nets" always live video chat site, Cutthroat.Networks.Alone.org to start a new pay site to utilize the content their services have amassed over the years. Site owner and pimp David Sommer's and Cutthroat.Networks.Alone.org has launched hundreds of videos with prostitutes and noted performers of this site's chat room users. It is no surprise "webcam sites" have been around as long as Cutthroat.Networks.Alone.org would have what appears to be many renegade prostitutes in their collection, claims Sommer's (I take issue with this renegade prostitute).

459

Uhmm! I just gotta stop here because I seem to be regressing into a cocoon-like isolationism state to collect my thoughts. I think we may have another, "failure to com mune cate" on Sommer's website page. The women I have seen on Cutthroat.Networks.Alone.org are what Sommer's defines as college educated. I am not suggesting they do not have a lone wolf or two, but to describe all these women as models (prostitutes) who are quick-witted, ingenious, college girls under his thumb ... I'll exercise my right by denouncing Sommer's assumption that he has nothing but high-end prostitutes in his lair, by stretching this truth far too generously.

These women have unsavory body tattoos and piercings in inappropriate places while others looked stoked; as if they were on some chemically induced drug. Others appeared to have limited movement, housed in confined cubicles while the vast majority seemed as if they came right off the streets. Still others seemed as though they were being monitored by what I describe as, "pimp-controlled," as shadows were observed outside the girl's cubicle. Let us read on, and see what other marketing strategies Sommer's is promoting.

"Webcams isn't a career," Sommer's implies. "Oops!" Here we go again with the "catch" phrase. "College girls graduate and go on to bigger and better things. (He's a visionary) "We've helped support teachers, psychologist, and researchers over the past." (This is as classic a statement as a vintage automobile gets). If, and this is a big IF; this class of clientele he claims to draw to his site is high-end prostitutes; I honestly wonder who is actually helping who here. We will ruminate that argument later. However, for now, let us stay on course. You have the choice of making the content available to mobile devices, IPhones, and Android in addition to the Mac, (Macintosh), and PC, (personal computers) for access. His team of pimps is hoping to bring the CNAO experience to as broad an audience as possible, while still keeping the "join free" and "chat" access to the main webcams, "To take perverts that much closer to the real LVN experience in real-time," Sommer's said.

"What live webcam site isn't in real-time"?

Allow the author to become unhinged with this observation. The term; "free," or "join free" is a catch phrase used by most webcam sites. Although it is true it cost the user nothing to sign up with one of these networks, don't think you are signing on and getting something for nothing. The phrase, "join free" is a ploy by most if not all of these webcam sites who use this as a marketing strategy to get traffic flowing onto their web page.

"Free," as defined in the dictionary means to: Relieve or rid of what restraints, confines, releases, liberates. Permanent removal of whatever binds, entangles, or oppresses', without charge. Instinctively, when the human brain sees free; they react to it as if free means free. Yes, it is so. It is free to sign up. However, once you register your information to gain access to these adult websites the ultimate goal of these sites is to get you to go the extra step and purchase tokens. Because it is after registering, where it gets a little troubling and sticky. Not only may there be a cost involved; but free is not liberating, but rather it enslaves the person into "SIN." Again, I will redress this later in the Chapter.

The CNAO Time Machine has soft-launched with an affiliate program, between software site enough.net and the Elevated X CMS (Our Flux Capacitor powered by Mojo hosts 1.21 Gigawatts).

"Talk about a mouthful of tech-o geek computer language ... Whew!" Left me with some homework assignment I'll say. Yeah! Let's see if we can make sense of this gobble-de-gook. Elevated X CMS merely implies adult, "Content Management System" software program used by entities of cam porn sites. It is reported that over two thousand adult websites use Elevated X for adult entertainment, (Pornography) sites. MojoHost is nothing more than another company that offers its products and services to registered users needing their technology for monitoring and storing information for its clients. MojoHost boasts 1.21 Gigawatts of power. Breaking this down in terms a layperson can wrap their arms around, we will use the light bulb as the example. A typical home may use a 100-watt light bulb. So if we have 1.21 Gigawatts, (billions of watts). It would be enough to light up 12.1 million light bulbs. "Is that a lot of watts or whaaat?"

MBASE is a "Model Based Architectures and Software Engineering" program that focuses on ensuring the projects product models. It is architecture, requirements, source code, etc., process models, task, activities, milestones, property standards. It covers cost, schedules, performance, dependability, and success models. Also, stakeholders, win-win, IKIWISI, (I will know it when I see it, business case, and are consistent and mutually enforcing. MBASE is an approach to the development of software systems that integrates the system process (PS), product (PD), property (PY), and success (SS), models, models that are documented elements. Also referred to as, artifacts or deliverables. Should you have made the discovery; after that you get lost in translation, you can file a complaint with the Federal Communications Commission.

The advantage of MBASE is that entities engaged in pornography can now broadcast their models, (prostitutes) to multiple sites generating more profits by networking with other webcam chat sites at the same time, in real-time. Prostitutes can also license their own live video to other websites for increased exposure, drawing in new customers (perverts) and increase sales from LVN. The prostitute has the choice of adding live chat from other LiveVideoNetworks.org websites to their own and charge what they want per minute to chat with other prostitutes. Another proclamation squeezes through the crack in the door by skillful and evil entities. "MBASE allows for independent pricing for each participating website. You can enable or disable any chat prostitute at any time. (They fail to mention; the prostitute can also ban perverts from their room without much cause). All sales across all sites recorded and credited in real-time. You have easy access to scheduling and your profile pages. "Here comes the carrot stick!" The prostitute can charge anything they want to for private, semi-private, and VIP modes.

What LVN and most other smut peddling entities fail to mention in their brochures or advertisements is the cost to you, the prostitute, to use their server and other incidentals. They certainly do not do this because they are nice people. Sometimes it requires the prostitute to buy their software to use that is compatible with the server the entity uses. Perhaps, they will have to purchase lighting and a better webcam to prostitute their bodies. LVN features "MiriStream" chat encoder;

(to convert a message into code from one system to another system) it recognizes all cameras seen by their computer's operating system and merges their live video, audio, and text chat into compressed stream. LVN though, chants with glee there is nothing to download and no special firewall or anti-virus rules that need configuring. The prostitute simply logs into the pervert's website and begins chatting with them.

A typical webcam network, or where the prostitute's room is, is where they operate from, whether in their private residence or in a studio setting of a pimp's server site. There we can envision the screen from which they are web-camming. You may see the top of the screen, yet not exclusive to all adult webcam sites the features; Chat, Camera Settings, Microphone Settings, Global Settings, (other countries throughout the world) Payment & ratio, Events, and Room Settings. These backgrounds are plain mainly to the prostitute.

However, the pervert visiting the site will likely see their Username, amount of money or tokens left in their account, user list. It is further sorted by level, ignore, ban, the balance of funds remaining in the customer's account. (Customer standing; location of the client, Member since, and language. "Blah, blah, blah, blah!" While you have a good vision of the prostitutes; in most cases in High Definition, the screen also accommodates the chat session.

This isn't exclusive to one single customer, but you also have other members visiting the same prostitute's room whose chat-talk you can view on the screen to see what has been said or asked of the prostitute. Members also exchange conversation with each other. Generally, the prostitute's audio is for her use only and turned on so everyone visiting her room can hear her. Seldom will a prostitute turn on audio where both parties; prostitute and member are on audio simultaneously voicing their potty mouth comments.

Cutthroat.Networks.Alone.org promotes their state-of-the-art software, (the entire set of program procedures and documentation associated with a system, especially a computer) with "Virtual Private Rooms," (ViPeR). This software allows your customers, (perverts) to watch and re-watch previously recorded video chat sessions for any amount of per minute you, and the prostitute agrees with the charges. Now you can understand why this has become a billion-dollar multi-layered industry. It is all about the money for pimps. The female flesh commodity is disposable goods after she has served their purpose. Women have to know the name of the game. Why they embark down this path of humiliation is beyond understanding?

Note of interest before I forge ahead. Clinging to these truths while typing the language and words embedded on these pages, I often wondered how many of the readers have a moral code that is scripturally based and not worldly. Of interest, is how the sex industry peddles its products and merchandise to the public via mass distribution, and advertising. Many of these promoters distributing their wares of pornography love to use catch phrases. Words like customers, viewers, your own visitors, models, and host, Etc.

It is using soft, polite words instead of "Perverts." Pervert means to cause to turn aside or away from what is good, or true or morally right. Corrupt.

Prostitute. "Devoted to corruption or improper purposes; money."

It is the best possible exemplification; either in reality or in conception. Nor would I define these entities as "companies," to lend it legitimacy. Rather, they are in the flesh peddling abyss of degradation to make profits for lost souls and pimps. They are someone who solicits women as nothing more than a prostitute. Misapplying and misusing the definition of words is nothing short of slick trick advertising in the pornography arena of smudged smut, (obscene matter, or language).

I am he who is responsible for the use of the word prostitute. Seldom will the entity identify their stable of on-line women as prostitutes; but misuse the word "model." Also, Cutthroat.Networks.Alone.org has now included as part of their service what they call LVN Satellite. "LiveVideoNetworksSat." Furthermore, LVN satellite promotes the service to service providers that could be the solution for companies who wish to provide for-profit services to their website customers, for businesses, and ISP'S, (Internet Service Provider's). Companies who want to run multiple sites, (a group of world wide web pages usually containing hyperlinks to each other and made available on-line by individual, company, educational institutions, government, or organization) to your customers, and provide multiple, billable services such as billing and MBASE services to them. Satellite license holders may resell LVN software, hosting, and support, Mbase services, billing, and other services, at any rate, they wish to charge including revenue sharing.

LVN Satellite includes three domains. A subdivision of the internet consisting of computers or sites usually with a common purpose as denoted in the Internet address by a unique abbreviation. .Com or, .net; domain name, licenses', fraud detection, hosting and support plan, transaction fees, custom programming, network-wide chat model sales comparison reports, and extensive overview put into context. It is all about the "MONEY!" Who are the victims? The naiveté who are damaged at the expense of the pimp who sells their flesh, and who are pimped on the streets, in motels, back alleys, or automobiles? Now some have journeyed their way into the outstretched tentacles of the internet to sell their wares under the control of their pimps. It's considered preferable than the streets because they are less likely to be harassed by the police. Are we to assume that if it were not for web-camming on the internet, these prostitutes would all be prostituting themselves on the street?

If you will recall at the beginning of the Chapter, I mentioned Eisha Thomas Instrument machines. Thomas had additional duties assigned by wiry David Sommer's to be in charge of and write public relations for CNAO including providing site maintenance, and optimization services via www.janitoroversite.com. This entity, on their advertisement pages, tempers itself within a positive light, despite questionable hiring practices including being an accessory to criminal activity by other entities using their software. LVN touts itself with self-praise. Examples include but not limited in scope and content. "Congrats to all beauties that have nominees at @showbiz awards tonight. We wish the best of luck to all of you. @babylove, LVN. Best of luck, @softwareteam – nominated for the best software company of the Year. I'm so fortunate to work with such an impressive group. (Your man Sommer's making the declaration) This website also feeds pervert's who visit their site, a running list of the top-ten prostitutes by their fictitious on-line prostitute name, and who LVN touts as the top-ten "babes," or what

I have come to call, "perverts ranking" based on some tokens they contribute to the prostitute.

Here is what Live, CNAO and 5.1 promotes as incentives to the prostitutes who contract for their services. LVN will provide the contracted prostitute, the following amenities:

- Free "Teaser" chat with the pervert, registered users or paying pervert. They offer actual private video chat. One pervert at a time, one-way video audio, and optional 2-way video audio chat, private video chat, with Passive viewers (voyeurism) and (1-chat pervert, and unlimited voyeurs). Call it for what it is.

  "Stalkers and Window peeping."

- Semi-Private Group chat (Unlimited Perverts).

- Semi-Private "Group chat," plus passive viewers, unlimited paying chat

- Perverts, and unlimited paid window peeping perverts).

- Private viewing or group viewing of previously recorded video chats, video

- clips, or movies. Free preview movie option.

Listed are the Network capabilities/abilities.

  o License to videotape and recorded content to other websites

  o Add licensed LIVE streams to your site instantly, display it organically and present it to your own customers as your own, complete with branding

- Stained "SIN," the pervert will love and enjoy:

- Wide-Screen, large format video

- High-quality sound (Not necessary to chat by keyboard)

- Macintosh and Personal Computer compatibility systems are user-friendly

- Internet Explorer, Firefox, Chrome, and Safari browser support

- Easy access "Start Private/Start Semi-Private" control buttons.

- Secure TIP function (Single click TIPS to your chat prostitutes). Adjustable video size and volume control with mute.

Entities insist on using the word "model" It sounds professional, clean; instead of calling them prostitutes. It's a marketing strategy to reign in more women. It is a slick trick marketing scheme.

This is what the Chat prostitute will love and benefit from their servers:

- Easy to set up and use video chat encoder (personal computer and McIntosh

- High-quality video broadcasting

- 1-Way and 2-Way "Cam to Cam" chat

- 3-Money-making chat modes plus free upsell mode

- Large text-chat window and adjustable font size

- Perverts information window

- Real-Time sales and earnings reports

- Private messaging functions

- Easy scheduling and instant online promotion

- Customizable profile pages (profiles page allows the pervert to view the prostitute's personal information related to age, weight, height, hair, and eye color … including a wish list of all things, etc.)

- Availability to access instant self-advertising

If LiveVideoNetworks.org were not offering enough incentives to draw women to their sites, they have sweetened additional options the prostitutes can choose from to procure for a COST to the prostitute of course; in addition to other software capabilities for their Virtual Private Rooms (ViPeR). Perverts can watch an ever-growing amount of "high quality," (Yeah, Right!) video chat playback for as long as the pervert wants to watch. For any amount you, the prostitute wants to charge them. Here comes the BIG marketing pitch.

"Of course, this means the chat prostitute makes, even more, MONEY thanks to the built-in commission system."

"That's right! Payback to the MAN for degrading and humiliating yourselves in front of perverts."

For an additional expenditure to the prostitute's wallet, they can choose between two options. You have the "ViPeR 1.1 Standard," or you can choose the "ViPeR 1.1 Pro." Listed again for comparative illustration purposes I have noted the difference between these two, however, slight in comparison they are to each other. The ViPeR Standard offers the following technology. When marketing, one has to put their best FACE, front and center on the product they are marketing. Nothing is more deceptive than with a young, innocent, looking prostitute on all fours, posing front and center on the video screen to capture the fantasies and imaginations of the perverts trolling (moving from one chat room to another), looking for what might fulfill their fanatic imaginations.

- The standard offers the prostitute to display videos at any rate per minute she wishes to charge

- Playlist support for multiple videos per room

- High resolution 264 video

- Add/remove live streams anytime-controlled by MBASE

- User-adjustable video size

- Audio volume and mute controls

Displays as separate area alongside live and scheduled chats with prostitutes to increase content awareness and improve SEO.

- Display other prostitute's recorded video chat on their site via MBASE

There is only a slight variation in the additional services the Pro delivers to perverts to view and, or prostitutes to utilize.

- It includes everything in the Standard including these features:

- Licensing to other websites via Mbase at any price the prostitute likes per

Minute.

- High Definition, 720p Video. High Definition and Wide-Screen support.

It displays free teaser trailers' (short film about prostitute's content.)

- Chat prostitutes commission program.

- Compatible with LVN.org, Logo/Advertising Overlay.

On September 3, 2012, LVN was ranked number 388,742 in the world according to the one-month Alexa traffic rankings and 4 out of 10 according to Google Page Rank. LVN. Org was founded twelve-years ago. It has the POTENTIAL to earn thirteen-hundred United States dollar in advertisement revenue per year. If the site were up for sale at the time of this writing, it would be worth approximately nine-thousand-seventeen U.S. dollars. Stuff Gate rates LVN a 3.0 out of a maximum of 5.0. There (IP) Internet Protocol is listed at location 62.919.413.211.

However, that designated location identifier can change within a twinkle of the eye if the evil empire is using (VPN) Virtual Private Network. Pimps use VPN to avoid being detected by people like me. In summary, LVN.org shows seven records in the (DNS) Domain Name System including 1 address (A) record. 2 (NS) name server's records, 1 (SOA) start of authority record, 2 (NX) mail exchange records, 1 (TXT) record. HTTP header responses of LVN shows how LVN responds to incoming Hyper Text Transfer Protocol while bracketed (HTTP) are one's from incoming clients. (E.g., web browsers) "This kind of information isn't shown by typical web browsers."

I googled, (ARIN) one of endless computer abbreviations used by the tech age. ARIN means. "American Registry for Internet Numbers." This requires internet operators to register their information with this agency in what is identified as (POC) usually a single "Point of Contact," via which the company can contact the register to ascertain if their email and data is current and up-to-date. Sometimes one can feel overwhelmed by abbreviations while using the computer, but teary not for one moment and don't get discouraged. Keep in mind; it was a learning process for me as well. Patience is a virtue … Always. Just Goggle, "what is, or who is," and Walla. (SEO) or, "Search Engine Optimization, for the novice user, this may prove intimidating. However, "POC" is nothing more than a strategies technique, and tactic to increase the number of visitors to a website by obtaining a high-ranking placement in the search results located in whatever site one decides to choose on a list of links provided by the search engine.

On the American Registry for Internet Numbers (ARIN), I located Nathaniel Raja's personal information, I already had most of his profile, however, now I was searching for an, (ID) identification number through which I could further identify and possibly track Nathaniel and Carrie. I ran this request on January 18, 2014. It revealed the point of handle contact information as RRC9-ARIN, Name on the registrar belongs to Nathaniel Raja, function; Nathaniel claims as, "general use," and contact type: "Person." Contact information lists the Company Name as … Live Video Networks.org Nathaniel's personal residence, followed by his email address. thunder@yahoo.com. Other information would contain home, and business phone numbers, registration date, and time, including when their information was last modified.

In my search for information that could provide additional leads or critical data on these alleged scammers, I used whatever links or web pages I felt useful in gleaning other intelligence. I have used, "Spokeo," "Domain Tools" "Checkmate," Arin.net," "Stuff gate," and a host of other helpful links in which to get information for this manuscript. Sometimes these applications charged a fee on some of these search engines. In rare cases, it will provide you the information without fees. In other settings, this link would allow the user a three or seven-day trial period. Even then, you were required to pay a minimal up-front fee for their services.

So you want to become a cam girl do you? Well here is how you can make the MOST money ever in the privacy of your own home as a real webcam prostitute. For the sake of being accused of misinformation, I wanted to substitute model for a prostitute because this is what they do. Here are some tips, tricks, and advice the pimps on website's you signed onto to promote your wares will help make plenty of cash for you … Even the young lass attending college can participate!

After all, we all feel this tendency to, "get wet and wild," right! So why not receive money for your naughty behavior. It is a "win, win" for all of us; except God will be watching. But then girl's, you made a conscience choice to leave the light and enter into the abyss for ALL eternity. That is unless you change your moral standards.

I guess we have to start living in sin to empower the women even more. "It is their body anyway," don't you agree? They can do what they want with their own bodies, even in the arena of prostituting themselves on adult websites in exchange for short-term financial gain. (First off, not all the women on webcam sites are making living wages. Now, LiveVideoNetworks.org is for anyone who wants to make MONEY in the live adult video chat or web cam business … "Not." In any industry, "do you like including adult entertainment, like Sodom and Gomorrah entertainment?" Sommer's and those of similar mindsets including but not limited to Nathaniel Raja and Carnal Carrie do. They offer chat coaching, and consulting. (Yep! They will show you how to be a good performing prostitute). This is not exclusive. "No, no, no, no!" This is relevant to any sinful person engaged or associated with prostituting women on the Internet, or outside of it.

I know Sommer's resides in Canada, but I believe he also has a crib in New York and Las Vegas. Cutthroat.Networks.Alone.org does not allow "gays, couples, or women to host LVN on their own servers. Their reasoning is that it may cause lag or latency issues. They maintain and monitor, (monitor is the buzzword; absolute control) their servers and cabinets at "given4network." The prostitute cannot sell their site, nor close their account, or even cancel out of LVN's relationship without written notification to close or transfer ownership of an account. Instead, it taunts". "Show me the money!" A send a private message when a tipping function, is built into the system to ENCOURAGE more tips from perverts who visit a webcam models site. The accounting system will then split the value of the tip between the prostitute and the site owner … any way they like.

Who controls the money that the prostitute generates for CNAO, or the "lion's share" of the proceeds from the flesh, humiliation, and degradation these females endure? LVN controls individual payouts per chat model. An automatic performer invoice generated, with calculated commissions; chat sales in per day, week, month, or year. Chat prostitute's performance tracking, promotional credits-set, and adjusted automatically, manage keywords and niche for models for each prostitute independently. Manage prostitute's photos, biographies, and descriptions. Tip reporting and tip split system. Then we are awestruck by this adjustable minimum payout threshold." It is micromanaging by the pimp. But then, what did you girls expect? It's all about money for these pimps.

Stepping through the threshold of the doorway ever so gingerly via Fed-Ex, are certain qualifications that determine the prostitutes earning potential. There is noted in their profile, a smart marketing strategy. In one of their brochures, this evil empire uses the sum of fifty-thousand dollars as an example for their breakdown on the payment schedule. Management explained the breakdown of how the entertainers receive their payments. "Somebody tell me how anyone prostituting themselves is going to take in fifty-thousand dollars per night let alone per month?" When a potential client sees that figure, what do suppose captivates her attention right away? That's right, the misleading fifty-thousand dollar per day earnings potential.

Management claims. "If you make under fifty-thousand you will get paid every two weeks." "Over fifty-thousand and the entertainer would receive a weekly paycheck. They inform the prostitutes who use their services that the return on any investments is dependent upon several factors including quality and quantity of prostitute's chat, marketing, promotion, and time spent online including other factors intentionally left out. Another interesting fact I learned in my research but does not necessarily apply to all cam sites. If the prostitute has her own cam site with LVN, and she, in turn, hires a stable of other prostitutes, she can put herself, or her girls in what is called a multicast mode.

However, you have to have the MBASE, "Model Based Architecture Software Engineering" system. This broadcasts to multiple websites simultaneously with the premise it will bring in more revenue to the prostitute. The entity informs the entertainer she can also charge any amount per minute to the pervert who elects to go, group, private, or VIP. Should the pervert ask the prostitute to go "solo private," it will cost him additional per minute of privacy with the prostitute.

LiveVideoNetworks.org uses the example of five-dollars per minute, but I have yet to see any prostitute charge that amount. The marketing strategy by these "slick pimps," (that's a fitting title) for what they do to fudge the figures and bait the hook to reel in prospective prostitutes. "Pays … pays … pays!" If the prostitute determines MBASE is profitable for her operation, then LVN demands a two-hundred-and-fifty-dollar minimum reserve deposit. I can assure you; these pimps will hard sell this most wonderful contraption. I will not bore you with statistics, reports, comparisons, etc. Most if not all these adult, webcam sites have a weapon at their disposal. They call this blocking or banning of unruly, disgusting, and abusive talk or behavior by perverts coming into their room. Also, LVN has a feature on its software they call, "GeoIP." This works by mapping the IP address of each user on any prostitute's website to known databases of millions of IP addresses worldwide within milliseconds. We have hypocrisy spoken here.

The polar axis is tilted ever so slightly as we meander through the amber meadows of time with its mysteries, and clichés; arriving at the castle of Carnal Carrie, also known as "carnalchatcams," as we address their alleged involvement in "scams," and fraudulent schemes.

473

Carrie operates her own cam site. This has been established. In this environment, rather than address money as currency, we speak regarding tokens as the medium of exchange between prostitutes and the pervert.

It is here where multiple options avail themselves to the pervert in which to choose from when interacting with online prostitutes. Most live video cams function on the same principle when determining the fee for services. The choices are simple. Open chat, group, private, and true private when interacting with the prostitute.

I have observed more than my share of perverts who appear to have insecurity issues. I base this observation on foul, dirty, filthy, degrading, and obscene language spoken by the pervert towards the prostitute. It is apparent we no longer embrace family values because if we did, the perverts would not have despicable potty mouth language, and there wouldn't be young impressionable girl's exposing their anatomy on the internet. Perverts who visit these adult cam sites on the internet are insecure, sick, scarred, lost souls. What these men (perverts) are doing by spending tokens on the prostitute is sending the wrong message, that it is alright for all participants to behave immorally. Man must have blinders on because he lusts in a vitiated state of human nature in which the self is estranged from God. Why the male has this penchant to dehumanize the female anatomy is plain insensitive, cruel, and sinful.

Before I explain private, I will break down token purchases in increments for live video network, just as I did in the previous Chapter. Actually, they are almost similar to www.legoflambcams.com.

- 200 tokens for $20.00

- 400 tokens for $40.00

- 600 tokens for $60.00

- 800 tokens for $80.00

- 1000 tokens for $95.00 and get 100 tokens free.

Carrie used MBASE, but when I first began this odyssey with Carrie, I eventually suspected Carrie had hired her own stable of women but was difficult for me to prove. These women appeared as if they were webcamming in substandard skanky cubicles. They were not; for the most part, attractive looking women of the evening, but they were performing on her website none-the-less. Private, meant other perverts could watch, provided they ponied up the same agreed upon price as the pervert who requested a private session with her initially.

Generally, Carrie would charge thirty tokens per minute. So if you bought two hundred tokens for twenty dollars. Two hundred tokens divided by thirty tokens per minute allows you approximately seven minutes with her performing whatever the pervert requested. If you deplete your token amount during the allotted time, a message will appear notifying you to purchase more tokens. The pervert then had to buy additional tokens if he wanted to continue the private session with her. In a perfect world, let us assume the closed session lasted an hour. Carrie would theoretically earn approximately one-hundred-eighty dollars for an hour's worth of work. But, this is not pure profit because Sommer's gets a commission because Carrie was using Sommer's live video network server. Unless …

If the prostitute elects to go true private; then it is just the two of you, without interference from other perverts inside her room. Prostitutes temporarily turn off the live video feed in the main room, and she takes the pervert who requested a true private to a separate room where there is no outside interference. Truly individual privacy is costlier; say, forty tokens per minute.

Given the scenario in the previous paragraph, two-hundred tokens divided by forty tokens per minute allows five-minutes alone with her. (Not figuratively, or physically speaking). If you were to spend an hour with her in true private, you would multiply minutes in increments. Example, twelve x five-minutes in an hour equals sixty x forty tokens per minute we derive at two-hundred-forty dollars an hour. This looks like easy money provided the prostitute could get a pervert to commit to that kind of real money, and they do. "Willy Nellie" the pervert has just tossed two-hundred-forty dollars into the abyss. Once the true private session has finished, the live video feed is connected again, role-playing and chat exchange commence with the other members and guests in her room.

Another application Carrie frequently used when communicating with me is what they call "imo messenger." It is an Android application from Google Play. Other times it is referred to as imo.im. You can message and call your friends and family free with imo messenger. Its features include:

- Free, high-quality voice calls

- Super fast and reliable messaging (much faster than SMS) (system management server)

- Group messaging and photo sharing

- Discover new people and content tailored to your interests

- Voice IMs (instant messaging) turn the Android into a walkie-talkie

- Multimedia attachments-audio, video, files

- Share location with friends using Google Maps and Places

- Searchable chat history accessible on mobile and the web

- Concurrent sessions on different devices

- Support for Facebook, Chat, Google, Talks, MSN. ICQ, AIM, Yahoo Messenger, Jabber, etc.

GoDaddy.com reported to be the largest domain registrar in the United States if not the entire world as noted on October 10, 2013. www. carnalcarriexxx.com. Carnal Carrie hosts from Weehawken, NJ, on a server with an IP address of 65.271.132.09 also located in Weehawken, New Jersey. It is projected to earn an estimated ten dollars on a daily basis. If Carrie considered selling their site today, it would probably be worth three-thousand-four-hundred dollars based on the daily revenue potential of the website over the last twelve-month period. According to GoDaddy.com, their Google page rank analysis, the (URL) Uniform Resource Locator, www.carnalcarriexxx.com currently has a page rank of 0/10. GoDaddy.com indicates that carnalcarriexxx.com receives an estimated 2168 visitors daily. They claim this is an enormous amount of traffic. From other sites I have visited, you could have that many and more just in one prostitute's room. The 2,168 daily visitors don't imply visits to her webcam site, but her website. And, they aren't necessarily paying clients.

Coming from where I sit, monthly revenue in the amount cited; approximately two-hundred-ten dollars a day would not come close to paying a person's monthly expenses. What may keep their collective heads above water would be the advertisement revenue and a controlling interest in other websites Carrie uses to promote her particular wares in graphic detail, which may not appear on Carrie's solely owned and operated website. Beyond what was covered as sources of revenue, it would strongly suggest to the author that Carrie and husband Nathaniel are indeed the folks; along with other co-conspirators who dirty their hands swindling unsuspecting victims.

A report by www.GoDaddy.com shows some other stats I find interesting. The report classifies this "motley crew" of visitors as, monthly unique visitors. This report goes on to indicate 72,076 monthly unique visitors, giving a sum total for the year of these unique visitors at 864,337. Alexa ranks Carnal Carrie's site at approximately 214,057. There is no other data to compare Carnal Carrie's visitors with other known pornography sites at this writing. However, I can tell you if I were to give the readers a rough estimate of say, 500,000 other porn sites, more than likely the numbers are right on target as web sites go.

Let's take a ride on the wild side shall we people? Suppose … Just suppose my intelligence gathering is spot on, and these perpetrators are who I allege as scammers. I have crossed the "T's," and dotted the "I's." A metaphor used on many an occasion. Starting with the hierarchy in relationship to people of interest in defrauding, and scamming, (a given) we will begin with "Guilt by Association." On the pyramid scheme, we have to begin with Carnal Carrie, and her husband. Owners, and operators of www.carnalcarriexxx.com, followed by, but not lagging far behind, is the flamboyant, charismatic David Sommer's, President of www.cutthroat.networks.alone.org. The duo conjoined misfits of Valerie Pamelosa, aka., Patti putts, and Jimmy Pamelosa, aka., jeremyfamou$187. Honorable mention goes to Sally, and Debra; Carrie's siblings. Allen Simple, an associate of David Sommers, authored guidelines for LiveVideoNetwork.org may also be a viable candidate or, at least, have knowledge of Raja's fraud network, and other player's names provided to IC3.

There was mention of other names, addresses, and phone numbers who appeared below Nathaniel's name when I powered on my "smartphone." This caught my attention and curiosity. This seemed to be an exceptional team of the ultimate outer circle of additional people of interest connected to Nathaniel, and Sommer's. With the names appearing on my Samsung smart phone. I used the computer, and began to Google "who is." The search engine produced a minimum of six or seven additional names associated with Nathaniel Raja, whose names and locations were given to IC3.

Well then; onto Wide World of Camming, Chapter 26.

Chapter 26

Wide World of Camming

WWW.legoflambcams.com

Come ... Come ... Come, into the harlot's lair,
this house, and its nasty reputation.
As far as East is to the West, come hither South
and North; we'll build a foundation.
Shadows of shame blinded by Christ stained blood for
all; a man sets site on riches and fame.
Woe ... Woe ... Woe ... Says the King of Kings; name
above all names, you blaspheme my name.
Jim Jacobs

Carefully examining the internet, I uncovered those who were performing acts of debauchery, showing all forms of lewd acts of immorality ... Moreover, they lacked understanding of the consequences of their actions, making folly of the messenger; these creatures of iniquity. I witnessed no shame or accountability, nor was their fear of the wickedness, and abominations displayed before the eyes' of the Lord their God. No reverence is given Him who is found in Heaven. "Whoever is ashamed of me and my words in this adulterous and sinful generation, the Son of Man will also be ashamed of him when Jesus comes back in the glory of His Father with the Holy angels. Mark 8: 38. And, I witnessed while in the abyss, another Sodom, and the likes of Gomorrah as in antiquity past. Woe. woe. woe, will be mankind as he endures the wrath of God.

The translation of John Calvin's Institutes of the Christian Religion, Volume I page 412, paragraph 3. Calvin writes about controlling our words. (a) Indeed, this precept even extends to forbidding us to affect a fawning politeness barbed with bitter taunts under the guise of joking. Some do this to crave praise for their witticisms to others' shame and grief because they sometimes grievously wound their brothers with this sort of impudence. Now if we turn our eyes' to the Lawgiver, who must in his own right rule over ears and heart no less than the tongue, we shall surely see that eagerness to hear detractions, and unbecoming readiness to make unfavorable judgments, are alike forbidden. For it is absurd to think that God hates the disease of evil speaking of the tongue, but does not disapprove of evil intent, in the heart.

Therefore, if there are any true fear and love of God in us, let us take care, as far as possible and expedient and as love requires, not to yield our tongue or our ears to evil speaking and caustic wit, and not to give our minds without cause to sly suspicion. But as responsible interpreters of the words and deeds of all, let us all sincerely keep their honor safe in our judgments, our ears, and our tongue. Let the love of our hearts become the sword of our tongues.

Whoever is familiar with Calvin may be wondering why I brought John Calvin and his works into this Chapter of the manuscript. I will explain his expository and how it relates to this Chapter. Allow me to forewarn the reader as to what I am about to inscribe on the following pages. Some of the content are distasteful and direct. For the reader to get a sense of the repulsive nature of pornography, (if you will) it has to be written in the setting where it was discovered in real-time using authentic dialogue. In this venue, I'm focusing on one of just thousands of times a thousand camming networks on the internet. This does not include dating sites, friendships, or the user's looking for companionship. This is strictly girl's web-camming for money on the internet.

Generally speaking, when an important news network assigns a reporter to go out into the field to do a piece; using human slave trafficking as our example, it requires the investigating reporter to assume a different persona to blend in with the story they are about to report. Undercover law enforcement agencies, covert operations, private investigators, and the like undergo a transformation to obtain information and gather evidence. My research, crusade, or mission statement, however you choose to define it, was no different.

"In order understand swine living in their natural habitat you do so by going directly to the source; their environment. Once you've arrived at the pig's habitat, you are now at liberty to watch, and observe their behavior. They furrow in the muck, and mire of filth, rolling around in the soggy mud to keep the biting insects off their tough skin and keep them cool. Swine are omnivorous creatures avidly taking in everything devouring almost anything that is eatable. Even when the pig is cleaned, it returns to the mud to wallow in it. Using this example, it lent credibility to my research. I was immediately banned by prostitute's when I used the metaphor of the swine. As far as I was concerned "camming and scamming" are synonymous.

There was reasonable cause to choose www.legoflambcams.com, as our poster child. First, it was one of the top cam networks on the internet. Second, I couldn't spend all my time and resources trolling from one site to another without sinking deeper into debt. Finally, I needed to establish a base where I could build repose, trust, and regularity for prostitutes to feel comfortable enough to share information about their chosen profession." Legoflambcams.com," is perhaps one of the most carefully guarded cam sites on the internet. I have always had bad vibes about this network and the folks behind the scenes ... management/pimps. There a maligned contentious bunch filled with treasure troves of secret information.

When asked by people why I was going to these dens of iniquity my answer was often terse. "If not now; when?" "If not, when; why not?" Tell me who should go? Who will learn of its immorality and its impact on society? Who is going to expose this out-of-control cancer and human condition of the heart? If you tell me the timing is not favorable for change, my response will be in the form of a question. "When is the right time?" If we as Christians are in the soul saving service for our Lord and Savior, then who goes into the belly of sin and darkness? Sin is not coming to you for sure. So, if someone has a grand scheme to reach out and engage the nefarious promiscuous purposes of the pimp peddling scavengers to fill me in. I wasn't stimulated, excited, titillated, or fascinated by what I was viewing. Actually, I had empathy for these girls and disdain for the pervert.

We are going to look into this network, www.legoflambcams.com. Here is what www.legoflambcams.com; squeal is all about in their advertisement campaign. Likened to the "belly of the beast," legoflambcams.com can never recruit enough fresh flesh to webcam for them. They claim to collaborate with their models as partners, (not) and the prostitutes are supposed to earn a lion's share; a larger percentage than other sites ... Not. They boast to be one of the biggest online webcam networks enticing men and women from all over the world. (Can you imagine, all over the world) Another false claim they want everyone to know is that they do their best to make sure all members are completely satisfied. That would be the perverts who are regarded as premium members This author is curious to know how you completely satisfy members. And what do they mean by completely satisfied? Do they have hands-on with the contingent of prostitutes in their stable?

A feature legoflambcams.com proudly boasts, is that their site offers more free features to the guest. However, it does not say with limitations over other website competitors. Spending money on tokens is optional. (Exchanging currency for what is referred to as tokens/points) Another claim made is that they are there to listen to the members and make them happy. "Another misnomer"! There are different account types on this site as well. However, overall, it's relatively standard for the majority of internet porn sites. A new pervert, which registers on legoflambcam.com site, can register as a guest, and create a username, and nickname.

Public relations are at a premium when you have been declared unequivocally by "LOLC," because the $19.99 you just spent on tokens, (200 tokens for $19.99) will be the best investment you ever made. However, should you disagree, you are to "Contact Support," and they will refund you your money back. (Good luck folks) NOTE: When you are a first-time premium member, "LOLC" limits the members buying power to two-hundred tokens a day. This remains in effect until the user has proven they are able to be a member in good standing. Additionally, it informs the pimps the frequency a member visits "LOLC." online. (Usually, a month before you will be given an increase in token purchases) Moreover, "LOLC" wants the member to feel they are protected from outside scrutiny as their credit card is billed discreetly (How pleasant to look after the pervert.) "We wouldn't want to embarrass the pervert now, would we?"

Pimps' who give themselves titles as if they were legitimate corporations such as, Chief Executive Officers, President, Chief Financial Officer, and other creative titles are nothing more than pimps who ingratiate themselves through the peddling of female flesh at the expense of women. These folks have nothing better to do than sit around the Chairman's conference table; "idol worshipping" their financial assets. They scheme to get the maximum profit from their models.

In a room setting, if the prostitute is not taking privates, true privates, or group shows, then she is in her room where perverts are able to chat with her at will. She replies via audio unless it is a private message sent by a pervert. The pervert must type out their comments, or questions to the prostitute. Rarely is there a live audio feed between the both parties. The powers that be, freely chase the "mother lode," for revenue their empire generates which comes from tips. They justify this form of payment by claiming that sending a tip is a way for perverts to transfer any amount of tokens to the prostitute while in her room. This statement by LOLC, in the author's mind, typifies pushing the envelope over the edge.

Perverts; the pimps claim, like to give tips after a private show, while others prefer to tip the prostitute while she is in public chat, for personal requests or just to be nice. They caution the pervert that tips do not change the rules for what prostitutes are allowed to do on their site, especially in public chat. The pimps want to remind the pervert that, "tips are gifts," so the pimp has sounded the alarm and cautioned the pervert. "Do not send any gratuities if you are asking for something in return from the prostitute," They claim this is not fair to the prostitute.

On another matter, the author believes the pimp was out to lunch when they made this announcement. "Just as in real life, tips cannot be reviewed or refunded." A feature is built into the program that allows pimps to send consecutive multiple tips by clicking the "click here to confirm," and "tip again" link at the bottom of the tip confirmation screen. There are many occasions when perverts will start tipping simultaneously just to see the prostitute (expletive) herself. (Sick)

Most, but not all prostitutes get creative in the multiple tips arena. They inform the pervert that if they form a solid "yellow wall" which is generated by non-stop tipping without being interrupted, and the yellow wall extends beyond ten, fifteen, or twenty tips received consecutively, they will (expletive) according to the number of long running yellow strips. Therefore, if the tipping creates a solid yellow wall, the prostitute takes (expletive) ten times. This is a form of self-abasement.

"What does LOLC offer as an incentive for the pervert to return to their site?" If the pervert is gullible enough to buy into this as a drawing card, he will not garnish my sympathy. For every ten tokens the pervert purchases, the pervert will receive one reward point. As the pervert accumulates more reward points, (Catch this now) certain options and features on the website become available to the perverts account. Moreover, the pimps will do their best to offer the pervert priority personal customer support for any issue that may arise. (A little far-fetched I do believe) Reward points never expire, and cannot be taken away. (Oh!) Future plans have them offering more features that will utilize reward points. Also, reward points cannot be transferred to anyone else … period.

Allow me to take you into a typical "chat room" on one of these live chat websites where the prostitute and pervert interact with one another. The Chat Room is the primary arena where perverts and prostitutes exchange dialogue. Once you have access to the website www.legoflambcams.com, you will have to click on a couple written instructions to access the homepage. If you have not logged off the main entrance, you will have to log in again to gain access to the prostitute's room, just enter as a guest, which does not allow you to dialogue with the prostitute or the pervert. Once on the webpage, you can click on any prostitute's picture on the homepage, and "Walla," you have just entered her chat room.

Here is where I get bent out of shape! If we just focus on "LegofLambCams" website, display. You notice between 1,100, upwards of 1,800 or more prostitutes online at any given time. And this is just one site amongst thousands operating 24/7. I will cover this later. I just wanted to let the viewer know how disturbing this trend is growing.

As I mentioned before, prostitutes and pimps will not allow a guest or " the principal members" to chat in their room. Only premium members are allowed to talk in the prostitute's chat room. If this does not create a little anxiety and pressure for other perverts visiting these sites to become a premium member and join this all-inclusive family of perverts, so they too can get a piece of the action, I don't know what will. I call this the carrot and stick trap.

Icon's such as "smiley face, roses, angry face and obscene images are a big part of the chat for the pervert. They enjoy incorporating them into their conversation to impress the prostitute or diminish her self-esteem. To insert a particular image, click on the icon of your choice and enter the Uniformed Resource Locator, (URL) you can also just enter the URL of the picture right into the chat. If you wanted to insert the Twitter logo, you would enter the URL. They ask the pervert not to post any inappropriate, pornographic, violent, offensive, or disturbing images in the chat room. (You have to be kidding me!) "These pimps are speaking from both sides of their mouth!" Moreover, they ask the pervert NOT to post pictures over, and over, DO NOT post photo's that are irrelevant, or disrupt the flow of the chat. Also, DO NOT annoy another pervert in the chat room. These rules were put in place so everyone can have more FUN to express him or herself. (This is another one of those; "are you kidding moment.")

The "pimps" have devised certain chat decorum so you can navigate around the site with more speed and efficiency. Examples of chat commands:

- /help or /? Get a list of available commands.

- /next or/: Go to the next prostitute's room.

- /prev or/p: Go to the previous prostitute's room.

- /last or/l: Go to the last room visited.

- /homepage or /: Go to the homepage.

- /prostitutes name /: Go to the prostitute's room. "Candice can" will take you to

Candace cans room.

LOLC has what is called the "Lounge." They created this to make the pervert think this was a privilege you earned to enter the room. It is nothing more than a room where you view another prostitute or the same prostitute whose room you had just left. "No more, no less."

- /pm: Send a private message to any online prostitute or pervert. (No one else can see it including members or guests)

- /whisper or /w: Send a Private Message (whisper) to the prostitute whose chat room you are currently occupying

- /me or /em: State in conversation that you are performing an action. (I've never seen anyone use this command).

What would an adult live video feed be without adding on advance commands? (You must enable these in your personal options.)

- /Tip: It is sending a tip to the prostitute in her chat room, or private message venue.

For example, tip 50, thank you! It sends a 50 token tip to the prostitute with the message. "Thank you!" The tip and message are displayed together in the chat room.

Tip Options:

- a: Anonymous tip

- p: Private gratuity. (Tip and message are not displayed in the chat room).

- m: Only the prostitute sees the tip message (tip is still shown in the chat room).

Premium Members can send private messages or PM's, to prostitutes or other perverts at any time. You can also view the webcam right in the private message window by clicking, view webcam at the top. You can re-size the window to change the size of the video. Moreover, you can have multiple open PM's watching different webcam feeds in each one. All this; only to pander to the pervert's insatiable appetite to view the prostitute entertaining the pervert's horrible cravings.

To make it easier for perverts to find prostitute's whereby, a pervert may become infatuated with one of the women, "LOLC" brainstormed an idea. It would allow the pervert to gain access to one of his favorite prostitutes by coming up with a list for the pervert who frequently visits an attractive prostitutes room. It is nothing more than a listing of prostitutes on the homepage, or below any chat room. Only prostitutes who are currently online are posted on the website. LOLC has made or programmed the homepage to indicate useful links at the top of the prostitute list. This is by no means the entire list, but it will give you a good indication of the various options available.

- The search box searches all online prostitutes by username, topic, or model tag.

- The new prostitutes link will toggle only showing other prostitutes.

- The settings link will bring up all of the options to filter and sort the prostitute list.

- The text list link brings up a text view of all models online.

- The pause link toggles the automatic refreshing the list.

- You can also set the number of prostitutes per page, and the current page you are currently browsing.

Color schemes also have significance in designing LOLC. It allows for the prostitute and pervert to know whether, you have elevated yourself in good standing with the prostitute. Yellow suggests the prostitute has just logged in, however; yellow slowly fades over time and disappears.

- Pink informs us the prostitute is on your friends list.

- Green signifies you are in the prostitute's room.

- Chat (no associated color) just takes you to the prostitute's chat room.

Links appear below each prostitutes Avatar. (Avatar is an electronic image that represents, and is manipulated by the computer user).

LOLC uses other language terminology the pervert needs to acclimate themselves to navigate themselves around other features. Commands you may have to execute to guide perverts in the process.

- A popup will open the chat room in a pop-up window.

- PM opens private message window (with webcam). The webcam is located on your computer right above the screen and centered.

- Profile opens the prostitutes profile.

- The menu opens the prostitute's menu containing useful links and information.

- When placing the mouse (the mouse is what navigates the cursor on the computer screen) cursor over an avatar, you can hover over the green camera icon in the top right corner of the avatar for a preview picture of the prostitute's current webcam feed. It refreshes itself about every thirty-second.

- HD icon informs the viewer the prostitute is broadcasting in High Definition video codec.

- Gold or silver crown shows the prostitute has previously finished in the top three in the "LegofLambCams" for the month.

- Yellow, "New Model" tag means she is a new recruit, a prostitute added to their site. Not something, I would care to have advertised for the whole world to see.

Cam Score: (The pimps can take their formula used for cam scores, liquefy it, and send it up in a helium balloon because it is not symmetrical on either side of the spectrum. When I hear the word, "By Default," I can feel the blood well up in my head. "Grrrrrrr!" How Cam Scores are derived at will not necessarily reflect the real deal. By default, (that dreaded word) the prostitute's standing, is a result of her end-of-month, "cam score." Perverts can change this order in their "prostitute list settings." Cam scores, as a rule, are calculated based on the performance of each individual prostitute on the site over a one-month cycle and updated several times each day. Every prostitute starts with a cam score of 1000, which LOLC" claims as the average cam score for every prostitute on "LOLC's" website. Prostitutes can improve their cam scores by earning tokens.

Notice the catch-all phrase? "Earn more tokens." Who are these pimps' that operate these flesh factories for perverts; identified as cesspool's neatly packaged as entertainer's providing a unique service. Parading themselves around on a computer screen, whoring themselves out to perverted, disgusting, and shameless feral rabbits on their video camera. Demanding the prostitute to do unthinkable sexual exploits against God's will. Earning more tokens requires longer hours in their room in front of the camera begging perverts to tip more money. I will elaborate on this issue shortly.

Friends List: With friends like these, it's becoming a way of life. (How sad) It allows you the option to add prostitutes and other perverts to your friends list, and then they become visible on the online friends list when other members log online. Other minute tidbits you may want to know. "Then again, maybe you don't give a Hoot." Nevertheless, for the sake of argument, I will do it anyway.

To send a private message, you must click on the person's username. Click the little people icon to bring up the options menu. Click the webcam icon to open a private message with a webcam, and click the open door icon to enter the chat room. A door that is closed signals the prostitute is in a private show. A closed door with a lock on it means the prostitute is in actual individual, and a secret door with a "G" means the model is in a group show. If the prostitute's door is faded, lets the observer know she is away.

If a prostitute's name appears online, but no door icon and no webcam icon, it means she logged-in, but not broadcasting her webcam at the moment. If a pervert's name is highlighted yellow, it means a message is on its way to him. Everyone; premium members, "necessary perverts," and guests have a special menu on the homepage. Premium members have more features on the list than do guests and primary perverts.

LOLC does not miss a cowlick with their caricature of informational instruction material to pass onto its prostitutes as they walk in step with their pimp masters. This is what I find hypocritical about this charade of adult live webcam sites.

"Adult vulgarity cannot be sent via SMS text message, so those words people chose to use will have asterisks substituted in its place. Example: "I feel like **** "To begin with, it lacks in civility." It is offensive, pretentious, and immorally crude to use any form of coarse language that belongs in the toilet. None-the-less, when you have founders of websites like LOLC digging in their heels cautioning prostitutes and perverts alike to abstain from obscene language when texting. Yet pimps let stand immoral behavior taking root in the prostitute's room, is hypercritical.

If this wasn't enough, I found it contemptible for the "pimps" who think they are doing the public a legitimate service, to encourage the perverts to bring a friend. That way the two of them can wallow in the muck and mire of these abominable atrocities, and drag them to their eternal destiny into the lake of fire (Hell) for eternity. It is obvious the "pimps" have no fear of Hell, or God's wrath and judgment. I would apply that to the perverts and prostitutes as well. They also tell the pervert not to post any pornographic or inappropriate material on their profile page.

"Not this again!" They must use the metaphor: "Do as I say, not as I do!"

The majority, if not all prostitutes create a profile page. Even perverts are allowed to create a profile page of their own on LOLC if they elect to do so. Why perverts would choose this option is beyond reasoning as well. I can see phantom in my mind. Sometimes these profiles can be a mirror of the soul of a prostitute. A typical outline contained in a prostitute's profile would include, but not limited to the following information.

- Username: Angel of Passion

- Cam Score: 3581

- Gender: Female

- Ethnicity: Caucasian

- Weight: 130 lbs., or if they are foreigners they use the metrics

- Height: 66."

- Country: U.S., Ukraine, Romania, Canada, UK, Polish, Asian, Russia, Mexico, Australia, and a variety of other countries

- Sexual Preference: Bi-curious. Why the majority of prostitutes choose this lifestyle choice is beyond my vegetative mind.

- Smoke: It is casual, abstinence, or smoke. Many smoke herbs, or other weed bearing plants, usually a by-product of marijuana

- Drink: Most will answer moderately to not at all. However, I have seen on numerous occasions, the prostitute getting drunk while performing.

- Drugs: They have either experimented or claim they are not using.

The profile may also reveal their body type, hair color, eyes', age, marital status, a photo gallery, their Twitter account, video clips, and of all things a "wish list." Some prostitutes may include some tokens it would cost the pervert to be added to the prostitutes "friends list, snap chat, or to get into their personal, "locked gallery," or "photo gallery." Some prostitutes are obsessed with the pervert rating them. I would image it squares with the overall Cam Score they receive at the end of each month.

Also, most prostitutes list their schedule on their profile page so the pervert knows when they will appear online. Their interests and hobbies are listed on their profile page as well. However, I have learned over time much of what the prostitute puts on her profile page is bogus anyway. About the only legitimate information, you would find trustworthy is what the prostitute has on her "wish list," that is available to the pervert. These are gifts she places on her wish list for perverts to buy for her.

Somehow, two plus two is not adding up to four. Believe me, when I say some of those consumer goods are not for the faint of heart. Some items are very high-end, expensive consumer products while some exclusive merchandise is excluded for obvious reasons.

The profile page of a pervert or prostitute is located at a (URL) Uniformed Resource Locator given in the example:

Those responsible for sitting around an executive table brainstorming ideas and ways to make quick cash from the flesh of women on adult webcam sites should feel convicted and ashamed. To promote this form of entertainment targeted at the male population is an abomination that each Pimp in the industry should be held accountable. For any adult flesh factory to advertise the lucrativeness of this sinful occupation is irreprehensible.

It is structured in tone and manner as to lend its legitimacy without realizing the consequences this has on women they enlist in this degrading market labeled entertainment. It is immoral, degrading, disgusting, abusive, and insensitive. When you advertise and highlight your sites in a manner that is in opposition to God's moral laws, you will be responsible for bringing his wrath down upon the innocent as well as the guilty of this nation. I challenge you to read Scripture and then tell me afterward I am mistaken.

Here is an example of how they promote and distribute their smut and reign people in who might otherwise have no interest in this debauchery. "While we try our absolute best to provide our members archived recordings of their private shows and chats on the site, they are not guaranteed, and archives should be considered a "BONUS." The group show link displays information for all current group shows, as well as any forthcoming group shows." Then they intentionally use language that suggests an appealing attraction to keep the perverts engaged.

"Prostitutes you may like is an elegant feature." You are instructed to input a prostitute you like and, based on her appeal, the system will then recommend other online models that YOU should check out. If the above paragraph isn't advertised to keep the pervert engaged and the prostitute to do what needs to be done to be in demand and liked, then I have no understanding of Scripture. Consider this cool addition to the site. The pimps flagrantly boast; based on the millions of interactions perverts and prostitutes exchange with each other on her website, that their system is able to guess "pretty accurately" what other prostitute's the pervert may like.

Instead of trolling (sort, roam, and search) through thousands of prostitutes online, this can be a "very useful tool," to narrow your search and find new prostitute's "YOU may ENJOY watching." It is only natural then for the pimps to devise a color scheme for this purpose. The green meter indicates the strength of a match. A green meter that is almost solid indicates a high match. Anything showing less than half-solid green indicates a weaker choice. It is this author's firm belief that the pimps put this system in place for one reason and one reason only. To prevent the pervert from trolling, or searching other prostitute's rooms. The more time a pervert spends searching and looking, the less likely it will become for the pervert to spend tokens on any one prostitute. It is all about profit … money … greed! This sounds more and more like a controlled environment no matter how you wiggle and giggle.

Now that I have given you some of the features, and inner workings of LOLC's webcam site, it is now time to take you inside a prostitute's room. I will attempt to explain as best I can without being too graphic as to what goes on inside her room that is no less an issue than the interaction between prostitute and pervert playing itself out day and night twenty-four hours a day, seven days a week.

Now the pimps of these adult webcam sites would like us to believe this is healthy … clean … wholesome entertainment for the general public at large. Addressing their women as models rather than what the ladies have signed a contract to do. The bottom line is to prostitute themselves on camera in front of an audience of perverts. So call it for what it is … Prostitution. However, I have disagreed with many LOLC prostitutes who argue that they are not prostituting themselves. They are merely providing entertainment.

"Very well, let's look at the definition of a prostitute."

Prostitute-1. To offer oneself indiscriminately for sexual intercourse, for money. 2. Devoted to corrupt, or improper purposes: DEBASE. It is a Man or Woman who engages in promiscuous sexual intercourse for funding. WHORE. Is a person (as a writer or painter) who deliberately debases his/her talents, in exchange for monies. However, the model will argue: "But there is no sexual intercourse involved!" I am not engaging in sexual intercourse!"

"This is a pointless argument. Until you read in the dictionary the definition of, "debase." I really don't believe these women appreciate the full extent of the meaning of what they have chosen for an occupation.

Debase. Reduces the intrinsic value of; to lower status … esteem … quality … character. Syn. DEBASE, VITIATE, DEPRAVE, CORRUPT, DEBACH, PERVERT, means to cause deterioration or lowering in quality or character. Debase. Implies a loss of position, worth, value, or dignity. Vitiate means a destruction of impurity, validity, or effectiveness by allowing entrance of a fault or defect. Depraved suggests moral deterioration by evil thoughts or influence. Debauch implies a debasing through sensual indulgence. Finally, pervert indicates a twisting or distorting what is natural or normal.

Any Man or woman who engages in this type of behavior degrades his/herself or is devalued as a person, and loses' self-esteem, and has a character or personality issue. I am not going to tidy this script to appeal to the sensitivity of female performers who made a conscious decision to choose this line of work. I am here to save soul's not pander to any popularity contest. Nor do I feel I'm sitting in judgment, or condemnation on anyone. That is God's work. I answer to a much higher power, and that is God. I'm telling you what the word of God says about iniquity. Should I be found negligent for failing to bring this to the forefront, I would be just as culpable in my sins as the pervert, pimp, and prostitute. I would be nailing Christ Jesus to the cross all over again. It's called discipleship; bringing the lost to salvation, through repentance, and Jesus Christ.

Logging online to LOLC, the first step I have to take is deciding what model's room I want to visit. I will tidy the verbiage here by substituting prostitute for a model even though I take offense to any of these adult webcam sites misusing the word model. Once I have made a decision on what room I would like to visit, I mouse over the "Avatar" with the models still photo showing, oh, and by the way, the pimp's want them to project the best appealing original photograph they have outside their room. I left click the mouse, and the models room is open to me. Depending on how I registered. Guest, primary, or premium member, will dictate what type of liberties I will be afforded. Will I be able to chat with the model or the other group members in the room with me? If you came into the room as a guest, you have no privileges other than sit, and observe.

For almost half the members (Toning it down now, rather than use the word pervert) who visit a model's room will come into her room as guests. After all, if they wait long enough, they will get rewarded with a "FREE" show at the expense of premium members who tips the model. As explained earlier, to become a premium member, you must purchase tokens. You can buy the bare minimum two-hundred tokens for $19.99, and you officially become a premium member on LOLC's website for life, regardless of how many times you log online to their website. There have been numerous instances where premium members have tipped $50 to $75 dollars' worth of tokens to the model in one transaction while the guest derives the benefits from the premium member's generosity. This can cause quite a stir amongst premium members, and guest.

When entering a model's room, it appears the founders; (pimps) selected a word that would not seem objectionable to new member's. The word is "TOPIC" It is mentioned uniformly in every model's room. The topic is the model's bread and butter, setting the stage for tips. From my understanding of how the goal works, the model will set a token goal that she wants to be tipped on the topic" when she is online. The model gives a set time to meet this topic goal. The "topic" always centers around tokens. The model establishes the value of the goal at twenty-six-hundred tokens. The goal is to reach the topic goal within one hour or the model signs out of her room, or the topic goal is reset at her discretion.

As a reward to the members who donate tokens to the model's account, she may offer to take an item of attire off. Then again, she may provide what she calls, A "Flash." It usually means revealing a private part of her body that covers her anatomy. She can suggest any amount of tokens to get the tips flowing into her account. Then again, some models will not bother with a topic, but will use other creative tools to solicit tokens. Some have used cards, numbers, wheel, raffles, or some models will disregard goals altogether some days. Instead, they employ their assets, mannerism's, and popularity to get tips flowing into their treasure chest.

Each token a member tips are worth five cents to the model's online time. If a member tips two-hundred tokens, the model stands to earn ten dollars. LOLC advertises' 60% return or six cents per token. However, this is not the final earned income the prostitute receives. If a model's choice is not to use a topic and decides to improvise using her flesh (used very loosely), she has that option. Moreover, if the model determines the tipping has been trickling in too slowly, she will go offline.

When the model has reached her topic goal, we will assume her room was occupied by, shall we say one-hundred visitors. As the model prepares to perform for her audience; just like a California mid-summer wildfire burning out of control, I notice an influx of gawking grazers beginning to enter the model's room who did not contribute anything. Hundreds of members and guests enter her room to view the spectacle that is about to unfold. They did not contribute to her topic. However, it didn't matter. There are no rules in place to keep them out. Maybe now we can all appreciate why I call them perverts. Men behaving badly; they lust after the flesh without guilt or conscience. These are disenfranchised caged creatures that cannot get their fill. "The fallen sin nature" of a man at his worst! This scenario plays itself out throughout the evening hours, and into the wee hours of the morning. Even as the model is performing, tokens can and do continue to increase the models token count. Before the model is through performing, her "token" account could go from 2600 to 3500 tokens quickly.

The Model has many ingenious methods she uses to market her intangible assets as a commodity to increase her earnings. If the model has a camera, an audio camcorder, or other electronic devices in her home, she can and often does make solo videos of herself performing inappropriate (expletive) acts. Many have done (expletive) videos, (expletive) video. Expletive completes this sentence.

Some models, when discovered by hardcore porn industry pimps, will travel to California, Arizona, New York, or any city promoting pornography for what is called "shoots." They go wherever the demand and money send them. The model then returns to her home base and sells the videos online to her members. The video is no longer than fifteen-thirty minutes in length.

Sometimes the model will do her self-made video's at home, and depending on content, quality, and duration of the film will sell them for two or three-hundred tokens per film or more. The model does not have to share the proceeds with LOLC. What she is unable to sell in her room, there will be a video display on her profile page with a brief description of the films content and price. She may also have recent sets of photographs for the member to choose from, and a section where comments about the models performance are encouraged.

Models have stooped so low as to sell (expletive), and another piece of personal attire to members is requesting such (expletive). (Expletive), they may have used during a performance, including (expletive) of all things. Many models hold raffles. The most popular reward includes the highest tipper for the month and tokens tipped in one evening by one member. Some models offer a special date with them or an all-expense paid trip to a location of her choice for one day, or whatever length of time the prostitutes sets. There have even been offers by foreign models who sweeten the deal by offering members an all-expense paid airfare to their country as incentives for high volume tips.

Personally, I felt the Hawaiian vacation and one evening with the model are deceptive and deceitful. It strongly indicates a form of swindling since winners do not appear to receive oversight. Ninety-percent of the models featured on LOLC have body tattoos imprinted somewhere on their anatomy. Displaying them as if they were a badge of honor or rite of passage. Is this liberating, setting them apart from modesty? Whenever I saw a tattoo on a model; what came to mind immediately was the sign of the beast. Some models have boyfriends or husbands. The powers that be actively discourage models from advertising this arrangement on their profile page. Why? It affects the bottom line in contributions and profit. LOLC wants to create the illusion and fantasy that the model might be available for courtship. If the model is in fact married, some husbands are unaware their spouse is doing this in secret and this posses' additional complications.

I have witnessed model's go outside the security of their homes with computer and accessories in hand; enter public venues such as a library, restaurants, mall's, vehicles parked in secluded areas, sneaking over to neighbors swimming pools under cover of night to broadcast themselves to members who visit her site. The truly successful model has been known to live in luxurious million dollar homes and drives top-of-the-line automobiles

Throwing caution into the wind. Any impressionable young girl who may be entertaining thoughts of entering the world of porn, let's be real. Of the thousands or more models signing a contract with LOLC, or any myriad of porn websites available, I would say a girls chances of becoming among the top 0.05% who consistently make high wages at the end of each month is rare … very rare.

If a young woman just out of school between the ages of eighteen to twenty-two years- old; the most impressionable age group the pimp has his sights zeroed in on, is nothing short of repulsive. They hire these young girls to put on display without concern for their innocence, and modesty. Subjecting them to be degraded, humiliated, debased, damaged goods as it kills heart and soul in the process.

Eventually, they become insensitive to what they are doing to themselves. Dead girls' walking! The vulgarity and the language spoken by many members towards the model in her room are nothing short of cruel, insensitive, and demeaning. The foul language is high, cold, and obscene. I had reservations about printing some of these words. It would serve no useful purpose, or would it? I decided to use discretion.

Some are far too graphic that it would be honorable just to leave it unsaid. When men speak of the women's anatomy or attacks her character with degrading, offensive connotations, I have to draw the line. There were many times I wanted to reach on into the computer screen and choke some of these perverts. These girls have experienced affliction by all the insensitive comments made to them night after night. It has to affect their self-esteem, self-worth, wholeness, and must leave them with a feeling of shame. If they are drinking while online, it is probably attributed to their need to deaden the pain of insults so when they do perform, or while sitting in their room (expletive) there is no shame. Imagine having to appear before a camera every day to expose the most intimate parts to a room full of inconsiderate, drunk, rowdy perverts.

With earnest intentions, I attempted to extend an invitation to as many models as humanly possible in the time I had, hoping I could bring these misguided people to a redeeming quality of Jesus Christ. However, the responses were met with laughter, suppressed snickering, or foul language. After that, I would be banned from their room, usually through the prompting of the members or both. The member's reaction to receiving discipleship was vicious and cruel. They did not want anyone interfering with his or her right to be the animals that he or she are.

How many models on LOLC who are enslaved by independent pimps I can't say? Especially models who have been showing themselves from other countries around the world exploited on American websites. I felt tremendous empathy for these young victimized girls. Their eyes' were lifeless and empty. Just as this heart reacted, when I determined them to be under the control of pimps.

"Did I expose legoflamb.com and carnalcarriexxx.com because I wanted to corrupt the innocence of wandering thrill seekers?" May it never be! However, if an older brother sister, or parent, wants to look into one of these sites to determine if their children or sibling appears in this abhorrent behavior, I would strongly encourage anyone to do so. It is only necessary to view their photograph (avatar) without imposing yourselves into their room to make an identification.

Use Google search, www.livewebcamsites.com. It will usually give the top ten sites. However, there are thousands of websites on the internet. Perhaps a visit to son or daughter's apartment or home for a snoop around for unusual items like chalkboards, wheel spins, raffle tickets, smoking implements, numerous (expletive), or a sophisticated keyboard, may be called for shortly. Model's make it an art form to conceal and lie to their member's so one should listen very carefully when they are talking. Eventually, words will catch them in their web of deception. I reveal this for the benefit and discernment of parents. Choices. Truth. What cost do we want to place on immoral behavior?

Be mindful blessed, this is not a manuscript of condemnation. No, no, no. Rather, its purpose and goals are for salvation of sinner's not yet saved. Those who continue to reject the saving grace of Christ. Romans Chapter 3: 23-24 For all have sinned and fall short of the glory of God, and are justified by his grace as a gift, through the redemption (serving to offset or compensate) that is in Christ Jesus. It is a Christmas gift Christ gave. It cost his creation nothing. It cost him his life. That is love!

It is by Christ grace that I am still here. For I should have long ended this pilgrimage in this tent. (body) However, Christ preserved another soul out of the abundance of his love for Jim Jacobs, that I may make straight this journey for us. The plea is that we together consider our moral compass and where found to be morally corrupt, begin to change direction by serving and obeying the "Great I Am," as children of the Most High.

Today, I face the final curtain call. The manuscript never has an ending, because it will always have a beginning. Another Author, another time, new venue, and a new dawn. It becomes a vicious cycle of never-ending stories. Successes', failure's, achievement's, and unresolved issues of the heart. We experience moments of euphoria and days of grief. Days of labor and times for relaxation. We develop friendships, but we can also experience betrayal. Man is constantly evolving. Each day there awaits new challenges. Nothing has been said that hasn't already been said in histories past. What isn't a constant, is man. We are all destined to die. The space we occupy will be taken by another. Therefore, who you are, what you've become; your plans, dreams, expectations, are all but vain; a chasing after the wind. God is in control, you would do well blessed, to come to this understanding.

To gain an understanding of life; to appreciate the notable secular point of view, all the reader has to do is turn to the book of Ecclesiastes in Old Testament of Scripture and read the teachings of Solomon to understand the meaning of work, life, and wisdom. Who you were or had become in life, will be but a distant memory, it will be as vapor... All is vain, striving after the wind.

"So, what does this all mean for you and for me?" As Dr. Meyer would ask at the conclusion of his sermon's. Perhaps the best way I can summarize this manuscript is explained by the vain motives of man's heart.

There was a man who accumulated much wealth in the land. In fact, he had so much wealth and amassed more land than he could manage even with the hired labor he hired to work the land. To show his gratitude to the Lord for all the blessings he received in his life, he determined to hold a raffle. The man whose name was drawn from the hat would qualify to claim as much land as would be his portion that he could claim beginning from sunrise to sunset.

With the formalities of a man's name drawn from the hat, the stage was set for the next day at sunrise for the gentleman to meet at a pre-determined starting point to begin his claim on whatever land he could stake out before sunset. The only restriction imposed on the participant was that it must be done on foot. He could bring whatever provisions were necessary for nutrition and water to keep his body hydrated.

The following day the towns people, the land owner, and the lucky winner met at the starting point just before sunrise. The gentleman who was already waiting for the owner and observers to arrive was in his early thirties, wore light clothing this day, and brought with him a canteen of water. He reasoned fewer provisions would make his claim on the land less burdensome to where it might weigh him down from claiming as much land as his eyes' could delight in. The day was mild, the Heavens were filled with the canvas of stars, as the sun was just beginning to rise in the East.

At sunrise, the owner gave the participant permission to begin, emphasizing once again to the gentleman he had to return to the finish line by sunset. With this, the gentleman took flight heading East, the sun would be in front. He began at a very brisk pace; a slow deliberate trot. Three miles into the trip, he was making great time, chewing up yard after yard of land. He thought, as he continued claiming more and more land that this was going better than even he expected. He wasn't tired, the temperature was relatively cool, and his strength had not diminished.

Seven miles into his trip and he still felt the vigor and stamina he had at the beginning. He was really feeling good about his conquest. Ten miles into his trip, he began to slow his pace, but overall his body strength was holding its own. The sun was just about overhead by now, reaching mid-day. He felt he still had plenty of water, even though it was about half full by now. Accessing his achievements thus far, he felt he could take possession of even more land. He far exceeded all expectations already in this challenge. But despite these gains, he pressed on, convinced that he could get another parcel or two of additional land.

Moving further East the man carved out for himself an additional seven miles, increasing his ownership of land to seventeen miles. By, now, the man was beginning to feel some of the energy draining from his body. Still, he thought if he could maybe claim another mile or two, he would have more land. And so, he went ahead another two miles, all the while the sun is moving West. After capturing another two miles, his strength beginning to weaken some, he decided it best that he return to the finish line.

He was feeling good about his achievements as he began the trip back. He was tired, but not so worn to sound any alarm bells. He was sure he could make it back well before sunset. Five miles into his trip back to the finish line, he began to take frequent sips of water. His body, especially the legs were beginning to feel heavy every step he took. However, he convinced himself he could make it back in time before the deadline. Therefore, onward he walked without a care in the world.

Another ten miles were traveled while walking directly into the afternoon sun. The heat was by now drawing sweat and perspiration from his body. He decided to rid himself of his shirt. The canteen of water was nearly empty by now. He was drinking more than even he realized. But he couldn't help this, as his body was being depleted of water and nutrients. Yet, he tried to remain positive. After all, he only had four miles before reaching the starting line.

Two miles to go and now his body is starting to cramp on him, His legs weak, the canteen empty, his feet filled with blister's, He remained confident he could negotiate the last two miles. One mile to go and he is beginning to hallucinate, becoming faint, lightheaded, and his steps are wobbly and unsteady. Only a mile to the end. He could make it, just a little further. Stumbling and falling, he could see the crowd assembled at the finish line. He had made it.

One-hundred yards from the finish line, the man collapsed and fell onto his face. The owner and the crowd went and gathered around him. As they were standing there looking down at the now lifeless body, the owner remarked to the crowd.

"You see this man lying here? This man could have had a reasonable portion of land for nothing," he declared. "But this man was greedy. He wasn't content with what was prudent and reasonable. He allowed vanity and his ego to dictate the outcome. "Man is his own worst enemy."

Lewdness, fraud, ungodliness, unrighteousness, bigotry, jealousy, lies, deceit, greed, murder, pride, and arrogance all have consequences. We just can't seem to get it right. We can't even live in harmony with ourselves, let alone live in harmony with the Lord, who has an abundance of blessings He wants to shower upon His children, but because we are at enmity with God, we shouldn't expect God's mercy. "I am not of this world!" I will rejoice when the Lord calls me home. I am what I am. Accept me for who I am. End of story; my business completed, and so we now draw the curtains.